TRADITION AND TECHNIQUE
IN
«EL LIBRO DEL CAVALLERO ZIFAR»

ROGER M. WALKER

TRADITION
AND TECHNIQUE
IN
«EL LIBRO
DEL CAVALLERO ZIFAR»

TAMESIS BOOKS LIMITED

LONDON

Colección Támesis

SERIE A - MONOGRAFIAS, XXXVI

© Copyright by Tamesis Books Limited
London, 1974

ISBN: 0 900411 86 4

Depósito legal: M. 34.375 - 1974

Printed in Spain by Talleres Gráficos de EDICIONES CASTILLA, S. A.
Maestro Alonso, 23 - Madrid

for

TAMESIS BOOKS LIMITED
LONDON

FOR MY PARENTS

CONTENTS

PREFACE

Considering its historical importance as the first indigenous romance in Spanish and its undoubted artistic interest, it is surprising that the Libro del Cavallero Zifar has attracted no full-scale literary study. This book attempts to fill part of that gap with a study of three fundamental literary aspects of the romance —its sources, its structure and its style— and an evaluation of it as a product of the rich heterogeneous culture of early fourteenth-century Toledo. Since many questions inevitably remain unanswered and many facets of the romance remain unexamined, this study makes no claim to completeness. It would, however, have been far more incomplete and imperfect but for the help, advice and encouragement of numerous people whose assistance it is a pleasure to acknowledge publicly.

No aspiring medievalist could have had better formative guides in his undergraduate days than Professor Eugène Vinaver and Professor J. W. Rees, of the University of Manchester; their influence on me is incalculable. I am especially indebted to Professor Rees for suggesting the Zifar to me as a potential research subject and for directing my work in its very early stages.

During my eleven years in the University of London I have been extremely fortunate in having colleagues, both in my own College (Birkbeck) and elsewhere, who have been willing to put their time and expert knowledge so unselfishly at my disposal. From the many I must single out for special thanks Professor Brian Dutton, formerly of Birkbeck College, who helped me with numerous widely divergent problems; Mr Jarīr 'Abū Haidār, of the School of Oriental and African Studies, who answered a number of queries in connection with Arabic names; Dr Robin Ostle, also of S.O.A.S., who read the whole of chapter 2 and thus saved me from several errors; and Dr Ralph J. Penny, of Westfield College, with whom I had useful discussions on the language of the Zifar. Out of the many other friends and colleagues in the University whose specialisms are remote from my own, but whose advice and encouragement have meant so much, I must mention particularly Professor Anthony Watson, my head of department, whose friendliness and generosity I have too often taken for granted; Mr Ian Gibson, of Birkbeck College; Professor James S. Cummins, of University College; and Professor J. E. Varey, of Westfield College, the editor of Tamesis Books.

xiii

Several people outside the University of London have also contributed information, answered questions and been generally helpful. I am indebted to the editors of the Modern Language Review *and the* Bulletin of Hispanic Studies *for permission to reproduce material in chapters 2 and 3 from articles of mine published in their journals. I should also like to record my gratitude to Professor Edmund de Chasca, formerly of the University of Iowa, for sending me on request a copy of his privately printed* Registro de fórmulas verbales en el «Cantar de Mio Cid», *and to Dr Colin Smith and Dr John Morris, the former of the University of Cambridge, for most generously allowing me to read and make use of the typescript of their as yet unpublished monograph* Reality and Rhetoric: an Aspect of Medieval Linguistics. *The extent of my debt to these three scholars will be apparent to any reader of chapters 5 and 6 of this book. I also wish to thank Mrs Margaret Chaplin, Mr F. W. Hodcroft and Dr I. R. Macpherson for providing me with useful information; and Miss Marilyn Olsen, of the University of Wisconsin, for a very fruitful correspondence and for sending me xeroxed copies of material difficult or impossible to obtain in this country.*

When I visited Canada in August 1970 I was fortunate enough to have a long discussion (accompanied by excellent hospitality) with my fellow zifarista *James F. Burke, of the University of Toronto. As Professor Burke's fascinating and thought-provoking book,* History and Vision: the Figural Structure of the «Libro del Cavallero Zifar», *came out when my own was in proof stage, I have only been able to take his findings into account in the odd very inadequate footnote reference. I hope to do his work more justice in my forthcoming review to be published in the* Modern Language Review.

In an earlier form this book was submitted and accepted for the Ph.D. degree of the University of London and, but for the vigilance, knowledge and conscientiousness of the external examiner, Professor Keith Whinnom, of the University of Exeter, many of its shortcomings might have gone unnoticed and been carried through to this final stage. I am deeply grateful to him.

Finally, three special debts of gratitude: first, to Birkbeck College, which made a very generous contribution towards the cost of publishing this book; second, to my wife, Pat, and my children, Julian and Sara, who have cheerfully put up with «Zif» as a member of the family for far too long; and third, to my friend and colleague Professor Alan D. Deyermond, of Westfield College, who has been a never-failing source of help and encouragement over a number of years. As the supervisor of my doctoral thesis, he expended a great amount of time and effort on my behalf with an unselfishness that those who know him will recognize as characteristic. He has read the whole of the revised and much altered version which makes up the present book and made further valuable suggestions. I can only hope that what follows reflects in some small way the excellence of the guidance he has at all times provided.

London, 1973.

R. M. W.

ABBREVIATIONS

A. TITLES OF JOURNALS AND SERIES OF STUDIES

AION, Sez. Rom.	*Annali dell'Istituto Universitario Orientale*, Naples, *Sezione Romanza*
BAE	Biblioteca de Autores Españoles
BÉHÉ	Bibliothèque de l'École des Hautes Études
BH	*Bulletin Hispanique*
BHS	*Bulletin of Hispanic Studies*
BJRL	*Bulletin of the John Rylands Library*
BRAE	*Boletín de la Real Academia Española*
CC	Clásicos Castellanos
CCMe	*Cahiers de Civilisation Médiévale*
CÉSCM	Centre d'Études Supérieures de Civilisation Médiévale
CFMA	Classiques Français du Moyen Age
CN	*Cultura Neolatina*
ELu	*Estudios Lulianos*
EMRLL	Elliott Monographs in the Romance Languages and Literatures
Fi	*Filología*
FMLS	*Forum for Modern Language Studies*
HBalt	*Hispania* (U. S. A.)
HR	*Hispanic Review*
HSCL	Harvard Studies in Comparative Literature
HSCP	*Harvard Studies in Classical Philology*
IUHS	Indiana University Humanities Series
KRQ	*Kentucky Romance Quarterly*
MLN	*Modern Language Notes*
MLR	*Modern Language Review*
MP	*Modern Philology*
N	*Neophilologus*
NBAE	Nueva Biblioteca de Autores Españoles
NRFH	*Nueva Revista de Filología Hispánica*
PLPLS: Lit. and Hist. Section	*Proceedings of the Leeds Philosophical and Literary Society: Literary and Historical Section*

R	*Romania*
REH	*Revista de Estudios Hispánicos*
RF	*Romanische Forschungen*
RFE	*Revista de Filología Española*
RHi	*Revue Hispanique*
RLC	*Revue de Littérature Comparée*
RPh	*Romance Philology*
RR	*Romanic Review*
SBE	Sociedad de Bibliófilos Españoles
SP	*Studies in Philology*
Sp	*Speculum*
TWAS	Twayne's World Author Series
UCPMPh	University of California Publications in Modern Philology
UNCSRLL	University of North Carolina Studies in the Romance Languages and Literatures
ZRP	*Zeitschrift für Romanische Philologie*

B. Titles of medieval Spanish works frequently referred to

Alex	*El libro de Alexandre*, ed. R. S. Willis, Jr
Apol	*Libro de Apolonio*, ed. C. C. Marden
Himnos	Berceo, *Himnos* (BAE 57)
Loores	Berceo, *Loores de Nuestra Señora* (BAE 57)
Milag	Berceo, *Milagros de Nuestra Señora*, ed. A. G. Solalinde
PCG	Alfonso X, *Primera crónica general*, ed. R. Menéndez Pidal
PFG	*Poema de Fernán González*, ed. A. Zamora Vicente
PMC	*Poema de Mío Cid*, ed. R. Menéndez Pidal
Sacr	Berceo, *Del sacrificio de la misa* (BAE 57)
SDom	Berceo, *Vida de Santo Domingo de Silos* (BAE 57)
Signos	Berceo, *De los signos que aparescerán ante del juicio* (BAE 57)
SLor	Berceo, *Martirio de San Lorenzo* (BAE 57)
SMill	Berceo, *Vida de San Millán de la Cogolla*, ed. B. Dutton
SOria	Berceo, *Vida de Santa Oria, virgen* (BAE 57)

For details of publication, see the Bibliography.

CHAPTER ONE: INTRODUCTORY

The *Libro del Cavallero Zifar* is by general agreement Spain's earliest surviving prose romance that has any pretensions to originality. As such it occupies an important position in the extant corpus of medieval Spanish fiction. It is true, of course, that the *General estoria* of Alfonso X at times draws on material that has already been given a fictionalized treatment in another language; but this material was still regarded as history, not literature. [1] There may also have been versions of the French Arthurian romances in the peninsula earlier than the Portuguese *Josep Abaramatia* of 1313; but these, if they existed, would almost certainly have been translations. The short chivalresque tales contained in the late fourteenth-century Escorial manuscript h-I-13 may antedate the *Zifar* in their original version; but these too are clear translations or adaptations of French works. [2] The *Zifar*, then, is the earliest extant piece of prose fiction in the peninsula that does not owe its existence to the ubiquitous French chivalric tradition. For this reason alone it is worth investigating.

Apart from its significance for the literary historian, the *Zifar* has its own very real intrinsic value and interest. The fact that it is, as Menéndez y Pelayo pointed out, «un *spécimen* de todos los géneros de ficción y aun de literatura doctrinal que hasta entonces se habían ensayado en Europa», [3] should be enough to awaken curiosity. The work contains not only accounts of knightly prowess, sensational adventures in the style of the Byzantine romance, and supernatural episodes both pagan and Christian, but also a long section of direct moral preaching which takes up a quarter

[1] The *Estoria de Tebas*, for example, derives from the French *Roman de Thèbes*.
[2] For example, *La estoria del rey Guillelme* (fls 32a-48a) is based on the *Guillaume d'Angleterre*, and *El cuento muy fermoso del enperador Otas de Roma, de la infante Florençia su fija e del buen cavallero Esmere* (fls 48b-99c) derives from a redaction of the *Chanson de Florence de Rome*. I am preparing an edition and study of the *Otas* which will examine more closely the question of the dependence of h-I-13 on French source material.
[3] *Orígenes de la novela*, ed. E. Sánchez Reyes, 4 vols (Edición Nacional, 2nd ed., Madrid, 1962), I, 295.

1

of the entire book. As well as all this, there are numerous didactic digressions, interpolated *exempla* and fables, *sententiæ* and proverbs, and even a few jokes. Such a mixture of disparate elements makes the *Zifar* a work of great fascination and offers a rich field to the potential researcher. What are the sources of this many-faceted book? How did the author come to write such a hybrid work? How did he try to reconcile and weld together this heterogeneous mass of material into a single whole? Did he in fact succeed in doing so? What kind of style and literary techniques did he have to evolve for his attempt at a new genre in Spanish? These are only a few of the more important questions that are raised by the *Zifar*. Some of them have been partially answered; others have not been answered at all; still others seem never to have been asked.

A. The extant texts of the «Zifar»

So far only four texts of the *Zifar* have come to light: two manuscripts and two printed editions. For all practical purposes, however, there are really only three versions, since the later printed text appears to be a simple reprint of the earlier one.

(i) *The Madrid Manuscript (M)*

Critics at the turn of the century regarded *M* as the later of the two manuscripts, dating from the fifteenth century. [4] Subsequently, however, after a more thorough investigation, C. P. Wagner came to the conclusion that *M* was in fact the earliest extant version of the *Zifar* and placed it in the fourteenth century. [5] Wagner's views on the dating of the manuscripts are now generally accepted.

M was discovered in 1882 in the library of the Dukes of Osuna, [6] and is now in the Biblioteca Nacional in Madrid (MS. 11,309; old number Ii-87). [7] Despite its obvious value as the oldest surviving version of the romance, the Madrid manuscript has many faults:

> *M* is a wretched manuscript; not only is it incomplete, and the hand crabbed and uneven, varying with the sharpening of the quill, but the text is filled with mechanical and psychological errors,

---

[4] See Charles Philip Wagner, «The Sources of *El Cavallero Cifar*», *RHi* X (1903), 5-104, at p. 8; Mario Schiff, *La Bibliothèque du Marquis de Santillane* (BÉHÉ 153, Paris, 1905), 388.

[5] *El Libro del Cauallero Zifar (El Libro del Cauallero de Dios)*, Part I: *Text* (Ann Arbor, 1929), viii, n. 4.

[6] José María Rocamora, *Catálogo abreviado de los manuscritos de la biblioteca del Excmo. Señor Duque de Osuna é Infantado* (Madrid, 1882), no. 140.

[7] For descriptions of the MS., see Wagner, «Sources», 8; Schiff, *Bibliothèque*, 388.

anticipations, inversions, omissions, especially homoiographa, and duplications. There is even one passage copied three times.[8]

(ii) *The Paris Manuscript (P)*

Although at one time regarded as a late fourteenth- or early fifteenth-century manuscript (and so earlier than *M*),[9] *P* is now reckoned to date quite definitely from the fifteenth century.[10] It is housed in the Bibliothèque Nationale in Paris (MS. Esp. 36).[11] By contrast with *M*, *P* is a beautifully produced manuscript, written on good quality paper in an elegant even hand and illuminated with no fewer than 242 fine miniatures.[12] The fact that it is so carefully produced is paradoxically a disadvantage when trying to establish the text of the *Zifar* original, since the scribe, with all his wits about him (unlike the bored, sick or senile copyist of *M*), has made considerable alterations to the language in order to make the work accord more with fifteenth-century usage. The ubiquitous *çertas*, for example, of *M* is in every case simply omitted or replaced by the more modern *çierto* or *por çierto*.[13] Some of the more obvious traces of juglaresque style, such as *ahévos*, are removed and the sentences in which they occur recast.[14] Archaic words and forms are replaced by more up-to-date ones: *estovo* for *estido*, *rato* for *pieça*, *çinquenta* for *çinquaenta*, *pensar* for *cuydar*, etc.[15] Whether all these differences between *M* and *P* are to be attributed to the latter's scribe or whether some were already present in the (lost) manuscript from which he was working, it is of course impossible to say. The fact remains, however, that the version of the *Zifar* preserved in *P* has a large number of modernized features.

---

[8] Wagner, *Cauallero Zifar*, ix; cf. also «Sources», 8. The poor quality of this MS. can be seen from the facsimile of fl. 174r in *Cauallero Zifar*, after p. 448.

[9] Wagner, «Sources», 8, says that «the writing is of the end of the 14th and the beginning of the 15th centuries»; Schiff, *Bibliothèque*, 389, believes that it was «écrit au XIV siècle»; Heinrich Michelant, *Historia del Cavallero Cifar* (Bibliothek des Litterarischen Vereins in Stuttgart CXII, Tübingen, 1872), 362, puts it even earlier: «Das aussehen des manuscripts im allgemeinen weist in die erste hälfte des 14ten jahrhunderts».

[10] Wagner, *Cauallero Zifar*, vii, n. 3.

[11] For descriptions of *P*, see A. Morel-Fatio, *Catalogue des manuscrits espagnols de la Bibliothèque Nationale*, 2 vols (Paris, 1882-84), no. 615; Michelant, *Cavallero Cifar*, 362-363; Wagner, «Sources», 7-8.

[12] Wagner, *Cauallero Zifar*, contains seven facsimiles of parts of *P*, one as a frontispiece and the others after pp. 126, 224, 256, 400, 404, 446.

[13] See ch. 2, section D (i) and appendix 1 below, and my article «The Genesis of *El libro del Cavallero Zifar*», *MLR* LXII (1967), 61-69, at p. 61.

[14] See ch. 5, section A below.

[15] I understand that Professor Jules Piccus is working on a full-scale comparison of the three extant versions of the *Zifar*.

(iii)   *The Seville Prints   (S' and S'')*

In the early sixteenth century the famous German printer Jacob Cromberger, based in Seville, published a new edition of the *Zifar* (*S'*) to which he gave the following detailed title:

> *Coronica d̄l muy esforçado y esclarescido cauallero Cifar nueua mente impressa. Enla qual se cuentan sus famosos fechos de caualleria. Por los q̄les & por sus muchas & buenas virtudes vino a ser rey de Menton. Assi mesmo enesta hystoria se contienē muchas & catholicas doctrinas & buenos enxēplos: assi para caualleros como para los otras personas de qualquier estado. Y esso mesmo se cuentan los señalados fechos en caualleria de Garfin & Roboan hijos del cauallero Cifar. En especial se cuenta la historia de Roboan, el qual fue tal cauallero que vino a ser emperador del imperio de Tigrida.* [16]

The colophon tells us that the printing was completed on June 9th, 1512. [17] The only known surviving copy of this edition is now in the Bibliothèque Nationale (Inv. Rés. Y² 259). [18]

Cromberger's press produced a second edition of the work in 1529 (*S''*). According to Simón Díaz, a copy of *S''* is preserved in the Biblioteca de Palacio in Madrid (VIII-2,054). Since it appears to be an unrevised reprinting of the 1512 edition, *S''* is of no importance for the purpose of establishing the text of the *Zifar*. [19]

Not surprisingly *S* has undergone even more extensive modernization than the fifteenth-century manuscript *P*. In his prologue the editor apologizes to his public that the work he is presenting has an archaic flavour; he has nevertheless made many changes. [20]   In Wagner's words, «he glossed, expanded, clarified, and on occasion omitted, in the interest of his reader». [21]   The spelling is modernized throughout: *h-* replaces *f-*,

---

[16]   I have transcribed the title from the facsimile of the title page of *S'* in Wagner, *Cauallero Zifar*, after p. 516. The version given in José Simón Díaz, *Bibliografía de la literatura hispánica*, 2nd ed., III, i (Madrid, 1963), no. 2259, is inconsistent in its modernization and in places inaccurate (e.g. *esto* for *esso*).

[17]   The colophon is transcribed in Wagner, «Sources», 6, and Menéndez y Pelayo, *Orígenes*, 294. Simón Díaz gives the date as June 19th, which seems to be a mistake.

[18]   See Bartolomé José Gallardo, *Ensayo de una biblioteca española de libros raros y curiosos*, 4 vols (Madrid, 1863-89), I, no. 532; Francisco Escudero y Perosso, *Tipografía hispalense* (Madrid, 1894), no. 164. Full descriptions of *S'* are to be found in Michelant, *Cavallero Cifar*, 359-360, and Wagner, «Sources», 5-6. A copy of *S'* was once in the library of Ferdinand Columbus; see Henry Thomas, *Spanish and Portuguese Romances of Chivalry. The Revival of the Romance of Chivalry in the Spanish Peninsula and its Extension and Influence Abroad* (Cambridge, 1920), 11, n. 3.

[19]   I have not seen the Palacio copy of *S''*. I base my assumption that it is a straight reprinting of *S'* on the information in Simón Díaz, *Bibliografía*, III, i, no. 2260.

[20]   The *S* prologue is printed by Wagner as appendix A of *Cauallero Zifar*, 517-518.

[21]   *Cauallero Zifar*, x.

4

-ud- replaces *-bd-*, *m* replaces *n* before a labial, and so on. The changes in vocabulary between *P* and *S* are even greater than those between *M* and *P*: *despues* for *desy*, *secreto* for *poridat*, *vezes* for *vegadas*, *con vos* for *conbusco*, *pareçer* for *semejar*, *plazer* for *sabor*, etc. [22] In view of this extensive revision *S* has only limited value as a reflection of what the *Zifar* author actually wrote. However, there are gaps in both *M* and *P* that can be filled only from *S*. [23]

B. THE TRANSMISSION AND DIFFUSION OF THE «ZIFAR»

The ancestry of the extant versions of the *Zifar* has been worked out by Wagner on the basis of a careful comparison of the three texts, and I can find no reason to question his findings. [24] There seems to be no doubt that with the *Zifar* we are dealing with a clear manuscript transmission, since the differences between the three versions seem due entirely to scribal errors or emendations; at no point can we postulate the intervention of any kind of oral transmission. In fact, two passages in the introductory matter reveal that the author felt that a written text was essential for the preservation of his work. In the Prologue he writes:

> E porque la memoria del ome ha luengo tienpo, e non se pueden
> acordar los omes de las cosas mucho antiguas sy las non fallan
> por escripto, e porende el trasladador de la estoria que adelante
> oyredes, que fue trasladada de caldeo en latín e de latín en romançe,
> puso e ordenó estas dos cosas sobredichas en esta obra (6.11-16). [25]

In the middle of chapter 1 he once again stresses the importance of the written text:

> E porque este libro nunca aparesçió escripto en este lenguaje
> fasta agora, nin lo vieron los omes nin lo oyeron, cuydaron

[22] Further major differences of vocabulary between *P* and *S* are listed in Wagner «Sources», 93-94.

[23] See Wagner, *Cauallero Zifar*, x.

[24] *Cauallero Zifar*, viii-xi.

[25] All quotations from the *Zifar* are from Wagner's edition. I have regularized the use of *u* and *v*, *i* and *j*, and added appropriate accentuation. Page and line numbers are given. The Prologue occurs in *M* and *P; S* has its own prefatory matter.

There is an interesting verbal similarity between the lines from the *Zifar* Prologue quoted here and part of the introductory matter to the fifteenth-century prosification of the thirteenth-century verse romance *Gilles de Chin*: «Pour ce que la mémoire des hommes deffault et passe par terminacion de vye et que touttes choses se délaissent et oublient qui ne les rédige et met par escript..., ay voulu transmuer de rime en prose chest présent traittiet...» (*La Chronique du bon chevalier messire Gilles de Chin*, ed. R. Chalon [Mons, 1837], 1-2; quoted in Georges Doutrepont, *Les Mises en prose des épopées et des romans chevaleresques du XIV° au XVI° siècle* [Bruxelles, 1939], 404). Further research might show this to be a *topos*.

algunos que non fueran verdaderas las cosas que se ý contienen, nin ay provecho en ellas, non parando mientes al entendimiento de las palabras nin queriendo curar en ellas (9.20-24).

These passages clearly rule out any possibility that the *Zifar* was orally *composed* by an improvising minstrel, like many of the old epics or sagas. There are, of course, other reasons for dismissing the idea of oral composition in the case of the *Zifar*. In the first place, it is of such a length that retention in the memory of the complexities of the story would be extremely difficult. Secondly, it is written in prose, and the *juglar* composers—in Spain at least—always worked in verse, using the rhythmic patterns and ready-made half-line formulaic units as a mnemonic aid in their task.

This does not mean, of course, that the *Zifar* was not *delivered* orally. Apart from the type of oral delivery that involved a considerable degree of improvised composition by the minstrel, there existed in the Middle Ages two other quite distinct methods of oral presentation, both based on an established written text: recitation by a professional *juglar* to a mass audience, and reading aloud by one individual (not a *juglar*) to another or to a small select group. In the past these two classes of dissemination have tended to be confused and bracketed together under the blanket title of «oral delivery» and contrasted with the modern practice of silent private reading. [26] In reality, however, they are quite distinct and involve quite different types of literature. [27]

The texts designed for recitation by minstrels are usually of manageable length, with a unilinear plot divided into clearly defined episodes, each with its own minor climax. The style of such works is lively and, above all, concrete. [28] In contrast, a work like the *Zifar*, with its enormous length, slow-moving plot, complex structure, high level of abstraction and constant moralizing, conflicts at every turn with the vivacity and actuality of mass oral literature. [29] If the *Zifar* was presented orally at all, it must

---

[26] See, for example, Ruth Crosby, «Oral Delivery in the Middle Ages», *Sp* XI (1936), 88-110; H. J. Chaytor, *From Script to Print. An Introduction to Medieval Vernacular Literature* (Cambridge, 1945), chs 2 and 4; Pierre Gallais, «Recherches sur la mentalité des romanciers français du Moyen Age. Les formules et le vocabulaire des prologues. I», *CCMe* VII (1964), 479-493; Albert C. Baugh, «The Middle English Romance: Some Questions of Creation, Presentation and Preservation», *Sp* XLII (1967), 1-31.

[27] Much of the material in this section was first delivered as a paper to the medieval section of the Association of Hispanists of Great Britain and Ireland at its Exeter meeting in April 1969. Some of the points are developed further in my article, «Oral Delivery or Private Reading? A Contribution to the Debate on the Dissemination of Medieval Literature», *FMLS* VII (1971), 36-42.

[28] See, for example, Crosby, «Oral Delivery»; A. C. Spearing, *Criticism and Medieval Poetry* (London, 1964), ch. 1.

[29] Similar arguments have been advanced to show that the *Libro de Alexandre* was not intended for public performance; see Ian Michael, «A Comparison of the Use of Epic Epithets in the *Poema de Mio Cid* and the *Libro de Alexandre*», *BHS* XXXVIII (1961), 32-41, at p. 41.

have been by the method of reading aloud either to a single person or to a small group, a method of diffusion very frequently practised in the intellectual and court circles of the Middle Ages. [30]

I believe that reading aloud, although a form of oral delivery, has a good deal more in common with private reading than it has with juglaresque performance. An author whose work is destined for this kind of presentation can assume a certain level of education, culture and sophistication in his audience, and does not need to impose on himself the restrictions of a simple plot and concrete texture. [31] Moreover, he can assume a situation in which any member of the listening group can request the reader to repeat a difficult passage or remind them of something that has gone earlier, things which the private reader can do for himself, but which the individual in a mass audience can never do. [32] The situational similarity of the private reader and the member of a small group being read to is underlined further if we accept H. J. Chaytor's contention that most people in the Middle Ages read aloud even to themselves. [33]

A passage in the *Zifar* itself seems to confirm that no distinction existed in the author's mind between private reading and reading aloud. The passage in question occurs in the account of Roboán's visit to the *Islas Dotadas*. When he asks about the family history of the empress of the islands, he is told that «don Yván fue casado con ella, segund podredes saber por el libro de la su estoria, sy quisiéredes leer por él» (458.15-17); this seems to be an invitation to private reading. A little later, however, a *donzella* fetches the book and reads aloud from it to Roboán:

[30] A miniature in the manuscript of Chaucer's *Troilus and Criseyde* in Corpus Christi College, Cambridge, shows the poet reading his work to a group of assembled courtiers.

[31] In a medieval context inability to read did not necessarily imply lack of learning or culture. Count Baldwin II of Guines, for example, was one of the most educated men of his day and the possessor of a fine library, but he never learned to read; he was rich enough to employ someone to do it for him. See Carlo M. Cipolla, *Literacy and Development in the West* (Harmondsworth, 1969), especially ch. 2. There were presumably other men who, although they knew how to read, rarely bothered to do so because their trained professional reader could do it so much better. A passage in Don Juan Manuel's *Libro de los estados* (ed. Pascual de Gayangos, *Escritores en prosa anteriores al siglo XV* [BAE 51], 311b) describes how the emperor, if he cannot sleep, orders «que leyan ante él algunas buenas hestorias de que tome buenos ejemplos». Dr Ian Macpherson (to whom I am indebted for the above reference) has also suggested to me that Juan Manuel himself may well have picked up most of his own material through hearing it read aloud, since he does not appear to work from a written exemplar but rather to be relying on a very good memory. Moreover, there is evidence to suggest that he composed his works by dictation. If this is so, we have a perfect example of a literate and literary man who could not (or did not) read or write. See Macpherson, «Don Juan Manuel: the Literary Process», *SP* LXX (1973), 1-18.

[32] At the end of the passage from ch. 1 quoted above, the author criticizes the public for not pondering on what is in his book: «non parando mientes al entendimiento de las palabras nin queriendo curar en ellas» (9.23-24). To be able to do this would seem to be the privilege of the private reader; but immediately before this the author talks of the *hearers* of his work. We must, then, accept the possibility that the individual members of a listening group could interrupt the reader when they wanted something clarified.

[33] *From Script to Print*, 10, 13-18.

E la donzella llevava el libro de la estoria de don Yván e començó a leer en él. E la donzella leyé muy bien e muy apuestamente e muy ordenadamente, de guissa que entendié el infante muy bien todo lo que ella leyé, e tomava en ello muy grand plazer e grand solaz; ca çiertamente non ha ome que oya la estoria de don Yván, que non resçiba ende muy grand plazer, por las palabras muy buenas que en él dizié. E todo ome que quisiere aver solaz e plazer e aver buenas costunbres deve leer el libro de la estoria de don Yván (459.16-24).

The identity in the author's mind between reading to oneself and having something read to one is clearly illustrated here. As the first part of the passage undoubtedly refers to reading aloud, *oya* in the latter half of the second sentence is to be taken literally. In the last sentence, however, the author now invites us not to have the story of Yván read to us, but to read it ourselves. [34]

It is my belief that the *Zifar* was originally composed for private reading *or* for reading aloud to a small company of educated people, two methods of diffusion that seem to have been largely undifferentiated in the author's mind. Phrases of direct address, such as «commo oyredes» or «como oyestes», do not exclude the possibility of private reading, as has been suggested: [35] such formulas persist into the sixteenth century as simple conventions. [36] Moreover, such phrases are not necessarily plural: *vós* was used in Old Spanish for the polite singular as well as the general plural. By avoiding clearly plural apostrophes such as *señores* or *amigos*, the *Zifar* author is able to address his work without difficulty to the private reader, the solitary listener or the members of a listening group.

Nevertheless, in view of the fact that literacy was still a rare accomplishment in the fourteenth century, even amongst the nobility and clergy, [37] it is probable that at first the *Zifar* was usually read aloud, and only came to be perused privately much later. This would seem to be borne out by the three texts that survive, spanning as they do some two hundred years, from the fourteenth to the sixteenth centuries. *M*, the earliest version, as we have noticed, is an inelegant manuscript, written

---

[34] Chaytor, *From Script to Print*, 15, quotes examples to show that in medieval languages «*legere, lire* and *read* might mean to read or to read aloud». The examples collected from the works of Berceo in Joaquín Artiles, *Los recursos literarios de Berceo* (Madrid, 1964), 28-34, show that both meanings were also carried by *leer* in Old Spanish.

[35] Crosby, «Oral Delivery», 100; Chaytor, *From Script to Print*, 11-12.

[36] See G. B. Gybbon-Monypenny, «The Spanish *Mester de Clerecía* and its Intended Public: Concerning the Validity as Evidence of Passages of Direct Address to the Audience», *Medieval Miscellany Presented to Eugène Vinaver* (Manchester, 1965), 230-244, at pp. 234, 241-242; B. W. Wardropper, «*Don Quixote*: Story or History?», *MP* LXIII (1965-66), 1-11, at p. 10. Even Crosby, «Oral Delivery», 98-100, admits that such phrases can be used simply as conventions.

[37] See Cipolla, *Literacy*, ch. 2.

8

in a careless hand on poor quality paper. It contains a number of marginal notes by the copyist and many corrections and additional notes in a second hand. It seems to me at least possible that M is a reader's working copy, a «script». P, on the other hand, is obviously intended for the eyes of a man of importance, not just those of a hired secretary: it is on good quality paper, neatly written and illuminated throughout with two-colour capitals and miniatures. This manuscript was clearly meant to be a fine addition to some rich man's library, an object of beauty as well as utility. The likelihood of a nobleman or bishop's being able to read his own books was greater in the fifteenth century, when P was copied, than in the fourteenth. [38] By the time S was printed, the practice of private reading was well established. [39] The editor of the Cromberger version was almost certainly referring to this practice when he wrote in his prologue: «que aunque tengan el gusto dulce con el estilo de los modernos, no de una cosa sola gozan los que leen los libros e historias» (Wagner, *Cauallero Zifar*, 517).

If one accepts that M is basically a «script» to be delivered, whilst P and S are «books» to be read, then it becomes easier to explain the great difference in the number of chapter divisions in the three texts. P has 220 chapters; S has 108; M has only 34. Wagner's suggested explanation of the discrepancy between P and S in this respect is convincing enough:

> Many of the chapter headings of S are longer than those of P, and seem to have been made up of several, or else they correspond to only the first part of the contents of the chapter.... We must suppose that the editor of S has deliberately cut down the number of chapters for the purpose of economizing space. It is to be noted that the divisions of S almost invariably coincide with some chapter division of P («Sources», 93).

Such inglorious economic considerations would presumably not affect the scribe of P, who had clearly been commissioned to produce a luxury

---

[38] A cautionary note is sounded by N. G. Round, «Renaissance Culture and its Opponents in Fifteenth-Century Castile», *MLR* LVII (1962), 204-215. Round's main point, however, is that there is no real flowering of humanistic (i.e. Latin) culture in Castile at this period; he admits the cultural pretensions of some great families such as the Mendozas. Crosby, «Oral Delivery», 100, n. 3, points out that «it is in the fifteenth century that direct address to the *reader* as opposed to the *hearer* first becomes at all common in popular literature».

[39] Edward M. Wilson, *Some Aspects of Spanish Literary History* (Oxford, 1967), 14-17, draws our attention to the chap-books that were printed for popular sale from the sixteenth century onwards, and refers to «the labourers who bought these trifles» (15), which suggests a higher incidence of literacy than we are perhaps tempted to suppose. A further interesting point occurs in Bernal Díaz del Castillo, *Historia verdadera de la conquista de la Nueva España*, ed. J. Ramírez Cabañas, 5th ed. (México, 1967), 531b, where the chronicler considers it worth remarking on the fact that Luis Marín, a member of Cortés' expedition, «no sabía leer». I am indebted to Prof. J. S. Cummins for this reference.

item without regard for cost; the headaches of the commercial printer were certainly not his.

But how do we account for *M*'s paltry 34 rubrics? Wagner offers no explanation, but merely says that «in *M* very much the same thing occurs. The chapter headings are as much longer than those of *P* as they are fewer in number» (*ibid.*). But is it not possible that the rubrics of *M* represent the divisions for a serialized reading of the work? In the first part, for example, dealing with the adventures of Zifar and his family, [40] there are ten headings in *M* (compared with 122 in *P*). [41] They occur at the following points in the story:

(*a*) When Zifar and his family leave their homeland and set out in search of better fortune.

(*b*) Immediately before the interpolated tale of the ill-fated Emperor.

(*c*) When Grima begins her own series of independent adventures after being separated from her husband and children.

(*d*) When the story returns to Zifar after relating Grima's adventures.

(*e*) When Zifar begins his reign as King of Mentón.

(*f*) When Grima returns to the story.

(*g*) When the two sons reappear on the scene.

(*h*) At the beginning of the episode of the treachery and rebellion of Count Nasón.

(*i*) At the beginning of the supernatural adventure of the Cavallero Atrevido in the Enchanted Lake.

(*j*) At the beginning of the final section dealing with the distribution of rewards and punishments and general tying up of ends.

It will be immediately apparent that all but one (i.e. (*b*)) of *M*'s rubrics introduce a new and quite distinct stage in the development of the narrative. The hypothesis that these chapter headings may represent reading breaks is strengthened by two other factors. First, eight of the nine chapters of *M* begin with the *incipit* formula «dize el cuento que», and the other, (*f*), with «segunt cuenta la ystoria». Secondly, all the sections close on a clear note of anticipation of what is to come next, dangling before us a tantalizing foretaste of what awaits us in the following episode, a technique that is reminiscent of that used in modern radio and television serials. [42]

---

[40] This covers two of the four books of Wagner's edition, *El Cavallero de Dios* and *El rey de Mentón*. This division of Zifar's adventures into two parts is a convenient one, but there is no sanction for it in any of the three extant texts. I have chosen this section of the romance for my investigation because *M* is at its most complete at this point.

[41] *M*'s rubrics occur at the following points: 40.4, 88.10, 94.7, 106.16, 164.11, 167.10, 178.18, 190.16, 226.17, 243.1. The second and fifth do not coincide with rubrics in *P*.

[42] It is worth noting that the *cantares* of the *PMC*, which presumably represent recitation periods, also end on a note of anticipation, especially the second (11. 2274-75).

At the end of (c), for example, Grima's thoughts—and consequently ours—return suddenly to her lost husband:

> E ella estava pensando en su marido sy lo podría fallar bivo, lo que non cuydava sy non fuese por la merçed de Dios que lo podría fazer (106.13-15).

The next chapter, (d), begins with a return to Zifar. M's chapter (g) ends with the honouring of the two sons which leads the author into a generalization about the qualities of «omes de buena sangre e de buen entendimiento» (190.8-9), contrasted with those «de vil logar e mal acostunbrados» (190.11-12) who «orgullesçen con sobervia, non queriendo nin gradesçiendo a Dios la virtud que les faze» (190.13-14). All this is a preamble to the last words of the chapter: «asý commo fizo el conde Nasón contra el rey de Mentón». At this point M has a break, and the next chapter, (h), begins the story of Nasón's treachery. In other cases the audience's appetite is further whetted at the end of a chapter by the use of a formula of direct address, such as «commo adelante oyredes» (e.g. 40.3) or «segunt que agora oyredes» (e.g. 226.16).

A further point of interest is that M's «dize el cuento que» formula is omitted in four places in P and five in S. [43] In one further case, (h), it is altered to «acaesçió que» in both later texts. This would seem to justify the assumption that the compilers of P and S were consciously attempting to tone down the sharply emphasized breaks of M, because these clearly signposted divisions, important for a serialized «public» reading, would appear artificial and superfluous to the private reader.

One problem remains: the episodes corresponding to the divisions in M vary quite considerably in length. We might perhaps expect them to be more uniform and correspond to a reading period of, say, one or two hours. On the other hand, we have no evidence that medieval man had the same concern for such artificially imposed symmetry as we have in the twentieth century, conditioned as we are by the half-hour or hour time-span of radio and television programmes. There is no reason to suppose that the reading period was not fixed according to the natural breaks in the material, whereas the modern tendency is to fit the material into a specified time limit. In other words, in the Middle Ages the last word lay with the author, not the impresario or, worse still, the sponsor. Whatever the reason for this lack of uniformity in the length of M's chapters, the fact remains that none of them would be too long to read at a single session or too short to be worth settling down for.

---

[43]   P and S omit the formula in (e), (g), (i) and (j); S omits it additionally in (a).

C. THE DATING AND AUTHORSHIP OF THE «ZIFAR»

(i) The Date

Until the discovery of the Paris manuscript the only known version of the *Zifar* was the 1512 Seville print. Not surprisingly this led early historians of literature to assume that the work was a sixteenth-century compilation, yet another decadent imitation of the *Amadís de Gaula*, and consequently more or less worthless. [44] Heinrich Michelant was the first to suggest that the *Zifar* in fact dated from the early fourteenth century. [45] Since Michelant all have agreed that this is the period in which the work was written.

The first attempt to date the *Zifar* more exactly was made in 1903 by C. P. Wagner. [46] He studied the historical material in the Prologue (contained in both *M* and *P*), which describes the translation from Rome to Toledo of the body of Cardinal Gonzalo García Gudiel, the first Spanish cardinal to be buried in Spain. This event must have taken place before 1303, the year of the death of Pope Boniface VIII, who gave permission for the removal of the remains and who is the only pontiff mentioned in the Prologue. On the basis of this evidence Wagner goes on to suggest that the accuracy of detail in the account implies that it was written very soon after the events it describes. This view is also expressed, rather more forcibly, by Ezio Levi:

> È tale la precisione, che noi non possiamo neppure per un momento dubitare che il «Prologo» sia stato scritto a distanza di tempo, o da scrittore estraneo a quegli avvenimenti. Queste pagine sono state certamente composte in quello stesso momento, e da uomo, che era a parte di quelle avventure. [47]

Wagner's case was given considerable support some years later by the publication of two articles by Erasmo Buceta which contain a great deal of additional historical data. [48] Buceta not only confirms a date earlier than 1303 for the translation of the body and the composition of the Prologue, but actually pinpoints the spring of 1301 as the time of the

[44] See, for example, P. de Gayangos, (ed.) *Libros de caballerías* (BAE 40), xlvii; George Ticknor, *History of Spanish Literature*, 3rd ed., 3 vols (London, 1863), I, 216-217. José Amador de los Ríos, *Historia crítica de la literatura española*, 7 vols (Madrid, 1861-75) does not mention the *Zifar*.

[45] *Cavallero Cifar*, 364.

[46] «Sources», 9-11. Cf. also *Cauallero Zifar*, xiv-xv.

[47] «Il giubileo del MCCC nel più antico romanzo spagnuolo», *Archivio della Reale Società Romana di Storia Patria* LVI-LVII (1933-34), 133-155, at p. 147.

[48] «Algunas notas históricas al prólogo del *Cauallero Zifar*», *RFE* XVII (1930), 18-36; «Nuevas notas históricas al prólogo del *Cauallero Zifar*», ibid., 419-422.

removal of the cardinal's remains. The Prologue tells us that King Fernando IV, Queen María de Molina and the Infante Don Enrique were in Burgos to pay homage to the body; according to Buceta, the only time the royal family was together in Burgos which fits in with other details in the Prologue was between March and May, 1301.

The only scholar to cast doubt on the date of 1301 for the composition of the Prologue is Gerhard Moldenhauer. In the introduction to his edition of the Spanish *Barlaam* he says that the *Zifar* Prologue:

> kann erst nach dem tode der königin Doña María de Molina († 1321) erfolgt sein, dann allerdings vermutlich bald. Von ihr heisst es in der einleitung s. 9: «e otrosi por ruego de Doña Maria, rreyna de Castilla et de Leon que era a esa sazon, que le enbio rogar, la qual fue muy buena dueña et de muy buena vida....» Die bestimmung der prologzeit schliesst nicht ohne weiteres zwingend die der abfassung der *Historia* [*del Cavallero Zifar*] in sich. Sie könnte vor- und nachdem entstanden, auch neu bearbeitet oder nachträglich erweitert sein. [49]

Wagner, however, at the time Moldenhauer was writing the above, was coming to the conclusion that the eulogy of Doña María de Molina started out as a marginal gloss, added to a post-1321 copy of the *Zifar* by someone familiar with the *Crónica de Fernando Cuarto*. The gloss «later came to be incorporated into the Prologue, in the midst of a sentence already too long» (*Cauallero Zifar*, xv). This explanation did not satisfy Moldenhauer, since he wrote a further article on the subject in 1931, still arguing for a later date for the *Zifar*. [50] To my knowledge, his thesis has received no further support from later critics.

The weight of the evidence, then, is very much on the side of Wagner's and Buceta's contention that the Prologue was composed *ca* 1301. If this is the case, there is no reason to question Wagner's other suggestion that the romance was written *ca* 1300, since «authors habitually write their prologues last» (*Cauallero Zifar*, xv).

(ii) *The Author*

There has been surprisingly little speculation about the identity of the author of the *Zifar* which, like so many medieval works, is anonymous. However, a certain amount of information can be gathered about him from the text itself, the attitudes it reveals and the values it upholds.

---

[49] *Die Legende von Barlaam und Josaphat auf der Iberischen Halbinsel. Untersuchungen und Texte* (Romanistische Arbeiten XIII, Halle, 1929), 103.

[50] «La fecha del origen de la *Historia del Caballero Zifar* y su importancia para la historia de la literatura española», *Investigación y Progreso* V (1931), 175-176.

There can be little doubt that the *Zifar* was written by a cleric. [51] In the first place, it is so evidently the work of an educated and well-read man, [52] and at the beginning of the fourteenth century there were few of these outside the ranks of the clergy. The knowledge of the Bible and hagiographic and devotional literature that is revealed in the book would in any case, seem to rule out lay authorship. Furthermore, the *Zifar*'s severe moral tone, its constant flights into a rather censorious didacticism, its basically anti-chivalric ethic, [53] and above all its overriding conviction that everything is directly attributable to the will of God, all this points to an ecclesiastical author. On the other hand, the worldly theme of the romance, with its stress on material ambition and earthly success, together with the evidence of wide non-devotional reading, seem to lead us away from the monastery and prompt us to look for our author among the secular clergy.

A few critics have suggested that the author of the *Zifar* came from Toledo. [54] A study of the language would seem to confirm this: there appear to be few, if any, traces of dialects other than Toledo-standard Castilian in the text. [55] Toledo, of course, was for many years the main centre of contact between the Moslem and Christian worlds, a largely bilingual city, and the home of the first great team of scholars devoted to making translations from Arabic into European languages. The number of clearly Semitic elements in the *Zifar* (see ch. 2 below) certainly indicates that the author had easy access to Arabic material, either in the original or in translation. Nowhere would such access be easier than in Toledo.

We are, then, in a position to assume with a fair degree of certainty that the author of the *Zifar* was an educated and well-read cleric, knowledgeable about the world and probably therefore a secular priest, who worked in or near a centre of Christian-Moslem contact, very likely Toledo. In view of this, it is worth investigating the claim of the only

[51] This suggestion was first made by Michelant, *Cavallero Cifar*, 364, and has been frequently repeated. See, for example, Wagner, «Sources», 11; Pedro Bohigas Balaguer, «Orígenes de los libros de caballería», *Historia general de las literaturas hispánicas*, ed. G. Díaz-Plaja, I (Barcelona, 1949), 521-541, at p. 533; María Rosa Lida de Malkiel, *La idea de la fama en la Edad Media castellana* (México-Buenos Aires, 1952), 259; Jules Piccus, «Refranes y frases proverbiales en el *Libro del Cavallero Zifar*», *NRFH* XVIII (1965-66), 1-24, at pp. 6-7.

[52] For evidence of this, see Wagner, «Sources», *passim*.

[53] See María Rosa Lida de Malkiel, *La idea de la fama*, 259-260, and *idem*, «Arthurian Literature in Spain and Portugal», *Arthurian Literature in the Middle Ages. A Collaborative History*, ed. Roger S. Loomis (Oxford, 1959), 406-418, at p. 414.

[54] Michelant, Wagner, Bohigas Balaguer; see n. 51 above.

[55] No study has been made of the language of the romance, although one was promised by Wagner (*Cauallero Zifar*, vii). I know of two linguistic articles that take the *Zifar* into account: H. Ramsden, «The Use of *A + Personal Pronoun* in Old Spanish», *BHS* XXXVIII (1961), 42-54; Edwin J. Webber, «A Lexical Note on *afortunado* 'unfortunate'», *HR* XXXIII (1965), 347-359. I am grateful to Dr R. J. Penny for a helpful discussion of the *Zifar*'s language.

man who has ever been suggested as a possible author of the work, since he fits our specifications exactly—a secular priest from Toledo.

It was Menéndez y Pelayo who, in an undeveloped aside, first advanced the theory that the *Zifar* was perhaps written by the Ferrand Martínez who appears in the Prologue as the man responsible for instigating, organizing and carrying out the transfer of the cardinal's body from Rome to Toledo. [56] Ferrand Martínez was Archdeacon of Madrid in 1300, a position he held until 1302. [57] What happened to him after that date is not known. Since the archdeaconship of Madrid was an office of some importance, Martínez was either a distinguished and able cleric or the scion of some noble family, privileged by birth to assume influential ecclesiastical rank. The absence of *don* before his name in the Prologue (where every other person mentioned is given this title) suggests that he was not a member of the aristocracy. This seems to be confirmed by the frequent stress that is laid on the gratitude and sense of duty he felt towards the cardinal for looking after him and bringing him up. [58] The church, of course, was almost the only way in which a man of lowly birth could improve his station in the Middle Ages; first by attracting attention to his academic potential so as to get himself an education, and then by taking holy orders and continuing to impress his superiors with his piety and learning. If an illiterate nobleman could become a bishop or abbot without too much difficulty, an illiterate peasant most certainly could not. On this basis, we can fairly safely assume that if the humble Ferrand Martínez could rise to be Archdeacon of Madrid, he would certainly have sufficient erudition—and stamina—to compose the *Zifar*. Furthermore, if he was a man who had pulled himself up from the lower classes, this would help to account for the emphasis on ambition and worldly success in the romance and the almost total absence of the aristocratic preoccupations of chivalric honour and courtly love. [59]

Ferrand Martínez' connection with Toledo is in no doubt whatsoever. We are told specifically that he was *natural* of that city (2.28), and he probably attended the cathedral school which seems to have been one of the best and most important of the period. [60] His mentor, Cardinal Gonzalo García Gudiel, was also a native of the city (2.26), and his family continued to exercise great influence there. The cardinal's sister, Doña Teresa, married Don Diego López Palomeque, «hijo de Gómez Díaz Palomeque,

---

[56] *Orígenes*, I, 294. The first miniature in the Paris MS. shows Ferrand Martínez in the company of Pope Boniface, the Archbishop of Toledo (the cardinal's nephew) and the Bishop of Burgos. There is a reproduction of this miniature in Levi, «Il giubileo», 136.

[57] See Buceta, «Nuevas notas», 422.

[58] 2.27, 2.32-34, 6.3-7.

[59] See n. 53 above.

[60] See P. E. Russell, rev. of José M. Millás Vallicrosa, *Las traducciones orientales en los manuscritos de la Biblioteca Catedral de Toledo* (Madrid, 1942), in *MLR* XLII (1947), 392-395, at pp. 394-395.

caballero principal de Toledo», [61] and their son was Archbishop of Toledo when Ferrand Martínez was Archdeacon of Madrid. Presumably, then, Martínez remained in the service of the archdiocese of Toledo most, if not all, of his working life. This means, of course, that he would be in a better position than most, even in Toledo, to consult the fine ecclesiastical libraries of the archdiocese, which contained not only Latin works but also many Arabic manuscripts and copies of the translations made at the behest of Don Raimundo, second Archbishop of Toledo (1126-52) and his successors. In this respect, it is particularly interesting that Cardinal García Gudiel, Ferrand Martínez' patron, was also active in fostering translations and that he himself owned a library of superb quality and great range, which included works from both the eastern and western cultural traditions. [62] As a native and inhabitant of Toledo, it is more than likely that Ferrand Martínez himself knew at least some Arabic. In view of this background, if the Archdeacon of Madrid is the author of the *Zifar*, its many Arabic features should not surprise us.

One further point of interest is Ferrand Martínez' relationship with the royal family of Castile. The *Zifar* Prologue tells us that the sovereigns of the time, Fernando IV and his mother Doña María de Molina, were very interested in the project to bring the cardinal's body back to Spain, and they urged Martínez to proceed with it (3.19-21). When he arrived in Burgos with the corpse, the royal family came out to meet the cortège (4.31-5.3). This does not prove, of course, by any means, that Martínez was intimate with the king and his relatives, but it does open up the possibility of sufficient contact to enable him to use the royal libraries, piled high, as we know, with Arabic manuscripts and translations accumulated by Fernando's grandfather Alfonso X.

Despite all this, no one (with the possible exception of Levi) [63] has seriously taken up Menéndez y Pelayo's fleeting suggestion that Ferrand Martínez may have been the author of the *Zifar*. Martín de Riquer, for example, after alluding to the possibility, adds hastily that «los argumentos que se pueden alegar a su favor no son tan numerosos, fuertes ni decisivos para que podamos dejarla de incluir entre las numerosas obras anónimas». [64] Nevertheless, the evidence points to the *Zifar*'s having been written by a man identical in every important respect with what we know or can reasonably surmise about the Archdeacon of Madrid: an educated cleric of non-noble birth, born and based in Toledo, probably at home in

[61]   Buceta, «Nuevas notas», 421.
[62]   A list of the books in the cardinal's library at the time of his appointment to the archbishopric of Toledo is contained in MS. 13022 of the Biblioteca Nacional; see Russell, rev. of Millás Vallicrosa, 394.
[63]   Levi, «Il giubileo», 147-148, writes: «Se l'autore non ne è proprio lo stesso arcidiacono di Madrid, Fernando Martínez, doveva almeno essere persona a lui vicinissima, e a parte d'ogni suo segretto e d'ogni suo intimo proposito.»
[64]   *El Cavallero Zifar con un estudio*, 2 vols (Barcelona, 1951), II, 335.

Arabic, and with easy access to richly stocked private, ecclesiastical and possibly even royal libraries.

So far, however,—and this would explain Riquer's caution—the only positive connection between Ferrand Martínez and the *Zifar* is a third-person mention of him in the Prologue. It is worth examining this Prologue further to see if it will yield other evidence to strengthen the claim of the archdeacon to be recognized as its author.

Although the Prologue is not written in the first person, it could hardly have been written by anyone who was not an eye-witness of the events described; the accuracy of detail seems quite incompatible with a second-hand account. We are told, for instance, that the archdeacon's journey cost a lot of money:

> todo el camino eran viandas muy caras por razón de la muy grant gente syn cuento que yvan a Roma en esta romería de todas las partes del mundo, en que la çena de la bestia costava cada noche en muchos logares quatro torneses gruesos (5.27-31).

The knowledge of such details as the exact price of fodder would seem to indicate that the author of the Prologue was a member of the group accompanying the cardinal's body on its journey back to Spain. The only person in that group who is named is Ferrand Martínez himself.

One quickly becomes aware also that the whole story is told from the point of view of the archdeacon: his promise to the cardinal, his determination to fulfil it, his attempts to enlist support for his mission from prominent lay and ecclesiastical figures, his success in getting the pope's permission to remove the body, his hardships on the journey, the considerable expenses he met out of his own pocket, and finally his triumphal return through Spain to Toledo. If this account was not written by Ferrand Martínez himself, then it was written by one who knew him intimately and admired him greatly. [65] But there are some points in the story that a eulogizing friend would surely have made much more of, but over which in fact a veil of modesty is at least partially drawn. The early part of the Prologue, for example, is carefully designed to stress the extreme difficulty, the near impossibility of the task undertaken by the archdeacon: the ruling of the *padres santos* that no body buried in Rome should ever be removed (3.4-6); the pope's blunt refusal to break this ruling even at the request of no less a person than the Archbishop of Toledo, the cardinal's own nephew (3.6-10); and finally the refusal of everyone else to risk the pope's displeasure by repeating the request (4.9). After all this, Ferrand Martínez' success in persuading Boniface to allow the body to be moved is described in the simplest of terms: «E commoquier que luego non gelo quiso otorgar el Papa, a la çima mandó gelo dar»

[65] Cf. n. 63 above.

17

(4.10-11). Who but the archdeacon himself would have felt it necessary to understate the great diplomatic achievement so much?

Moreover, one senses in the Prologue a feeling of quiet pride and delight that would be out of place in anyone but Ferrand Martínez himself. The account of the honour done to the cardinal's body is lovingly lingered over; the names of the important people who came out to meet the cortège are all painstakingly given; the various ranks of society that paid their respects are carefully catalogued. The arrival at Burgos illustrates this well:

> E ante que llegasen con el cuerpo a la çibdat de Burgos, el rey don Ferrando, fijo del muy noble rey don Sancho e de la reýna doña María, con el infante don Enrique su tío, e don Diego, señor de Vizcaya, e don Lope su fijo, e otros muchos ricos omes e infançones e cavalleros le salieron a resçebir fuera de la çibdat, e le fizieron mucha onrra (4.31-5.3).

One gains the impression that the honour accorded the prelate reflects very much on the man who has brought him home against such great odds. Once again the indirect, but quite unmistakable, way in which this is conveyed seems to point to the archdeacon as the author of the Prologue.

The evidence that Ferrand Martínez wrote the Prologue is, then, reasonably strong. [66] But this goes only part of the way towards establishing that he also wrote the romance. However, the two compositions share certain stylistic idiosyncrasies which would seem to suggest that they are the work of the same man. [67] But the strongest argument in favour of a common author is, perhaps paradoxically, the almost total irrelevance of the main part of the Prologue (the account of the transfer of the cardinal's body) to the story of Zifar and his family. If the romance was written by someone other than Fernand Martínez, what reason could he possibly have for prefacing it with a long account of the exploits of the archdeacon? [68] It is surely more reasonable to conclude that if Martínez wrote the Prologue he also wrote the *Zifar*.

One final piece of speculation. It is possible that the romance had already been written by the archdeacon before his journey to Rome, perhaps as a private exercise in sublimating his desire to get on in the world and

---

[66] Martínez' choice of the third person rather than the first for his narrative may be compared with the practice of other historians such as Julius Caesar and Jean Froissart (in his rubrics at least). On the other hand, it may simply be another of the archdeacon's attempts at modesty.

[67] The occurrence of *çertas/çiertas* three times in the Prologue (2.3, 6.2, 6.22) is probably the strongest piece of evidence. The very frequent use of this form of the emphatic particle, which is rare elsewhere in medieval Spanish, is one of the most striking features of the *Zifar*'s style; see ch. 2, section D (i) below.

[68] The only link between the material of the Prologue and the romance is an exhortation to remember noteworthy deeds (6.11-20); cf. Levi, «Il giubileo», 153-154. The editor of S omitted the Prologue presumably because of its irrelevance.

to be accepted by the rich and powerful on equal terms. The *Zifar*, after all, is a classic example of the «rags-to-riches» story. The success of his mission earned him the acclaim and the entrée he so much wanted, and he decided to consolidate it by seeking fame as an author, «publishing» his romance and introducing it with the true story of his achievement, liberally sprinkled with famous names to show the world the circles in which he now moved. This, of course, is the purest speculation. What is more than speculation, however, is the considerable evidence that points to Ferrand Martínez, the Archdeacon of Madrid, as the author of the *Zifar*. [69]

D. THE FORTUNES OF THE «ZIFAR»

(i) *The Fourteenth Century to the Seventeenth Century*

There seems little doubt that the *Zifar* enjoyed considerable popularity during the later Middle Ages and for quite some time afterwards. Apart from the two manuscripts that survive, we have information about two others that are now lost. One of them was formerly in the possession of Marguerite of Austria, [70] and the other possibly formed part of the library of the Conde de Haro. [71] Yet another manuscript must have existed if Pedro IV of Aragon ever got the copy he ordered from his scribe Eximeno de Monreal. In a Latin letter, dated 27 October 1361, the king asks Eximeno to complete his commission as quickly as possible. [72] Whether the manuscript in the Marqués de Santillana's library was the one now known as *M*, as Schiff assumes, is perhaps open to some doubt. [73]

The popularity of the *Zifar* in the later Middle Ages can also be deduced from references to it and its use as a source by other writers. In one of the glosses to his translation of the *De Regimine Principum* (*Regimiento*

---

[69]   The only other suggestion about the circumstances under which the romance was written is made by Levi, who believes that «l'autore abbia scritte le pagine del *Caballero Cifar* durante le soste del suo viaggio, appunto per distrarre la mente dalla funebre immagine che accompagnava i viandanti e dal funebre compito che costituiva il loro quotidiano dovere» («Il giubileo», 153).

[70]   See Michelant, *Cavallero Cifar*, 360-361, and Wagner, «Sources», 94. Michelant states that this was the MS. from which the printer of *S* worked, but gives no real evidence to corroborate this assertion.

[71]   An entry *El libro del caual[ler]o cifar* appears in a list of eight book titles attached to a MS. of the *Libro del Arçobispo de Sevilla;* the list seems to be a library catalogue. The owner of the library is not mentioned, but copies of four of the eight works in the list are to be found in the remnants of the Haro library in the Biblioteca Nacional. See Wagner, «Sources», 94-95.

[72]   «Bene recolimus vos nobis pridem, dum eramus in regno Aragonum, retulisse qualiter infra breves dies proficeretis scribere librum militis vocati Siffar [*sic*], quem ex jussione nostra ab aliquo libro consimili abstrahere debebatis» (quoted by Moldenhauer, *Barlaam*, 103, n. 2; cf. Wagner, *Cauallero Zifar*, xiv).

[73]   Schiff, *Bibliothèque*, 388-389; cf. Wagner, *Cauallero Zifar*, viii, n. 4.

de los príncipes) Fray Juan García de Castrogeriz puts Zifar on the same level as two of the most famous of all medieval heroes, Amadís and Tristan. [74] Fray Juan's translation dates from before 1350. Amongst the writers who probably drew on the *Zifar* for their own compositions are to be numbered two of the giants of fourteenth-century Spanish literature, Juan Ruiz, the Archpriest of Hita, [75] and the Infante Don Juan Manuel. [76]

Perhaps the greatest testimony to the *Zifar*'s high reputation in the fourteenth and fifteenth centuries, however, is the fact that it was printed in the early sixteenth. It has been pointed out that a very small proportion indeed of all the literature composed in Spanish before 1500 found its way into print. [77] Furthermore, the romance must have retained its popularity to some extent at least if Cromberger felt it worth his while to reissue it in a second edition in 1529. I have discussed elsewhere the frequently propounded (but usually unsubstantiated) hypothesis that Cervantes knew the *Zifar* and based his characterization of Sancho Panza on the Ribaldo, Zifar's squire. [78] Taking all the available evidence into account, it seems quite likely that Cervantes had read the work. If this is so, it means that the *Zifar* was read and enjoyed for the extraordinarily long period of some three hundred years.

(ii) *The Nineteenth and Twentieth Centuries*

The *Zifar* has suffered from rather severe neglect since medieval literary studies began in earnest in the last century. It seems that we have here a classic example of what happens when critics devote their attentions almost exclusively to the undoubted masterpieces of the past and write distorted histories of literature around those works that appeal to modern sensibilities, without regard for the historical importance or contemporary popularity of minor creations. Keith Whinnom has made this point very forcibly:

> the acknowledged classics of Spanish literature stand, perhaps not far removed from, but not often at, the beginning of a new tradition. In other words, there is no necessary connexion between literary merit and historical importance.

[74] See R. Foulché-Delbosc, «La plus ancienne mention d'*Amadis*», *RHi* XV (1906), 815; Wagner, *Cauallero Zifar*, xiv.

[75] See A. D. Deyermond and Roger M. Walker, «A Further Vernacular Source for the *Libro de buen amor*», *BHS* XLVI (1969), 193-200; Walker, «Juan Ruiz's Defence of Love», *MLN* LXXXIV (1969), 292-297.

[76] Moldenhauer, *Barlaam*, 103, writes: «Ein quellen verhältnis zwischen der *Historia* [*del Cavallero Cifar*] und D. Juan Manuel ist zweifellos vorhanden, und zwar hoffe ich an anderer stelle eine abhängigkeit des D. Juan Manuel von der *Historia del Cavallero Cifar* nachweisen zu können.»

[77] Keith Whinnom, *Spanish Literary Historiography: Three Forms of Distortion* (Exeter, 1967), 10.

[78] «Did Cervantes Know the *Cavallero Zifar*?», *BHS* XLIX (1972), 120-127.

And again:

> One criterion which the modern critic almost consistently ignores and which he ought never to neglect to apply is the esteem in which a writer was held by his contemporaries. [79]

Now, the *Zifar*, as we have seen, is a work which begins a whole tradition of fictional writing, which seems to have directly influenced at least three of Spain's greatest authors, which was read for the phenomenal period of some three hundred years, and which was printed twice when such «acknowledged classics» of medieval literature as the *Poema de Mío Cid* and the *Libro de buen amor* had long been consigned to oblivion; such a work surely deserves attention.

The critical fortunes of the *Zifar* can be traced very quickly. We have already noted how the great literary historians of the nineteenth century, such as Amador de los Ríos and Ticknor, ignored it or dismissed it with contempt. The only two attempts to rehabilitate the work in the last century were made by Heinrich Michelant who edited it, even if imperfectly, [80] and Gottfried Baist who set it firmly in its place as the oldest example of chivalric fiction in Spanish. [81]

The early years of the twentieth century produced two fundamental studies that have remained the basic plundering ground, acknowledged or unacknowledged, of the great majority of literary historians since. These studies are C. P. Wagner's long article on the sources (1903) and Menéndez y Pelayo's more general section on the *Zifar* in the first volume of his *Orígenes de la novela* (1905). The remarks on the *Zifar* in the already mentioned surveys of Spanish romances of chivalry by Sir Henry Thomas, William J. Entwistle and, to a lesser extent, Pedro Bohigas Balaguer, derive almost entirely from these two earlier scholars. The more general and wide-ranging histories of literature, if they mention the work at all, tend simply to repeat a few of the major points advanced by Wagner and Menéndez y Pelayo: the curious mixture of narrative, didactic, hagiographic, realistic and fantastic elements; the apparent lack of structural cohesion; the relationship between the *Zifar* and the legend of St Eustace; the anticipation of the creation of Sancho Panza in the Ribaldo. [82]

---

[79] *Spanish Literary Historiography*, 13 and 14.

[80] See, for example, Menéndez y Pelayo's scathing remarks in *Orígenes*, I, 293, n. 2; Schiff, *Bibliothèque*, 389, dismisses it as «une mauvaise édition».

[81] «Die Spanische Litteratur», *Grundriss der Romanischen Philologie*, ed. Gustav Gröber, 3 vols (Strasburg, 1898), II, 440.

[82] See, for example, Angel Salcedo Ruiz, *La literatura española* (Madrid, 1915), I, 319; Henry Thomas, *Spanish and Portuguese Romances*, 13-20; William J. Entwistle, *The Arthurian Legend in the Literatures of the Spanish Peninsula* (London-Toronto, 1925), 71-75; M. Romera-Navarro, *Historia de la literatura española* (New York, 1928), 39; J. Hurtado y J. de la Serna and Angel González Palencia, *Historia de la literatura española*, 5th ed. (Madrid, 1943), 111 and 473; Angel Valbuena Prat, *Historia de la literatura española*, 3rd ed. (Barcelona, 1950), I, 233; P. Bohigas Balaguer, «Orígenes de

This absence of a substantial body of critical work on the *Zifar* is even more surprising in view of the fact that for the last forty years scholars have not even had the excuse of the lack of a reliable text on which to base their researches. In 1929 Wagner made his most significant contribution to Hispanic scholarship when he published his edition of *M* with its lacunae filled from *P* and *S*, and with notes of all the significant variants from the two later texts. After this one might have expected a spate of work on the *Zifar*; but it did not come. This may have been due at least in part to Wagner himself who, in the preface to his edition, promised a companion volume which would contain «all the critical apparatus except the variants: paleographical, textual, and other notes, a new study of the sources and literary relationships of the *Zifar*, a grammar and a glossary» (vii). Unfortunately this second part remained unpublished at Wagner's death in 1964. It is to be hoped that someone will bring to press the material that this most eminent *zifarista* devoted over half a century to amassing.

Whatever the reason, apart from the articles of Buceta, Levi and Moldenhauer on the dating of the work, almost all that has appeared in recent years is a few short studies on various aspects of the romance. Some points in Wagner's article on the sources have occasioned a certain amount of disagreement. The famous folklorist Alexander Haggerty Krappe wrote two pieces on the supernatural episodes of the *Islas Dotadas* and the Enchanted Lake, in which he contradicted Wagner's findings completely. [83] Three attempts have been made to show that the main story of the hero's adventures does not depend so heavily on the Eustace legend as Wagner believed: Angel González Palencia and I suggest an Arabic source for Books I and II of the *Zifar*, [84] and Erich von Richthofen traces parallels with the stories of Floovant and Octavian. [85] The question of French influence has been reopened recently in a desultory article by Jole Scudieri Ruggieri, [86] and Martha Alfonso draws unconvincing conclusions from a comparison between the *Zifar* and Ramón Llull's

los libros de caballería», 531-533; Agustín Millares Carlo, *Literatura española hasta fines del siglo XV* (México, 1950), 166; Richard E. Kandler and Kessel Schwarz, *A New History of Spanish Literature* (Baton Rouge, 1961), 162; James R. Stamm, *A Short History of Spanish Literature* (New York, 1967), 63. Two recent histories of literature are honourable exceptions, providing valuable short assessments of the *Zifar*, which take into account the work of critics later than Menéndez y Pelayo and Wagner: Juan Luis Alborg, *Historia de la literatura española*, 2nd ed., I (Madrid, 1970), 316-319, and A. D. Deyermond, *A Literary History of Spain: The Middle Ages* (London-New York, 1971), 157-158.

[83] «Le Mirage celtique et les sources du *Chevalier Cifar*», BH XXXIII (1931), 97-103; «Le Lac enchanté dans le *Chevalier Cifar*», BH XXXV (1933), 107-125.

[84] González Palencia, *Historia de la literatura arábigo-española*, 2nd ed. (Barcelona, 1945), 345-346; Walker, «The Genesis of *El libro del Cavallero Zifar*», MLR LXII (1967), 61-69.

[85] *Estudios épicos medievales con algunos trabajos inéditos* (Madrid, 1954), 45-68.

[86] «Due note di letteratura spagnola del s. XIV. 1) La cultura francese nel *Caballero Zifar* e nell'*Amadis*; versioni spagnole del Tristano in prosa. 2) 'De ribaldo'», CN XXVI (1966), 233-252.

Félix. [87] The sources of the *Castigos del rey de Mentón* and the relationship of the *Flores de filosofía*, the nucleus of the *Castigos*, to other similar books of wisdom have been fairly frequently discussed. [88] Wagner himself reassessed some of his own findings in the light of new evidence on the *Castigos e documentos*. [89]

More specifically literary studies on the *Zifar* have also been relatively scarce. The first extensive piece of criticism of the post-war era is to be found in Justina Ruiz de Conde's important, but neglected, book *El amor y el matrimonio secreto en los libros de caballerías* (Madrid, 1948), in which the *Zifar* author's attitude to love and marriage is studied in relation to other romances of chivalry. [90] Three years later there followed a short, but provocative, *estudio* by Martín de Riquer, appended to his edition of the *Zifar*. [91] Other critical studies have concentrated on single aspects of the romance. The statement that the *Zifar* lacks unity, made by Wagner in 1903 and repeated as a truism through successive surveys of chivalric literature, was first challenged by Justina Ruiz de Conde, who demonstrated a basic structural pattern in the work, but did not develop the point very extensively. Further work in this field has been done by K. R. Scholberg and myself. [92] James F. Burke has made two interesting attempts to relate parts of the *Zifar* to the medieval exegetical tradition of allegory and typology, [93] and Edward J. Mullen has made a study of all the supernatural elements in the work. [94] The author's considerable

[87] «Comparación entre el *Félix* de Ramón Llull y el *Caballero Cifar*, novela caballeresca a lo divino», *Estudios Lulianos* XII (1968), 77-81.

[88] See Helen Peirce, «Aspectos de la personalidad del rey español en la literatura hispano-arábiga», *Smith College Studies in Modern Languages* X, 2 (Jan. 1929), 1-39; Miguel Zapata y Torres, «Breves notas sobre el *Libro de los çien capítulos* como base de las *Flores de filosofía*», *ibid.*, 43-54. The introductions to the following editions also contain relevant material: *Dos obras didácticas y dos leyendas*, ed. Hermann Knust (SBE XVII, Madrid, 1878); *Mittheilungen aus dem Eskurial*, ed. H. Knust (Bibliothek des Litterarischen Vereins in Stuttgart CXLI, Tübingen, 1879); *Castigos e documentos*, ed. Agapito Rey (IUHS 24, Bloomington, Ind., 1952); *Poridat de las poridades*, ed. Lloyd A. Kasten (Madrid, 1957); *El libro de los cien capítulos*, ed. A. Rey (IUHS 44, Bloomington, Ind., 1960); Maestre Pedro, *Libro del consejo e de los consejeros*, ed. A. Rey (Zaragoza, 1962).

[89] «The *Caballero Zifar* and the *Moralium Dogma Philosophorum*», *RPh* VI (1952-53), 309-312.

[90] The section on *Zifar* covers pp. 35-98.

[91] Two vols (Barcelona, 1951). The *estudio* is in II, 325-341.

[92] Scholberg, «The Structure of the *Caballero Cifar*», *MLN* LXXIX (1964), 113-124; Walker, «The Unity of *El libro del Cavallero Zifar*, *BHS* XLII (1965), 149-159. See also Ricardo Arias y Arias, *El concepto del destino en la literatura medieval española* (Madrid, 1970), 222-248.

[93] «Symbolic Allegory in the Portus Salutaris Episode in the *Libro del Cavallero Cifar*», *KRQ* XV (1968), 69-84; «The Meaning of the *Islas Dotadas* Episode in the *Libro del Cavallero Cifar*», *HR* XXXVIII (1970), 56-68. Burke's book *History and Vision: the Figural Structure of the «Libro del Cavallero Zifar»* (London, 1972), published while the present work was in proof, is a fascinating attempt to interpret the *Zifar* as a figure of the redemption of man.

[94] «The Role of the Supernatural in *El Libro del Cavallero Zifar*», *REH* V (1971), 257-268.

artistry as a story-teller, revealed in the interpolated *exempla*, has been discussed by Amado Alonso, K. R. Scholberg and J. B. Avalle-Arce; but all three confine themselves to the consideration of a single tale. [95] Scholberg has also contributed a short article on humour in the work. [96] Finally, Jules Piccus, in addition to his work on the proverbs (see note 51 above), has analysed the author's obsession with advice and advisers. [97]

The role of the sea, of Africa and of lions in the *Zifar* and the reflections of everyday real life in the romance have been taken into account in various thematic studies on medieval Spanish literature. [98] Aspects of the work's style have been discussed in a broader medieval context by John H. R. Polt and Armando Durán. [99] A useful, although somewhat incomplete, classification of the interpolated tales in the *Zifar* is to be found in John E. Keller, *Motif-Index of Mediaeval Spanish Exempla* (Knoxville, Tenn., 1949), and the proverbs in the work are listed in Eleanor S. O'Kane, *Refranes y frases proverbiales de la Edad Media (BRAE* anejo II, Madrid, 1959).

It would be wrong to close this brief survey of *Zifar* criticism without some mention of the three contributions of one of the greatest Hispanic medievalists, María Rosa Lida de Malkiel, none of which is very extensive, but all of which make valuable points. In her classic work, *La idea de la fama en la Edad Media castellana* (México-Buenos Aires, 1952), she discusses the generally anti-chivalric tone of the *Zifar* (259-261). In the addendum she wrote to the Spanish translation of Howard R. Patch, *The Other World*, she analyses the supernatural and fantastic elements in the *Zifar*. [100] Finally, her essay «Arthurian Literature in Spain and Portugal» sets the work concisely within the framework of the Spanish

---

[95] Alonso, «Maestría antigua en la prosa», *Sur* XIV, no. 133 (1945), 40-43 (deals with the story of the Wind, Water and Truth); Scholberg, «A Half-Friend and a Friend and a Half», *BHS* XXXV (1958), 187-198; Avalle-Arce, «El cuento de los dos amigos» in *Deslindes cervantinos* (Madrid, 1961), 163-235, especially pp. 169-175.

[96] «La comicidad del *Caballero Zifar*», *Homenaje a Rodríguez-Moñino* (Madrid, 1966), I, 157-163.

[97] «Consejos y consejeros en el *Libro del Cauallero Zifar*», *NRFH* XVI (1962), 16-30.

[98] Alberto Navarro González, *El mar en la literatura medieval castellana* (La Laguna, 1962), *passim;* Margaret Sampson, «Africa in Medieval Spanish Literature: its Appearance in *El Caballero Cifar*», *Negro History Bulletin* XXXII, 8 (Dec. 1969), 14-18; Sturgis E. Leavitt, «Lions in Early Spanish Literature and on the Spanish Stage», *HBalt* XLIV (1961), 272-276; J. Rubió y Balaguer, *La vida española en la época gótica* (Barcelona, 1943), *passim*.

[99] Polt, «Moral Phraseology in Early Spanish Literature», *RPh* XV (1961-62), 254-268; Durán, «La 'amplificatio' en la literatura caballeresca española», *MLN* LXXXVI (1971), 123-135.

[100] *El otro mundo en la literatura medieval*, trans. J. Hernández Campos (México-Buenos Aires, 1956). The appendix (369-449) is entitled «La visión de trasmundo en las literaturas hispánicas». The *Zifar* is dealt with on pp. 409-412.

chivalric tradition and pays particular attention to its few reflections of the Arthurian material. [101]

The only attempt at a full-scale critical study of more than a single aspect of the *Zifar* is, so far as I know, the unpublished doctoral dissertation of James F. Burke, [102] which discusses the allegorical interpretation of names, [103] the chivalric and heroic ideal, parody, the epic structure and aesthetic bases of the work. Many valuable points are made by Burke and I have availed myself of his findings at a number of points in the following pages. Unfortunately, however, his study is rather uneven and at times lacks a firm evidential basis, especially in the chapter on parody.

Such, very briefly, is the state of *Zifar* studies.

E. THE AIMS OF THE PRESENT STUDY

In this book my aim is to present a more thorough literary study of the *Zifar* than has hitherto been attempted, together with a reassessment of the work of other critics and of my own earlier articles. Before embarking on the literary study proper, however, it is necessary to devote a chapter to the origins of the work, so as to set it in its true context of the Hispano-Arabic tradition.

The critical assessment of the work begins with two chapters on the vexed question of its heterogeneity and supposed lack of unity. The first traces the complex structural patterns in the three books of adventures (I, II and IV); the second attempts to tackle the more difficult problem of the integration of the didactic third book, the *Castigos del rey de Mentón*, into the work as a whole.

Chapters 5 and 6 are devoted to the almost totally neglected area of the *Zifar*'s style. Just as the material of the romance is taken from an almost bewildering variety of sources, similarly its style appears to be an amalgam of many different influences: the juglaresque epic, the learned *mester de clerecía*, the prose of the chroniclers and translators, the precepts of the medieval rhetoricians, and Arabic literary conventions. The first of the two chapters on style is concerned with the author's considerable debt to the techniques of the «oral» poets; the second is devoted entirely to a study of the binary expressions in the work, which illustrate the

---

[101] *Arthurian Literature in the Middle Ages. A Collaborative History*, ed. Roger S. Loomis (Oxford, 1959), 406-418.

[102] *A Critical and Artistic Study of the «Libro del Cavallero Cifar»*, Ph.D. diss. of the University of North Carolina at Chapel Hill, 1966 (*Dissertation Abstracts* XXVII [1966-67], 2525-A). Burke's recent book, *Vision and History* (see n. 93), is not a reworking of this dissertation, but a detailed development of one aspect of his earlier study.

[103] This section has since appeared in a revised form as «Names and the Significance of Etymology in the *Libro del Cavallero Cifar*», *RR* LIX (1968), 161-173.

variety of models used by the author better than any other single feature.

My basic purpose throughout has been to give long overdue recognition to a remarkable artist who, out of a mass of miscellaneous materials and literary models, not only gave birth to the Spanish prose romance, but also created, to all intents and purposes, Spanish literary prose. The *Zifar* undoubtedly has its faults and its *longueurs*, some of them serious; but despite its weaknesses it remains one of the most extraordinary and, in many ways, most exciting creations of medieval Spanish literature.

CHAPTER TWO: SEMITIC ELEMENTS IN THE *ZIFAR* [1]

A. THE AUTHOR'S CLAIM

In the Prologue to the *Zifar* the author makes the simple statement that «la estoria ... fue trasladada de caldeo en latín e de latín en romançe» (6.13-15). [2] There is a further reference to the work's being a translation in the first chapter of the romance:

> E porque este libro nunca aparesçió escripto en este lenguaje fasta agora, nin lo vieron los omes nin lo oyeron, cuydaron algunos que no fueran verdaderas las cosas que se ý contienen (9.20-22).

At the end of the book the author calls himself a translator as he draws a final moral from the story he has just told: «Onde dize el traslaudador que bien aventurado es el que se da a bien, e se trabaja sienpre de fazer lo mejor» (516.5-6). [3]

In view of the fact that the *Zifar* was almost certainly written at the very beginning of the fourteenth century by an author who had strong connections with Toledo, for long a centre of contact between the Christian, Moslem and Judaic worlds, it is rather difficult to understand why successive critics have dismissed the unequivocal statement in the Prologue as a simple convention to which we are not expected to attach any credence. C. P. Wagner asserts categorically that «we must not take seriously the statement that the *Cifar* is a translation from the Chaldean». [4] William J. Entwistle assumes that the writer of the Prologue is different from the author of the

---

[1] Some of the material in this chapter first appeared in my article «The Genesis of *El libro del Cavallero Zifar*», *MLR* LXII (1967), 61-69.

[2] The Prologue is omitted from the Seville edition and replaced by a shorter *apologia* in which the publisher explains why he thinks it worthwhile reproducing such an old work. No reference is made to the book's being a translation; we are merely told that the author's name *sub silentio jacet* (Wagner, *Cauallero Zifar*, 517).

[3] *S* substitutes *sabidor* for *traslaudador*.

[4] «The Sources of *El Cavallero Cifar*», *RHi* X (1903), 5-104, at p. 11.

rest of the romance «which he [i.e. the prologuist] supposes to have been translated from Chaldean into Latin, and from Latin into Spanish». [5] The use of the word «supposes» suggests that Entwistle is not prepared to take the claim at its face value; he does not, however, concern himself with the problem further. Erich von Richthofen follows the same line and commits himself firmly to the view that the prologuist's assumption was erroneous:

> El autor del prólogo supuso equivocadamente que el libro había sido traducido en otro tiempo del caldeo al latín y de esta última lengua al español. [6]

Other critics have given more detailed reasons for refusing to accept the statement that the *Zifar* is a translation. They suggest that we are here dealing with a common *topos* used by innumerable writers of romances of chivalry to give their work an air of mystery from the outset, a device that is parodied and at the same time brilliantly exploited by Cervantes in the *Quixote*'s Cide Hamete Benengeli. [7] Sir Henry Thomas discusses this *topos* at length in connection with several romances, including the *Zifar*. It is a little curious, however, that whilst he is prepared to concede that there may be some truth in Martorell's claim at the beginning of the *Tirant* that he translated the work first from English into Portuguese and then from Portuguese into Catalan, he dismisses the *Zifar* author's statement as «the usual pretence». [8] A little later Thomas quotes the extraordinary explanation of the origins of the *Sergas de Esplandián* offered by Garci Rodríguez de Montalvo in the prologue to the *Amadís de Gaula*:

> por gran dicha paresció en vna tumba de piedra, que debaxo de la tierra en vna hermita, cerca de Constantinopla fue hallada, y traydo por un vngaro mercadero a estas partes de España, en letra y pargamino tan antiguo que con mucho trabajo se pudo leer por aquellos que la lengua sabían. [9]

Thomas quite rightly asserts that this is simply a piece of blatant mystification; but he then, unjustly to my mind, goes on to equate it with the *Zifar* author's straightforward claim about the genesis of his own work. [10]

---

[5]   *The Arthurian Legend in the Literatures of the Spanish Peninsula* (London-Toronto, 1925), 72.
[6]   *Estudios épicos medievales con algunos trabajos inéditos* (Madrid, 1954), 49.
[7]   See E. C. Riley, *Cervantes's Theory of the Novel* (Oxford, 1962), 205-212.
[8]   *Spanish and Portuguese Romances of Chivalry* (Cambridge, 1920), 33.
[9]   *Amadís de Gaula*, ed. Edwin B. Place, I (Madrid, 1959), 9.
[10]   «This is of course mere bluff, such as we have seen employed in *El Cavallero Cifar* and *Tirant lo Blanch*» (*Spanish and Portuguese Romances*, 65). It is also perhaps a little odd that Martorell's claim, which Thomas is prepared to consider fairly seriously on pp. 33-34, is here dismissed as «mere bluff».

28

Martín de Riquer, writing specifically about the *Zifar*, follows the same line:

> Todo el mundo está de acuerdo en que no hay que tomar en serio la afirmación que se hace en el prólogo según la cual la novela fue traducida del caldeo al latín y del latín al romance. Se trata de un frecuente procedimiento de los autores de *romans* y libros de caballerías que pretendían dar autoridad a sus obras fingiendo que eran versiones de relatos escritos en lenguas extrañas y de prestigiosa antigüedad, recurso que se satirizará en el *Quijote* con Cide Hamete Benengeli. [11]

But surely there is a great difference between the *Zifar*'s simple statement that the work is a translation and Montalvo's absurd charade of tombs in Byzantine hermitages, bibliophile Hungarian merchants and barely decipherable scripts. Although the fiction of a work's being a translation from some esoteric language (Riquer's «lenguas extrañas») is virtually standard in later romances of chivalry, [12] this does not necessarily mean that all such claims are spurious. [13] It is even reasonable to suppose that the very fact that the first prose romances in Spanish were translations (usually from the French) inspired later authors to establish the convention of pretended translation.

The most valid reason, however, for examining in more detail the author's claim for the genesis of the *Zifar* is that a number of other medieval Spanish works of undisputed Arabic origin contain a clear statement to that effect. In the prologue to the *Libro de los engaños*, for example, we read: «Plogo e tovo por bien que aqueste libro fuese trasladado de arávigo en castellano para aperçebir a los engaños e los asayamientos de las mugeres». [14] The introductory material to Alfonso X's *Lapidario* contains the phrase «mandóselo trasladar de arábigo en lenguaje castellano»; [15] and in the preface to the same king's *Libro de las cruzes* we read: «mandólo

---

[11] *El Cavallero Zifar con un estudio* (Barcelona, 1951), II, 335.

[12] See, for example, José Simón Díaz, *Bibliografía de la literatura española*, 2nd ed., III, ii (Madrid, 1965), nos. 6646, 6967, 6969, 7048, 7077, 7177, 7233, 7245, 7303, 7314.

[13] The assurance with which modern critics dismiss earlier authors' claims concerning the genesis of their works was recently paradoxically undermined when a number of reviewers accepted at face value George Macdonald Fraser's assertion that his supposed memoirs of a Victorian soldier, published as *Flashman* (London, 1969) and *Royal Flash* (London, 1970), were a faithful transcription of papers found in an attic in a house at Ashby, Leicestershire, despite the fact that the protagonist, Flashman, is derived quite openly from Thomas Hughes' novel *Tom Brown's Schooldays*, and that *Royal Flash* is a fairly obvious parody of Anthony Hope's *Prisoner of Zenda*. Even *Who's Who* objected to the publishers that Fraser's invented entry for Flashman was too accurate a pastiche for comfort and might mislead the general public.

[14] Ed. John E. Keller, 2nd ed. (UNCSRLL 20, Chapel Hill, 1959), 3.14-16.

[15] I have used, because of its availability, the modernized version of María Brey Mariño (Odres Nuevos, Madrid, 1968), 11.

trasladar de arávigo en lenguage castellano». [16] Another work emanating from Alfonso's court, *El libro conplido en los iudizios de las estrellas* of Aly Aben Ragel, uses a similar formula: «traslató-lo de lengua aráviga en castellana». [17] If statements such as these are taken at their face value, why not the *Zifar* author's assertion that «la estoria ... fue trasladada de caldeo en latín o de latín en romançe»? The reason probably lies in the use of *caldeo* rather than *arávigo* and in the mention of an intermediary version in Latin.

To take the question of *caldeo* first. In the prologue to the *Lapidario* we learn that Abolays, to whom the Arabic source is attributed:

> era hombre que amaba mucho los gentiles y señaladamente los de tierra de Caldea, porque de allí fueran sus abuelos; y como el sabio sabía hablar aquel lenguaje y leía su letra, pagábase mucho de buscar sus libros y de estudiar por ellos (*ed. cit.*, 10).

A little later we are told that Abolays, having found an interesting book on astronomy and related sciences, «trasladólo de lenguaje caldeo en arábigo» (11). There is no doubt in this case that *Caldea* is Syria and *caldeo* is Syriac. [18] Another clear instance of *caldeo* meaning Syriac is to be found in the famous introduction to the *Libro de las estrellas de la ochava esfera*, in which the editorial role of Alfonso X is described. Here we read that «mandó trasladar de caldeo et de arábigo en lenguaje castellano el rey don Alfonso». [19]

On the basis of this evidence are we justified in supposing that the *Zifar* had a Syriac original? This would certainly present problems, since there could have been very few people in Spain in the fourteenth century who knew Syriac well enough to undertake a full-scale translation. On the other hand, there is a good deal of evidence to show that *caldeo* was often used simply as a synonym for *arávigo*, particularly outside the scholarly circle of Alfonso el Sabio's court. One has only to look at medieval chronicles to discover that the Moslem invaders are referred to indiscriminately as *Sarrazeni*, *Arabici*, *Ysmaeliti* and *Caldei* (as well, of course, as *pagani*). [20] The *Libro de Apolonio* also contains an example of *caldeo* that almost certainly means Arabic:

---

[16]   Ed. Lloyd A. Kasten and Lawrence B. Kiddle (Madrid-Madison, 1961), 1.b.20-21.

[17]   Ed. Gerold Hilty (Madrid, 1954), 3.a.28-29.

[18]   See John E. Keller, *Alfonso X, el Sabio* (TWAS 12, New York, 1967), 142.

[19]   *Antología de Alfonso X el Sabio*, ed. A. G. Solalinde, 5th ed. (Austral 109, Madrid, 1965), 180.

[20]   For *Caldei* = Arabs, see, for example, *Cronica Visigothorum*, ed. R. Menéndez Pidal, in *Reliquias de la poesía épica española* (Madrid, 1951), 22.14, 23.24, 24.7, 24.8, 24.10, etc.; *Cronica Najerense*, ed. A. Ubieto Arteta (Textos Medievales 15, Valencia, 1966), 46, 47, 56, 57, etc. Cf. also the entry under *Caldaei* in Du Cange, *Glossarium Mediae et Infimae Latinitatis*, II (Niort, 1883), 283: «Saraceni. Ita Saracenos Hispanicos non semel vocat Sebastianus Salamanticensis Episcopus in Historia a Sandovallio edita.»

> Ençerró se Apolonio en sus cámaras privadas,
> Do tenié sus escritos e sus estorias notadas.
> Rezó sus argumentos, las fazanyas passadas,
> Caldeas e latines tres o quatro vegadas. [21]

There is little doubt, then, that we are entitled to interpret *caldeo* in the *Zifar* as meaning Arabic.

The problem of the Latin intermediary version is rather more puzzling, but once again a study of other early Spanish texts sheds some light on the matter. The *Calila e Digna*, of undisputed Arabic provenance, closes thus:

> Aquí se acaba el libro de Calina e Digna, e fue sacado de arávigo en latýn, e rromançado por mandado del infante don Alfonso, fijo del muy noble rrey don Ferrnando en la era de mill e dozientos e noventa e nueve años. [22]

The work's latest editors, Keller and Linker, state categorically that «del texto de 'Abdallah ben al-Muqaffa' procedió directamente el castellano del siglo XIII, conocido con el título de *Calila e Digna*» (*ed. cit.*, xx). To support their rejection of the Latin intermediary they quote the colophon of a third manuscript of the *Calila* (now lost) which reads:

> El libro de Calila e Dimna, que fue sacado del arábigo en latín romanizado, por mandado del Infante Alfonso, fijo del Rey don Fernando, en era de mil trescientos ochenta y nueve [23].

This clears up the problem: «latín romanizado» simply means Castilian; the Latin intermediary has disappeared with the conjunction. [24]

Another work in which the question of a Latin intermediary arises is the Pseudo-Aristotle *Poridat de las poridades*. In this case, however, the Latin version is alleged to have come between Greek and Arabic

[21] Ed. C. Carroll Marden, I, 2nd ed. (EMRLL 6, Princeton, 1937), st. 31. The Latin *Historia Apollonii Regis Tyri*, ed. Alexander Riese (Lipsiae, 1871), 6.3-6, reads: «et aperto scrinio codicum suorum inquirit omnes quaestiones actorum omniumque paene philosophorum disputationes omniumque etiam chaldaeorum.»

[22] Ed. John E. Keller and Robert W. Linker (Clásicos Hispánicos XIII, Madrid, 1967), 371.

[23] Keller and Linker, xxii. The quotation is from Martín Sarmiento, *Memorias para la historia de la poesía* (Madrid, 1775), 339.

[24] Earlier critics who have also rejected the possibility of a Latin intermediary are listed in Alvaro Galmés de Fuentes, «Influencias sintácticas y estilísticas del árabe en la prosa medieval castellana», *BRAE* XXXV (1955), 213-275, at p. 230. Cf. also Consuelo López-Morillas, «A Broad View of *Calila e Digna* Studies on the Occasion of a New Edition», *RPh* XXV (1971-72), 85-96, at pp. 86-87. Both Galmés de Fuentes and López-Morillas support this view.

versions. In the early pages of the *Poridat* the finding of the original is described in the words of the Arabic translator Yahya ibn al-Batrik:

> et començé con ayuda de Dios et con ventura de Miramomelín [his patron, the caliph al-Ma'mun] a trasladarlo de lenguage de gentiles [*v.l.* griego] en latín e de latín en arávigo. [25]

This, of course, is an extremely unlikely place for a Latin intermediary to turn up. In the introduction to his edition of the *Poridat*, Lloyd A. Kasten clears up the mystery and, in the process, provides information of great value for solving the problem of *latín* in the *Zifar:*

> Nos choca la traducción al latín, que parece ser un error del traductor castellano. El texto árabe emplea la palabra *rumi*, que se habrá confundido con *romano*, es decir latín. Si es verdad lo que dice Yahya sobre este punto, la lengua original de su hallazgo podría ser el griego. El *rumi* se presta a dos interpretaciones. El término a veces se aplica al griego bizantino u otra lengua de los cristianos de aquel imperio; otras veces se refiere al siriaco. En este caso se ha creído que significa esta última por haberse empleado mucho esta lengua como medio de transmisión entre el griego y el árabe (*ed. cit.*, 13).

We are now in a position to decipher the probable meaning of the *Zifar* author's claim that his work was «trasladada de caldeo en latín e de latín en romançe». The *Calila* evidence suggests the possibility of «latín romançado» or some such phrase in the original text of the *Zifar*, which an early copyist has misread. Such a misreading must have taken place before the composition of *M*, since at this point *M* and *P* give identical readings, and *P* does not derive directly from *M*. [26] This hypothesis is perhaps unlikely, but the variations in the *Calila* colophons do show that scepticism is justified in the matter of supposed Latin intermediary versions of works translated from Arabic into Castilian in the thirteenth and fourteenth centuries. [27] The information on the *Poridat* translation provided by Kasten is even more significant. If the *Zifar* were originally Syriac (which *caldeo*, strictly speaking, means), it would be likely to enter Spanish through an Arabic intermediary, not a Latin one. But if *caldeo* can be used to mean both Syriac and Arabic, and if *rumi*, Syriac or Byzantine Greek, can be misinterpreted as *romano*, Latin, then the possibilities of turning a Syriac-Arabic-Romance transmission into an Arabic/Syriac-Latin-Romance transmission are easily explicable. The confusion, which

[25] Ed. Lloyd A. Kasten (Madrid, 1957), 31.13-15.
[26] For the relationship of *M* and *P*, see Wagner, *Cauallero Zifar*, ix.
[27] Cf. Gonzalo Menéndez-Pidal, «Cómo trabajaron las escuelas alfonsíes», *NRFH* V (1951), 364-380, who suggests that even in the twelfth century the Toledan translators probably did not render their Arabic or Hebrew originals directly into Latin, but worked from an intermediary version in Castilian.

must have been initiated at least two stages before *M* in the manuscript tradition, probably began with a misreading which resulted in Syriac-Arabic-Romance becoming Latin-Arabic-Romance. A later copyist, regarding such a transmission as unlikely, presumably altered the order of the first two terms, thus giving us the reading of *M* and *P*, Arabic-Latin-Romance.

I suggest, then, that the *Zifar* author's claim that the ultimate source of his work is *caldeo* deserves much more serious attention than it has received in the past. It has already been established that the romance has clear connections with Toledo, a largely bilingual city with a long tradition of translation and adaptation of Arabic works. It will, I trust, prove more fruitful to examine the *Zifar* within this tradition rather than within that of the French chivalric romance with which it has really very little in common. [28] The rest of this chapter will be devoted to showing the considerable influence of Arabic language, style, literary forms and modes of thought on the work.

B. THE NAMES OF CHARACTERS

Even a cursory glance at the *Zifar* reveals that few of its characters bear obviously Romance names; on the contrary, many, such as Rubén, Farán and Gamel, have names that are clearly Semitic. [29] What is more significant, however, is that in almost every case where an Arabic etymon is traceable the name is a singularly appropriate one, summing up salient characteristics or highlighting personal destiny. The *Zifar* author seems to have been well aware of the custom that is still common in Islamic countries of bestowing on people names and titles that have a real significance.

Over forty years ago Angel González Palencia suggested that the name Zifar «es el nombre árabe que equivale a *viajero*, que es la característica del · caballero». [30] The root *s-f-r* indeed expresses the basic idea of «(to) journey». [31] Thus the knight Zifar is in name as well as in fact «el caballero andante». [32]

---

[28] See, for example, the remarks of María Rosa Lida de Malkiel, «Arthurian Literature in Spain and Portugal», *Arthurian Literature in the Middle Ages. A Collaborative History*, ed. Roger S. Loomis (Oxford, 1959), 406-418, at p. 414; Justina Ruiz de Conde, *El amor y el matrimonio secreto en los libros de caballerías* (Madrid, 1948), 97-98.

[29] Despite the clearly Semitic ring of these names, Jole Scudieri Ruggieri rather unconvincingly attempts to derive Rubén from French Robin and relates Farán to the Faran(t) or Ferrant in the *Prose Tristan* («Due note di letteratura spagnola del s. XIV. 1) La cultura francese nel *Caballero Zifar* e nell'*Amadís*; versioni spagnole del Tristano in prosa. 2) 'De ribaldo'», *CN* XXVI [1966], 233-252, at p. 237).

[30] *Historia de la literatura arábigo-española*, 2nd ed. (Barcelona, 1945), 345-346. This book was first published in 1928.

[31] Cf. the English loan-word «safari».

[32] The term «cavallero andante» is not used in the *Zifar*, but the hero is referred to at least twice as «un cavallero viandante» (45.9, 108.1).

33

4

González Palencia also pointed out that Grima is a form of Karīma, «nombre corriente entre las mujeres musulmanas», but he did not explain the meaning of the name or its particular appropriateness to Zifar's wife. [33] The root *k-r-m* has the basic meanings of «nobility» and «generosity», qualities which Grima possesses to a marked degree. It is also possible, however, that the name derives not from *k-r-m* but from *gh-r-m*, which expresses the multiple ideas of «obligation», «punishment», «passion»; in short, perhaps, «loving dedication whatever the cost». This concept sums up Grima's unswerving loyalty through many trials and sufferings even better than *k-r-m*. In this respect it is interesting that the lady who rules over Galapia is also called Grima, although this does not help us to decide between *k-r-m* and *gh-r-m* as the source of the name, since the qualities inherent in both roots are equally applicable to the lady of Galapia and to Zifar's wife.

The knight's two sons also have Arabic names. Roboán is the Spanish version of Roboam, [34] who appears in the Old Testament as the son of Solomon. [35] For Zifar's son this is a particularly appropriate name, since Roboam means «he who enlarges the people»: it is Roboán who leaves home and the safety of his father's kingdom to carve out an empire for himself and thus extend the territories of his family. Garfín's name derives from the Arabic *'arif* which numbers amongst its many meanings «prince» or «leader». The development of the initial *'ain* to *g* was common in the Mozarabic dialects of the Toledo area; the final *-ín* can be explained as the Spanish diminutive suffix. [36]

This concern to make names reflect something inherent in the characters who bear them extends also to many of the minor figures in the work. Zifar's notorious ancestor Tared, for example, who was driven out of his kingdom by his subjects «por malas costunbres», has an eminently suitable name, since the Arabic *tarīd* means «expelled» or «banished». Rodán, the aggressor who is attempting to conquer Galapia, may well take his name from *radā*, a root containing the ideas of «wickedness», «viciousness». The name of Farán, the evil counsellor of the rebel king of Safira, could be connected with the Arabic verb *farā*, «to lie», «to deceive». Elsewhere in the *Zifar* we read:

---

[33] *Literatura arábigo-española*, 346. J. Scudieri Ruggieri, «Due note», 237, suggests that the «nome di Grima... ricorda il masc. *Griman* nel *Girart de Roussillon* e nell'anglosassone *Eger and Grime*».

[34] Ernest Langlois, *Table des noms propres de toute nature compris dans les chansons de geste imprimées* (Paris, 1904), 565, gives seven examples of the name used to denote *sarrasin*.

[35] Cf. *Zifar*, 307.4-5, «Roboán, fijo de Salamón». This identity of name between the son of Zifar and the son of Solomon was first noted by Jules Piccus, «Consejos y consejeros en el *Libro del Cauallero Zifar*», NRFH XVI (1962), 16-30, at p. 26, n. 8. Piccus does not, however, discuss the meaning of the name.

[36] See James F. Burke, «Names and the Significance of Etymology in the *Libro del Cavallero Zifar*», RR LIX (1968), 161-173, at pp. 164-165.

E a la una seta dellos [i.e. of the Jews] dixieron fariseos, e a la
otra seduçes, e a la otra eseos; ca los fariseos tomaron el nonbre
de Farán, que fue fuera de la fe de los judíos, e asý los fariseos
eran defuera de la fe, e traýan pedaços de cartas en las fruentes
e en los braços diestros, porque se acordasen de la ley .... E esto
fazían por engañar las gentes e que los non entendiesen que eran
partidos de la fe (330.18-331.1). [37]

This tendency to use descriptive and meaningful nomenclature is also
seen very clearly in the purely Romance names in the *Zifar*. Names
such as Cavallero Amigo, Cavallero Atrevido, Nobleza, Fijo de Bendiçión
and Fortunado are particularly appropriate for the persons who bear
them, synthesizing as they do a salient characteristic. All these names,
in fact, suggest translations from the Arabic: *ṣādiq*, «friend», for example,
is a common Moslem name; Fijo de Bendiçión recalls the Arabic practice
of naming people *ibn-*, «son of», and could be a translation of *ibn-Barak*. [38]
Finally, in this respect, it is perhaps worth noting that the two sons of
Roboán, Fortunado and Fijo de Bendiçión, are both reported to have
books written about their exploits in *caldeo*. [39]

Another aspect of this preoccupation with descriptive names is the
importance attached to titles in the *Zifar*. Throughout the earlier part
of Book I the protagonist is always called «el cavallero Zifar»; but after
his deliverance of the city of Mentón the townspeople and the king agree
that he is truly an agent of God «e de allý adelante le dixieron el cavallero
de Dios» (154.7-8). [40] After this he is never again referred to as Zifar
but always as «el cavallero de Dios». A little later the King of Mentón
dies and Zifar succeeds him. Henceforth his title is «el rey de Mentón»;
he is never again known as «el cavallero de Dios». Similarly Roboán
is always referred to as «el enperador» after his accession to the throne
of Tigrida. The Ribaldo, the constant companion of Zifar and later of
Roboán, after being knighted is always known as «el cavallero Amigo».
When he is further ennobled he is referred to invariably as «el conde Amigo».
Never once does the author forget the new titles he has assigned to his
characters. [41]

Many characters in the *Zifar*, then, have what E. R. Curtius calls

[37]   This point is also made by Piccus, «Consejos e consejeros», 26, n. 8.
[38]   See Américo Castro, *España en su historia. Cristianos, moros y judíos* (Buenos
Aires, 1948), 72.
[39]   Fortunado, «del qual ay un libro de la su estoria en caldeo, de quantas buenas
cavallerías e quantos buenos fechos fizo» (477.18-19); Fijo de Bendiçión, «de que
dizen que ay fecho un libro en caldeo, en que cuenta toda la su vida e muchos buenos
fechos que fizo» (516.2-4).
[40]   The title itself recalls the common Arabic name Abdullah, «slave of God».
[41]   An interesting illustration of the author's meticulousness in this respect is to be
seen on pp. 510-511, where Seringa addresses the Ribaldo as «Cavallero Amigo» throughout
their interview because she is not in a position as yet to know of his new title of «Conde
Amigo».

«speaking names». [42] But most of these names are only meaningful to a person who understands Arabic, since the author never once explains them. Other characters, as we have seen, have Romance names that are quite clearly «speaking names», but which suggest by their unusual form that they are translations from an alien language. Consequently we are already in a position to lend more credence to the author's statement that his work is a retelling of an original in *caldeo*. We can almost certainly reject the idea that these oriental names are included simply to give an exotic flavour to the narrative, a common enough practice in medieval literature, since in the *Zifar* they have a clear symbolic significance to anyone with an understanding of Arabic, whereas this is not the case with the strange names we find in other European epics and romances. [43] Nor does it seem a very likely hypothesis that the Castilian author of the *Zifar* invented these Arabic names himself; it is more reasonable to assume that he took them over from a Semitic source. [44]

C. The names of places

Semitic place names crop up over and over again in the *Zifar*. To some extent this is to be expected since the stories of both the father and the son are set in the east. Zifar is a «cavallero de Yndias do andido predicando sant Bartolomé apóstol» (8.6-7); his lineage is traced back to Shem, the eldest son of Noah and the founder of the Semitic race. [45] Tigrida, the country of which Roboán becomes emperor, takes its name from the river Tigris. [46] The kingdom of Çafira which he later conquers is «la más postrimera tierra poblada que sea contra oriente» (503.15-16). With

---

[42] *European Literature and the Latin Middle Ages*, trans. W. R. Trask (New York, 1953), Excursus XIV «Etymology as a Category of Thought», 495-500, at p. 495.

[43] See, for example, C. J. Lofmark, «Name Lists in *Parzival*», *Medieval German Studies Presented to Frederick Norman* (London, 1965), 157-173; Jean Richard, «La Vogue de l'Orient dans la littérature occidentale du Moyen Age», *Mélanges offerts à René Crozet* (Poitiers, 1966), I, 557-561, especially p. 557. Many oriental or pseudo-oriental names are listed in Langlois, *Table des noms propres* and in Louis-Fernand Flutre, *Table des noms propres avec toutes leurs variantes figurant dans les romans du Moyen Age écrits en français ou en provençal et actuellement publiés ou analysés* (Publications du CÉSCM II, Poitiers, 1962).

[44] A small detail that perhaps supports this assumption is contained in the following sentence: «E fállase por las estorias antiguas que Ninbros el valiente, visnieto de Noé, fue el primero rey del mundo, e llamávanle los cristianos Nino [? *PS* Ninoe]» (36.21-24). It would surely be odd for a Christian author, if composing his own material, to give the Semitic name as the usual form and refer to the *cristianos* as if they were foreigners.

[45] India was part of the Moslem empire from the early eighth century; see Steven Runciman, *A History of the Crusades*, 2nd ed. (Harmondsworth, 1965), I, 19.

[46] This name has different forms in the three extant texts: *M* Trigrida, Triguiada; *P* Trigida; *S* Tigrida. The name of the river varies accordingly: *M* Trigris, Triguis; *P* Trigris; *S* Tigris. I accept the view of María Rosa Lida de Malkiel, addendum to H. R. Patch, *El otro mundo* (México-Buenos Aires, 1956), 410, n. 11, that the *S* readings must be the correct forms.

this setting it is not surprising that there are many references to places that fell within the boundaries of the Islamic empire. Therefore we should certainly not attach too much significance to mentions of Mecca, Ethiopia or Babylon, for example, since almost any educated medieval man in Western Europe (especially if he came from Toledo) would know of such places. [47]

There are, however, two other types of place name in the *Zifar* that are much more interesting: pure Arabic names for parts of the world that had perfectly good Spanish ones; and imaginary place names that have a symbolic value in terms of the story.

If we examine the *Zifar*'s two geographical digressions (chs 202 and 225) we are led to the inevitable conclusion that the author is using Arabic geographical sources. [48] We read, for instance, that «sabios antigos dizen que Fisón es el río que llaman Nilo, a que dizen en arávigo al-Nil e en ebrayco Nilos» (443.24-25). «Tierras de Çin» (444.13, 504.22) is a clear reference to China, for which the Arabic name is *ṣīn*. When he is describing the division of the world into three parts—Europe, Asia and Africa—, the author again uses many recognizably Arabic names instead of their Romance equivalents, and many others that are probably Arabic but which bewildered copyists have rendered indecipherable. «Al-Fares [*M* Alsares]» (504.20-21) is clearly the Arabic *(bilād) al-fārs*, Persia; «Alçinde [*M* Agas]» (504.23) is *al-sind*, the Indus; «Tanjat-ally-adia [*P* Tangad aladia]» (505.14-15) is certainly connected with Tangier, for which the Arabic name is *tanja;* «syerras que dizen Gameldaron [*P* Guiberdaran]» (505.1) suggests a derivative of *jabal*, «mountain».

A particularly interesting phrase in the second of these geographical digressions is «tierras que dizen Alar Vire [*P* Arquibia; *S* Alarquebia] que quiere dezir 'la grant tierra'» (504.8-9). In its original form this place name must have been *al-'arḍ al-kabīra*, the usual Arabic term for the *continens* as opposed to islands, peninsulas, etc., but which literally means «the great (or big) land», as the *Zifar* author tells us. Since «la grant tierra» is mentioned between references to Brittany and Gascony, it clearly means France. [49] Now, one can accept without much difficulty that even a Spanish writer should use the Arabic names for parts of Asia and Africa, but it is somewhat surprising to find him extending this practice to places in Christian Europe. We can thus fairly safely assume

[47] For an account of the contribution of medieval Moslem geographers to western knowledge, see John Kirtland Wright, *The Geographical Lore of the Time of the Crusades. A Study in the History of Medieval Science and Tradition in Western Europe* (New York, 1925), 77-87.

[48] Wright, *Geographical Lore*, 77-87, mentions a number of Arab geographers who worked or were known in Spain, among them the famous al-Idrīsī.

[49] The name *Tere major* given to France in the *Chanson de Roland* (Digby MS. 23, ll. 600, 1532, 1667) seems to be a reflection of *al-'arḍ al-kabīra*, especially as it is twice used by Saracens and the third time by the traitor Ganelon as he swears allegiance to the Moorish king.

that these geographical digressions in the *Zifar* are based on the works of Islamic geographers.

Apart from the Semitic names for real places in chapters 202 and 225, there are other purely imaginary places in the romance whose names have interesting symbolic meanings if they are interpreted in terms of an Arabic root. It is easy, for instance, to relate the kingdom of Garba (486.24) to *gh-r-b*, «strange», «foreign», «west», [50] and to see in the name of Toribia (243.12), where Zifar's second wife dies, a derivative of *t-r-b*, «earth», «dust», «tomb». [51]

The examples just quoted may possibly be coincidental, but there is one very interesting case of a country that alters its name when its symbolic role in the story changes. Zifar is separated from his wife and children in or near Mella in the kingdom of Falac (85.4). The root *f-l-q* expresses the ideas of «misfortune», «distress» and «splitting». At this stage the country is appropriately named. When Zifar's sons meet their parents again after an interval of many years, they tell them that they were brought up by kind foster-parents in Mella in the kingdom of Falit (181.26) or Fallid (187.7). The root *f-l-t* contains the notions of «freedom» and «escape». It is particularly interesting that both *P* and *S* change *M*'s Falit/Fallid to Falac so as to make the sons' account consistent with the story of the separation of the family told earlier.

In no case of a place name with a recognizable Arabic root does the *Zifar* author give us a clue to its symbolic meaning. There are, however, at least four examples of places with Romance names for which an etymological commentary is supplied. The King of Mentón is being besieged in Grades, «e dízenle asý porque está en alto e suben por gradas allá» (117.7-8); the Cavallero Amigo is sent on a mission to the city of Paludes, so called «porque está çercada de lagunas que sallen de las Aguas Mistas» (490.21-22); as he returns the Cavallero Amigo is captured and taken to the city of Altaclara, «e dízenle asý porque está en alto logar, ca paresçe de muy grand tierra» (492.8-9); the principal city of Çafira is Monteçaelo, «e este nonbre tomó porque es la tierra de color de çielo» (503.13).

It is certainly very curious that, if the *Zifar* is a Castilian original (as Riquer, for example, dogmatically asserts), [52] its author should take the trouble to explain the etymology of some of his Romance place names whilst giving no clue whatsoever towards helping his audience to understand the symbolic meaning of those derived from Arabic. Is it not more reasonable to suppose that the work is, as its author says, a translation

[50] Burke, «Names», 171, relates Garba to *k-r-b*, «worry», «care», «grief», «since the author moralizes concerning the weakness of the kings in not standing firm against the false persuasions of Count Farán».

[51] For other examples, see Burke, «Names», *passim*.

[52] «Es evidente que el *Zifar* se escribió directamente en castellano» (*Cavallero Zifar*, II, 335).

or adaptation of an original in *caldeo*? If the romance was intended for a readership in the area around Toledo where it was written, then at least some of the etymological subtleties of the Arabic «speaking names» would presumably have been appreciated and understood when it first appeared. This was not, however, the case with the later copyists: in all the extant versions the Arabic place names have suffered considerable mangling. Burke suggests very plausibly that the four explanations of Romance names may well be later interpolations by scribes who, ignorant of Arabic, joyfully seized on something they could understand and explained what is already fairly obvious. [53] It is a further possibility that at least some of the apparently Romance names started life as derivatives of Arabic near-homonyms which became corrupted in transmission. [54]

D. STYLISTIC FEATURES

(i) *Çertas*

One of the most striking stylistic features of the *Zifar* is the very frequent use of the word *çertas* (or occasionally *çiertas*). In the four books of the work it occurs no fewer than 346 times. [55] On the other hand, there are only 33 examples of *çiertamente*. [56] *Çierto* appears twelve times, but in every case it has been supplied by Wagner from the later manuscript *P*; *çierto* never appears in *M*. If we assume, then, that what occurs as *çierto* in Wagner's text would have been *çertas* in the original, and that *çiertas* is merely a rare variant, we arrive at a total of 358 examples of *çertas* in the four books of the *Zifar*. [57] But this figure must have been even higher in the original version, since large sections of the text, particularly in Book IV *Los hechos de Roboán*, are missing from *M* and have to be supplied from *P* or, occasionally, *S*. [58] Neither *P* nor *S* uses *çertas*, which their redactors, conscious of the need to modernize the

[53] «Names», 172.
[54] Burke, «Names», 171-172, suggests that the name of the King of Çafira probably comes from the Arabic *safir*, «mediator», since it is he who explains to Roboán why he and his fellow king rebelled. The *Zifar* author, however, explains the name as if it were Romance: «e porende le dizen âquella tierra Çafira, que tomó el nonbre de çafir» (507.16-17). There seem to be two weaknesses in Burke's argument: it is the king, not his country, that acts as mediator; and the land of Çafira in fact contains many marvellous sapphires. Nevertheless, this illustration does remind us of the possibility of a shift of meaning through homonymy.
[55] The form *çiertas* occurs three times only: 35.21, 198.8, 509.7.
[56] All occurrences of *çertas*, *çiertas*, *çierto* and *çiertamente* are listed in appendix 1.
[57] In the author's Prologue there is one example of *çertas* (6.22) and two of *çiertas* (2.3, 6.2).
[58] The three major *lacunae* in *M* that have to be filled from *P* cover the following sections of Wagner, *Cauallero Zifar*: 403.16-422.32, 454.13-463.24, 486.14-496.31. In these sections there is no example of *çertas* or *çiertas*, but there are three occurrences of *çierto*, four of *çiertamente* and two of *por çierto*.

work for their own day, regarded as an archaic form. In these later versions *M*'s *çertas* usually appears as *çierto* or *por çierto* (forms never found in *M*); but in many cases the ubiquitous *çertas* is simply omitted or a different word such as *ca (S que)* substituted for it. [59]

Bearing all this in mind we can safely assume that the original *Zifar* contained even more examples of *çertas* than survive in the text established by Wagner. The following table shows the distribution of *çertas* and *çiertamente; çiertas* and *çierto* are regarded as variants of *çertas:*

BOOK	NUMBER OF PAGES	NUMBER OF EXAMPLES OF «ÇERTAS»	NUMBER OF EXAMPLES OF «ÇIERTAMENTE»
I	154	148	2
II	90	81	4
III	125	55	11
IV	135	74	16 [60]

By far the highest incidence of *çertas* is in the sections of rapid exchange of dialogue. Once again regarding *çertas, çiertas* and *çierto* as one, we find that out of the 303 occurrences in Books I, II and IV—leaving Book III aside because of its special nature and the rarity of passages of dialogue in it—no fewer than 275 appear in conversation:

BOOK	NUMBER OF «ÇERTAS»	NUMBER OF EXAMPLES IN DIALOGUE	NUMBER OF EXAMPLES NOT IN DIALOGUE
I	148	145	3
II	81	71	10
IV	74	59	15
	303	275	28 [61]

[59] One rather extreme example will serve to show the extent of these changes. The section of *M* contained on p. 215 of *Cauallero Zifar* has five examples of *çertas;* four of these are simply omitted from *P* and *S,* and the other is changed to *estonçe.*

[60] The table appears to show a fairly sharp decline in the use of *çertas* as the work progresses and an increase, although much less marked, in the use of *çiertamente.* Two things, however, should be borne in mind: *a)* the commonest use of *çertas* is in rapid exchanges of dialogue, which is not a notable feature of Book III, except in the interpolated *exempla; b)* the fact that Book IV, although almost as long as Book I, contains only half the number of examples of *çertas,* must be seen in relation to the incompleteness of *M* at this point. About 28 per cent of the text of Book IV in *Cauallero Zifar* (38 pages out of 135) has been supplied from *P* which, as we have seen, is much more sparing in its use of the emphatic particle, even in its more modern form *çierto.* Nevertheless, there is a clear increase in the use of *çiertamente* as the work progresses.

[61] The corresponding figures for Book III are: 14 occurrences of *çertas* in real dialogue (i.e. in *exempla*) and 41 occurrences in the course of Zifar's direct teaching.

It is interesting to note that of the 28 cases where *çertas* is not used in dialogue the majority in fact introduce a general comment on the action or a maxim from the author. [62]   In other words, the use of *çertas* in the course of the actual narrative is very rare.

Çertas, then, is used almost exclusively in dialogue, where by far its commonest function is to open a speech, particularly in reply to a question; its use is that of an emphatic particle.   The following table gives an idea of the frequency of *çertas* in certain types of stock phrases used at the beginning of speeches in the *Zifar*:

BOOK	TOTAL «ÇER-TAS»	TOTAL IN DIALOGUE	«(E) *çertas*», *dixo/dixieron*	«*Çertas, señor/ amigo*, etc.», *dixo/dixieron*	«*Çertas, sý/non*», *dixo/dixieron*
I	148	145	87	16	3
II	81	71	33	10	3
IV	74	59	22	16	1
			142	42	7
303	275			191 [63]	

The above table shows that about 92 per cent of the examples of *çertas* in Books I, II and IV are to be found in dialogue, and that some 70 per cent of these occurrences in dialogue consist of the simple stock phrase «'Çertas', dixo» or one of its slight variants.   In the very great majority of cases where *çertas* is the opening word of a speech it occurs in this kind of set expression.   One further point: *çertas*, whether in dialogue or not, is invariably either the first word of a sentence or clause or preceded only by some insignificant conjunction such as *ca* [64] or, more frequently, *e*. In all cases the function of *çertas* in the *Zifar* is simply that of an emphatic particle.

One is bound to ask why the author of the *Zifar* should be so fond of this particular word and its use in this rather specialized way.   *Çertas* is a rare word elsewhere in medieval Spanish literature: considerable research has revealed only thirteen other occurrences, [65] only two of which

---

[62]   E.g. 14.5, 77.16, 133.5, 202.11, 203.24, 228.12, 234.23, 390.7, 397.14, 397.24, 398.10, 468.5, 502.15, 508.12, 509.7, 515.15.   Almost all the examples in Book III can be classified in this way because of the very nature of the book.

[63]   Of the 14 cases of *çertas* used in true dialogue in Book III 9 are of this type.

[64]   It is interesting to note that after *ca* the author seems to prefer to use *çiertamente;* of the 33 examples of *çiertamente* 12 occur after *ca*: 210.4, 253.18, 295.9, 308.15, 385.2, 411.2 *(ca bien ç.)*, 411.20, 421.18, 428.10, 431.28, 451.13, 459.20 (cf. also *que ç.* 322.27). *Çertas*, on the other hand, is found only 5 times after *ca*: 198.8 *(çiertas)*, 200.22, 326.3 *(çierto*, supplied from *P)*, 424.8, 484.7.

[65]   «Certas nacido es en tirra/aquel qui en pace i en guera/senior a a seer da oriente/de todos hata in occidente», *Auto de los reyes magos*, 23-26 (ed. D. J. Gifford and F. W. Hodcroft, *Textos lingüísticos del medioevo español*, 2nd ed. [Oxford, 1966], 37); «Dubdar

follow the *Zifar*'s ubiquitous «'Çertas', dixo» construction. [66] There are a number of examples of the more widespread *çierto*, but nowhere is it used to anything like the same extent as *çertas* in the *Zifar*. We would seem, then, to be dealing here with something unique in medieval prose style.

The origins of the word *çertas* are not at all mysterious. Corominas *(DCELC,* I, 795) traces it to the Old French *certes* and mentions the cognate Provençal and Old Catalan forms *certas* and *certes*. This may explain the formal origin of the word, but it does not help at all to explain why the author of the *Zifar*—alone, it seems, among medieval authors—should have used it in an almost obsessional fashion. If we accept, however, the probability of Arabic influence on the work, then an explanation is possible. The use of an emphatic particle to introduce speech is a widespread Semitic stylistic device. We know it best perhaps in the biblical «*Verily,* I say unto you», but it is equally common outside the Scriptures. The Arabic emphatic particle *'inna* is mostly used to introduce an affirmative statement or after *qāla* (= *dixo)* to introduce a noun clause. [67] The use of *çertas* in the *Zifar* certainly corresponds very closely indeed to the use of *'inna* in Arabic. As there seems to be no other satisfactory explanation of why the compiler of a medieval Spanish romance should use an alien stylistic feature to such a marked extent, we are once more obliged to take seriously the possibility of a Semitic original for the *Zifar*.

podriamos çertas, si debiessemos dubdar/si nos podria don Xpo maior piadat far», Berceo, *Loores,* 135-136, BAE 57, 97; «Çiertas nom preçio menos que una emperadriz», *Libro de Alexandre,* 371d (composite numbering) ed. Raymond S. Willis Jr (EMRLL 32, Princeton-Paris, 1934), 70; «Bien tien que yago muerto e çertas ey grant mal», *ibid.,* 1573b; «Certas tod el poblo mientre que cata de facer el mandado de principe... entende de facer a las veces servicio de grado, a las veces de debda», *Fuero juzgo* (quoted in V. Fernández Llera, *Gramática y vocabulario del «Fuero juzgo»* [Madrid, 1929], 130); «Çiertas non lo tengo por bien», *Primera crónica general,* ch. 740, ed. R. Menéndez Pidal (Madrid, 1955), II, 438; «Estonçe rrespondio la bendita virgen: 'Çiertas yo deseo bevir'», *De Santa Catalina* (ed. Hermann Knust, *Geschichte der Legenden der h. Katharina von Alexandrien und der h. Maria Aegyptiaca* [Halle, 1890], 291); «Çertas, don Rodrigo, esta batalla cuesta a nos muy cara», *Crónica de 1344* (ed. R. Menéndez Pidal, *Reliquias de la poesia épica española* [Madrid, 1951], 203, nn. to 1.13); «e çiertas asy fue, que ansi gelo dixieron e el ansy lo cuidava», *Crónica de 1344* (quoted by R. Menéndez Pidal, *Homenaje a Menéndez y Pelayo,* I [Madrid, 1899], 442); «'Certas', dixo el cavallero, 'aun mas fazia'», *Libro de Josep de Abarimatia* (ed. Gifford and Hodcroft,*Textos lingüísticos,*101); «'Çiertas', dixo Galvan, 'es el mejor honbre e mejor cavallero que vos'», *Demanda del santo grial,* ch. 393 (ed. Adolfo Bonilla y San Martín, *Libros de caballerías,* I [NBAE 6, Madrid, 1907], 314); «Certas no que todo amor/de si debe proceder», Alfonso Enríquez, *Razonamiento,* 39-40 (ed. Francisca Vendrell de Millás, *Cancionero de Palacio (Manuscrito no. 594)* [Barcelona, 1945], 256); «certas yo me faria antes pieças que le envias mi filla», *Libro de Marco Polo,* ed. R. Stuebe (Leipzig, 1902), 9. Mrs Margaret Chaplin, Professor Brian Dutton, Mr F. W. Hodcroft and Professor J. W. Rees have all been kind enough to send me examples of *çertas* which they have found in the course of their work.

[66] These are the examples quoted from the *Josep de Abarimatia* and the *Demanda* in n. 65. A few lines before the *Josep* example cited there is an instance of *çierto* used in exactly the same way: «'Çierto', dixo el cavallero, 'sennor, sy'».

[67] See W. Wright, *A Grammar of the Arabic Language,* 3rd ed. (Cambridge, 1962-64), I, 284-285 and II, 47.

(ii) «*Dixo el sabio*», etc.

There are at least thirty-five occurrences of phrases such as «dixo el sabio» or «palabra es del sabio» used to introduce *sententiæ* in the *Zifar*. There appear to be seven basic types of these clichés, with variants:

(*a*) «palabra es del sabio/de los sabios»: 7.5, 14.12, 51.16
«palabra es de Salamón»: 321.18
«la palabra del sabio que dize asý»: 487.23 [68]

(*b*) «onde dize el/un sabio»: 23.23, 326.16-17, 334.30-335.1, 341.2, 361.2, 363.10, 398.7
«onde dize Salamón»: 325.27, 339.16
«onde dize el filósofo»: 307.24, 516.13

(*c*) «ca dize el/un sabio»: 263.18, 264.19, 331.18, 502.8
«ca dize el filósofo»: 300.11

(*d*) «e dize otro sabio»: 263.19-20, 263.22

(*e*) «e sabios antigos dizen»: 443.24
«segunt dizen los sabios antigos»: 38.3
«las opiniones de los sabios que dizen»: 348.24-25

(*f*) «e por esto dixo un sabio»: 318.26
«e en esta razón dixo un sabio»: 316.27
«es verdat lo que dixo el sabio»: 135.16
«asý commo dixo [Tulio] un sabio»: 303.15-16
«onde dixo [Abu Ubeyt] un sabio»: 38.9-10
«e asý se conplió la palabra del sabio que dixo»: 470.27

(*g*) «ca sobre esto dixieron los sabios»: 270.18-19
«e porende dixieron los sabios»: 308.21.

Phrases such as these are a clear echo of the Arabic commonplace *wa-qāla -l-ḥakīm*, «thus spake the sage», which occurs with almost monotonous frequency in Semitic wisdom literature. Examples of similar phrases abound in medieval Spanish works that are translations or adaptations of Arabic originals, such as the *Calila e Digna*, the *Poridat de las poridades* and the *Libro de los cien capítulos*. The *Disciplina clericalis*, written by a Spanish Jew and drawing heavily on Arabic sources, contains many Latin versions of similar phrases. [69] It is not, therefore,

---

[68] Cf. also «palabra es de la Santa Escriptura» (281.19, 304.19) and «dizen las palabras santas» (301.21).

[69] Pedro Alfonso, *Disciplina Clericalis*, ed. Angel González Palencia (Madrid-Granada, 1948). The equivalent phrases are, for example, «dixit alius philosophus», «dixit Socrates», etc.

surprising to find examples of such clichés in the Castilian translation of the Arabic *Flores de filosofía*, most of which is incorporated virtually *verbatim* into the *Zifar's Castigos del rey de Mentón*.[70] There are, in fact, seven ocurrences of such phrases in the *Flores:*[71]

> (*a*)   «e en esta rasón dixo un sabio» *(ley* IV, p. 21)
> (*b*)   «e sobre esto dixieron los sabios» *(ley* V, p. 22)
> (*c*)   «e por esso dixo un sabio» *(ley* VIII, p. 27)
> (*d*)   «e dixo un sabio» *(ley* XVII, p. 43)
> (*e*)   «ca disen los sabios» *(ley* XXXIII, p. 68)
> (*f*)   «e dixo el sabio» *(ley* XXXIII, p. 68)
> (*g*)   «e dixieron los sabios» *(ley* XXXV, p. 73).

Five of these—(*a*)-(*d*) and (*f*)—are carried over into the *Zifar*.[72] One of the others, (*e*), appears simply as «ca dizen»,[73] and (*g*) occurs in a section of the *Flores* not used by the *Zifar* author. In other words, we cannot attribute the frequency of these phrases in the *Zifar* simply to the fact that it reproduces virtually the whole of the *Flores*. The *Castigos* contains seventeen other occurrences of similar expressions which cannot be traced to the *Flores*. It is possible, of course, to ascribe the commonness in the *Castigos* of «dixo el sabio» and similar phrases to the general influence of the style of wisdom literature with which the *Zifar* author was undoubtedly familiar; but the fact that there are thirteen other examples of this kind of phrase in the other three books of the work, which are not overtly didactic, seems to be further evidence of an Arabic original.

(iii)   *«Dize el cuento»*, etc.

It is possible that the frequent use of phrases such as «dize el cuento» (33 occurrences),[74] «dize la escriptura» (10 occurrences),[75] and «cuenta la estoria» (2 occurrences)[76] may be a reflection of the common Arabic expression *wa-qāla -l-kitāb*, «the story relates». Too much importance should not be attached to this, however, since «dize el cuento» is also very common in texts that have no connection whatsoever with Semitic

[70]   Wagner, «Sources», 31-36.
[71]   Quotations and page references are from the edition of Hermann Knust, *Dos obras didácticas y dos leyendas, sacadas de manuscritos de la biblioteca del Escorial (SBE* XVII, Madrid, 1878). The *Flores* occupy pp. 11-83.
[72]   The distribution of these in the *Castigos* is as follows: *a*) 316.27; *b*) 270.18-19; *c*) 318.26; *d*) 264.19 (adapted to «ca dize un sabio»); *f*) 361.2 (adapted to «onde dize un sabio»).
[73]   «Ca dizen» is the reading of *M; P* and *S* give «ca suelen dezir los omes».
[74]   11.5, 17.16, 24.17, 40.6, 88.11, 94.10, 98.2, 106.19, 164.11, 178.20, 190.20, 226.20, 243.3, 256.7, 259.11, 266.25, 271.16, 283.15, 330.13, 332.12, 346.7, 368.10, 370.14, 375.17, 376.25, 418.36, 429.19, 438.6, 444.20, 478.12, 506.4, 514.6, 515.17.
[75]   6.23, 27.20, 290.25, 306.13, 331.20-21, 345.13, 361.22, 368.25-26, 372.15, 509.23. «Dize (en) la Santa Escriptura» is not included.
[76]   9.4, 167.14.

sources, such as numerous later romances of chivalry. [77]   Nevertheless
it is worth noting that the *Disciplina clericalis*, for example, introduces
many of its stories with «dictum est/fuit» or «relatum est»; that «dizen
que» is used in a similar way with great frequency in the *Calila e Digna;*
and that the bulk of the tales in the *Thousand and One Nights* open with
«It is related that».   Finally, R. S. Willis has suggested that even the use
of «dice la historia» in *Don Quijote* may be a reminiscence of this Arabic
stylistic trait:

> the vestigial form of the *isnād*, the chain of authorities that
> introduces and authenticates the text of the *hadith*, or record
> of an action or saying of the Prophet....   The presupposition
> is, of course, that the most authentic truth is that which emanates
> from Mohammed, and the chain seeks to reach back as close to
> him as possible. [78]

Of the twenty-seven interpolated *exempla* in the *Zifar* thirteen are
introduced by «dize el cuento» and one by «dize la escriptura»; a further
one begins «e dize asý».   The other main use of these *incipit* phrases in
the *Zifar* is to indicate that we are about to follow the adventures of a
different character from the one we have just left.   In view of the other
stylistic features of the *Zifar* that are unmistakably Semitic, it is perhaps
legitimate to regard «dize el cuento» as a further indication of an Arabic
original. [79]

(iv)   «*Pensar en el coraçón*», etc.

Since Arabic has no genuine reflexive pronouns, one of the ways of
expressing the reflexive idea is to use the word *nafs*, «soul» or «spirit»,
acompanied by a pronominal affix. [80]   Alvaro Galmés de Fuentes points
out that in medieval Spanish works that are straightforward translations
from the Arabic, such as the *Calila e Digna*, the construction with *nafs*
is frequently rendered not by the normal Spanish reflexive but by an
expression such as «pensé en mi coraçón» or «aviendo esta contienda
con mi alma». [81]

---

[77]   The Spanish *Tristán*, for example, begins almost every chapter with «dize el
cuento».
[78]   *The Phantom Chapters of the «Quijote»* (New York, 1953), 101.   Cf. E. C. Riley,
Cervantes's Theory of the Novel, 210.
[79]   The use of these phrases as an element of the author's style and narrative technique
is discussed below in ch. 3, section D and ch. 5, section B (i).
[80]   See Wright, *Grammar*, II, 271-272, 280-282.
[81]   «Influencias sintácticas y estilísticas del árabe en la prosa medieval castellana»,
BRAE XXXVI (1956), 65-131, at pp. 97-98.   This monograph, to which frequent
reference will be made, appeared in four parts: *BRAE* XXXV (1955), 213-275 and
415-451, XXXVI (1956), 65-131 and 255-307.

The *Zifar* abounds in phrases involving *coraçón*, most of which clearly draw on the symbolic associations of the heart as the seat of courage, intellect and emotion. [82] There are some others, however, which convey little, if anything, more than an intensive reflexive: «pensó en su coraçón» (14.23, 29.7, 175.19-20, 232.19-20, 273.14-15); «conçibe en su coraçón» (236.14-15); «perjuró en su coraçón» (13.21); «he propuesto en mi coraçón» (176.23); «júdguelo en su coraçón» (465.25-26); «asosiegue el tu coraçón» (205.16-17); «venir a coraçón» (35.18, 267.20-21, 382.26, 383.16). The only possible symbolism that could be involved in these cases is that of the heart as the the innermost part of the being, a concept which is, of course, implicit in the Arabic *nafs*.

Since such phrases are not confined to medieval Spanish works that have a known Arabic original, [83] their presence in the *Zifar* is not in itself proof of direct Semitic influence or origin; but they take on rather more significance if we consider them alongside the many other traces of Arabic stylistic conventions that are to be found in the work.

(v) *The Expression of an Indefinite Personal Subject*

On the expression of an indefinite personal subject Galmés de Fuentes writes:

> La clara tendencia personalizadora de la lengua árabe determina que en ella sean escasas las formas propias para la expresión de un sujeto indeterminado y general. Por el contrario, el árabe habilita desde los primeros tiempos distintas formas personales, que permiten un juego de intervención entre el escritor y sus lectores como interlocutores posibles, reemplazando a pronombres o sustantivos indefinidos para expresar la idea de un sujeto indeterminado; para realizar tal función se sirve el árabe, ante todo, de la 3ª persona del plural, 3ª persona del singular y 2ª persona del singular (99).

In his subsequent account of the survival of these three ways of expressing the indefinite personal subject in Spanish, Galmés de Fuentes quotes the following examples from the *Zifar:*

> E el enperador mandó que levasen âquél e troxiesen al segundo (31.4-5)

> E estonçe mandó la señora de la villa que pensasen dél e que·l diesen todas aquellas cosas que·l fuesen mester (50.4-5)

---

[82] These are discussed in ch. 5, section B (iii) below.
[83] See C. C. Smith and J. Morris, «On 'Physical' Phrases in Old Spanish Epic and Other Texts», *PLPLS: Lit. and Hist. Section* XII, part v (1967), 129-190, at pp. 169-170, where such phrases in epic and *clerecía* works are discussed.

E maguer que el enemigo omildoso sea, non le deven tener en poco; ante lo deve ome temer (146.9-10)

Pero dos maneras son de omes largos: a los unos dizen desgastadores e a los otros francos (356.8-9)

E proveetvos muy bien de todas las cosas que vos fuere mester ante que entredes en la guerra; ca poco valen las armas en la lid sy ante que entre en ella non ha buen acuerdo e sea bien aperçebido de cómmo ha de usar dellas (361.14-18). [84]

Arabic has no indefinite third-person pronoun corresponding to the French *on*, German *man* or Latin *quisquam, quidam, quisque, quisquis*, etc. When Arabic does not use a person of the verb to express the indefinite subject, it avails itself of a generalized noun such as *rajul* or *'insān*, «man», «humanity». These words always function as nouns in Arabic; they never degenerate into simple pronouns. [85] Galmés de Fuentes shows how *rajul* and its synonyms are translated into Old Spanish by *omne* which, he asserts, functions quite differently from its French counterpart *on*. Whereas *on* undergoes considerable phonetic reduction and completely loses its original substantival function, *omne* remains a full noun. In the words of S. Kärde:

> *omne* n'a acquis, à être employé de cette façon, aucune signification nouvelle qui le distingue nettement du substantif *omne*. Par conséquent, là où un grammairien reconnaît la valeur pronominale de *omne*, un autre pourra la contester et trouvera que *omne* est équivalent à «l'homme» ou à «un homme». [86]

Furthermore, Galmés de Fuentes points out some instances in which French *on* is rendered in a Spanish translation not by *omne*, but by the third-person plural form of the verb.

All this emboldens one to suggest that the common use of *ome* as an indefinite subject in the *Zifar* may be a further reflection of an Arabic source. Not surprisingly, in view of the findings of Galmés de Fuentes, many of the examples of this structure are to be found in those sections of the *Castigos del rey de Mentón* that derive directly from the *Flores de filosofía*. [87] But there are very many other occurrences of *ome* or *el ome* used to express an indefinite subject elsewhere in the *Zifar*. [88]

[84] This is the only example of the third-person singular construction in the *Zifar*, and it only occurs in *M; P* and *S* insert *ome* before *entre*.

[85] See Galmés de Fuentes, «Influencias», 126.

[86] *Quelques manières d'exprimer l'idée d'un sujet indéterminé ou général en espagnol* (Uppsala, 1943), 14 (quoted in «Influencias», 129).

[87] E.g. 270.13/19/23, 271.9, 279.8/18, 280.1, 281.24, 282.7/12, 291.1/3/7/8/13/16/23/24/25, etc.

[88] E.g. 16.4, 27.21, 75.4, 127.17-18, 127.20, etc.

(vi) *Paranomasia*

Paranomasia, the juxtaposition of words with the same morphological root, plays a much more important part in Semitic languages than it does in European languages, where the tendency is to seek as much lexical variety as possible. Galmés de Fuentes (283-291) studies various types of paranomasia in Arabic and shows how they are reflected in the style of works translated from Arabic into Spanish. The first type is what he calls *figura etimológica*, in which the verb and one of the surrounding nouns have the same morphological root. The *Zifar* contains numerous examples of this device: for example, «fazer algunt mal fecho» (75.5) «posaron en una posada» (188.7), «fízole cavalgar en el cavallo del cavallero» (196.26), «non le podría peor nasçençia nasçer» (206.10-11), «acátalos con fermoso catar» (302.4).

Another type of paranomasia frequent in Arabic is the repetition of the same verb with various subjects or the linking of two or more clauses by the repetition of the verb. These devices are not usual in the Romance languages on account of the *horror aequi*, but they are found very often in Spanish translations from Arabic. They also occur in the *Zifar:*

> E guárdete Dios non te contesca commo contesçió a un asno con su señor (109.5-6) [89]

> El dolor va enpós del que fuye, e çertamente el que fuye non fuye sy non con dolor que siente e tiene ya consigo, e fuye de otro mayor que va en pos él (113.26-28)

> ca sy del bien usare, puede le durar, e sy non usare del bien, puede lo perder (309.27-29)

> E commoquier que de los otros me espediese, de vós non me podía espedir maguer quisiese (388.17-19).

(vii) *Parataxis*

The juxtaposition of clauses and sentences connected only by the simple copulative *e* is a prominent feature of early Spanish prose from Alfonso X onwards. [90] J. Oliver Asín states categorically that this is due to the influence of Arabic; [91] but a certain caution is advisable here,

---

[89]   Cf. the almost identical construction in 259.5-6, 370.11, 372.13, 373.17-18.
[90]   See *Antología de prosistas españoles*, ed. R. Menéndez Pidal, 8th ed. (Austral 110, Madrid, 1964), 17.
[91]   *Historia de la lengua española*, 3rd ed. (Madrid, 1939), 65-66.

since parataxis is also common in Old French and Middle English p rose.[92] However, Galmés de Fuentes makes three important points which considerably strengthen Oliver Asín's thesis. First, parataxis is not so widespread in Old French texts as it is in the Spanish translations from the Arabic (268). Secondly, it falls into disuse much more quickly in French that it does in Spanish, where examples can be found well into the Golden Age (272). [93] Thirdly, in those parts of Alfonso X's works where Latin sources are being used «aparece ausente el estilo paratáctico» (269).

Classical Arabic syntax relies very heavily on parataxis, using the two inseparable conjunctions *wa* and *fa* to link together its juxtaposed clauses and sentences. *Wa* is equivalent to the simple copulative «and». *Fa* is rather more emphatic and implies some clear connection, either of sequence or causality, with the preceding clause; it is usually translated «and so», «and therefore» or «for». [94] In view of this, it is tempting to look no further for the origin of the ubiquitous *e* and *ca* in the *Zifar*'s paratactic structures. Parataxis is so common in the romance that virtually every page provides perfect examples; it is sufficient to quote just two:

> E el fijo fízolo asý, e desý el padre sacó luego segurança de la otra parte e apaçiguólo muy bien. E otro día fizo matar un puerco e mesólo e cortóle la cabeça e los pies, e guardólos, e metió el puerco en un saco e atólo muy bien e púsole so el lecho, e enbió por su fijo que se veniese en la tarde. E quando fue a la tarde llegó el fijo e acogióle el padre muy bien e díxole de cómmo el otro le avía asegurado, e çenaron (18.20-27)

> ca non eres tú ome para dezir al rey mi padre ninguna cosa, nin él para te responder. Ca tú eres ome estraño e non sabemos quién eres. Ca mala venida feziste a esta tierra, ca mejor fizieras de folgar en la tuya (406.12-16). [95]

* * *

There are numerous other stylistic and syntactical features of Old Spanish which, according to Galmés de Fuentes, reflect Semitic conventions. Many of these also occur in the *Zifar*, but a detailed investigation of them

---

[92] See, for example, Peter M. Schon, *Studien zum Stil der frühen französischen Prosa (Robert de Clari, Geoffroy de Villehardouin, Henri de Valenciennes)* (Analecta Romanica 8, Frankfurt am Main, 1960), 150; Margaret Schlauch, «The Art of Chaucer's Prose», *Chaucer and Chaucerians. Critical Studies in Middle English Literature*, ed. D. S. Brewer (London, 1966), 140-163, at p. 144.

[93] Margaret Schlauch, *art. cit.*, points out that much of Chaucer's more artistic prose is not primarily paratactic.

[94] Wright, *Grammar*, I, 290-291.

[95] J. F. Burke, *A Critical and Artistic Study of the «Libro del Cavallero Cifar»* (unpubl. diss. of the University of North Carolina at Chapel Hill, 1966), 127-133, discusses the literary effectiveness of the *Zifar*'s paratactic syntax.

would enlarge this study beyond tolerable limits. [96] Already enough evidence has been produced to show that some of the more incontrovertibly Arabic features to be found in Old Spanish are abundantly represented in the *Zifar*. None of them, of course, taken by itself, is indicative of very much; but the presence of so many seems to show beyond reasonable doubt that the author was familiar with the stylistic and syntactical conventions of the Semitic languages. This is one more reason for taking seriously the claim in the Prologue that «la estoria ... fue trasladada de caldeo».

E. THE MORAL TONE

Earlier critics have pointed out that in many respects the tone and spirit of the *Zifar* do not fit into the usual pattern of European romances of chivalry. The clearest statement of this is probably María Rosa Lida de Malkiel's:

> the *Zifar* clashes with the Arthurian narratives. Its religion is robust and by no means mystical; its protagonists are moral and middle-class, with stray gleams of humour. Not even in the last part, a trifle less pedestrian and didactic, are there traces of courtly love or of pure chivalric honour. [97]

Other scholars stress the work's powerful didactic element and its extraordinary mixture of different literary genres, two features which also set it apart from the more typical romance of chivalry. Menéndez y Pelayo, for instance, calls the *Zifar* «un *spécimen* de todos los géneros de ficción y aun de literatura doctrinal que hasta entonces se habían ensayado en Europa». [98] Is it not possible that at least some of the puzzling points about the work's moral tone may, in fact, be reflections of Islamic and Arabic rather than Christian and European ideals?

---

[96] One may note in passing the use of a preposition and a tonic form of the personal pronoun instead of *ý*, as in «corríale la tierra e fazíale mucho mal en ella» (190.22-23; cf. «Influencias», 82-86); the tonic form of the personal pronoun used to express simple accusative or dative relationships, as in «salieron a él» (20.1-2), «yo perdoné a ellos» (23.4), «grant bien quería ella a él» (26.22; cf. «Influencias», 78-82); the infinitive used in place of an abstract noun, as in «perdió la fabla, el oýr e el ver» (26.4-5; cf. «Influencias», 260-262); the *non... synon* construction used to express the concept of *sólo*, as in «non guardan a su amigo synon demientra pueden fazer su pro con él» (17.23-24; cf. «Influencias», 296-298).

[97] «Arthurian Literature in Spain and Portugal», 414.

[98] *Orígenes de la novela*, ed. E. Sánchez Reyes (Edición Nacional, 2nd ed., Madrid, 1962), I, 295. Cf. P. Bohigas Balaguer, «Orígenes de los libros de caballería», *Historia general de las literaturas hispánicas*, ed. G. Díaz-Plaja, I (Barcelona, 1949), 532: «En él se hallan cabida, en forma que no se da en ninguna otra obra, todos los géneros y tendencias de la literatura española de fines del siglo XIII o principios del XIV, desde el apólogo oriental hasta las narraciones del cicle bretón».

In the first place, chivalry was not confined to the Christian nations of the Middle Ages, but also existed amongst the Moslems. *Al-futuwwa* was a religious brotherhood dedicated to more or less the same ideals as the European orders of chivalry: the service of God and the protection of the weak. [99] But whereas Christian chivalry—in literature at least—became involved with an egocentric desire for personal honour and with the fundamentally anti-religious doctrines of courtly love, the Islamic variety remained practical and spiritual. The perfect knight of the type of Lancelot or Gawain feels it a point of honour to fight any other knight he comes across so as to confirm his position as the greatest champion of all and to make himself more worthy of his lady's love. Zifar, on the other hand, fights only when he has to, when there is no other way out. His opponents tend to be arrogant bullies who take advantage of the weak, such as the lady ruler of Galapia, or the old, such as the King of Mentón. The Moslem *fatā* could be of any age between eighteen and forty, married or unmarried; the typical European knight of literature is always young, rich, handsome and unmarried—characteristics which fit him to be a courtly lover rather than the humble servant of a religious ideal.

Secondly, courtly love, the basis of the ethic of the typical romance of chivalry, was evolved—or at least came to prominence—amongst the heretical Cathars of southern France. [100] Although it is unlikely that Catharism can provide a complete explanation of the origins and cult of courtly love, it is surely not merely coincidental that both flourished in the same society at the same time. At the very least, they are manifestations of the same sensibility, a sensibility which differed strikingly from that of the religiously orthodox feudal societies of the rest of Europe. The Cathars accorded much less importance to authority in general and upheld a more permissive attitude to sex and a belief in the ennobling effects of chaste love, freely entered into and not hedged around with prohibitions and taboos. Theirs was, in other words, a matrist religion. Christianity and Islam, on the other hand, are both patrist religions serving patrist societies which preach the subjection of women, respect for authority and the sacredness of property (which includes conjugal rights). Broadly speaking, then, medieval Moslem and Christian writers would uphold the same set of social and religious values. This is one possible reason why so much literature written by Moslems and Jews (who are also patrists) found a congenial home in the patrist atmosphere of medieval Castile. It may well be this fusion of Christian and Islamic patrism in the *Zifar* that

[99] See W. B. Ghali, *La Tradition chevaleresque des Arabes* (Paris, 1919). Burke, *A Critical and Artistic Study*, 53-58, also discusses the possible influence of Arabic chivalric ideals on the *Zifar*. For European chivalry, see Sidney Painter, *French Chivalry* (Ithaca, 1940) and Edgar Prestage (ed.), *Chivalry. A Series of Studies to Illustrate its Historical Significance and Civilizing Influence* (London, 1928).

[100] See Denis de Rougemont, *Passion and Society*, 2nd ed. (London, 1956), especially Books II and III.

distinguishes it so clearly from the romantic productions of the *matière de Bretagne*. [101]

Thirdly, perhaps the most important anomaly in the *Zifar* that can be cleared up if we suggest an Arabic source is the hero's second, bigamous marriage to the daughter of the King of Mentón whilst his first wife is still alive. Marriage to the princess is, of course, necessary to the story; without it Zifar could not inherit the throne of Mentón. [102] At the same time, the author must have felt that adulterer and bigamist was hardly a suitable role for such an exemplary moral hero as Zifar. To resolve his difficulty he allows the marriage to take place, but introduces the rather unconvincing two-year vow of chastity, which the new wife, even more unconvincingly, accepts. Before the two years are up, however, the queen obligingly dies and leaves Zifar free to reclaim his first wife and make her his royal partner. The whole sequence gives the impression of a rather embarrassed compromise on the part of the Castilian author. If the *Zifar* is seen as an adaptation of an Arabic original, however, it is easy to realize how the problem arose: an Islamic hero would face no moral dilemma whatsoever if he chose to take a second wife, since his religion encouraged polygamy. A relic of the earlier version seems to survive in the presentation of the hero's second marriage as the express will of God. The hermit, with whom Zifar stays after the loss of his family, reports that in his vision of the knight's future greatness he was told by the heavenly voice:

> Dy al tu huésped que ora es de andar; e bien çierto sea que ha de desçercar aquel rey e ha de casar con su fija, e a de aver el regno después de sus días (121.28-122.3).

It is very unlikely that this divine encouragement to commit bigamy is the independent creation of a Christian author.

F. The sources

So far we have looked only at the internal evidence provided by a number of proper names, certain stylistic features and some aspects of the moral tone that suggest an Arabic source for the *Zifar*. An examination of the subject matter of the romance reveals further likely debts to Semitic

[101] For a discussion and definition of patrism and matrism, see G. Rattray Taylor, *Sex in History* (London, 1953).

[102] Many folk-tales and several medieval romances (which often, of course, have their remote origins in folk-tales) preserve this relic of primitive matrilinear societies, where succession to a throne is through the female line. See Margaret Schlauch, *Chaucer's Constance and Accused Queens* (New York, 1927).

literature, which can be conveniently studied under three headings: the didactic element, the supernatural episodes, and the story of Zifar's adventures.

(i) The Didactic Element

It has long been recognized that the author of the *Zifar* was familiar with Islamic wisdom literature, on which he drew freely for his many moralizing passages. The most striking example of this borrowing occurs, as we have seen, in the *Castigos del rey de Mentón*, which incorporate practically the whole of the *Flores de filosofía* almost *verbatim*. The *Flores* themselves derive from the longer *Libro de los cien capítulos*, [103] which «guarda estrecha relación con otras obras didácticas en prosa del siglo XIII o principios del XIV, muy particularmente con *Bocados de oro*, *Poridat de las poridades*, *Castigos e documentos*, y las *Siete partidas* de Alfonso el Sabio». [104] All these works, of course, when they are not simply translations from the Arabic, draw heavily on Semitic originals. Traces of all of them (and of some others such as the *Barlaam e Josapha*) can be found in the didactic sections of the *Zifar*.

The problem facing anyone who tries to identify precise sources in this confused mass of moralizing literature has been clearly stated by Agapito Rey: «Los frecuentes paralelismos verbales pueden obedecer a la comunidad de fuentes más que al influjo directo de un texto sobre otro.» [105] C. P. Wagner has tried to attribute certain parts of the *Castigos del rey de Mentón* that do not derive from the *Flores* to specific sources in other works of the same type, notably the *Siete partidas* and the *Castigos e documentos*; [106] but the commonplace nature of the various precepts, the multiplicity of thirteenth-century wisdom books that draw on the same basic material, and the consequent impossibility of saying with any certainty whether the *Zifar* is using one or other of the vernacular versions or is drawing independently on the «comunidad de fuentes», makes the exercise an almost impossible one. [107] All we can say with confidence is that the *Zifar* author was undoubtedly familiar with oriental wisdom literature in Spanish translations (as any educated man in Toledo at that period must

[103] See Miguel Zapata y Torres, «Breves notas sobre el *Libro de los cien capítulos* como base de las *Flores de filosofía*», *Smith College Studies in Modern Languages* X, 2 (Jan. 1929), 43-54.

[104] *El libro de los cien capítulos*, ed. Agapito Rey (IUHS 44, Bloomington, Ind., 1960), vii.

[105] *Cien capítulos*, vii.

[106] «Sources», 31-40.

[107] Wagner, «Sources», 31, says that «excepting in the case of a few Biblical allusions, we need not look beyond the Spanish didactic works of the thirteenth century for the sources of this part of the *Cifar*». Later, however (44), when talking of these works, he says that «to examine any two of these texts, is to be confronted by a mass of parallel passages, often strikingly similar», without considering the possibility of a common Arabic (or Latin) source.

have been, and as his use of the Castilian version of the *Flores* proves); but whether he knew the Semitic originals of these translations is a question that cannot really be answered.

The same difficulty arises over the attribution of the interpolated tales and fables in the *Zifar*. There were so many collections of stories and *exempla* in the Middle Ages, in Latin, in Arabic and in the vernacular languages, all making use of a common stock of traditional material, that it is impossible to say with any certainty precisely where the *Zifar* author took his tales from. It is true that many of them are of undisputed oriental origin, and some of them appear not only in the *Zifar*, but also in other works of clear Arabic provenance, such as the *Disciplina clericalis* and the *Castigos e documentos*. [108] We shall probably never know whether the *Zifar* author took his *exempla* directly from a Semitic source or whether he drew them from a number of works in various languages.

One feature of the *Zifar*'s technique of story-telling, however, the interpolation of tales within tales, is undoubtedly Arabic in origin. The typical oriental collection of fables or *exempla* takes the form of a frame story in which the characters relate tales to each other. This basic structure is often enormously elaborated by making the protagonists of the tales themselves tell other tales, whose characters in turn narrate yet more stories, and so on. One of the most fully developed examples of this technique is the *Thousand and One Nights*. [109] At the beginning of the work the author introduces the story of King Shahryār and Shahrazād. Shahrazād begins by telling the tale of the Fisherman and the Jinnī, which is followed by the Fisherman's relating the story of the Wazīr of King Yūnān and Rayyān the Doctor. Both the King and the Wazīr then tell their own tales, the former of Sinbād and the Falcon, the latter of the Prince and the Ogress. After all this we return to Shahrazād's story of the Fisherman and the Jinnī. And so the elaborate and, to the western reader, confusing process winds on.

Many of the oriental collections of tales that were translated or adapted into Spanish follow the technique of the frame story, but usually, like the *Libro de los engaños*, avoid the interpolation of tales within tales. An exception, however, is the *Calila e Digna* which follows the traditional highly complex structural pattern of the original Sanskrit *Panchatantra*. [110]

In three places the *Zifar* has the protagonist of an *exemplum* himself telling a story. In chapter 5 Zifar relates the famous tale of the Father, the Son and the Half-Friend; in the following chapter the Father tells the story of the Whole Friend. At the beginning of the *Castigos* Zifar instructs

[108]   For an account of the other versions of the *exempla* in the *Zifar*, see Wagner, «Sources», 74-90 and John E. Keller, *Motif-Index of Mediaeval Spanish Exempla* (Knoxville, Tenn., 1949).
[109]   I have used the English translation of Sir Richard F. Burton, *The Book of the Thousand Nights and a Night*, repr. and ed. Leonard C. Smithers, 12 vols (London, 1894).
[110]   For a discussion of this point, see Keller, *Alfonso X*, 56.

his sons with the tale of the King and the Preacher (ch. 124), and follows it immediately with the tale of the King (the same king) and the Apothecary (ch. 125). The next chapter is devoted to the fable of the Hunter and the Lark, which is told by the Apothecary to the King. Finally, there is a good example of tales within tales at the end of the *Castigos*. In chapter 171 Zifar relates the story of the Moorish King and his Steward; chapters 172 and 173 contain the fable of the Wolf and the Leeches and the tale of the Cardinal and the Pope, both put into the mouth of the Steward. In this use of the technique of multiple levels of narration in *exempla* it is tempting to see Arabic influence on the *Zifar* author; but again, it may be second-hand.

(ii) *The Supernatural Episodes*

Critics have already suggested that oriental features are to be found in the supernatural episodes of the *Zifar*. In the adventure of the Cavallero Atrevido and the female ruler of the Enchanted Lake (chs 110-117) A. H. Krappe has found many parallels in folklore and literature, both generally oriental and specifically Arabic, for the seven basic motifs that he discerns in the episode. [111] María Rosa Lida de Malkiel, however, asserts that «Krappe's analysis does not carry conviction», since «the author of the *Zifar* in inserting other extraneous stories does not freely combine individual motifs, but on the contrary adheres in each instance to a single continuous source». [112] Nevertheless, this does not really invalidate Krappe's point, since there may well have been an oriental story which combined all or most of the seven motifs but which is now lost to us, or which has eluded the search of the folklorists. Krappe himself makes a similar point at the end of his article:

> À l'époque qui précède l'invention de l'imprimerie, il faut compter avec deux genres de sources, toutes deux également hors de notre portée: les sources perdues et les sources orales .... Pour ce qui est des sources écrites perdues, il est vain de s'en occuper. Pour les sources orales, il en est autrement. C'est qu'elles ne sont pas perdues, mais sont aujourd'hui aussi vivaces que jamais .... Naturellement, il est impossible d'affirmer catégoriquement que tel récit oral recueilli de nos jours est la source *directe* de tel épisode d'un roman médiéval quelconque .... Ce qui nous suffit, c'est de signaler le *type*, le thème général

---

[111] «Le Lac enchanté dans le *Chevalier Cifar*», *BH* XXXV (1933), 107-125. Wagner, «Sources», 29, in answer to whom Krappe wrote his article, confesses himself baffled by this «obscure allegory».

[112] «Arthurian Literature in Spain and Portugal», 414. Three years before, however, Mrs Malkiel had cited Krappe's article without adverse comment, calling it «la discusión de fuentes y paralelos de este episodio en el folklore y en la literatura» (addendum to Patch, *El otro mundo*, 410, n. 10).

(que j'ai appelé *motif* dans l'étude qu'on vient de lire) et d'affirmer que notre auteur a puisé dans un conte oral appartenant à ce type (124-125).

Krappe has also contributed an excellent, if somewhat tetchy, article on the other main supernatural episode in the *Zifar*, the adventure of Roboán on the *Islas Dotadas*, in which he demonstrates the many parallels that exist between this story and stories in the *Thousand and One Nights*, the *Seven Vizirs* and earlier Indian stories. [113] He objects to the persistent habit of many medievalists of claiming to find «partout l'influence des romans bretons et les fées celtiques» (99), a habit which has come in for increasing criticism in recent years. [114] In view of the considerable Arabic influence on other aspects of the *Zifar*, Krappe is probably right when he says:

> Les romans bretons et les maîtresses-fées ne sont donc pour rien dans cet épisode du *Chavalier Cifar* qui n'est qu'un récit oriental d'origine indienne et apporté en Espagne par les Arabes (103).

On this occasion Mrs Malkiel agrees with Krappe that the *Zifar* author started out from an oriental source. [115]

The two principal marvellous episodes in the *Zifar* are, then, likely to be of eastern origin; the various Celtic parallels can be ascribed either to universal folklore motifs or to elements in Celtic mythology that are themselves of oriental provenance.

(iii) *The Story of Zifar*

Hermann Knust was the first to trace the similarities between the first two books of the *Zifar* and the widely circulated and highly influential medieval legend of the Roman general Placidus, later to become St Eustace. [116] Knust's findings were more fully investigated by Wagner

---

[113] «Le Mirage celtique et les sources du *Chevalier Cifar*», *BH* XXXIII (1931), 97-103.

[114] F. Carmody, «Les Sources orientales du *Perceval* de Chrétien de Troyes», *RLC* XXXIX (1965), 497-545, shows—conclusively, to my mind—that many of the so-called Celtic elements in Chrétien's romances are in fact oriental. He attacks the Celticists for their over-zealous desire to attribute everything «soit à des textes irlandais perdus et entièrement hypothétiques, soit à des textes celtiques déjà marqués d'influences continentales» (519). Cf. the similar approach and conclusions in Silvestro Fiore, «Nouvelles considérations sur la fusion des éléments orientaux et cambriens dans la formation du roman courtois», *AION, Sez. Rom.* XI (1969), 33-51. Both the popularity of the east as a «pays de merveilles» and also the very real knowledge of the east possessed by medieval Europeans are surveyed by Jean Richard in «La Vogue de l'Orient» (see n. 43 above).

[115] «Arthurian Literature», 414.

[116] *Dos obras didácticas y dos leyendas*, 88-93. Knust also points out the similarities between the Eustace story and the William of England legend and discusses the relationship of these works to the German romances *Die gute Frau, Wilhelm von Wenden*

who concluded firmly that the «author of the *Cifar* has used as the skeleton of his story, the primitive Placidus legend». [117] Wagner's conclusion has been universally accepted by later critics, [118] with three notable exceptions whose views on the matter will be examined in detail later. First of all, however, a long overdue revaluation of Wagner's evidence must be made.

The story of Placidus as found in the Latin and Greek versions of the *Acta Sanctorum* is told in outline by Wagner («Sources», 14-17). I reproduce his outline below, noting the few points at which the Spanish version of the legend (which Wagner says the *Zifar* author must have used) differs from the earlier accounts: [119]

> Placidus [Sp. *Plácidas*] is the commander of the forces of the Emperor Trajan [Sp. *Troyano*]. He is not a Christian, but is of a charitable and noble disposition, and has a good wife, and two boys that he has brought up with the greatest care. He is very fond of hunting, and one day, while in pursuit of a fine stag, he becomes separated from his companions. The stag turns and faces him, and he beholds between its horns the sign of the cross. Filled with wonder he stops, and hears the stag speak, saying he is the Christ, who has appeared to him in this form that he may be turned to Christianity, and go to the Bishop of Rome and be baptized. Placidus believes, and hastens home to tell his wife of the miracle; but Christ has already appeared to her in a dream, and she is ready to believe also. At night they go to the Bishop with their children, and all are baptized. Placidus receives the name of Eustathius [Sp. *Eustacio*], while his wife is called Theospita [Sp. *Teóspita*], and his two sons Agapius [Sp. *Agapito*] and Theospitus [Sp. *Teóspito*]. [120] On the next day Eustathius goes again into the forest, and again meets the stag. He is told that he is to be tried like Job, but that he must not lose courage and he will receive his reward. With this the vision disappears.

and *Der Graf von Savoien* and the Middle English *Syr Isambrace* (93-104). The various treatments of the Eustace legend known to Knust are examined on pp. 107-121. A much more detailed study of the ramifications of the legend and related stories is provided by A. H. Krappe, «La leggenda di S. Eustachio» *Nuovi Studi Medievali* III (1926-27), 223-258.

[117] «Sources», 13-29; the quotation occurs on p. 29.

[118] See, for example, Menéndez y Pelayo, *Orígenes*, I, 296; Entwistle, *The Arthurian Legend*, 72; Thomas, *Spanish and Portuguese Romances*, 14; Ruiz de Conde, *El amor y el matrimonio secreto*, 39; Bohigas Balaguer, «Orígenes de los libros de caballería», 532.

[119] The Spanish version of the legend, *De un cavallero Plácidas*, has been edited by Knust, *Dos obras*, 123-157. Wagner's belief that this was the main source for the *Zifar* is based on the point that the forms of the names of Eustace and his family (90.26-91.1) coincide with those in the *Plácidas* («Sources», 29). This is true of the names of the wife and the sons, but not of the husband, who is called Eustacio in the *Plácidas* and Eustachio in the *Zifar*. Eustachio is the reading of *P* and *S; M* calls him Auestechio.

[120] Wagner, «Sources», 15, n. 1, points out that the spelling of these names varies considerably in the different Latin versions.

His trials begin with the loss of his slaves [Sp. *toda su conpanna ... asý servientes commo cavalleros*] and his cattle by a pestilence; and when he has retired with his family to a safer place, thieves break into his home and take all that he has. With the loss of his wealth his friends begin to look down upon him, and, rather than endure their scorn, he sets out for Egypt with his wife and children.

After two days [Sp. time not specified], they come to the sea, and seek a passage on one of the foreign ships in the harbour [Sp. *fallaron ý una nave*]. They have no money for the fare; but the captain, seeing the beauty of Theospita, offers to retain her for pay, and on the indignant refusal of Eustathius has him thrown into the sea. He makes his way to the land, and weeping and lamenting, goes on his way with his children.

Before long he comes to a certain river that is so swollen with the recent rains [Sp. *tan grande e tan ancho;* no mention of rains] that he dares not ford it with both boys. Leaving one on the bank, he takes the other across on his shoulders. When in mid-stream, he is horrified to see a lion bear off one child and a wolf the other before he can do anything to prevent them. In despair, and likening himself to Job, he goes on alone to a certain town, Badyssus [Sp. *Dadisa*] by name, where he is able to earn a living by working in the fields. He does not know that shepherds [Sp. *caçadores*] have rescued one of his children from the lion, and ploughmen [Sp. *carvoneros*] the other from the wolf, and that both are living in the same village, unknown to each other.

Theospita, meantime, is kindly treated by the Barbarian captain, who does not approach her. He dies soon after they reach his country [Sp. he tries to get into bed with her and *tomóle un mal tan fuerte que lo mató luego*], and she lives alone in the garden of a certain rich man [Sp. the sailors, terrified by the death of their captain, give her as a servant to a rich woman, who gives her a garden to live in].

During this time the Barbarians invade Roman territory, and the Emperor sends soldiers in all directions to look for Placidus to lead his troops. Two of them, Antiochus and Achacius [Sp. *Antiocus* and *Agnachis*], former soldiers [Sp. *amigos*] of Placidus, come to Badyssus. Placidus himself entertains them; but in answer to their enquiries, claims to know nothing of the man they seek, until they recognize him by a certain scar on his forehead. They tell him that he is to be raised to his former high estate, and clothe him in fitting raiment sent by the Emperor. They go back to Rome with him, where he is received with great pomp, and placed again in command of the army.

When recruits are called for, the two sons of Eustathius are sent from their village, as the most able and soldierly in the place. They come under the notice of the General, who makes them a part of his bodyguard.

The army sets out, and crosses the Hydaspes [Sp. *Jaspes*] river and comes to the town where Theospita is living; and it so happens that the tent of the General is pitched in her very garden. She herself entertains her two sons, who, in her presence, fall to relating stories of their childhood. [121] From their stories they discover their relation to each other, and she recognizes them as her boys. Upon this she goes to the General, to tell him her story, and to beg him to take her to Rome. They recognize each other, and she tells him that their children are alive. After the general rejoicing, the Barbarians are defeated, and the army returns in triumph to Rome, where it is found that Trajan has been succeeded by Hadrian [Sp. *Adrien*] who is intolerant towards Christians.

The sacrifice of victory is celebrated in the temple of Apollo. Placidus does not sacrifice, and when taken to task by the Emperor, proclaims his Christianity. The Emperor orders him and his family to be cast into the arena, as prey for a lion; but the beast refuses to touch them. All recognize the miracle but Hadrian, who orders a brazen ox to be heated, and Eustathius and his family to be cast into it. They enter praying. On the third day, when their bodies are taken out, they are found intact, and not a hair of their heads singed. Their bodies are reverently borne away by the Christians, and given fitting burial, and a chapel is consecrated to their memory.

Wagner notes six points at which the Placidus story coincides with that of the first two books of the *Zifar:*

(*a*) A knight, who has lost honour in his own country, sets out with his wife and children to seek his fortune elsewhere.

(*b*) The knight loses his wife and children.

(*c*) The knight and his wife pass through independent series of adventures.

(*d*) The children are found by strangers and brought up in the same town.

(*e*) The mother finds her two children and her husband.

(*f*) The knight, who has reached a position of great honour, becomes reunited with his family.

On the face of it, this is an impressive list of correspondences; but, since Wagner wrote his study of the *Zifar*'s sources, A. H. Krappe has

---

[121] In the Spanish version one of the sons says that they were both rescued by herdsmen, which coincides with the Latin accounts but not with the version of the rescue told earlier in the Spanish story: «E los porquerisos que andavan de la una parte e de la otra del rrío guardando ganados, libraron a mí del león e a mi hermano del lobo» (Knust, *Dos obras*, 148).

demonstrated that both the legend of St Eustace and the *Zifar* are members of an enormous family of stories, eastern and western, ancient and medieval, Christian and non-Christian, all deriving ultimately from a lost Indian archetype. [122] It is worth reproducing Krappe's reconstruction of the contents of this archetype:

> Un re buono e pio viene cacciato dal suo regno. Senza offrire resistenza, se ne va in esilio con sua moglie e due figliuoli gemelli di tenera età. La moglie gli viene rapita da un pirata. Seguitando la sua strada, arriva ad un fiume. Mentre lo passa, uno dei figli è rapito da un lupo, l'altro è portato via dalla corrente. Sono salvati, l'uno da un pastore, l'altro da un pescatore. Vengono allevati probabilmente nello stesso luogo e si riconoscono presto o tardi. Il padre, dopo un certo tempo, viene eletto re. I ragazzi ignorando affatto di chi sono figli, entrano al suo servizio. Il rapitore arriva in questo paese, non è riconosciuto dal re. Durante il suo soggiorno alla corte, il re mette i due giovani a sua disposizione per custodire le sue merci. Narrandosi, la notte, le loro avventure e forse riconoscendosi in quest'occasione quali fratelli, la loro conversazione è intesa dalla madre tenuta prigioniera sulla nave del rapitore. Segue il riconoscimento e una scena di mutua tenerezza. Sono sorpresi dal pirata che torna dalla corte, e vengono accusati da lui di aver voluto far violenza a sua moglie. Per giustificarsi raccontano le loro vicende al monarca, il quale non tarda a riconoscere in essi la propria moglie e i propri ragazzi. Il rapitore riceve la punizione che merita (251-252).

It will be noticed that the six parallels between the Zifar and the Placidus legend pointed out by Wagner are all to be found in this archetype. The only minor difference lies in the initial status of the hero: in the archetype he is a king, in the *Zifar* and the story of St Eustace he is a knight. [123] Furthermore, although Wagner himself notes eight major points of divergence between the *Zifar* and the saint's life, [124] he does not mention the very important facts that the entire setting of two works is different and that there is no echo in the romance of the long sections at the beginning and end of the *Plácidas* dealing with the hero's conversion and martyrdom, events which in fact occupy the hagiographic writer for nearly half his work. [125] Thus, if we assume with Wagner that the *Zifar*

---

[122] «La leggenda di S. Eustachio». Krappe (225-230) lists 59 versions of the basic story which he classifies as follows: 3 lives of saints; 10 Middle-Eastern stories; 6 Indian stories; 16 medieval European stories; 20 folk-tales of diverse origin; 4 ballads.

[123] These are not the only versions of the story that present the hero as a knight rather than a king; see Krappe, «Leggenda», 230-231.

[124] «Sources», 21-29.

[125] In Knust, *Dos obras*, the conversion occupies pp. 123-133 and the martyrdom pp. 152-157, i.e. 17 pages out of a total of 35.

is based directly on the Spanish version of the Eustace legend, we have to explain not only why the *Zifar* coincides more closely with the Eustace archetype than with the hagiographic sub-type represented by the *Plácidas*, but also why, for no reason that can be deduced from Wagner's theory, the *Zifar* author has invented a mass of Arabic proper names with allegorical significance and deliberately cultivated various features of Semitic style which are certainly not present in the *Plácidas*. [126] In view of the great number of versions of the same basic story collected by Krappe, it is unwise to postulate direct imitation by the *Zifar* author of one version from which it diverges in many fundamental respects.

It is true, of course, that there is a specific reference to the Eustace legend in the *Zifar*. In chapter 42 the knight's prayer for guidance includes these words:

> asý commo ayudeste los tus siervos bien aventurados Eustachio e Teóspita su muger e sus hijos Agapito e Teóspito, plega a la tu misericordia de ayuntar a mí e a mi muger e a mis fijos que somos derramados por semejante (90.25-91.3).

But this passing reference is not in itself sufficient evidence to justify the postulation of a direct imitation of the Eustace story by the *Zifar* author. Since this particular hagiographic legend was one of the most widely known in the Middle Ages, the romance-writer could easily have been struck by the similarities between it and his own source and added this comparison to Zifar's prayer. In the *Plácidas* the hero, after the loss of his family, also uses a comparison in his appeal to God:

> Buen sennor Dios, non me dexes a la cima nin desprecies mis lágrimas, ca bien me nienbra que me dexiste que sería tentado como Job; enpero sy él perdió sus rriquesas e sus posesiones, al de menos fincóle un muradal en que pudiese ser e yaser, mas yo so en tierra estranna con otra tanta coyta commo él ovo (139).

The story of Job clearly has various points of contact with the Eustace legend, but it is not its source. In view of the other clearly oriental elements in the romance, it is not unreasonable to look for the source of the first two books of the *Zifar* amongst the more purely eastern versions of the basic story outlined by Krappe, which originated in India.

In this connection it is interesting to note that Hippolyte Delehaye quotes the St Eustace story as an excellent example of what he calls *roman d'aventure*, a classification that embraces many of the lives of saints

---

[126] In the *Plácidas*, for example, there is not a single instance of *çertas* (or *çierto*) nor any echo of the «dize el sabio» or «dize el cuento» type of expression.

composed in the Middle Ages. [127] After outlining the main features of the Eustace legend, he goes on to say:

> Le sujet n'est autre chose qu'un des thèmes préférés du roman grec, dont les origines orientales sont connues. Cette famille composée du père, de la mère et de deux fils, dispersés d'abord puis réunis après une succession d'incidents caractéristiques, se retrouve dans toutes les littératures. Elle paraît d'abord dans les contes indiens et les a suivis dans leurs migrations coutumières (318-319).

These «migrations coutumières» are translations of oriental stories into Arabic whence they were rendered into Latin and the European vernacular languages. In other words, the Eustace story follows a route identical to that of the *Zifar*, but, it would seem, quite independently. The *Plácidas* owes a very great deal to the Latin Christian tradition; the *Zifar*, on the other hand, seems much closer to the oriental roots of the legend. [128]

Before passing on to a consideration of a possible direct Arabic source for the *Zifar*, it is necessary to deal with suggestions of Erich von Richthofen concerning the genesis of the romance. [129] In a rather confusing study Richthofen attempts to show that the *Zifar* derives from the story of the French epic hero Floovant, which in the course of time had assimilated to itself elements from the legend of Octavian. Since he finds in the *Zifar* echoes of episodes that are found only in the French *Chanson de Floovant* and of others that are found only in the Italian prosifications of the *Reali di Francia* and the *Storie di Fioravante*, Richthofen is obliged to suggest that the Spanish author either had access to two versions or to a lost *refundición* which had already fused the various elements from the different traditions.

Richthofen discerns eight major parallels between the Floovant-Octavian story and the first two books of the *Zifar*. These parallels, however, appear rather less convincing after a closer examination of the details of the two works. First, both heroes are descended from kings; but whereas Floovant is the son of a king, Zifar's royal ancestor Tared died several generations before. Secondly, both heroes leave their homeland in search of adventure, but the reasons for their departure are different. Floovant is exiled by his father for insulting his tutor; Zifar leaves his home of his own accord and because of misfortune for which

[127] *Les Passions des martyrs et les genres littéraires* (Bruxelles, 1921), 317-319.

[128] It is worth noting that amongst the many other lives of saints in the *roman d'aventure* tradition may be numbered *El cuento muy fermoso del enperador Otas e de la infante Florençia su fija* and *Un muy fermoso cuento de una sancta enperatriz que ovo en Rroma*, both of which are contained in the same MS. (Escorial h-I-13) as the *Plácidas*. This MS. also has a version of the William of England story, which shares many of the features of Krappe's archetype and the hagiographic *romans d'aventure*.

[129] *Estudios épicos medievales*, 45-68.

he is in no way to blame. Thirdly, both heroes are welcomed at a foreign court where they distinguish themselves by feats of arms against an enemy. Once again, however, the circumstances are rather different: Floovant arrives at the court of the King of Ausai, whose daughter he has just rescued from three Saracens; his welcome is thus assured; Zifar enters the court of Galapia (ruled over by a woman) without anything to recommend him. Fourthly, both knights are accompanied by squires; but whereas Floovant's squire Richier is with him from the outset and is already a fully-fledged *escuer*, Zifar meets the Ribaldo (who is a peasant, a fisherman's servant) only after he has lost his family. Fifthly, both men lose their wife and children, but for quite different reasons. Floovant repudiates his family; Zifar is involuntarily separated from his wife and sons through a series of misadventures. Sixthly, both heroes marry foreign princesses as a reward for their bravery. Whereas, however, Zifar marries the daughter of the King of Mentón, whom he has served in battle, Floovant rejects marriage with the princess he has rescued and whose father he has served, and marries the sister of his former enemy. Seventhly, both men inherit a kingdom and are finally reunited with their wife and children; but Floovant succeeds to his father's realm, to which he is the legitimate heir, whilst Zifar acquires Mentón through his marriage to the princess. Finally, both squires marry. Richier, however, marries the princess whom Floovant rescued and then spurned; the Ribaldo marries the daughter of a count, who has no other role in the story.

There are, then, significant differences between the *Floovant* and the *Zifar* in their treatment of the eight major motifs they have in common. Moreover, the majority of the motifs themselves are traceable to the Eustace archetype established by Krappe. [130] The few elements shared by the two stories but missing from the archetype, such as the feats of arms and the figure of the squire, can easily be explained by the influence of the medieval epic and chivalric tradition, which both the French poet and the *Zifar* author could have drawn on quite independently. After all his efforts, Richthofen himself has to admit that «Cierto que en la novela española los hechos particulares han sufrido un desplazamiento y los episodios se hallan trabados entre sí de otra manera que en la tradición de Floovante». [131]

---

[130] Krappe, «Leggenda», 228, includes *Octavian* among the medieval versions of the story.

[131] *Estudios épicos medievales*, 51. Some of Richthofen's subsidiary points with which he attempts to show close imitation of the Floovant story by the *Zifar* are very doubtful. For example, comparing two battles he mentions that the encounter takes place in a specific spot («A l'isue dou bois»; «arrivò presso a Balda»; «llegaron a aquella villa»); that the knights are armed with lances and swords (!), and that they ask God's help before the battle. In the episode of the loss of the children (which occurs only in the *Reali* and *Storie* versions of the Floovant story) Richthofen traces the common motifs of arrival at dusk («la sera»; «a ora de terçia») at a fountain where the family stop and eat. According to Richthofen, the woman then goes to sleep, which is certainly not the

Two other critics have challenged Wagner's theory that the first part of the *Zifar* derives from the Placidus story. Angel González Palencia categorically asserts that «es indudable que el esqueleto del cuento lo forma el relato de *Las mil y una noches*, según espero demostrar pronto, más bien que la leyenda de Plácidas o de San Eustaquio». [132] The *relato* to which he refers is *El rey que lo perdió todo*, known in its English version as *The Tale of the King Who Lost Kingdom and Wife and Wealth and Allah Restored Them to Him*. [133] Unfortunately González Palencia never wrote his promised study of the *Zifar*'s debt to this story. At more or less the same time A. H. Krappe arrived independently at a similar conclusion in his study of the legend of St Eustace. Wisely, however, he puts forward his views with rather more caution than González Palencia. He does not discount the influence of the hagiographic versions of the legend, but he adds that «*M4* [*Zifar*] e *M5* [*Boeve de Hamstone*] hano subito inoltre l'influsso d'una versione orientale, affine a *NP1* [the *Tale of the King*]». [134] To be more specific about the relationship of the *Zifar* and the *Tale* would be rash, in view of the frequency of such tales of separation and reunion in the eastern tradition. Krappe himself lists

case in the *Zifar:* here it is the knight who sleeps whilst his wife delouses him. In the Italian stories both the children are taken at this point, one by a giant/robber and the other by a lion; the mother wakes up and chases the lion thinking it has already eaten the other child. In suggesting that the *Zifar* version is virtually identical at this point Richthofen has clearly misread the text: Grima does not wake up (she was not asleep); she simply «volvió la cabeça» on hearing her child's screams. Zifar gives chase to the lion, but he does not return to find that in his absence Grima has lost the other child, as Richthofen asserts (59); the younger son is lost later in the town to which Zifar and his wife repair after leaving the fountain.

[132]   *Literatura arábigo-española*, 345. Cf. also Juan Hurtado y J. de la Serna and Angel González Palencia, *Historia de la literatura española*, 5th ed. (Madrid, 1943), 111.

[133]   The *Tale* forms part of Sir Richard F. Burton, *Supplemental Nights to the Book of the Thousand Nights and a Night* (Benares [i.e. London], 1886), I, 319-331. It is reprinted in Smithers' edition of Burton's translation (see n. 109 above), IX, 213-222. It was alleged by Thomas Wright early this century that Burton plagiarized most of his *Nights* and his *Supplemental Nights* from the translations made by his friend John Payne a few years earlier, *The Book of the Thousand Nights and One Night*, 9 vols (London, 1882-84), and *Tales from the Arabic of the Breslau and Calcutta Editions of the Book of the Thousand Nights and One Night not Occurring in the Other Printed Texts of the Work*, 3 vols (London, 1884); see Thomas Wright, *The Life of Sir Richard Burton*, 2 vols (London, 1906), II, 105-127, and *The Life of John Payne* (London, 1919), 70-88 and 181-186. Although the allegation has been repeated by others since Wright, those most competent to judge the issue seem to be agreed that Burton's work is an independent translation and that his dependence on Payne is minimal. For a summary of the dispute and a reasoned assessment of Burton's case, see Fawn M. Brodie, *The Devil Drives. A Life of Sir Richard Burton* (London, 1967), 300-311 and 341-343. Most critics now agree that Burton's version is more accurate and all (including Wright, who, incidentally, knew no Arabic) agree that in the many scabrous passages the uninhibited Burton is much nearer to the meaning and spirit of the original than the timid Payne.

[134]   «Leggenda», 253-254. Krappe calls the *Tale Schah Bakht*. It is in fact one of a group of 32 stories listed by Burton under the general heading of *King Shah Bakht and his Wazir Al-Rahwan*. It is clear, however, that Krappe is referring to the *Tale*, since his footnote (226, n. 2) gives a precise reference to Burton's text in the *Supplemental Nights*.

six from India and ten from the Semitic world (including four in the *Thousand and One Nights*), [135] all of which he regards as sufficiently similar to be classified as versions of the basic Eustace archetype. A further invitation to caution is the extremely tangled web of chronological and textual problems surrounding the *Nights*. In fact, it could well turn out that the *Nights* version of the *Tale* is later than the *Zifar*. Nevertheless, a close comparison of the content of the *Tale* and the first two books of the Spanish romance shows that the similarities between them are far more numerous and significant than those that exist between the *Zifar* and either the Placidus legend or the story of Floovant. There seems little doubt that Krappe's postulation of influence by a *versione affine* is reasonable and will stand further investigation.

It is undeniable that both the *Tale* and the *Zifar* include more of the essential features of Krappe's archetype than either the *Plácidas* or the Floovant-Octavian group of stories. The following are the most important:

(*a*) The hero is from India.

(*b*) He is married with two sons.

(*c*) He is obliged by adverse circumstances to leave his homeland with his family.

(*d*) He loses his sons on the journey.

(*e*) The sons are rescued by humble people and brought up together.

(*f*) The wife is kidnapped by lecherous sailors.

(*g*) The hero becomes king of a foreign city.

(*h*) His wife, after a series of independent adventures, arrives in a ship at the city of which her husband has become king.

(*i*) The two sons come to the city and enter the king's service, without either of the parties being aware of their blood relationship.

(*j*) Their mother, hearing the story of their adventures, recognizes them as her sons.

(*k*) The compromising situation in which the three of them are found arouses suspicions of criminal sexuality, and they are taken before the king for trial.

(*l*) When, as a defence, they tell their story to the king, he recognizes them as his long-lost family.

(*m*) The story ends with the execution of a felon.

Moreover, the *Tale* and the *Zifar* coincide in a considerable number of minor details, which are not mere commonplaces of the archetype. Significantly, none of them occurs in the *Plácidas* and only a couple echo motifs in the Floovant story:

[135] Apart from the *Schah Bakht*, which is of Persian origin, there are two Arabic stories, which Krappe calls *Cogia Muzaffer* and *Il Gioielliere* and a Jewish tale, *Il pio Israelita* («Leggenda», 226).

65

6

(a) The fleeing family lose their horses.

(b) The abduction of the wife comes later than the loss of the sons. [136]

(c) The ship in which the wife is carried off is laden with rich goods.

(d) When she realizes the captain's designs on her, the wife wants to throw herself overboard to escape dishonour, but she is stopped from doing so and imprisoned to prevent any further attempt.

(e) The king of the city at which the hero arrives after the loss of his family has no sons, only daughters.

(f) It is suggested that the hero should marry the king's daughter. [137]

(g) After the mother has recognized her sons, all three faint away in each other's arms.

(h) The body of the executed felon is burned and his ashes scattered.

(i) The reunited family is presented to the king's subjects and received with acclaim.

These points of contact between the works seem to be far too numerous to be purely coincidental or completely ascribable to their common archetype. Krappe's thesis, that there is a close link between the first half of the *Zifar* and some version of the tale which we can now know only in the form it takes in the *Thousand and One Nights*, appears to be unchallengeable. In fairness it must be admitted that there are a number of differences between the two, but, as a closer examination will show, these are not as disturbing as the differences between the *Plácidas* or the Floovant legend and the *Zifar*, which have been discussed above. Even if one were to go so far as to claim with González Palencia that the *Tale* itself (and not some *versione affine*) was the source of the *Zifar*, many of these differences could still be explained quite simply on grounds on genre: the *Tale* is, after all, a short story, whereas the Spanish work is a full-scale romance. Other divergences could be attributed to the shift from a Moslem and Arabic ethic to a Christian and European ethic and to the moral pattern that the *Zifar* author has imposed on his work, probably under the influence of the very popular legend of Placidus. And the remainder could be seen simply as the result of the romance-writer's search for greater dramatic effect. Let us examine some of these differences:

(a) The hero of the *Tale* is a king at the outset; Zifar is only a knight. This simple change fits into the European feudal picture and also helps to underline the main theme of the work, the progression from poverty and humiliation to wealth and power of a noble God-fearing family.

[136] In almost all the versions of the story studied by Krappe, the abduction of the wife precedes the loss of the sons; in only seven does it follow, and of these five are oriental (Indian or Middle-Eastern) and only two are European; see «Leggenda», 238.

[137] According to Krappe, «Leggenda», 248, apart from the *Schah Bakht* and the *Zifar* there is only one other version of the story, *Boeve de Hamstone*, in which «è l'eroe che va esposto alla tentazione di rimaritarsi».

66

(*b*) The hero's wife is his cousin in the Arabic version. To avoid any suspicion of contravening the strict Christian laws of consanguinity, Grima is not related to Zifar by blood.

(*c*) In the *Tale* the hero is forced to leave his homeland through the aggression of a neighbouring king, assisted by his own treacherous vassals. With Zifar reduced to the rank of knight, this element is no longer applicable and it is sufficient to show the hero incurring the king's displeasure. In both cases, however, it is noticeable that the hero in no way contributes to his own downfall.

(*d*) The loss of the family's horses on the way to a new life is due to the activies of highwaymen in the Arabic. In the *Zifar* it is the result of a curse on the hero which causes all his horses to die at ten-day intervals. The latter version is certainly more dramatic and is used by the Spanish author to provide the motive for the king's coolness towards Zifar.

(*e*) In the *Tale* the two sons are lost together: they wander off when their father, having forded the river with them, has gone back to collect their mother. In the *Zifar* the boys are lost at different times and in different circumstances: one is seized by the lion and the other strays off in search of his mother. The introduction of the lion could well reflect the author's knowledge of the *Plácidas* and spacing out the loss of the two sons is easily explicable as a simple case of elaboration. In any event, it makes no significant difference to the development of the story, since both boys are immediately brought together again in the care of the same foster-parents.

(*f*) The circumstances in which the hero's wife is lured on to the boat differ in the two versions. In the *Tale* the owner of the island where the unfortunate couple are resting deliberately arouses the captain's lust by telling him of the lady's beauty. She is asked to go on board to attend to a woman who is alleged to be in childbirth. The *Zifar* author connects the episode more firmly with his basic narrative thread, the flight of the family. Zifar asks the sailors if they will ferry them across the water; they set sail with Grima but without him. The superfluous character of the owner of the island is eliminated and the ominous ill luck of the hero intensified, since he must blame himself to some extent for his latest misfortune.

(*g*) In the Arabic tale when the hero arrives at the city he is eventually to rule, the old king is already dead and the question of his successor is a vital issue. In the *Zifar*, the knight serves the King of Mentón for some time before the latter dies. This elaboration may be due simply to the Spanish author's imitating a widely used motif of European romances of chivalry. [138]

(*h*) In the *Tale* the old king has two daughters; the King of Mentón has

---

[138] Cf. Don Quixote's outline of the ideal progress of a knight in Part I, ch. 21.

only one. In both cases the number of royal offspring is directly related to the necessities of the story: the two daughters will be married to the hero's two sons at the close of the tale; Zifar will marry the princess of Mentón.

(*i*) The Arabic hero is chosen to succeed to the throne of the foreign city by the curious process of being picked out by the late king's elephant. [139] If this motif was present in the *Zifar* author's source, he would presumably have rejected it as being too fantastic, too oriental, and out of keeping with the sober tone of his own composition. Zifar becomes King of Mentón through the slower, but more credible, method of serving the old king and marrying his daughter.

(*j*) One of the most interesting differences between the two stories is that although Zifar, a Christian, marries the princess whilst his first wife is still alive, the hero of the *Tale*, a Moslem, does not remarry because of a promise he had made to his wife that he would not marry anyone else but her. Although this second marriage produces moral difficulties for Zifar (and his author), it is obviously necessary for the development of the plot and for getting the hero accepted as King of Mentón. It has been noted above that a second marriage would be perfectly acceptable for a Moslem hero, which suggests that the motif could well have been present in the *Zifar*'s immediate source. If this is the case, then that source could not have been the *Tale*.

(*k*) The adventures of the two wives on the ship differ significantly. In the compact Arabic tale the lady arrives at her husband's city still in captivity. In the *Zifar* Grima is freed from her captors through divine intervention and left in sole charge of the ship under the guidance of Christ. This change is presumably the invention of the Christian author. It also allows him to introduce an independent series of adventures for Grima before her eventual arrival in Mentón.

(*l*) In the *Tale* the wife herself overhears the conversation of the two young men which convinces her that they are her sons. In the *Zifar* Grima receives a report of their conversation from a *donzella*. This again seems to be a simple case of elaboration either by the Spanish author or his immediate source.

(*m*) When the mother and her two sons are found asleep together, this creates trouble for them in both stories. In the *Tale*, however, they are accused by the captain of conspiring to rob him. In the *Zifar* they incur the charge of sexual immorality, which carries the sentence of burning at the stake. This is not only more dramatic, but also closer to the archetype, once again suggesting that the *Zifar*'s immediate source is a *versione affine* to the *Tale*, not the *Tale* itself.

(*n*) The trial of the captain at the end of the Arabic tale is paralleled by the trial of the treacherous Count Nasón who has rebelled against the

---

[139] Krappe, «Leggenda», 246, says that this is a survival from the Indian original.

lordship of Zifar. This change is explicable in two ways. First, the captain has disappeared from the scene a long time ago in the *Zifar*. Secondly, the shift of emphasis, from a human-interest story about a divided family in the *Tale* to an account of the social and political advancement of the family in the *Zifar*, is underlined by the alteration of the husband's condemnation of the wife's abductor to the king's condemnation of the last person to oppose his right to rule. The depression of his status to that of knight at the beginning and his exaltation to undisputed overlord at the end enables the *Zifar* author to impose his rags-to-riches pattern more clearly upon his material.

(*o*) After the trial the ashes from the burned body of the felon are scattered in the air in the *Tale*. In the *Zifar* Nasón's ashes are cast into a lake. This change allows the author to introduce the supernatural episode of the Cavallero Atrevido and the Enchanted Lake, which has no counterpart in the Arabic tale.

(*p*) To round off the story of the ultimate happiness of the reunited family the Arabic author marries the new king's two sons to the two daughters of the old king. The *Zifar* author avoids this conventional happy ending, probably because he already had plans for extending his work to include the adventures of Roboán. If Roboán were married at this stage he would have no excuse for setting out on his own, since there can be no question of his being driven from his home as his father and mother were.

G. CONCLUSION

In view of the evidence gathered in this chapter we must surely now take very seriously the author's statement in his Prologue that the *Zifar* was «trasladada de caldeo». Obviously *trasladada* must be given quite a wide interpretation: there is no question of the romance's being a straightforward translation. Its sometimes uneasy mingling of eastern and western, Moslem and Christian elements suggests that it is an adaptation of an Arabic work, modified, enlarged and moulded to fit the taste of a Christian, Castilian society at the beginning of the fourteenth century. Nevertheless, as we have seen, a very great deal remains that points unmistakably to Arabic inspiration; indeed, certain aspects of the *Zifar* (particularly the names) make sense *only* in terms of an ultimate Arabic source. Books I and II, then—which, it will be remembered, are not divided in any of the three extant versions of the *Zifar*—would seem to be based directly on an oriental narrative, not the *Tale* in its *Thousand and One Nights* version, but one closely related to it and probably a good deal longer. To this basic source, elaborated with many additions and interpolations, the Castilian author has added a reworking of the *Flores de filosofía*, interspersed with borrowings from other sources in wisdom literature, [140] to serve as an introduction to the last part, *Los hechos de Roboán*, which, one suspects, is a product of his own imagination, but based very closely, as we shall see in the next chapter, on the structural pattern of Books I and II. [141]

This last book is much nearer to what we regard as the typical romance of chivalry, with its unmarried and younger hero of noble status, its hints of courtliness in the relationship between Roboán and Seringa, the more elevated rank and behaviour of the squire, the traditional kind of mysterious trappings (such as the emperor who does not laugh and the marvels of Çafira), and the visit of the hero himself to the Other World. In chapter 206 the Arthurian story of Yván is mentioned, which suggests the hero of Chrétien's poem, although, as Mrs Malkiel points out, the plot seems to correspond more to Marie de France's *Lanval* and *Graelent*. [142] In chapter 211 there is a reference to Venus as the goddess of love (476.12), and in chapters 212 and 213 there are two interpolated lyrics in the courtly tradition. [143] We have also noticed that the incidence of *çertas* is much less in this last book, although we have to take into account the incomplete state of MS. *M* at this point. All in all, we seem somewhat closer to the world of the true chivalric romance in Book IV than anywhere else in the *Zifar*.

Despite the differences between Books I and II and Book IV and, particularly, between Book III and all the rest, there can be little doubt that the whole enormous compilation is the work of one author. One cannot agree with Bohigas Balaguer when he suggests that the differences between the first and last parts may be due to «el retoque posterior de un refundidor, más aficionado a lo maravilloso y a lo sentimental que quien concibió la obra». [144] Despite these differences, the moral tone is still the same, the use (or abuse) of *çertas* is still far greater than in any other medieval Spanish work, and certain stylistic tricks are common throughout the whole romance. Above all, the complex system of structural parallels that is followed in all four books should convince us that the *Zifar* is the product of a single highly original and highly trained mind. [145]

---

[140] For an account of these, see Wagner, «Sources», 36-40.

[141] Cf. Wagner, *Cauallero Zifar*, viii, n. 8: «It is possible that the *Zifar* which has come down to us in *M* may not be the first redaction by the author, which may well have ended with the section of the book which I have called *El Rey de Menton;* in which case the Prologue would belong to the earlier form, since the concluding sentences do not make mention of the *Castigos*, or of *Los Hechos de Roboan*, but only of the adventures of *El Cauallero de Dios*.»

[142] «Arthurian Literature in Spain and Portugal», 408, n. 2.

[143] These two lyrics have been edited and studied in Brian Dutton and Rogeı M. Walker, «El *Libro del Cauallero Zifar* y la lírica castellana», *Fi* IX (1963), 53-67.

[144] «Orígenes de los libros de caballería», 533.

[145] K. R. Scholberg, «The Structure of the *Caballero Cifar*», *MLN* LXXIX (1964), 113-124, at pp. 119-120, also disputes Bohigas' theory, citing as evidence the «almost monotonous frequency» of *çertas* and some other linguistic features, such as the constant use of *dixo* throughout to introduce direct speech.

CHAPTER THREE: THE STRUCTURAL UNITY OF THE *ZIFAR*

I. THE THREE BOOKS OF ADVENTURES [1]

A. CRITICAL VIEWS AND THE PROBLEM OF UNITY

C. P. Wagner, the first scholar to undertake extensive critical work on the *Zifar*, makes an almost casual reference to the romance's supposed lack of structural unity: «In such a work as this we must not look for unity: and so it is that the *Cifar* falls naturally into three divisions, each quite independent of the others.» [2] Almost without exception later critics have accepted this judgment, regarding the work as little more than a collection of heterogeneous elements put together without any great skill and without any apparent unity of structure and purpose. Menéndez y Pelayo, writing a few years after Wagner, says that «la fábula principal ... es muy desordenada e incoherente», adding that «el contraste no puede ser más grande ni menos hábil la fusión de elementos tan discordes como el bizantino y el céltico». [3] Sir Henry Thomas describes the *Zifar* as «immature and transitional», and refers to «the author's lack of a unity of purpose». [4] G. T. Northup asserts that «the *Cifar* is not a typical romance of chivalry but a book of miscellaneous content», [5] whilst William J. Entwistle goes further and declares that «it is no single work». [6] The same line is followed by Aubrey Bell who states that the *Zifar* «does not succeed in blending its heterogeneous ingredients». [7] The ranks of the detractors have been swelled by at least three eminent modern critics.

---

[1] Some of the material in this chapter first appeared in my article, «The Unity of *El libro del Cavallero Zifar*» *BHS* XLII (1965), 149-159.
[2] «The Sources of *El Cavallero Cifar*», *RHi* X (1903), 5-104, at p. 13.
[3] *Orígenes de la novela*, ed. E. Sánchez Reyes (Edición Nacional, 2nd ed.; Madrid, 1962), I, 296 and 302. This volume was first published in 1905.
[4] *Spanish and Portuguese Romances of Chivalry* (Cambridge, 1920), 11 and 19.
[5] *An Introduction to Spanish Literature* (Chicago, 1925), 93.
[6] *The Arthurian Legend in the Literatures of the Spanish Peninsula* (London-Toronto, 1925), 72.
[7] *Castilian Literature* (Oxford, 1938), 47.

According to María Rosa Lida de Malkiel, the *Zifar* «es un no logrado maridaje de narración didáctica y de novela caballeresca». [8] Erich von Richthofen is a little less severe, but he too feels that «los dos últimos libros no guardan con el primero [i.e. Wagner's I and II] más que una relación ideal». [9] Most recently Otis H. Green has described the romance as «a rather amorphous yet remarkable work». [10]

None of these critics, however, takes the trouble to define exactly what he understands by unity, and we are consequently unable to assess with any precision how each of them thinks the *Zifar* falls short of the ideal. The word «unity» is capable of so many interpretations that it is, without definition, virtually useless as a component of critical vocabulary. In the words of Arthur K. Moore:

> The term is a philosophical puzzle and a logical pitfall. Predicable in one sense of almost nothing and in another of perhaps everything, it is a will-o'-the-wisp which can seldom be apprehended without some expense to probability. [11]

In general terms, modern critics may be said to profess allegiance to either the Aristotelian or the Coleridgean concept of unity, concepts which are themselves so different that even now some indication of the critic's loyalties is essential if we are to understand his terms of reference. In his *Poetics* (ch. 8) Aristotle sets out his own almost impossible ideal of unity:

> Thus, just as in the other imitative arts each individual representation is the representation of a single object, so too the plot of a play, being the representation of an action, must present it as a unified whole; and its various incidents must be so arranged that if any one of them is differently placed or taken away the effect of wholeness will be seriously disrupted. For if the presence or absence of something makes no apparent difference, it is no real part of the whole. [12]

Coleridge's theory of «organic unity», on the other hand, is part of the Romantic reaction against the rigidity of Aristotle and of classicism in general:

> The form is mechanic when on any given material we impress a predetermined form, not necessarily arising out of the properties of the material, as when to a mass of wet clay we give whatever

[8]   *La idea de la fama en la Edad Media castellana* (México-Buenos Aires, 1952), 259
[9]   *Estudios épicos medievales con algunos trabajos inéditos* (Madrid, 1954), 50.
[10]   *Spain and the Western Tradition. The Castilian Mind in Literature from «El Cid» to Calderón*, I (Madison, 1963), 12.
[11]   «Medieval English Literature and the Question of Unity», *MP* LXV (1967-68), 285-300, at p. 286.
[12]   *Aristotle, Horace, Longinus. Classical Literary Criticism*, ed. and trans. T. S. Dorsch (Harmondsworth, 1965), 43.

shape we wish it to retain when hardened. The organic form, on the other hand, is innate; it shapes as it develops itself from within, and the fullness of its development is one and the same with the perfection of its outward form. [13]

Despite their notable divergences, these two definitions of unity agree that unity resides above all in formal perfection, based on some sort of logical development, either imposed from outside (Aristotle) or growing from within (Coleridge). Medieval romances, however—and, indeed, medieval literature in general—appear to our modern eyes prolix, formless and confused, conforming to neither the «mechanic» nor the «organic» concept of unity. In the words of Eugène Vinaver:

> The knights-errant whom we try to follow as they make their way through a forest—that ancient symbol of uncertain fate— are apt to abandon at any time one quest for the sake of another, only to be sidetracked again a moment later. They behave as though this were an accepted mode of living, requiring no apology or explanation. [14]

Clearly such rambling works are unlikely to possess either Aristotelian or Coleridgean unity, with the result that the founders of medieval studies in the late nineteenth and early twentieth centuries had little hesitation in condemning them as obscure and incoherent; and the disciples and imitators of those scholars have, for the most part, repeated their masters' verdict.

In recent years, however, there has been a marked swing in the opposite direction, and a spate of studies devoted to demonstrating the unity of certain medieval works has appeared. Unfortunately most of the writers of these studies have failed just as signally as the early detractors to define their terms and establish a concept of unity that would be generally applicable to medieval literature. This has resulted in the almost comic situation of a work that was previously regarded as devoid of unity now being credited with as many as four or five different kinds of unity. [15] The reason for this is the growth of knowledge about and enthusiasm for allegorical interpretation, for going beyond the literal level of the narrative to discern elaborate tropical and anagogical patterns that would almost certainly have been beyond the grasp of the audience for which the works were intended in the first place. [16] As Moore so rightly points out, the

---

[13] Quoted by Moore, «Medieval English Literature», 290.

[14] *Form and Meaning in Medieval Romance* (Presidential Address of the Modern Humanities Research Association, 1966), 8.

[15] Moore, for example, examines the conflict of interpretations concerning the unity of *Beowulf*, *Piers Plowman*, the *Parlement of Foules* and Malory.

[16] See Moore, «Medieval English Literature», 295. Cf. Gillian Beer, *The Romance* (The Critical Idiom 10, London, 1970), 18.

romances at least «usually have no significance beyond the literal level, and their unity is demonstrable, if at all, in descriptions of self-evident relations» (296).

Where, then, if anywhere, are we to look for the theoretical basis for a concept of unity applicable to medieval romance? It seems clear that one existed, since there is no evidence to suggest that the writers of the Middle Ages were any less concerned with or less proud of the formal aspect of their works than writers of any other period. [17] But if both our modern notions of unity refuse to function when faced with the prolixity of a medieval romance, and if oversubtle allegorical and thematic interpretations simply lead to more confusion, we must necessarily look elsewhere for the source of the structural principles that motivated medieval authors in the composition of their works. A good place to start would seem to be contemporary literary theory.

The *Artes Poeticæ*, the medieval manuals of composition, give very detailed precepts for the elaboration and ornamentation of the various parts of a literary work, but unfortunately they do not lay down similar clear guidelines for the structuring of the work as a whole. With the exception of a few remarks on how to begin and how to end a composition, these rhetorical handbooks say almost nothing on the subject of *dispositio*, the arrangement and patterning of the material. Nevertheless, the influence of these treatises was so widespread that we are justified, I think, in seeking to explain at least some of the structural complexities of medieval romance as extended applications of some of the rhetoricians' precepts on stylistic elaboration. [18]

The most fundamental lesson taught by the *Artes Poeticæ* is the expansion of one's material by means of *amplificatio*. [19] Although the

---

[17]   In the opening lines of his *Erec et Enide*, for example, Chrétien de Troyes speaks with pride of the «molt bele conjointure» of his work (1. 14). The striking similarities between this *exordium* and the beginning of the *Libro de Alexandre* have been well studied by Ian Michael, «A Parallel between Chrétien's *Erec* and the *Libro de Alexandre*», *MLR* LXII (1967), 620-628.

[18]   The scarcity of advice on the subject of structure in the *Artes Poeticæ* is convincingly explained by Douglas Kelly, «The Scope of the Treatment of Composition in the Twelfth- and Thirteenth-Century Arts of Poetry», *Sp* XLI (1966), 261-278. Kelly points out that Matthew of Vendôme and Everhard the German say nothing about *dispositio* because they are essentially grammarians, concerned with teaching the basic skills of versification and stylistic ornamentation. Geoffrey of Vinsauf and John of Garland, however, are true rhetoricians and, as such, concerned with *dispositio;* but they could not legislate at any great length on this topic because of the infinite number of possible subjects and possible arrangements of *materia*. They do, nevertheless, stress the need for careful organization within the poem and insist that ornamentation should always be subordinated to the structural plan the author has worked out for his material. A. C. Spearing, *Criticism and Medieval Poetry* (London, 1964), 67, sounds a cautionary note about the practice of seeking to explain the structure of medieval works in terms of extended applications of stylistic precepts. His strictures, however, seem somewhat overstated and a little unjust to some eminent critics.

[19]   See Edmond Faral, *Les Arts poétiques du XIIe et du XIIIe siècle. Recherches et documents sur la technique littéraire du Moyen Age* (BÉHÉ 238, Paris, 1924), ch. 2.

theorists were almost exclusively concerned with stylistic elaboration, it is not unreasonable to suppose that medieval authors, trained as they were in rhetoric, when they came to write romances, might have elevated (or perverted) amplification into a structural principle. Leisurely elaboration, after all, seems to spring from a medieval habit of mind. It is not without significance that, whereas for the classical rhetoricians of ancient Rome *amplificatio* meant the ennoblement of one's material, «raising acts and personal traits above their dimensions», it came to signify the simple stretching out of one's material to Geoffrey of Vinsauf and his fellow-preceptists of the Middle Ages. [20] If the theorists themselves could make such a fundamental change, why should the authors not have taken the next logical step and turned a stylistic device into a structural one? Two eminent scholars have, in fact, sought to explain the prolixity and complexity of much medieval literature in terms of one or other type of *amplificatio*.

Dorothy Everett suggests that the device of *interpretatio* might have provided the inspiration for a certain type of medieval structural pattern. [21] *Interpretatio* is one of the most basic forms of amplification: it consists of saying the same thing in many different ways. [22] Everett applies her theory to Chaucer's *Book of the Duchess* and attempts to explain the parallelism of episodes, the repetition of the same basic situation under slightly different circumstances, in terms of *interpretatio*. This parallelistic technique, not unnaturally, leads to a quite distinct kind of structural organization from that which we would expect to find in a modern novel. This point has been developed by Robert M. Jordan:

> Narrative structures composed in this way—based on the coordinate ordering of more or less fixed units of narrative— are particularly difficult to contain within the strictures of modern novelistic theory. A narrative composed according to the additive, repetitive principle of «letting the same thing be covered in many forms» is bound to be uncongenial to the expectations and criteria of a literary aesthetic which values economy, relevance, and organic unity of effect. The structural principles of juxtaposition and parallelism produce a form of narrative more expository than dramatic, more inclined to «tell» than to «show». [23]

[20] See Vinaver, *Form and Meaning*, 11-12.

[21] «Some Reflections on Chaucer's 'Art Poetical'», *Essays on Middle English Literature*, ed. Patricia Kean (Oxford, 1955), 149-174.

[22] For definitions of *interpretatio*, see Geoffrey of Vinsauf, *Poetria Nova*, 11. 219-225; id., *Documentum de Arte Versificandi*, II, § 29; Everhard the German, *Laborintus*, 11. 309-312. Editions of all these treatises are included in Faral, *Les Arts poétiques*.

[23] «Chaucerian Narrative», *Companion to Chaucer Studies*, ed. Beryl Rowland (Toronto-New York-London, 1968), 84-102, at p. 96. Cf. the same author's *Chaucer and the Shape of Creation. The Aesthetic Possibilities of Inorganic Structure* (Cambridge, Mass.-London, 1967), *passim*.

As we shall see, the most fundamental structural pattern that emerges from the *Zifar* is an elaborate parallelism of episodes and motifs, an intricate interplay of what Nevill Coghill has aptly described as «forestastes and echoes». Such a structure may be unfamiliar, even incomprehensible, to us, but we are not entitled to deny its unity out of hand.

Eugène Vinaver also traces one of the basic structural features of medieval romances to one of the many forms of *amplificatio*. He believes that the origin of the tapestry-like interweaving of episodes is to be found in the device of *digressio*. [24] Discussing the complexity of the *Suite du Merlin*, he writes:

> The result is an elaborate fabric of extended narrative sequences, curiously unlike any modern novel in appearance, and well in keeping with the contemporary rhetorical devices known as *digressio ad aliam partem materiæ* and *digressio ad aliquid extra materiam*. [25]

Vinaver also makes the interesting point that *digressio* is an invention of the Middle Ages that has no exact counterpart in classical rhetoric. [26] Thus once again we have a stylistic device peculiar to medieval rhetoric (like *amplificatio* = elaboration, not ennoblement) being put forward by an eminent critic as the basis of one of the characteristic structures of medieval romance. As we shall see, the interweaving of separate sets of adventures *(digressio ad aliam partem materiæ)* is an essential feature of the *Zifar*, and pure digressions *(digressio ad aliquid extra materiam)*, in the form of *exempla* or moral commentaries, are to be found everywhere.

A third source that has been suggested for the complex structure of medieval literary works is the technique of the so-called «university» sermon as set out in the *Artes Prædicandi* which, unlike the *Artes Poeticæ*, have a good deal to say about *dispositio*. [27] A. C. Spearing, in the course of a fascinating analysis of *Piers Plowman*, structurally one of the most baffling of all medieval poems, shows how the constant repetitions and digressions, the shifts from homily to narrative and back again, can be explained in terms of the recommended sermon structure. [28] Spearing

---

[24] For definitions of *digressio*, see *Poetria Nova*, 11. 527-553; *Documentum*, II, §§ 17-21; *Laborintus*, 11. 325-328.

[25] Introduction to *Le Roman de Balain*, ed. M. Dominica Legge (Manchester, 1942), xiii. See also Vinaver, *The Works of Sir Thomas Malory*, 3 vols (Oxford, 1947), I, lii: «each episode appeared to be a digression from the previous episode and at the same time a sequel to some earlier unfinished story.»

[26] *Le Roman de Balain*, xiii, n. 1.

[27] See Th.-M. Charland, *Artes Prædicandi. Contribution à l'histoire de la rhétorique au Moyen Age* (Publications de l'Institut d'Etudes Médiévales d'Ottawa VII, Paris-Ottawa, 1936), 2ᵐᵉ partie.

[28] *Criticism and Medieval Poetry*, ch. 4.

makes the important point that the preacher tried to combine instruction with literary elegance:

> They [the sermons] were often intended to be preached to a mixed congregation of clergy and layfolk, educated and illiterate people; and we may note that the repetitive patterning of the «university» method, which would offer aesthetic pleasure to the upper layers of such an audience, would also serve to hammer home the main points of the preacher's message to the lower layers. Such sermons borrow from the *ars prædicandi* not a complete scheme but a general principle of structure: a method of organization by which a sermon ... becomes an independent meditation closely and constantly related to a single *thema*. And within this larger structure there will be an interweaving of sub-themes, involving frequent reappearances of the same sets of words and ideas (76).

Now, one of the most striking features of the *Zifar*, and the one which is perhaps least congenial to a twentieth-century reader, is its repetitiousness. Time and time again we return to the same moral commonplaces applied to different sets of circumstances, very much, it would appear, in the style of the «university» sermon. The flow of narrative is frequently interrupted so that the author can deliver himself of a homily on a sub-theme that has arisen out of his story, and in many cases this homily is illustrated, in the precise manner of the preachers, with an uplifting *exemplum*. The whole enormous compilation, after wending its labyrinthine way, at the end arrives back at the point from which it started, the trite text (or *thema*) of «act virtuously and you will be rewarded». [28a] This too is typical of the medieval sermon, as Spearing reminds us:

> The preacher or poet of Christian orthodoxy cannot leave us with an original message of his own: his aim must be to revitalize for us a commandment whose very familiarity may have deadened it as a motive for action (77).

All three of these attempts, then, to explain the complex structure of medieval works and justify it in medieval terms give us valuable pointers for an assessment of the unity of the *Zifar*. Without having recourse to the over-sophisticated techniques of allegorical interpretation and confining ourselves to Moore's «self-evident relations», we now have a theoretical position from which to defend the *Zifar* author's attempts to impose a logical pattern on his mass of material, a pattern which differs greatly from modern novelistic technique, but which is no less valid for that. [29] The *Zifar* may be, to use Iris Murdoch's word,

---

[28a]   J. F. Burke, *Vision and History (passim* but especially ch. 3), argues that the entire structure of the *Zifar* is based on the University sermon.

[29]   See Vinaver, *Form and Meaning*, especially p. 23.

«crystalline» fiction; its author may well have surrendered to the temptation to allow «myth» to take over and falsified human character and the fortuity of real life by an oversubtle attention to occult patterns of meaning and events. [30] But before we condemn him from our twentieth-century standpoint we should remember that medieval creative and intellectual activity generally is characterized by artificial order and repetitive patterning. Their Gothic cathedrals are built of symmetrically repeated structures; [31] their arts of memory depend on the cultivation of a series of clearly arranged mental images; [32] their theology reaches its zenith in the phenomenal architecture of St Thomas Aquinas' *Summae*. All these things, together with other manifestations of their desire for order, such as the codes of law, chivalry and love, are reflections of their all-pervading world picture, a picture based on the principles of balance and harmony, in which all the diverse elements of life can be reconciled. In the words of C. S. Lewis:

> A Model must be built which will get everything in without a clash; and it can do this only by becoming intricate, by mediating its unity through a great, and finely ordered, multiplicity. [33]

Perhaps it is here above all, in the influence of the Model, that we should seek the ultimate explanation of the labyrinthine structure of medieval romance.

B. THE BASIC PARALLELISM OF STRUCTURE

The first critic to see the *Zifar* structurally as anything more than a haphazard collection of chivalric, hagiographic, fantastic and didactic elements was Justina Ruiz de Conde in her book *El amor y el matrimonio secreto en los libros de caballerías* (Madrid, 1948). [34] Her important findings, however, have been inexplicably ignored by subsequent critics who have pronounced on the *Zifar*'s structure. Although Mrs Malkiel reviewed the book favourably, [35] she makes no reference to it in any of her writings on the *Zifar*. Otis H. Green includes it in his bibliography and mentions it in a general footnote (which he appears to have borrowed

---

[30] Iris Murdoch, «Against Dryness. A Polemical Sketch», *Encounter* XVI, 1 (Jan. 1961), 16-20.

[31] See Erwin Panofsky, *Gothic Architecture and Scholasticism* (Latrobe, Pa., 1951).

[32] See Frances Yates, *The Art of Memory* (London, 1966), especially chs 3-5.

[33] *The Discarded Image. An Introduction to Medieval and Renaissance Literature* (Cambridge, 1964), 11.

[34] As the title implies, this book is not concerned primarily with structure, but there is an important section devoted to this topic in connection with the *Zifar* on pp. 46-57.

[35] *RPh* III (1949-50), 224-225. In the course of her review Mrs Malkiel mentions the «discretas observaciones sobre la estructura y correspondencias del *Cifar*» (225).

from Wagner), [36] but makes no use of its conclusions in his section on the *Zifar*. In his article on the structure of the romance K. R. Scholberg does not refer at all to Ruiz de Conde's work, but he arrives independently at some of the same conclusions. [37]

Ruiz de Conde *(El amor*, 46-48) summarizes briefly the contents of the three books of adventures (I, II and IV) and shows that they are all constructed according to the same five-part pattern: [38]

   (i)   An initial situation.
   (ii) A first set of «aventuras de plano real».
   (iii) A supernatural episode.
   (iv) A second set of «aventuras de plano real» (except in II).
   (v)   A final distribution of rewards and punishments. [39]

This clear parallelism in the organization of the three books of adventures is Ruiz de Conde's main point; but, as she is not primarily concerned in her work with problems of structure, she does not go on to develop her findings in great detail. She does add one or two other interesting points to her analysis of the *Zifar*'s structure, but these are not specifically connected with the basic five-part pattern and will be dealt with later. My immediate purpose is to examine more thoroughly the plan which she establishes for the three books of adventures.

(i) *The Initial Situations*

Books I, II and IV each begin with a problematical situation which is the clear starting point for the development of events in that particular book. These opening sections are contained in Book I, chapters 1-10, Book II, chapters 80-81, Book IV, chapters 176-179. Ruiz de Conde lists these situations (46-48), but does not comment on their real structural importance.

The point of departure for the adventures of Book I is the failure of Zifar to make good in his own country because of his misfortunes: «atán fuerte fue la fortuna del marido que non podía mucho adelantar en su casa asý commo ella [Grima] avía mester» (9.7-8). All the knight's horses die

---

[36] Cf. Green, *Spain and the Western Tradition*, I, 98, n. 101, and Wagner, «The *Caballero Zifar* and the *Moralium Dogma Philosophorum*», *RPh* VI (1952-53), 309-312, at p. 312, n. 17. Apart from anything else, the page references (identical in both notes) to J. Ruiz de Conde, *El amor y el matrimonio secreto*, are wrong.

[37] «The Structure of the *Caballero Cifar*», *MLN* LXXIX (1964), 113-124.

[38] Like all recent critics she accepts Wagner's division of the original very long first book into two separate books (see *Cauallero Zifar*, xii), a division which I hope the present chapter will show to be totally justified.

[39] This pattern may be a reflection, conscious or unconscious, of the common structure of many «university» sermons: the *thema* + a tripartite *divisio* + a return to the *thema* in the conclusion. The close relationship between the initial situation of each book of the *Zifar* and the final distribution of rewards and punishments is examined below.

when he has had them for ten days, with the result that the ruler of the country finds him too expensive to employ in his wars despite the fact that he is the finest soldier in the land. Zifar's curious misfortune stems from a curse placed on his family as a punishment for the «malas costunbres» of one of his ancestors, King Tared (ch. 20). Thus Zifar's reasons for leaving his homeland are partly due to economic considerations (he wishes to find regular employment so that he can support his wife and children), and partly due to dynastic ambition (he wishes to restore the family to its former royal status). It is this dual impetus that dictates the knight's actions throughout the rest of Book I; and at the end of the book we find him, after many labours and tribulations, rich and respected and about to become heir to the throne of Mentón.

In Book II the initial situation is once again the mainspring of much of the action that is to follow. In this instance in particular Ruiz de Conde appears not to have fully appreciated the real structural significance of the carefully established opening sequence. In her summary of the events of Book II (47) she puts forward Zifar's vow of chastity as the main point of interest in the early chapters, whereas it is surely the hero's second marriage to the King of Mentón's daughter which stimulates and complicates subsequent events. If Zifar had not married the princess, he would not have become King of Mentón, and Grima, his first wife, would not have had to keep secret her relationship to him and narrowly escape death at the stake because of having to keep it secret. Furthermore, if Zifar had not inherited the crown of Mentón, it is unlikely that Grima or their sons would ever have come to Mentón, since it is made quite clear that it is the report of the new ruler's many virtues which prompts the members of his family, quite independently, to seek him out. [40] At the end of Book II the family of Book I, which seemed to have been finally given up for lost when Zifar married again, is not only reunited but accorded royal status in its own right by the citizens of Mentón.

The circumstances that spur Roboán into action at the beginning of Book IV are similar in many ways to those which influenced his father earlier. He finds himself, as the younger son, without real position or power and so, with the ambition of the family strong within him, he decides to set out and seek his fortune. If he had been the elder son, he would have become a count and his father's heir; he would not have left Mentón or met his future wife Seringa or served the Emperor of Tigrida, whom he eventually succeeds. By the end of the last book Roboán has done what he set out to do: he has proved himself as a knight, raised the status of his family to an even greater height, and ensured the continuation of the noble line of Zifar through the birth of his son, Fijo de Bendiçión.

[40] Grima is advised to go to Mentón by the «ome bueno» she meets in Ester (ch. 83); the two sons are sent to Mentón by their foster-parents so that they may be knighted by the famous king (ch. 90).

All three books of adventures, then, open with a situation in which a character is faced with an important dilemma. The rest of the book is largely concerned with the protagonist's attempts to find a solution to his problem, and by the end of the book he has successfully accomplished the aim he set himself.

Besides sharing a common function of providing motivation for the later events in the book they introduce, these three opening sections also share a common structural pattern. It has already been pointed out that each book begins with a presentation of the protagonist's dilemma —Zifar's misfortune in I, his bigamous remarriage in II, and Roboán's position as the younger son in IV. After he has appreciated the real difficulty of his problem, each of them then discusses it with the other person or persons most closely concerned with him—Zifar with Grima in I, with his second wife in II, and Roboán with his parents in IV. As a result of the discussion a major decision is reached, and the people involved proceed to act upon it—Zifar and Grima foresake their homeland in I, Zifar and his second wife swear a vow of chastity in II, and Roboán sets out in search of fame and fortune with his parents' approval in IV. The progression from the initial situation to the main action follows the same smooth course in each of the three books of adventures.

The parallel construction of the three openings is further strengthened by the inclusion of a prophecy or near-prophecy which will be fulfilled by the end of the book. In Book I Zifar tells Grima of his grandfather's death-bed prediction that one day a member of the family would recover the royal status they had held in the past:

> «E sy yo fuere de buenas costunbres», dixe yo, «¿podría llegar a tan alto logar?» E él me respondió reyéndose mucho, e díxome asý: «Amigo pequeño de días e de buen entendimiento, dígote que sý, con la merçed de Dios, si bien te esforçares a ello e non te enojares de fazer bien: ca por bien fazer bien puede ome subir a alto lugar» (34.8-13).

It is made quite clear that it is because he does «fazer bien» that Zifar achieves regal status at the end of Book I.

Book II's introductory material does not contain a real prophecy; but Zifar tells his new wife, when making his vow of chastity, that he will only be able to re-enter a state of grace if he does penance for two years:

> «El yerro», dixo el rey, «fue tan grande que yo fis a Nuestro Señor Dios, que non puede ser emendado amenos de me mantener dos años en castidat» (166.18-20).

This voluntary abstention from sexual intercourse is necessary to wipe out the sin of having entered into a second marriage whilst his first wife

81

is still alive. It would obviously be impossible in such a moral work for an adulterer and bigamist to achieve—with God's clearly signified approval—the greatness achieved by Zifar. He must endure two years of self-imposed chastity before he can be allowed to reclaim his true wife and his sons. The knight's words, then, have a very similar function to a prophecy: they are a clear statement that if certain conditions are fulfilled a certain result will ensue. At the end of Book II Zifar's «prophecy» comes true: the price has been paid, the sin forgiven, and God tells him directly that he may now acknowledge his first family publicly before the citizenry of Mentón (ch. 119).

At the beginning of Book IV Grima makes a prediction about her son Roboán. When she is about to take leave of him as he sets out on his travels, she announces her belief that one day he will become an emperor: «ca me semeja que de todo en todo ha de ser un grant enperador» (383.13-14). By the end of the last book the prophecy has been fulfilled and Roboán has duly ascended the imperial throne of Tigrida.

Finally, to underline even more clearly the parallelism between the three opening situations, the author includes in the two later ones a specific reference to the first. In Book II, after his marriage to the princess and his accession to the throne, Zifar suddenly remembers Grima, but more significantly he specifically recalls what she said to him at the beginning of Book I when he told her of his grandfather's prophecy:

> Este rey estando un día folgando en su cama, vínosele emiente de cómmo fuera casado con otra muger, e oviera fijos en ella, e cómmo perdiera los fijos e la muger. Otrosý le vino emiente las palabras que·l dixiera su muger quando lo él contara lo que·l acaesçiera con su avuelo (165.8-12).

At the beginning of Book IV we again have a reference back to the opening chapters of Book I. As they discuss Roboán's request to leave home, Zifar says to Grima:

> E reýna, véngasevos emiente que ante que saliésemos de nuestra tierra, vos dixe el propósito en que yo estava, e que quería seguir lo que avía començado, e que lo non dixiésemos a ninguno ca nos lo ternían a locura. E vós respondístesme asý, que sy locura o cordura, que luego que me lo oyérades dezir vos subió al coraçón que podría ser verdat, e consejástesme asý: que saliésemos luego de la nuestra tierra (382.27-383.6).

The *Zifar* author's concern for balance and symmetry is already evident, then, from a study of the openings of the three books of adventures In each one he first establishes his main character as a man with a great problem, and then goes on to describe how he confronts this dilemma and comes to a decision upon which he can act, after winning the support of those close to him. The end of each book shows that the decision was fully justified. But this care for structure is not confined to the individual books: the three initial situations are bonded together not only by their similarity of plan (dilemma—discussion—decision) but also by the important position accorded to the prophecy in each of them, and by the deliberate recollection at the beginning of Books II and IV of the significant events in the opening chapters of Book I. [41]

(ii) *The Adventures on the Natural Plane*

Justina Ruiz de Conde entitles the second part of each book «aventuras de plano real». These quite extensive sections cover Book I, chapters 11-43, Book II, chapters 82-109, and Book IV, chapters 180-204. A close examination of these series of adventures reveals that not only do they occur in the same place in each book (between the initial situation and the supernatural episode), but also that they are built up largely from a set of motifs that is common to all of them.

First, they all begin with an arrival in a new and strange land. In Book I Zifar and his family make their first stop, after leaving their home, at Galapia (ch. 11); in Book II Grima reaches the dominion of the King of Ester (ch. 82); in Book IV Roboán enters the kingdom of Pandulfa (ch. 180). There is a further point of interest about these arrivals: they mark only a temporary settling place for the wanderer concerned, not the permanent haven where he will receive his ultimate reward. Moreover, these arrivals also fulfil an important structural function, since they focus our attention immediately on the person who is to occupy the centre of the stage for much of the book. Book I is primarily concerned with Zifar and, to a lesser extent, with his family; in Book II Zifar is a much more passive figure and the adventures mainly involve Grima and, later on, their sons; the attention throughout Book IV centres on Roboán.

Books I and IV also have a second series of «aventuras de plano real», following the supernatural episode. [42] These later adventures are not as extensive as the first set—Book I, chapters 51-76, Book IV, chapters 213-226. They too begin with the opening up of a new phase in the main character's life, but this time it does not involve his arrival in a strange land. The second group of adventures in Book I starts with Zifar's meeting the

---

[41] There is also an interesting parallel in the use of the phrase «venir emiente» in both the passages quoted from the opening sections of Books II and IV. This could be interpreted as a further subtle link between the three initial situations, but such a hypothesis must be advanced with caution in view of the great reliance of medieval authors on formulas; see Spearing, *Criticism and Medieval Poetry*, especially p. 23. The *Zifar* author, as we shall see in chs 5 and 6, relies heavily on set phrases and formulas.

[42] For a possible explanation of why Book II lacks a second set of earthly adventures, see n. 62 below.

invaluable Ribaldo (ch. 52), who is to remain his constant companion even after the knight becomes King of Mentón. The second series of adventures in Book IV opens with Roboán's taking on the new responsibilities of Emperor of Tigrida (ch. 215).

All five sets of «aventuras de plano real», then, begin with the onset of a new and important stage in the protagonist's history which takes the form of either his arrival in a new country or his acceptance of new companions and a new role in life.

A second example of the close parallelism that exists between these five groups of adventures is to found in their inclusion of the test motif: the protagonist has to undergo some kind of trial to mark his entry into a new phase of life. In the first series of adventures in Book I, before Zifar can be admitted to Galapia he has to prove his courage by doing battle with the nephew of the count who is besieging the city (ch. 12). In Book II Grima is faced with the extremely disquieting realization that her husband is married to another woman and that she must overcome her natural feelings so as not to prejudice his position (ch. 87). In the early stages of Book IV Roboán's patience and chivalry is put to the test by the impertinent lady-in-waiting Gallarda upon his arrival in Pandulfa (ch. 181). In the second set of adventures in the first and last books the hero's assumption of a new role in life is again conditional upon his passing a test. Zifar, who underwent a physical trial of his courage and fighting skill when he arrived in Galapia, now has his patience and tolerance tried out by the Ribaldo's cheeky cross-examination (ch. 54). Roboán, on the other hand, who was submitted to the latter type of test when he first came to Pandulfa, is now called upon to prove his soldierly ability and capacity for making decisions against the rebel kings before he is allowed to take up his position as emperor unchallenged (ch. 216).

A third motif which all five sets of adventures have in common is war. In the first series of Book I Zifar takes a leading part in freeing Galapia from its aggressor, injuring the count who is leading the invading army and capturing his son (ch. 25). In the second group of adventures he engages in a succession of battles in connection with the relief of Mentón from the investment of the King of Ester: he defeats in turn one of the king's sons, his nephew and his other son (chs 65-68), and in the final confrontation helps in the overthrow of the king himself (ch. 76). In Book II Garfín and Roboán are appointed by their father to crush the revolt of Count Nasón. In the ensuing battle the elder son captures the count (ch. 99) and his brother defeats the count's nephew (ch. 104). In Book IV Roboán overcomes the army of the King of Grimalet to deliver Pandulfa in the first series of adventures (ch. 188), and he quells the rebel Kings of Garba and Çafira in the second (ch. 223). These wars are the nucleus of the five sets of adventures, representing in each case a significant victory for the heroes, a corresponding improvement in status, and a further assurance that God is on their side. The victories won by Zifar and Roboán in the latter part of Books I and IV are literally the crowning point of their lives: as a result of their «fechos de armas» in these wars they achieve royal status as king and emperor respectively.

A fourth point of comparison between the five groups of adventures is the importance of the role of women in them. In Book I it is a female, the ruler of Galapia, who first gives the unemployed—and allegedly unemployable—Zifar a chance to prove his worth. Later in the same book the princess of Mentón offers the knight the chance to fulfil his grandfather's prophecy. Grima has a key role in Book II after her arrival in Mentón, particularly in the task of reuniting the family. Her courage, patience and devotion are a constant support to her husband throughout these first two books, and even when they are apart her virtue remains absolutely constant. In Book IV an important part is played by Seringa. It is she, as ruler of Pandulfa, who gives Roboán his first free-lance military command; and falls in love with him. Their love provides a kind of framework for the whole of the last book: at the end Roboán returns to marry her.

A fifth motif that recurs in all five sets of knightly adventures is marriage. Early in Book I an eminent citizen of Galapia suggests marrying his two daughters to Zifar's sons. The knight rejects this offer, although it would have brought him honour, because he knows that his destiny is still unfulfilled and that as yet he must make no new ties (ch. 18). There is, however, one marriage in this first series of adventures: the lady ruler of Galapia marries the son of her former enemy and so ensures a lasting peace (ch. 37). At the close of Book I the marriage of Zifar to the princess of Mentón is arranged (ch. 77). The wedding takes place at the very beginning of Book II. Zifar is also reunited with Grima in this second book, and when his second wife conveniently dies he is able to acknowledge Grima before his subjects (ch. 118). Book IV once again follows closely the pattern of Book I. In the first set of adventures Count Rubén, a high-ranking member of the court of Pandulfa, proposes that Seringa and Roboán should marry (ch. 194). But, as in the corresponding section of Book I, the offer is turned down because the hero feels that he has not yet proved himself sufficiently. In the later adventures of Book IV marriage once more crowns a successful life when Roboán finally comes to claim Seringa (ch. 227).

An analysis of the five sets of «aventuras de plano real» provides more evidence that the *Zifar* author was aiming at a clear symmetrical structure for his work. The use of the same group of motifs, as we have seen, is not confined to the first series of earthly adventures in each of the three books or to the two series in the same book, but is common to all five. In this way the most extensive sections of the whole huge work are neatly welded together by a system of parallels, of foretastes and echoes. It now remains to examine whether the other two parts of the five-part pattern of each book established by Ruiz de Conde show similar evidence of careful structural planning.

(iii) *The Distribution of Rewards and Punishments*

Although many medieval romances end unhappily (including some of the best known such as the stories of Alexander and King Arthur), the *Zifar*'s three books of adventures each close with a settling of accounts in which the good are rewarded for their virtue and given ample recompense for their sufferings, and the wicked are exemplarily punished. This explosion of poetic justice is, of course, closely related to the initial situation of each book: the frustrations and problems which drove the protagonist to make the great change in his life are all resolved; the prophecies are fulfilled; the rewards gained are the logical climax of the preceding events. Those who have helped the hero on his way are suitably repaid; those who have tried to hinder God's purpose for him are justly dealt with.

At the end of Book I the King of Ester, the aggressor against Mentón, is defeated and flees the field; Zifar, the main agent of victory, is promised the hand of the princess and the position of heir to the throne. Book II closes with Zifar's whole family receiving their well-earned reward after their many sufferings and deprivations. Now that his second wife is dead, Zifar is able to present Grima and his children to the citizens of Mentón, who have no hesitation in accepting them as their rulers. Thus Zifar becomes king in his own right and on his own merits instead of, as before, king as the result of patronage. Garfín, the elder son, is given the confiscated county and title of the rebel Nasón, and his younger brother achieves his ambition to become a knight errant. The faithful Ribaldo is given large sums of money. Even the minor characters are not forgotten: the hermit who predicted great things for Zifar is sent the wherewithal to build a monastery,[43] and the fisherman is remembered by his former employee, the Ribaldo. Book IV ends with Roboán's victory over the rebels who disputed his right to the throne of Tigrida and with his marriage to Seringa. During their first year together she bears him a son, thus ensuring the continuity of the noble house of Zifar. To round off the whole work, the various members of the family are reunited at the very end when Roboán takes his wife and son to visit his parents and his brother in Mentón.

The final chapters of each book, then, are devoted to achieving the morally satisfying «and-so-they-lived-happily-ever-after» kind of ending.

---

[43] One recalls the similar case of the monk Pelayo and Count Fernán González in the *PFG*; see J. P. Keller, «The Hunt and Prophecy Episode of the *PFG*», *HR* XXIII (1955), 251-258, and Edward J. Mullen, «The Role of the Supernatural in *El libro del Cavallero Zifar*», *REH* V (1971), 257-268, at p. 261.

These concluding sections are carefully related to the events of their particular book, as we have seen, and the author also strives to link them to each other by using similar motifs in at least two of them. Thus we get the recurrence of such themes as the defeat of rebellious vassals, the accession to a throne, marriage, the reuniting of separated loved ones. Like the initial situations, these endings are also explicitly linked through the motif of the monastery of the Holy Spirit which Zifar asked the hermit to build at the end of Book II and which is visited by Roboán at the close of Book IV. [44] Once again, then, we see the author's concern for structural cohesion within his enormous compilation.

(iv) *The Supernatural Episodes*

The central part of each of the three books of adventures is devoted to a supernatural interlude. These fantastic episodes are quite extensive, covering Book I, chapters 44-50, Book II, chapters 110-117, and Book IV, chapters 205-213. These full-scale excursions into the marvellous have been much to blame for the critical commonplace that the *Zifar* lacks unity.

The main obstacle to any attempt to show the integration of the supernatural episodes into the *Zifar* as a whole is the fact that elsewhere the author appears to have deliberately avoided the magical trappings, enchanted castles, fantastic automata, strange races of men and beasts, that one normally associates with a romance of chivalry. The prevailing tone of the *Zifar*, then, outside the three marvellous adventures, is one of sobriety and «realism». J. Rubió y Balaguer has noted a number of reflections of the everyday life of early fourteenth-century Spain in the romance. [45] Apart from these details of contemporary reality, the author also includes numerous touches that give his work a surface appearance of verisimilitude, despite the basic unreality of the plot as a whole. To use C. S. Lewis' convenient terms, the *Zifar* lacks «realism of content» but abounds in «realism of presentation». [46] A few examples will serve to illustrate this point. When Grima meets her husband again after their long separation she has difficulty in recognizing him:

> porque la palabra avía canbiada, e non fablava el lenguaje que solía, e demás que era más gordo que solía e que le avía cresçido mucho la barba (177.16-19).

A similar «realistic» detail is present in the following passage from the early part of Book IV:

[44] This point is developed below, pp. 99-100.
[45] *La vida española en la época gótica* (Barcelona, 1943), 22, 41, 60, 105, 119, 200-202, 245.
[46] *An Experiment in Criticism* (Cambridge, 1961), ch. 7, especially pp. 57-59.

Asý que era redrado Roboán de la tierra del rey su padre bien
çient jornadas, eran entrados en otra tierra de otro lenguaje que
non semejava a la suya, de guisa que se non podían entender sy
non en pocas palabras (386.25-387.2). [47]

When Garfín sees a caged lion in Mentón, his brother warns him to keep
away from it in case the same thing should happen to him as happened
when he was a child, an event from which he still bears the scars
(dentelladuras) as a reminder. This conversation serves in yet another
way to increase the verisimilitude of the work, since it is overheard by
a girl who knows the story of Zifar's family misfortunes and who
immediately reports to Grima that her sons may be in Mentón. [48]

Since the author of the *Zifar* seems to have been at some pains to
present his material as realistically as possible within the conventional
framework of the romance, any supernatural episode will naturally tend
to seem out of place and threaten to destroy this carefully created illusion
of reality. Why, then, should the author run the double risk of disrupting
the unity of his work and of shattering belief in its reality by introducing
a lengthy excursion into the realm of the fantastic at the very centre of
each of his three books of adventures? There are, I think, two possible
explanations.

In the first place, the intervention of the marvellous in heroic narrative
was a firmly established tradition. The germs of this, of course, lie in the
epic, but the major development takes place in the romances which, from
Chrétien de Troyes onwards, are characterized by what Gillian Beer
neatly describes as «a serene intermingling of the unexpected and the
everyday». [49] The medieval public would expect at least some other-
worldly colouring in a work about a noble knight. The hero of the
romance, like the hero of the epic, is a special individual, a man with the
finger of destiny pointing at him, someone who is in degree if not in kind
different from the rest of us. An obvious and effective way for the author
to convey this is to introduce the supernatural into the account of his
hero's life and deeds.

A second probable reason for the inclusion of these fantastic episodes
in the *Zifar* is a simple, but eminently praiseworthy, desire to bring into
the narrative as much variety as possible. To break the monotony of

[47] According to H. J. Chaytor, *From Script to Print. An Introduction to Medieval
Vernacular Literature* (Cambridge, 1945), 26-29, this emphasis on language differences
between people of diverse races and countries is rare in medieval literature: mutual
understanding between Frenchman and Saracen, Greek and Roman, Norman and Saxon,
tends to be assumed. For the state of language study in the Middle Ages, see Bernhard
Bischoff, «The Study of Foreign Languages in the Middle Ages», *Sp* XXXVI (1961),
209-224.
[48] Other examples of realistic details and a discussion of the *Zifar*'s realism are to be
found in James F. Burke, *A Critical and Artistic Study of the «Libro del Cavallero Cifar»*,
Ph.D. dissertation of the University of North Carolina at Chapel Hill, 1966, 116-118.
[49] *The Romance*, 10.

repeated battles, misfortunes and chivalric adventures, relieved only by didactic sermonizing and the odd *exemplum*, the author inserts at three clearly defined points a highly coloured and exciting episode on the supernatural plane. (This practice might be compared perhaps with the tendency of contemporary novelists to include at least one similarly highly coloured and exciting bedroom-scene in their work).

Whatever his reasons, the *Zifar* author decided to incorporate some fantastic adventures and was then faced with the problem of integrating them harmoniously into his romance. Not the least of his achievements is his success in fusing them into the work as a whole without undermining its structural cohesion or seriously impairing its verisimilitude.

We have already seen, in Ruiz de Conde's analysis, that the «aventuras de plano fantástico», as she calls them, are enclosed by «aventuras de plano real»; the characters involved in them are not transported permanently to the Other World. Thus, before each incursion into the marvellous we are firmly in the world of man, and it is to this world that we shall return when the fantastic adventure is over.

Moreover, there is a good deal of evidence of careful preparation on the part of the author before he moves the action on to a supernatural plane: the change from the real world to the world of fantasy is never done abruptly. Here and there throughout the work there are brief glimpses of the supernatural which prepare us for the longer and more developed marvellous episodes at the centre of each book. In Book I, before Grima's strange adventures on the boat (chs 44-50) we have, apart from the mysterious death of Zifar's horses after ten days (chs 2, 11, 38), two intrusions of the specifically Christian supernatural: the raising from the dead of the lady ruler of Galapia through the direct intercession of the Virgin (ch. 30) and—significantly only two chapters before the beginning of the main supernatural episode—the heavenly voice addressing the knight on the river bank (ch. 42). In this way we become accustomed to the direct intervention of the deity in Zifar's affairs before we are plunged into the extensive account of the miraculous rescue of Grima from the sailors by Christ and the Virgin. Soon after the return to the real world a last intrusion of the supernatural occurs in the hermit's vision of the future greatness of Zifar (ch. 56), which fulfils the dual structural role of recalling the opening prophecy of the knight's grandfather and the hero's reasons for setting out, and also of reminding the reader of the continuing existence of a guardian deity which helps to stamp the mark of destiny on the family of Zifar.

These hints of the marvellous are more frequent in the first book than in the others, since by the time we get to Book II we have already been through one full-length supernatural episode and so we are less surprised when the action moves once more on to this plane. Nevertheless, before the strange adventure of the Cavallero Atrevido and the Enchanted Lake (chs 110-117), we have one further reminder: Grima arrives at the kingdom of Ester still aboard the boat «que guiava Nuestro Señor Jesu Cristo» (167.15-16). And shortly after the conclusion of the Cavallero Atrevido story a voice from heaven addresses Zifar once more, telling him that the time has come for him to acknowledge his family before the subjects of Mentón (ch. 119).

In Book IV there is no specifically supernatural happening before the main other-worldly adventure of the *Islas Dotadas* (chs 205-213). However, there is a building of an atmosphere of tension and mystery just before Roboán goes to the islands. The geographical position of Tigrida is described in terms of the «mysterious orient», and stress is laid on its proximity to the earthly paradise from which man is cut off by a wall of fire (ch. 202). The whole sequence of events leading up to Roboán's banishment from Tigrida to the islands overflows with elements of mystery —the emperor who never laughs, the terrible fate awaiting those who ask him why he is so solemn, the unexplained inability of the emperor to pardon Roboán when he falls into the trap of asking the question (chs 203-204). After Roboán's return from the *Islas Dotadas* and his accession to the throne of Tigrida, we are again reminded of the strange world with which the hero has been connected. Before his battle with the rebels a voice from heaven urges him to use the magic banner he has brought back from the islands (ch. 224).

Just as we are systematically prepared for the visits to the supernatural plane, similarly we are prepared for the return to the natural world which is to take place after the fantastic interlude is over. Each of the three extensive supernatural episodes is brought back to earth temporarily in the middle so that our minds will not become too accustomed to moving on the other-worldly plane and receive a jolt when the final return is made. In Book I Grima's journey on the ship guided by the Christ Child is broken by a nine-year sojourn in Orbín, where she occupies herself with ordinary everyday things before continuing her travels on the same mysterious vessel (chs 46-49). The adventure of the Cavallero Atrevido in Book II is interrupted so that St Jerome's *exemplum* about love can be related (ch. 115). Roboán also hears a story from the world of men whilst on the *Islas Dotadas*, the fable of the Wind, Water and Truth (ch. 209). In this way the author tries to ensure that we never completely lose sight of the real world which we have temporarily left and which we are to re-enter before very long.

It is also noteworthy that even the fully-fledged supernatural adventures of the Enchanted Lake and the *Islas Dotadas* are comparatively restrained when compared with the fantastic episodes in other medieval works of a similar type. [50] This restraint becomes abundantly clear when we

[50] For an account of such episodes in Spanish chivalric fiction, see María Rosa Lida de Malkiel, «La visión de trasmundo en las literaturas hispánicas», addendum to

realize how few of the established marvellous elements of the romance tradition the *Zifar* contains: there are no pagan gods, allegorical figures or magicians interfering with the course of events; no strange human species such as giants, dwarfs, invisible men or even wild men; no strange automata such as mechanical trees and birds or moving statues; no fantastically decorated tents, chariots or saddles; no magic beds, lamps, cloths or clothes; no truly fabulous beasts such as dragons, unicorns or griffons; no enchanted gardens with miraculous trees and plants. [51] The only other-worldly beings in the *Zifar* are the fairy mistresses of the Cavallero Atrevido and Roboán, and they are given the stamp of credibility —for a fourteenth-century reader at least—by being associated firmly with the orthodox Christian supernatural system. The sense of the marvellous in both the lake and the islands is conveyed more by the richness and luxury of the bejewelled buildings and furniture than by any really magical apparatus. [52] The truly fantastic elements are few. The most remarkable feature is the speeding up of time in the lake kingdom to such an extent that plants, animals and human beings reach maturity in seven days; but even this does not depend on any mechanical or magical aids. The Cavallero Atrevido's horses which turn into a goat and pig, and the strange steed which bears the helpless Roboán away from the islands, lose something of their awesomeness because we are already familiar with the equally inexplicable and unexplained enchantment of Zifar's horses on the earthly plane. Similarly, the pennant which makes Roboán invincible rather pales into insignificance beside some of the truly wonderful weapons wielded by medieval chivalric heroes. The *Zifar*'s supernatural episodes, then, are distinctly underplayed by normal romance standards.

Thus we can see that the author has gone to considerable trouble to make sure that the transitions from the natural to the supernatural plane and back again do not take the reader by surprise. Within the earthly adventures there are hints of forces and worlds outside everyday human experience; and when the characters become involved in an extensive supernatural episode, the author not only takes care that our credulity is not overstrained by the use of the most extravagant fantastic elements at his disposal, but also brings the protagonist—and the reader—back to earth briefly (either physically or metaphorically) in the middle of the episode.

H. R. Patch, *El otro mundo en la literatura medieval*, trans. J. Hernández Campos (México-Buenos Aires, 1956), 408-426.

[51] The great range of marvellous elements in the French *roman* is classified in Edmond Faral, *Recherches sur les sources latines des contes et romans courtois du Moyen Age* (Paris, 1913), 307-388.

[52] The only jewels with magical properties in the work are those found by Roboán in Çafira, which is not, overtly at least, an other-worldly kingdom. This is a further illustration of the author's subtle mingling of realistic and fantastic elements in both the primarily earthly and primarily supernatural planes of his work.

A further illustration of the author's desire to impose unity on the various elements of his story is the way in which the three supernatural interludes increase gradually in degrees of incredibility. The main marvellous episode of Book I involves what for the medieval reader would be the «real», that is Christian, supernatural. The same is true of all the fantastic elements in this first book, with the exception of the curse on Zifar's horses. It would require little effort for the fourteenth-century man to accept God's direct intervention in the affairs of human beings as possible, if perhaps rather uncommon in such a dramatic form as we see here. It is also significant that in this case the supernatural manifests itself in the world of men: Grima does not travel to the Other World. The return to earthly reality which, as we have seen, occurs in all the fantastic interludes, in this case is a physical return: Grima lands at the kingdom of Orbín. Thus the supernatural in Book I is kept as down-to-earth as possible.

The other-worldly adventure in Book II demands rather more suspension of disbelief on the part of the reader, since it involves a supernatural system that is not Christian. By this stage, however, the reader has been gently acclimatized to the idea of a marvellous element in the work and is now willing to accept the Enchanted Lake episode, particularly as it concerns a strange character with an awe-inspiring name who plays no part in the main story. Again there is a return to the earthly plane in the middle, but this time it is only in the form of St Jerome's *exemplum*, not a physical return as it was in Book I. Nevertheless, it is an *exemplum* involving real people and a real human situation, and it is attributed to a well-known figure from the world of men.

By Book IV the author has led us so skilfully into accepting the marvellous that he can now transport the central character of his narrative to a completely fantastic Other World. Although the brief descent to the natural plane in the middle of the episode is still there, it is in this case even more abstract than in Book II: again it takes the form of an *exemplum*, but not this time about human beings; instead we hear the fable of the Wind, Water and Truth. However, by having gradually accustomed the reader to the idea of supernatural interludes in the story, by the systematic building up of an atmosphere of mystery immediately before the *Islas Dotadas* episode and, finally, by including the devil, a figure from the orthodox Christian supernatural system, in his pagan Other World, the author manages to carry us with him into total acceptance of the highly imaginative adventure in the middle of Book IV.[53]

[53] A comparison might be made here with the *Poema de Mío Cid* where the poet uses a very similar technique. In the first *cantar* he sticks almost exclusively to well established historical facts so that his audience will be convinced that it is the true story of the Cid they are hearing. Having lulled them into this belief, the author then proceeds in the second and third *cantares* to introduce more and more legendary and downright fictional elements into his narrative in order to give us his own personal interpretation

There is one further point of interest with regard to the structural function of these «aventuras de plano fantástico». Participation in such episodes naturally thrusts the protagonist into the spotlight and gives him increased stature in our eyes. Grima is not the leading character in Book I, which is devoted almost entirely to Zifar, but she does play a considerable part in Book II. By making her the centre of the fantastic adventure in the first book, the author prepares us for her emergence as a major figure in Book II, since the brief intensity of a spectacular episode of this type impresses itself on our mind and imagination as much as the longer but somewhat less sensational adventures on the natural plane.

Book II is in many ways a transitional book which, although still concerned primarily with Zifar, is also intended to prepare us for the emergence of Roboán as the central character of the work in succession to his father. Consequently, since their work is almost over, neither Zifar nor his wife must be emphasized too much or the delicate balance would be destroyed. It would be a mistake to give the supernatural adventure to Garfín, as he would then assume more importance than his younger brother. The elder son's chief role is to take over the duties of Zifar in Mentón and leave Roboán free to set out in search of adventures. It would perhaps seem logical, therefore, to give the supernatural episode to Roboán himself. The fact that the author does not do this is presumably because he felt it would be too early to thrust the hero of Book IV into the limelight at this stage and overshadow prematurely the importance of his father. There is still a long way to go before Roboán actually sets out on his adventures: the *Castigos del rey de Mentón*, in which the great Zifar displays his accumulated wisdom, is still to come, and the fact that the *Castigos* is addressed to his sons will be sufficient to make the transition from Zifar to Roboán as the leading character smooth and unhurried. However, as the author seems clearly to be committed to a system of structural parallels that demands a supernatural adventure in the middle of the earthly episodes in each book, he has to find a suitable protagonist for an excursion into the marvellous at this point. It is for this reason, I think, that the Cavallero Atrevido is brought into the story. Apart from his role in the episode of the Enchanted Lake he plays no part in the romance at all. He appears to be used simply to get the author out of a dilemma in which he found himself at this juncture, caught between the demands of his structural pattern for a supernatural adventure and the lack of a suitable protagonist for such an adventure amongst the major characters.

In Book IV the undisputed main character is Roboán; he holds the centre of the stage throughout. There can be no danger now of

of the Cid's deeds and character. But because of his careful establishment of a real historical basis early in the poem, the audience (and a considerable number of later scholars) are willing to accept the later events as part of the same historical truth.

overemphasizing his importance if he is also made the protagonist of the supernatural episode in the book. It is Roboán, therefore, who visits the *Islas Dotadas*. [54]

A further point of interest is that the three marvellous episodes are linked thematically with the rest of the book in which they occur. These adventures on the supernatural plane are not in fact digressions which can be abstracted from the book without damaging it, but an intrinsic part of it. Grima's rescue from the sailors not only concerns one of the main characters of the first book, but also underlines its principal theme, the nearness of God to Zifar and his family. By this direct confrontation of a member of this family with Christ himself the message is emphasized and made absolutely clear.

The adventure of the Cavallero Atrevido, which Wagner calls an «obscure allegory», [55] and which Scholberg says is «unnecessary and foreign to the affairs of Cifar or his family», [56] in fact fits admirably into the overall thematic scheme of Book II. When the ashes of Nasón, the traitor and rebel, are cast into the lake, they provoke a violent tempest, the report of which brings the fearless knight to investigate. He too will prove to be a traitor and, like Nasón, he will be punished. The lake kingdom clearly represents the home of treachery, which, together with its opposite, loyalty, is one of the most important themes of Book II. A. H. Krappe stresses this point in his analysis of the episode:

> Trahison, démon hideux, y arrache le coeur à deux traîtres
> .... Sans doute l'auteur de notre compilation a-t-il voulu faire
> entendre que le Chevalier Sans Peur aurait mérité leur compagnie,
> son aventure galante avec la pucelle inconnue constituant, aux
> yeux des rigoristes et du beau sexe, une noire trahison. S'il
> n'est pas puni plus exemplairement, c'est évidemment pour
> qu'il revienne conter ses aventures qu'on n'aurait pas apprises
> autrement. La perte de sa belle maîtresse et de sa sinécure
> est sans doute une punition assez grave. [57]

[54] A similar pattern is to be noted in the *Zifar*'s battle scenes: they always concern the leading character in the particular book in which they occur. Zifar, the protagonist of Book I, fights all the battles in that book. Similarly, the battles in Book IV concern Roboán alone. In the transitional Book II we are being prepared for the shift of emphasis from Zifar to Roboán. The father fights no battles in this book; and the warlike exploits are left to his sons. But it is Garfín, not his brother, who captures the rebel leader Nasón; Roboán has a less important victory over the count's nephew. This point is stressed by Zifar after the battle: «Amigos, sy Garfín traxo buen presente para ser más conplido, Roboán nos trae lo que menguava, e éste es el sobrino del conde» (214.25-215.1). It is also worth noting that the Ribaldo, who plays no military part in Zifar's battles in Book I and who acts merely as an emissary for Roboán in Book IV, takes an active role in the fighting in Book II. All this appears to be part of the author's elaborate plan for bringing Roboán into the picture gradually, but not putting him in the centre of the stage too early.

[55] «Sources», 29.

[56] «The Structure of the *Caballero Cifar*», 123.

[57] «Le Lac enchanté dans le *Chevalier Cifar*», *BH* XXXV (1933), 107-125, at p. 109.

In Book IV, as in Book I, the supernatural episode concerns a leading character in the work. But the adventure is further connected with the main narrative thread of the work by other links. Roboán undergoes the same test as the emperor he is to succeed and, as Scholberg says, «it is an integral part of the process whereby Roboán becomes the favourite of the Emperor of Trígida and eventually inherits the crown». [58] Moreover, it is as a result of his stay on the *Islas Dotadas* that Roboán comes into possession of the marvellous banner which makes him invincible in his later battles.

The foregoing analysis shows clearly that the *Zifar*'s three major supernatural episodes are carefully integrated into the overall structure and tone of the particular book in which they occur. But, as we saw earlier, the author is concerned not only with establishing a unity for each book within itself, but also with fusing the three books of adventures together into a coherent whole. Consequently we shall find that the three fantastic episodes are linked *to each other* by the use of a set of identical motifs and by cross references, in the same way as the five sets of earthly adventures are linked together.

Justina Ruiz de Conde points out that water plays an important part in all three marvellous adventures: [59] Grima's rescue takes place at sea; the Cavallero Atrevido enters an underwater kingdom; Roboán crosses the sea in a «batel syn remos» to reach the islands. This similarity of setting shows that the *Zifar* author was well acquainted with the common folkloric idea of the Other World as a place either across the water or under it. [60] Secondly, in each of these episodes the protagonist comes into possession of fabulous riches. Grima's ship is laden with precious merchandise, chiefly clothes and jewels (ch. 45). The treasures of the Enchanted Lake (ch. 112) and the *Islas Dotadas* (ch. 206) are of the usual fantastic size that one finds in descriptions of Celtic or Oriental Other Worlds. [61] It is also interesting that the riches of the islands are specifically compared with those of the lake: «Ca bien valié esta baxilla tanto o más que la que fue puesta delante del Cavallero Atrevido quando entró en el lago con la Señora de la Trayçión» (460.34-461.2). Thirdly, all three adventures in the Other World involve the protagonists with remarkable children. Grima's ship is guided by the Infant Jesus, and both the Cavallero Atrevido and Roboán become the fathers of redoubtable sons—Alberto Diablo (so called because of the demonic connections of his mother), who is born after only seven days' gestation, and Fortunado. Of the former we are told:

---

[58]   «Structure», 124.
[59]   *El amor y el matrimonio secreto*, 49.
[60]   See Howard Rollin Patch, *The Other World according to Descriptions in Medieval Literature* (Cambridge, Mass., 1950), *passim*.
[61]   See Patch, *The Other World*, *passim*; Faral, *Recherches sur les sources latines*, 351-358.

> Aquéste fue muy buen cavallero de armas, e mucho atrevido e muy
> syn miedo en todas las cosas, ca non avía cosa del mundo que
> dubdase e que non acometiese (242.9-11).

Destined to become equally famous is Fortunado:

> del qual ay un libro de la su estoria en caldeo, de quantas buenas
> cavallerías e quantos buenos fechos fizo después que fue de
> hedat e fue en demanda de su padre (477.18-20).

Apart from the motifs of water, fabulous jewels and extraordinary
children, which can be considered as specifically designed to give an
appropriate air of the other-worldly, there are other constant motifs in
these episodes that are particularly interesting because they are not only
common to all three supernatural adventures, but also clearly mirror
the group of motifs that we have already discerned in the five sets of
«aventuras de plano real».

First, we saw that each series of events on the natural plane begins
with the arrival of someone in a new land or their acceptance of new
responsibilities and companions. In the supernatural episodes these two
alternatives are combined: the central figure not only enters a new realm
but clearly begins a new phase in his life with new friends and, in the case
of the Cavallero Atrevido and Roboán, new duties as a ruler.

Secondly, the new world brings with it a series of trials and tests to
which the protagonist has to submit in order to show whether or not he is
worthy of his destiny. Grima's courage is tested when she is carried off
by the sailors, and her faith is put on trial when God speaks to her and
tells her what to do after her captors have killed each other in a quarrel.
The Cavallero Atrevido is forbidden to speak to the inhabitants of the lake
kingdom and told that he must remain faithful to his fairy mistress if he
is to be worthy of sharing the wonders of the underwater paradise. Roboán
is repeatedly warned to be very careful whose advice he listens to, lest he
too should lose his loved one and his dominion over the *Islas Dotadas*.
Grima comes through triumphantly because she is helped by God, but
the two men lose their advantages and have to return to the world of
ordinary mortals with all its sorrow and pain, because they failed to
recognize the devil in his disguise when he tempted the fearless knight
into infidelity and Roboán into foolishly asking for the enchanted horse
that will prove his undoing. The test, then, forms an important part of
the initiation of a man into a new life on the supernatural plane as on the
natural plane. The only difference is that the heroes always succeed in
passing the test in this world, whereas in two cases out of three they fail
in the Other World.

Thirdly, in all three supernatural episodes women have a significant part to play, just as they do in the earthly adventures. In each of the other-worldly sequences there are two women with roles of central importance. In the first of these the protagonist is herself a woman, and she is advised and guided throughout by another woman, the Virgin Mary. The Cavallero Atrevido marries the lady of the lake and it is she who controls his fate, punishing him for his infidelity with the temptress, the other prominent female character in this episode. A similar situation exists in the supernatural adventure in Book IV: Roboán marries the mistress of the other-world kingdom, and he too is tempted by a beautiful woman who causes him to lose his happiness.

Fourthly, marriage is a constant motif in the fantastic adventures as in the earthly adventures. In Books II and IV the mortal hero contracts marriage with the fairy ruler of the marvellous land to which he is taken. Perhaps one might even say that Grima, like a nun, undergoes a form of marriage with God during her voyage; when she lands in Orbín she sets up a religious house, like a good wife, and when she leaves Christ again goes with her. It would be imprudent, however, to try to push the parallel too far.

Finally, the ending of the three marvellous episodes, with their distribution of rewards and punishments in strict accordance with the protagonist's deserts, again reflects the pattern of events on the natural plane. Grima reaches a safe haven in Orbín and is left in possession of the considerable riches on the ship. When she leaves Orbín Christ is once more her guide until she reaches Mentón, where she will be reunited with her husband and children. She has survived the test of her faith and courage; her unerring trust in God yields its reward. On the other hand, both the Cavallero Atrevido and Roboán are violently expelled from their paradise because they have not withstood the trial of their integrity: both have allowed themselves to be deceived by the devil into surrendering to their base desires—lust in the case of the fearless knight and greed in the case of Roboán. As we have seen, treachery and ingratitude are similarly repaid in the world of men.

* * *

With all the above evidence before us, it is surely impossible now to subscribe to the traditional view that the *Zifar* is a work without unity. Each of the three books of adventures is built up on the same basic pattern of an initial situation, which sets the action in motion, followed by a first series of adventures on the earthly plane, a supernatural episode and a second set of earthly adventures (except in Book II). [62] Each book ends

---

[62] The absence of a second series of earthly adventures in Book II admittedly upsets somewhat the ultraprecise balance I have claimed to find in the *Zifar*. I can only suggest that since *El rey de Mentón* is a transitional book with no absolutely clear central character, the author would have some difficulty in choosing a protagonist for such a

8

with the distribution of rewards and punishments. Within this pattern
there are many other parallels: the same elements occur in each of the
initial situations; the same motifs are used in each of the five sets of
«aventuras de plano real»; and the supernatural episodes have many
common features. Unity is further ensured by the coincidence of many
of the motifs in the fantastic adventures with those in the earthly adventures.
Moreover, great care is taken to fit the other-worldly episodes into the
tone and structure of the particular book in which they occur, mainly
by subtle preparation for the change from one plane to the other and by
thematic links between the supernatural episodes and the main body of
earthly adventures.

C. OTHER STRUCTURAL LINKS

Besides the complex parallelistic structuring there are several other
devices used by the author to ensure that the whole enormous compilation
has its own overall unity.

First of all, the same characters figure throughout, sometimes in the
foreground, sometimes in the background, but always present. In Book I
the obvious hero is Zifar himself, but for certain periods the centre of the
stage is occupied by his wife and their two sons. This is the beginning
of the process whereby Zifar is gradually replaced as the principal character
by Roboán. In Book II the stories of Zifar, Grima and the boys are
continued independently until their reunion. After this the two brothers
begin to play a more active role than their father, taking command of his
army against the rebellious vassals and preparing us for Roboán's emergence
as the central figure in Book IV. The *Castigos del rey de Mentón*
(Book III) completes the process. When the last book opens, we have
witnessed Roboán's initiation and education, and we are ready to see
how he will follow his father's teaching and example. But even in Book IV
Zifar is still present in the background. Not only does Roboán take
leave of his father and mother at the beginning of the book and return
with his wife and son to visit them at the end, but the pattern of his life
and career constantly recalls that of his father in Books I and II. [63]
Throughout Book IV the noble spirit of Zifar is reflected in the actions,
speech and thoughts of his son.

One of the minor characters, the Ribaldo, also plays an important

set of adventures. I have already put forward a similar reason for the choice of the unknown Cavallero Atrevido to face the perils of the Enchanted Lake rather than a member
of the family. By the end of the first series of earthly adventures in Book II the family
is reunited, Zifar has reached the zenith of his power, Garfín and Roboán have proved
themselves. In fact, the stage is already set for the *Castigos* and the adventures of
Roboán in Book IV.

[63] See the tabulation of this in Scholberg, «Structure», 120-121.

part in establishing a sense of continuity and unity between the various sections of the romance. This is not such a weak argument as Scholberg maintains. [64] Zifar meets the lively peasant about two-thirds of the way through the first book and he is thereafter the constant companion first of the knight and then of Roboán. He takes a significant role in the transitional second book, where the change from one hero to another is being gently brought about. It is not by chance that whereas the Ribaldo takes no part in Zifar's battles in Book I, and merely acts as adviser and ambassador to Roboán in Book IV, he plays a very active role in the fighting in Book II. When Zifar appoints him to accompany Roboán on his wanderings, a clear tangible link is forged between father and son and their adventures.

The links between the various books are also strengthened by direct references to previous happenings. In chapter 177, for example, when Zifar and Grima are discussing Roboán's request for permission to leave home and seek his own fortune, the knight recalls his own beginnings and reminds Grima that she was all in favour of their setting out. She admits that she does not want to lose her son, but she recognizes the logic of her husband's argument and finally agrees that Roboán should go. The connection between the lives of father and son is further underlined in the reader's mind by this reminiscence of the very beginning of the work. And this is not all: in the course of his adventures Roboán twice recalls his own setting out and his parents' farewells. When he is knighted by the Emperor of Tigrida, «menbrósele de lo que·l dixiera su madre quando se della partió, que el coraçón le dava que sería enperador, e creçióle el coraçón por fazer bien» (440.28-441.2). A little later, when he arrives at the *Islas Dotadas*, he is reminded once again of his departure from home by the *donzellas* who welcome him: «E Nuestro Señor Dios, al que vós tomastes por guiador quando vos despedistes del rey vuestro padre e de la reýna vuestra madre, vos quiso enderesçar e guiar a este logar» (457.33-458.1).

A further recurring theme is provided by the monastery which Zifar orders to be built. The periodic reappearance of this motif has been studied in some detail by Scholberg. [65] In the hermitage where Zifar first meets the Ribaldo the hermit has a vision of the knight's future greatness. He communicates his dream to Zifar and asks him to remember the place where the prediction was made (ch. 56). At the end of Book II, when he has become King of Mentón, Zifar sends the Ribaldo with gifts of money to the hermit so that he can build a monastery (ch. 120). In Book IV, after ascending the throne of Tigrida, Roboán decides to make a pilgrimage to the monastery founded by his father (ch. 216); but he has to postpone his visit owing to the rebellion of the Kings of Garba and

---

[64] «Structure», 114.
[65] «Structure», 115-117.

99

Çafira. He carries out his plan, however, at the end of the book, after the rebellion has been put down and he has married Seringa (ch. 229). In Scholberg's words, «the hermitage-monastery serves as a unifying point: future success is foretold there and it is brought to mind at the culmination of the good fortune of both father and son» (116).

These cross-references show up the author's concern for overall unity, a concern which is also revealed by the frequent indirect echoes of themes and events in other books of a rather more subtle type than the groups of common motifs in the basic five-part parallelistic plan we have already examined. These free-ranging motifs, as we might call them, perform the dual function of binding the three books of adventures more closely together in our minds and of giving a certain amount of flexibility to what otherwise might seem an over-rigid and rather unimaginative schematic pattern.

The marriages of Zifar and Roboán provide an excellent topic for a closer examination of the free-ranging or multi-purpose motif. The fact that both heroes marry twice underlines the basic and closely worked out similarity of pattern in the life stories of the two men. But the location of the two marriages within their parallel biographies is very different. Zifar is already married to Grima when the story opens, and he marries the princess of Mentón at the beginning of Book II, just *before* he becomes king. Roboán, on the other hand, remains a bachelor for a considerable period, and only takes a wife for the first time half-way through Book IV when he marries Nobleza, the Empress of the *Islas Dotadas*. His second marriage, to Seringa, occurs right at the end of Book IV, just *after* he has become Emperor of Tigrida. In terms of a different pattern, however, we can see that both father and son go through the same exactly parallel threefold cycle of first love, second love, return to first love, which does not coincide with the pattern of their marriages:

ZIFAR

    (a) Early life: already married to Grima.
    (b) Change of status: marries the princess and becomes king.
    (c) Final settling down: reunited with Grima and becomes king in his own right.

ROBOÁN

    (a) Early life: meets and falls in love with Seringa.
    (b) Change of status: marries Nobleza and becomes Emperor of the *Islas Dotadas*.
    (c) Final settling down: marries Seringa and becomes Emperor of Tigrida.

Within this scheme, then, Roboán's first marriage balances his father's second marriage; but it also continues the tradition of marriage in the supernatural episodes and links the marvellous adventure of Book IV with that of the Cavallero Atrevido in Book II, since he too marries the ruler of the fairy kingdom to which he is taken.

The similarity between Zifar and Roboán is also underlined outside the limits of the basic parallelistic structure by the fact that they both have two sons. Again there is a great difference in the circumstances in which these sons are born and in the part they play in the story. At the beginning of the work Zifar's two sons, both born to his first wife Grima, are already growing up and, of course, they take an increasingly important part in the story in Book II until the younger one emerges as the central figure of the later part of the work. Roboán's sons, however, are born to different mothers and play no role in the story whatsoever. But the author clearly wishes us to see Roboán as the father of two sons, thus providing a further point of similarity to Zifar. It is interesting to note that both of Roboán's sons are introduced into the story by a very similar form of words (see ch. 2, n. 39 above).

Justina Ruiz de Conde has rightly pointed out that enchanted horses are a constant feature of all three books of adventures. [66] In Book I Zifar's horses die after he has had them for ten days as a result of the curse on his family; in Book II the theme recurs with the two horses that turn into a goat and a pig as the Cavallero Atrevido is hurled unceremoniously from the Enchanted Lake; and in the last book it is a marvellous horse which carries Roboán away from Nobleza and his happy life on the *Islas Dotadas*. Although the motif is common to all three books, there are nevertheless interesting differences in the circumstances surrounding the three appearances of these enchanted beasts. In the first instance, the bewitched horses belong entirely to this world: they are ordinary horses that have been tampered with from the supernatural plane. [67] Any horse that comes into Zifar's possession immediately becomes affected by the curse. The horses of the Cavallero Atrevido, on the other hand, seem perfectly normal whilst they are in the marvellous world of the lake, but go through an extraordinary metamorphosis as soon as they set hoof in the world of men. The last of the enchanted horses confines its activities entirely to the fantastic world of the *Islas Dotadas:* it does not bring Roboán back to this world, but simply drops him in the boat that will return him to Tigrida. Thus, once again, flexibility and variety temper the rigidity of the parallelistic structure.

[66] *El amor y el matrimonio secreto*, 49-50.
[67] This, of course, fits in with the whole «realistic» tone of Book I which, as we saw, has no actual visit to the Other World and a main supernatural adventure that is entirely Christian.

These few examples are, I hope, enough to show that the author of the *Zifar* not only constructs his work according to a highly symmetrical parallelistic pattern, but that he also is capable of introducing other correspondences that cut across the divisions of the basic pattern, form new patterns, and bind the three parts of the work that concern chivalric action with further subtle links.

D. INTERWEAVING

It is well known that the interweaving of several strands of independent adventures with different protagonists is a marked characteristic of medieval romance in general. The most extreme examples of this technique are probably to be found in the great French Arthurian cycles. In the section of the so-called Vulgate Cycle known as *La Queste del Saint Graal,* for instance, we follow the fortunes of each of the four Grail-seekers in turn, leaving Lancelot to take up with Boorz, then abandoning him and retracing our steps to find out what is happening to Galaad or Perceval, returning briefly to Lancelot, and so on. This technique of *entrelacement* has been likened by Ferdinand Lot to a tapestry in which all the threads are so inextricably interwoven that «si l'on tente d'y pratiquer une coupure tout part en morceaux». [68] Eugène Vinaver, as we saw in the early part of this chapter, suggests that this process originated in the rhetorical device of *digressio ad aliam partem materiæ:*

> To the bewilderment of the reader unaccustomed to works of this type, narrative threads are interwoven in such a way as to make each story seem at one and the same time a continuation of one series of events and a digression from another. [69]

The *Zifar* author also avails himself of this structural device when he has to describe the adventures of Zifar, his wife and his children, after the break-up of the family. Although this technique of narrative clashes with modern ideas on novelistic structure, [70] the interweaving is much less complicated and multi-levelled than in many of the French romances of about the same date. In this respect and, as I hope to show, in his handling of the transitions from one protagonist to another, the Spanish author seems to exhibit surprisingly modern attitudes. He appears to have been somewhat worried by the blatant toing and froing of medieval romance in general and consequently to have soft-pedalled his own indulgence in the practice.

[68] *Etude sur le «Lancelot» en prose* (BÉHÉ 226, Paris, 1918), 28.
[69] *Le Roman de Balain*, xiii-xiv.
[70] One excepts, naturally, such works as J. R. R. Tolkien, *The Lord of the Rings*, which is a deliberate imitation of medieval romance not only in structure, but also in content and to some extent style.

In most medieval narratives a change of direction is almost invariably indicated quite openly. In fact, authors seem to make a deliberate point of emphasizing a break rather than trying to conceal it. The usual signpost is a rather crude formula of the type «Now we leave X and return to Y». Examples of this kind of cliché can be found in romances in many languages throughout the Middle Ages. They occur, for instance, in the thirteenth-century *Libro de Apolonio:*

> El rey Antioco vos quiero destajar,
> Quiero en Apolonio la materia tornar (62ab)

> Mas dexemos a ella su menester usando,
> Tornemos en el padre que andava lazdrado (433cd).

The French *Queste*, also dating from the thirteenth century, uses a very similar formula, but without the element of direct address:

> Si lesse ore a tant li contes a parler d'aux et parole de Galaad

> Mes atant lesse ores li contes a parler de lui et retorne a Perceval. [71]

In the fifteenth century Sir Thomas Malory is still using the same device:

> So leve we sir Launcelot in hys londis and hys noble knyghtes with hym, and returne we agayne unto kynge Arthur and unto sir Gawayne

> Now leve we the quene in Amysbery, a nunne in whyght clothys and black ... and now turne we from her and speke we of sir Launcelot du Lake. [72]

In the *Zifar* a similar formula to the above is used seven times when the narrative is about to change direction. All of them occur in Books I and II:

> Aquí dexa de fablar la ystoria del señor de la hueste, e fabla de la señora de Galapia (64.10-11)

> Agora dexa la fabla de todo lo acaesçido e fabla del Cavallero Zifar (83.21-22)

> Agora dexa la ystoria de fablar del Cavallero Zifar e fabla de su muger (94.7-8)

---

[71] *La Queste del Saint Graal (Roman du XIIIᵉ siècle)*, ed. Albert Pauphilet (CFMA 33, Paris, 1949), 55 and 71. The break in the narrative is underlined even further in these cases by the use of the *incipit* formula «Or dit li contes» immediately afterwards.

[72] *The Tale of the Death of King Arthur*, ed. Eugène Vinaver (Oxford, 1955), 49 and 82. Further examples of transitional phrases from Old French and Middle English romances are to be found in Ruth Crosby, «Oral Delivery in the Middle Ages», *Sp* XI (1936), 88-110, at p. 107, especially nn. 1 and 2.

Dexa la ystoria de fablar de la dueña e fabla de lo que contesçió a su marido el Cavallero Zifar con el hermitaño (106.16-18)

Agora dexa la ystoria de fablar del rey e de la reýna, e torna a fablar de la muger del cavallero (167.10-11)

Aquí dexa la ystoria de fablar del rey e de la reýna e de la dueña, e fabla de sus fijos (178.18-19)

Aquí dexa la ystoria de fablar de la conpaña del rey e fabla de un cavallero atrevido (226.17-18).

It is important to note, however, that all these occurrences of the formula in the *Zifar* are chapter headings; there is no example of this type of cliché in the actual text of any of the three extant versions of the romance. Furthermore, all the cases quoted are taken from manuscript *P*. In the oldest manuscript *M* there is not a single instance of this formula used as a rubric. At two of the points where *P* employs the formula (64.10-11, 83.21-22) *M* has no rubric at all. This is not surprising since, as we saw earlier (ch. 1, section B), *M* has chapter headings only when there is a significant alteration in the direction of the narrative. At neither of the points quoted above is this the case: we are simply moving from one character to another within the same episode. In the other five cases *M*'s rubrics are worded quite differently from those of *P*. All this suggests strongly that the chapter headings are the work of copyists, not of the author. This seems to be borne out further by the fact that in one rubric (167.10-11) Zifar, now King of Mentón, is referred to as a *cavallero*. It has already been shown (ch. 2, section B) how the author scrupulously refrains from referring to any of his characters by a title that has been superseded. At this point Zifar is *always* called «el rey (de Mentón)».

If the *Zifar* author eschews the usual cliché, how does he prepare his readers for the major changes of direction that are necessarily involved in an interwoven structure? An examination of those points at which a character who has been off-stage for some time re-emerges shows, I think, that the author is rather more subtle in his linking technique than many other medieval writers. Instead of baldly telling us that he is now going to deal with someone different, he makes sure that a mention of the character about to reappear is brought in at the close of the previous episode. If we look at the four places at which the members of Zifar's family successively return to the centre of the picture after the separation, we shall see this technique illustrated perfectly.

(*a*) At the end of chapter 43, which describes the adoption of Zifar's two sons by the *burgés* and his wife, we read:

E todos punavan en fazer merçed e plazer a aquellas criaturas, e más el padre e la madre que los porfijaron, ca ellos eran muy

plazenteros, e de muy buen donayre, e muy linpios e bien
acostunbrados, maguer moços pequeños, ca asý los acostunbrara
e los nodresçiera aquella buena dueña que los falsos levaron
en la nave, de que agora vos contará la estoria en cómmo pasó
su fazienda (93.27-94.6).

The following chapter takes up the story of Grima. The break in the
narrative flow is clearly indicated in this case by the final words of chapter 43
—«de que agora vos contará la estoria en cómmo pasó su fazienda»—
but the skilful reminder of the links between the sons and the mother,
despite their separation, is artistically more satisfying than the later
interpolated chapter heading of *P*—«Agora dexa la ystoria de fablar del
Cavallero Zifar e fabla de su muger»—which does not even get the *dramatis
personæ* right, since chapter 43 is concerned not with Zifar but with his
sons.

(*b*) After a few chapters the author abandons Grima and returns
to Zifar. Once again the character due to reemerge is mentioned, as
naturally as possible in view of the artificiality of the method of
entrelacement, immediately before his reappearance. At the end of
chapter 50 we are told that Grima:

> estava pensando en su marido sy lo podría fallar bivo, lo que
> non cuydava sy non fuese por la merçed de Dios que lo podría
> fazer (106.13-15).

(*c*) In chapter 82 the story of Grima is taken up once again. At the
end of the previous chapter Zifar enters into a vow of chastity with his
second wife:

> ca la su entençión fue por atender algunt tienpo por saber de su
> muger sy era muerta o biva (167.7-9).

(*d*) Grima and Zifar come together in Mentón, although they cannot
at first acknowledge one another. The final words of this section read:

> E en la noche [Grima] ývase para su ospital, e todo lo más estava
> en oración en una capiella que ý avía, e rogava a Dios que ante
> que muriese que·l dexase ver a alguno de sus fijos, e señaladamente
> al que perdiera en aquella çibdat ribera de la mar; ca el otro,
> que levara la leona, non avía fuzia ninguna de lo cobrar, teniendo
> que lo avía comido (178.12-17).

In the next chapter (ch. 89) the long-lost sons reappear on the scene.

It will be noticed that in the last three of these four cases there is no
unequivocal statement that the protagonist is about to change (except
of course in the rubrics of *P*). The new direction, neatly prepared for

by the links just discussed, is indicated simply by the *incipit* formula
«dize el cuento que», [73] whose use is not confined to the points at which
the threads of an *entrelacement* are picked up again. [74] It would seem,
then, that the *Zifar* author, by understating rather than overemphasizing
the violent changes of direction in his story, reveals a care for narrative
flow that is moving towards much more modern novelistic ideals than
one would perhaps expect to find at the beginning of the fourteenth
century. [75]

E. DIGRESSIONS

Within the overall parallelistic and interwoven structure of the *Zifar*
there are many true digressions *(digressiones ad aliquid extra materiam)*
which, from a modern viewpoint, would seem to damage the work's
cohesion. Even Justina Ruiz de Conde, the first critic to recognize any
real structural pattern in the romance, as we have seen, is worried by
these digressions:

> Porque preciso es reconocer que a veces parece que el autor ha
> perdido su camino, o al menos que el camino es muy difícil
> de reconocer; y se continúa la lectura, enfrascándonos en las
> nuevas aventuras, un poco con la impaciencia de volver a
> reunirnos con los protagonistas. Lo que éstos dicen o hacen
> está tan sobrecargado de elementos aparentemente ajenos a la
> trama, innecesarios para la acción, que las voluminosas 516
> páginas quedarían reducidas a mucho menos de la mitad, si de
> ellas se entresacaran los comentarios, digresiones morales,
> geográficas, religiosas y de toda clase, cuentos y ejemplos de todo
> tipo, cuyo peso hace temblar la propia unidad del libro. [76]

It is my belief, however, that every episode, adventure, situation, description
and digression has its due function and justification within the complex
unity of the whole. A close analysis of the elements that go to make up
Book I, *El Cavallero de Dios*, should support this belief.

The first book begins naturally enough with a short description of
the hero's wife and two sons, and then goes on to stress how God watched

---

[73] In the case of *(c)* the formula is «segunt cuenta la estoria».

[74] «Dize el cuento» is used to introduce interpolated tales (e.g. 17.16, 88.11, 256.7,
259.11, 266.25, etc.), supernatural adventures (e.g. 226.20), and to indicate the resumption
of the narrative after a digression (e.g. 11.5, 40.6, 243.3, etc.).

[75] Armando Durán, «La 'amplificatio' en la literatura caballeresca española»,
MLN LXXXVI (1971), 123-135, compares what he calls the «*entrelacement* necesario»
of the *Zifar* with the «*entrelacement* artístico» of the *Amadís* and the absence of *entrelacement* of any kind in the *Tirant*.

[76] *El amor y el matrimonio secreto*, 52. She does go on to acknowledge, however,
that such cutting would have «destruido la historia del *Cauallero Zifar*».

over the whole family and, seeing their worth, after «grandes trabajos e grandes peligros» (9.19), brought them to a noble position in life. In one paragraph we are introduced to the protagonists and to the theme of the romance. Everything that comes about later in the first book concerns the members of the family and illustrates God's concern for their welfare.

The first passage that could conceivably be termed a digression occurs at this point. The author breaks off to insist on the useful lessons that can be derived from reading his work, drawing on the familiar medieval symbol of the nutshell and the kernel, a variety of the *corteza-meollo topos*. This exhortatory section, which occupies the rest of chapter 1, has much in common with the *prothema* recommended by the preceptists of the *Artes Prædicandi*. The appeal to the audience to attend well and the citation of authorities, for example, recall common elements in the preacher's *prothema*. [77]

In chapter 2 we return to the narrative proper, with a description of Zifar's great qualities as a man and as a soldier and an account of how his unfortunate inability to keep his horses alive for more than ten days, combined with the back-stabbing of jealous rivals, prevents him from enjoying the favour of the king which, on merit, he clearly deserves. This situation prompts the author to introduce his first moral digression, concerning the obligations of overlords towards their vassals. This short homily can easily be justified on structural grounds. In the first place, it arises naturally out of what has gone before: the author is merely generalizing from the particular, like the preacher, and giving the stamp of universality to one of the basic themes of his first book, the quest by Zifar and his family for a just overlord who will accord them the honour they deserve. [78] Secondly, the digression is overtly linked with the main narrative by the equation of Zifar with the ideal vassal at the beginning (12.17), and by the return to the particular case of the knight and his king at the end, using the formula «asý commo contesçió a este rey» (13.17). Thus, it can be said that this digression does not seriously harm the work's unity in any way.

The second chapter ends with an account of the king's lack of success in his wars because of his refusal to go back on the promise he has made to himself and his evil advisers not to call on Zifar's help. This too provokes a short digression, again in the form of a moral comment by the author. This time there is no clear structural link between the narrative and the general point that stubborn adherence to the wrong decision is to be deplored; but the digression is so short (ten lines) and it arises so naturally out of the situation just outlined that it cannot be held to impair

[77] See Charland, *Artes Prædicandi*, 123-135.
[78] Cf., for example, Zifar's answer to Grima when she persuades him to stay for a while in Galapia: «ca ya veo que avemos mester bienfecho de señores por la nuestra pobredat en que somos» (47.25-27).

the cohesion of the work. Furthermore, its relevance becomes apparent as the story proceeds, since the importance of recognizing good and bad advice and advisers is one of the major preoccupations of the *Zifar* author. [79]

Having established the basic starting point for his story, the worthy knight and his family cursed by misfortune and lack of recognition, and having introduced some of his main themes in the narrative itself or in short digressions that are carefully related to the narrative, the author moves into the real beginning of his story in chapters 3 and 4. Zifar, recognizing the hopelessness of his position, appeals to God for guidance and is overheard by his wife, who asks him to confide his troubles to her. This provokes a discussion between the two of them about whether it is preferable to bear one's troubles alone or to share them with a friend. This, in its turn, leads into the first extensive digression in the work (17-32), in which Zifar tells his wife the tales of the Half-Friend and the Whole Friend to illustrate his point that before a man confides in another person he must be sure that the latter deserves the title of friend. These two *exempla* seem, at first sight, to be quite extraneous and to present a real threat to the work's unity. However, a closer examination reveals that once again the author has taken considerable trouble to integrate the digression into the total structure of his romance. In the first place, the story of the Half-Friend is put into the mouth of Zifar, not narrated directly by the author himself, [80] and it is linked to the hero's previous discourse by the connecting formula «asý contesçió» (17.10). The careful way in which these stories are worked into the narrative has already been noted by Scholberg:

> The story of the Half-Friend ... is intertwined with the main narrative and could only be removed by doing violence to the text. Moreover, it is intimately related with the following story of the Complete Friend, for it is the father in the first story who tells this tale to his son. [81]

Secondly, the fact that these *exempla* are related by Zifar to his wife tells us something important about their relationship, for when he does decide to confide in her (ch. 7) he puts her, by implication at least, on the same ideally high level of the almost impossibly loyal friends depicted in the tales. Through this digression, then, we appreciate the full extent of the love and trust the knight and his wife have for each other. Thirdly, the

---

[79] See Jules Piccus, «Consejos y consejeros en el *Libro del Cauallero Zifar*», NRFH XVI (1962), 16-30.

[80] Of the 28 interpolated *exempla* in the *Zifar* only two are narrated directly by the author: the fable of the Wolf and the Lamb (ch. 99) and the story of the Man and his Daughter (ch. 115).

[81] «A Half-Friend and a Friend and a Half», BHS XXXV (1958), 187-198, at p. 191.

interpolation of *exempla* at such an early stage in the story prepares us for the emergence of Zifar as a teacher and counsellor, one of his most important roles, [82] culminating of course in his long moral discourse to his sons, the *Castigos del rey de Mentón*. Finally, these stories impress upon us the high store which the hero sets by true friendship, and explains his stance of aloof loneliness in the work, loneliness that is only alleviated by his wife and later by the Ribaldo. As we shall see, both these profound friendships are severely tested in the same way as the «proeva de los amigos» in the *exempla*. In view of all this, it is possible to say that the unity of the *Zifar* is not really impaired by this long digression, but is perhaps even enhanced by it. [83]

In chapter 8, after deciding that Grima deserves his trust, Zifar tells her of the origins of the family's misfortune and of his grandfather's prophecy that he would be the one to restore their honour and position through his «buenas costunbres». Chapter 9 is devoted to Grima's reaction to what her husband has just told her. Both confess to feeling instinctively that the old man was right and they decide, without further discussion, to set out in search of better fortune. This immediate empathy fully justifies Zifar's trust in his wife and, to my mind, also justifies the time spent by the author on defining and illustrating just what he means by a true friend. The basic situation from which the story will develop, the moral issues that it will involve and the relationship between the major characters have now been established by a skilful combination of self-revelation, dialogue, description, digression, comment and *exemplum*. The process, by our standards, is a slow, ponderous and complex one; but its inner cohesion should not be doubted.

The stage is now set for the real action to begin, but before it does the author introduces another digression (ch. 10), a detailed historico-geographical description of India. Once again, however, the digression flows smoothly from the main stream of the narrative and flows equally smoothly back into it at the close. It opens with a reference back to Tared, the royal ancestor of Zifar, who lost his kingdom «por sus malas costunbres» (36.4-5) and so handed on a legacy of poverty and degradation to his descendants. The kingdom, it appears, was in India, and at this point the author begins to parade his geographical and historical knowledge, giving us due warning by the use of the formula «asý commo oyredes» (36.14-15). At the end of the digression we return to Tared the «mal

---

[82] Zifar's advice is sought and given on many occasions in Book I: e.g. 50.1-2, 53.9ff., 55.17, 69.24ff., 71.13ff., etc. The *huésped* with whom Zifar lodges in Galapia in fact accuses the knight of being «mejor para predicador que non para lidiador» (51.20).

[83] There is a further digression within a digression in the first tale. Before embarking on the story proper, Zifar discusses the three types of friend (17.21-18.1). The connection between this little sermon and the tales it introduces is obvious and recalls the practice of the preacher once again. See J. B. Avalle-Arce, *Deslindes cervantinos* (Madrid, 1961), 172.

acostunbrado» (39.26) and the hopes that reside in Zifar the «bien acostunbrado en todas cosas» (40.1). The details given of the descent of the hero from a son of Noah establish, objectively as it were, the greatness of Zifar's family; previously we have heard it only from the perhaps prejudiced lips of his grandfather: we now see clearly the magnitude of the family's loss. Similarly, the emphasis on the misdemeanours of Tared, for which his heirs have to suffer, also serves to give an honourable motivation to Zifar's ambitions for himself and his family. [84]

When all this is said, however, can we defend as relevant in any way the wealth of detail about the parts of India and the races who live there? Is this not an unpardonable affront to the work's unity? The fact that such apparently gratuitous chunks of erudition occur in many medieval works, not least in romances, is not in itself a justification, but it does suggest a line of enquiry. C. S. Lewis, in the course of a discussion of this trait shared by so many authors of the Middle Ages, makes this interesting comment:

> Poets and other artists depicted these things because their minds loved to dwell on them. Other ages have not had a Model so universally accepted as theirs, so imaginable, and so satisfying to the imagination.... Merely to imitate or to comment on the human life around us was therefore not felt to be the sole function of the arts. The labours of men appear on Achilles' shield in Homer for their own sake. In the Mutability cantos or the Salone they appear not only for their own sake but also because of their relation to the months, and therefore to the Zodiac, and therefore to the whole natural order. This does not at all mean that where Homer was disinterested the later artist was didactic. It means that where Homer rejoiced in the particulars the later artist rejoiced also in that great imagined structure which gave them all their place. Every particular fact and story became more interesting and more pleasurable if, by being properly fitted in, it carried one's mind back to the Model as a whole. [85]

This passage helps to explain the presence of the digression on India and other similar ones in the *Zifar:* [86] the author is attempting to set the elements

---

[84] A medieval reader would also not miss the point that Tared is in the same figural relationship to Zifar as Adam is to Christ. Adam and Tared (Ar. «banished») not only lose their inheritance because of their wickedness, but also pass on the consequences of their action to their descendants until the moment of redemption comes with the goodness and sacrifice of Christ and Zifar; see A. D. Deyermond, «*Exemplum, Allegoria, Figura*», *Iberoromania* (in press). This and other possible figural elements in the *Zifar* are fully explored in James F. Burke, *Vision and History: the Figural Structure of the «Libro del Cavallero Zifar»* (Tamesis, London, 1972).

[85] *The Discarded Image*, 202-203.

[86] E.g. the *mapa mundi* in ch. 225 and the geographical lore in ch. 202.

of his story in their due place in the march of history and the complex order of the physical world.

When the action of the story finally begins in earnest with the family's departure from their homeland (ch. 11), there are no digressions of any kind for some time. Chapters 11-37 are concerned with Zifar's stay in Galapia, his efforts to raise the siege of the city, the ultimate defeat of the besiegers and the establishment of peace through the marriage of the female ruler to the son of the aggressor. The development of this part of the romance is leisurely and the purely military action is frequently suspended for councils, debates and negotiations; but none of these respites can really be termed digressions, since they are all relevant to the gradual unfolding of the story, helping to carry the plot forward to its *dénouement* and create an atmosphere of suspense. The nearest one gets to a digression in this section is the miraculous resuscitation of the lady of Galapia through direct divine intercession (ch. 30). But the fact that this episode directly involves one of the principal actors presupposes its relevance. It also functions as a reminder of the nearness of God to the hero at all times and, as we have seen, prepares us for the extensive excursion into the supernatural a little later.

The account of the siege of Galapia, then, develops slowly but logically, without sidetracking of any kind. The contrast between the clear structural line at this point and the many digressions and divagations of the early chapters is striking but explicable. The location of the characters in their geographical, historical, social and moral setting, and the establishment of the ethical bases of the story that is about to unfold, are obviously more amenable to the flowering of all kinds of digression than an account of military and diplomatic endeavours.

The next section of Book I (chs 38-43) deals with the break-up of the family, the successive loss of the elder son, the younger son and finally the wife in a violently rapid series of misfortunes which gains immensely in dramatic impact by contrast with the elaborately drawn-out account of the siege of Galapia that has just ended.

There is, however, one digression in this section in the form of an *exemplum* delivered by Zifar to his wife (ch. 41). After the loss of their children Grima gives way to near despair and urges her husband to leave the accursed land «do nos Dios tantos enbargos fizo e quiere fazer» (88.4-5). Zifar points out that one cannot escape God's will by simply moving to a different place and, by way of illustration, tells the story of the Roman Emperor who, attempting to avoid the death by lightning that had been prophesied for him, built an underground shelter. One day, however, he was caught in a storm and struck down as he hurried to his refuge. From this Zifar draws the moral that «ese mesmo Dios es en un lugar que en otro, e ninguno non puede fuyr de su poder» (89.4-5). At first sight, it may seem difficult to defend a digression at this point; it

111

appears to weaken the impression that one would otherwise get of the inexorable march of fate manifested in the successive loss of the two boys and then their mother. But what is lost in impact is gained in subtlety. In the first place, the fact that Zifar narrates a story to his wife during their last conversation together before separation balances perfectly his *modus operandi* during their first recorded conversation, when he told her the tales of the Half-Friend and the Whole Friend. The poignant contrast between Grima's faith on that occasion and her despair after losing her children is more clearly brought out by this simple structural parallel. Secondly, the story of the Emperor, besides reminding us of the past, also looks forward to the future. An *exemplum*, of course, represents a universal truth illustrated by something fixed in the immutable past which gives it the status of a guide for one's conduct in the future. Here we see what inevitably happens when a man seeks to frustrate the will of God by human action. Consequently, when Zifar and Grima also attempt to escape their destiny by flight, we are prepared for the misfortunes of separation to overtake them. Thirdly, the story and its moral, in the mouth of Zifar, not only remind us of his role as a teacher which increases in importance as the work goes on, but also illustrates his unshaken faith in God and his determination to accept whatever lies in store for him, the qualities for which he is finally rewarded. This prepares us for the next element in the work, God's message of comfort to Zifar after the loss of his wife (ch. 42), which shows vividly the continuing support of heaven for the knight's endeavours. The tale of the Emperor, then, although a digression, serves a very real structural purpose.

Grima's adventures on the boat (chs 44-50) are much less of an overt digression then the supernatural adventures of Book IV and particularly Book II. This first book concerns not just Zifar but the whole family. Consequently, what happens to Grima is to be regarded as an essential part of the narrative. We have already studied in some detail the way in which the marvellous episodes are carefully prepared for and integrated into the rest of the book in which they occur, but one further point is worth making about this one: Grima's miraculous rescue from the sailors is a concrete example of the general help which God has just promised to Zifar.

In chapter 51 we take up the knight's story again with his arrival at the hermitage and his meeting with the Ribaldo. There is an immediate digression. When the future squire declares his intention of trying to provoke Zifar, the hermit tells him the story of the Ass and the Lap Dog (ch. 53). Once again, however, the digression can be shown to underline rather than impair the structural unity of the work. First, it is integrated into the context of the conversation between the hermit and the Ribaldo. The former expresses doubts about the latter's proposal, from which he draws a generalized moral statement and illustrates it with his tale. The *exemplum* itself is introduced by a series of formulaic expressions: «commo contesçió», «¿cómmo fue eso?», «yo telo diré»:

> «Deso he yo miedo», dixo el hermitaño, «que la tu proeva sea non buena; ca el loco en lo que cuyda fazer plazer a ome, en eso le faze pesar; porende non es bien resçebido de los omes buenos. E guárdete Dios non te contesca commo contesçió a un asno con su señor». «¿E cómmo fue eso?» dixo el ribaldo. «Yo telo diré», dixo el hermitaño. (109.2-8).

Secondly, there are striking parallels between the narrative situation at this point and the one obtaining in the early part of the work when Zifar tells his wife the stories on friendship. In both cases the *exempla* are put into the mouth of an, as it were, qualified teacher; in both cases the knight is about to set out with a companion who will render him absolute devotion; and in both cases the *exempla* introduced concern, in their different ways, a test of love. [87] Thirdly, as in the case of the stories of the Friends and of the Roman Emperor, the universal truth exemplified in the tale is tested and proved in the subsequent action. The Ribaldo, like the ass, is humiliated for his impertinence. Once again the elaborate interplay of foretastes and echoes in the digression adds to the overall cohesion of the work.

The next ten chapters (chs 54-63) are devoted, with one exception (ch. 56), to showing the growth of the relationship between the knight and his new companion. In modern terms, much of this section would probably be regarded as a digression or at least as an interlude in the main action, and thus a threat to the work's overall unity. A closer examination of these chapters, however, reveals that they have a clear structural cohesion. The long debate between Zifar and the Ribaldo (ch. 54) serves a number of purposes. The peasant's taunts and questions about the disasters suffered by the knight and those awaiting him in the future not only reveal the peasant's grasp of the realities of life, but also provide a severe test of Zifar's protestations of stoical endurance and fortitude. To be mocked for one's misfortunes is harder to bear than the misfortunes themselves. Towards the end of the discussion we begin to feel, however, that the hero is in danger of crossing the narrow barrier between resignation and apathetic despair, and here the Ribaldo takes on a more positive role by urging the knight to use his arms again in the service of the King of Mentón. This marks the turning point in Zifar's fortunes; from now on things begin to get better. The knight, then, is saved by the Ribaldo and, persuaded out of his lethargy, he decides to leave the passive existence of the hermitage and re-enter the world of action for which he was destined, with the peasant as his squire (ch. 55).

---

[87] Note also the similarity of the *provar/proeva* wording.

9

The next chapter (ch. 56) concerns the hermit's vision about the future glory of Zifar. This, of course, indicates divine approval for the knight's projected course of action and, presumably, for the Ribaldo's part in turning him away from despair. Moreover, the hermit's vision has another structural function: it looks back to the prophecy of Zifar's grandfather and to the earlier promises of protection given by God to the knight and his family, and it also looks forward to the hero's accession to the throne of Mentón.

The two companions, taking leave of their former life, set out together with the basis of their relationship already firmly established. The next few chapters are devoted to consolidating their relationship in the real world, away from the sheltered existence of the hermitage. The devotion they have professed is severely tested in chapters 58-60 in which, at great personal risk, each saves the other's life. Since the action is in no way advanced by this episode of the double rescue, which is quite self-contained and which has no later repercussions in the story, one is tempted to regard it as a digression. Nevertheless, it has its structural *raison d'être*. It recalls vividly to our minds the high ideals of friendship set out in the two *exempla* at the beginning of the book, and thus further strengthens the parallelism between Zifar's initial *salida* with Grima and the opening of this new phase in his life in the company of the Ribaldo.

After this the two men set out in earnest for Mentón, but before they reach their destination the author introduces another pause in the main line of action. The purpose of this digression is to illustrate a further important aspect of the Ribaldo's character, his practical sense. Chapters 61-62 describe the squire's skill in providing himself and his master with food and protecting them from the hazards of the journey. In chapter 61 he kills a deer and builds a fire to keep off marauding wolves. The next chapter contains the famous episode of the turnip stealing and the Ribaldo's astute answers to the owner of the field when he is caught. [88] Apart from providing some comic relief, these escapades illustrate the worldly *savoir faire* of the squire, which makes him the perfect complementary foil to the idealistic knight. They also prepare us for the occasions in the future when the practical sense of the Ribaldo will be applied to the (perhaps) nobler ends of military strategy.

The ten chapters devoted to the beginnings of the Ribaldo's career as a squire, although containing many digressions and tangential episodes, illustrate once again the author's concern for careful preparation and painstaking efforts to establish the basic situation before embarking on a major new phase in his narrative. The rest of the first book (chs 63-79) deals with Zifar's services to the King of Mentón, and is quite free from

---

[88] The artistic value of this episode is studied in K. R. Scholberg, «La comicidad del *Caballero Zifar*», *Homenaje a Rodríguez-Moñino* (Madrid, 1966), II, 157-163, at pp. 161-162.

digressions of any kind. In tone and pace it resembles very much the earlier account of the knight's activities in Galapia. The military action is frequently interrupted for discussions, tactical planning, reports, negotiations, and so on; but, although the development may be slow and leisurely in the extreme, the single narrative thread is at no point broken or even tangled.

I hope that this fairly detailed examination of the digressions in Book I of the *Zifar* has shown that all the apparently superfluous elements have in fact a very real relevance to the overall action and theme of the work, and furthermore that they are an essential part of the complex structure based on balanced parallelisms and the constant interplay of foretastes and echoes. I believe that a similar analysis of the digressions in any of the other books of adventures would lead to a similar conclusion.

When all this has been said, however, the fact remains that the most powerful unity possessed by the *Zifar* is an internal one: the steady but sure progression of the family from rags to riches, from poverty to power, from humiliation to honour. At the beginning Zifar is a poor knight, dogged by fate and suffering misfortune because of the sins of one of his ancestors. By his virtue, courage and perseverance through many trials —physical, mental and spiritual—, by submitting himself at all times to the will of God, he emerges victorious and regains royal status for himself and his family. He learns kingship the hard way, in the school of experience. He then lends his position, his wealth and, above all, his experience to his son, who uses them as a stepping-stone towards even greater power and honour. Roboán becomes an emperor; but his triumph is as much his father's as his own, owing as it does so much to Zifar's help and advice set out in the *Castigos del rey de Mentón*, which is central to any proper understanding of the work. The *Castigos* is based on Zifar's experience in Books I and II, and the extent to which Roboán heeds its counsels determines his success or failure in Book IV. In the next chapter we shall examine the ways in which this much maligned third book can be fitted into the elaborately patterned structure that we have traced in the three books of adventures.

CHAPTER FOUR: THE STRUCTURAL UNITY OF THE *ZIFAR*

II. THE «CASTIGOS DEL REY DE MENTON»

A. THE INTEGRATION OF THE «CASTIGOS» INTO THE NARRATIVE

The *Castigos del rey de Mentón*, which occupies chapters 123-175 of the *Zifar*, is a long homily delivered by Zifar, now King of Mentón, to his two sons, Garfín and Roboán. Most critics have chosen to ignore this rather curious section of the romance, and those few who have concerned themselves with it at all have simply pointed to its apparent irrelevance and expressed scarcely concealed annoyance at the way it interrupts the narrative, presenting this as further evidence of the author's deficient sense of unity. Sir Henry Thomas, for instance, sees the *Castigos* as «a parenthesis, due to the author's succumbing entirely to the didactic tendency of his times». [1] Menéndez y Pelayo implies censure when he says that with the *Castigos* «la narración se interrumpe por completo». [2] Even K. R. Scholberg, who recognizes a certain structural cohesion in the *Zifar* as a whole, asserts that «for the modern reader, the section most difficult to relate to the others is without doubt the middle, the *Castigos del rey de Mentón*». [3] All these criticisms may, from a twentieth-century viewpoint, seem reasonable enough; but, considering the amount of evidence brought forward in the last chapter to testify to the author's concern for structural and tonal cohesion in the work, we should perhaps look more closely at the *Castigos* to ascertain whether it is as damaging to the unity of the *Zifar* or as grossly irrelevant as it appears. It is surely unlikely that the careful and skilled architect of the books of adventures would bisect his romance with a long abstract sermon without some consciousness of what he was doing.

[1] *Spanish and Portuguese Romances of Chivalry* (Cambridge, 1920), 17.
[2] *Orígenes de la novela*, ed. E. Sánchez Reyes (Edición Nacional, 2nd ed., Madrid, 1962), I, 310.
[3] «The Structure of the *Caballero Cifar*», *MLN* LXXIX (1964), 113-124, at p. 117. Scholberg does go on, however, to make a few points in an endeavour to show how the *Castigos* can be related to the rest of the work.

Once again it is Justina Ruiz de Conde who gives us a starting point for an examination of the structural role of the *Castigos* which, she says:

> es el puente entre las otras dos partes de la obra. Hay que leer el libro último relacionándolo con el de *Los Castigos* para poder ver la continuidad del *Cauallero Zifar* y poder, además, entender el verdadero significado de *Los Hechos de Roboan*. [4]

She does not, however, develop this point in her brief study of the *Zifar*'s structure. Nevertheless, her suggestion that the *Castigos* is in some way integrated into the three books of adventures and is not merely a tasteless and unnecessary digression is a valuable one, and one which deserves closer investigation.

In the first place, the *Castigos* is introduced into the work as naturally as possible. The situation existing at the end of Book II leads easily and logically into the didacticism of Book III: Garfín is made governor of the lands formerly belonging to Count Nasón and is told by his father that «has a ser rey después de mis días» (252.1); Roboán, the younger son, asks permission to leave home «para trabajar e para ganar onrra» (253.22). With his sons on the threshold of adult responsibilities, the time has come for Zifar to pass on his great experience as a knight, a king and a man. Their courage and military prowess have been proven in the wars against Nasón and his rebels; they must now be given wisdom so that, like their father, they may conform to the pattern of the ideal medieval hero, who combined the qualities of *fortitudo* and *sapientia*. With this moral and practical guidance they will reach even greater eminence than their father, as he himself tells Roboán: «E segunt por mi entençión es, çierto so e non pongo en duda que has a llegar a mayor estado que nós» (253.24-26). He decides that on the following day he will begin to instruct them «tan bien en fecho de cavallería commo en guarda de vuestro estado e de la vuestra onrra quando Dios vos la diere» (254.2-3). At the end of the *Castigos* Garfín assures his father that he and his brother will always try to act according to the precepts they have been given:

> E fío por la su merçed [de Dios] que estos dos escolares que vós castigastes e aconsejastes, que deprendieron bien la vuestra leçión, de guisa que obrarán della en quanto vos acaesçiere, mucho a serviçio de Dios e de vós (380.4-7).

We shall study later to what extent the counsels of Book III are a reflection of Zifar's experiences in Books I and II, and to what extent Roboán is guided by the specific points of his father's teaching during his adventures

---

[4] *El amor y el matrimonio secreto en los libros de caballerías* (Madrid, 1948), 41.

in Book IV. It is sufficient for the moment to note that, in intention at least, the *Castigos* is firmly integrated into the rest of the work. [5]

A second way in which the author prepares us for this long excursion into didacticism is his insistence right from the start of the romance on Zifar's skill as a teacher and adviser. As early as the end of the Prologue we are told that, as well as his many other qualities, the knight is «conplido de buen seso natural» and «de buen consejo» (8.13-14). In chapter 2 he is again described as «de muy sano consejo a quien gelo demandava» (11.6) and praised for his «buen seso natural» and his «buen consejo» (12.10-11). To emphasize this aspect of the hero's character and fix it firmly in the reader's mind, the author almost immediately proceeds to show Zifar in action as a teacher and counsellor. Chapters 5 and 6 contain the extensive stories of the Half-Friend and the Whole Friend, which are both told by the knight to his wife. In chapter 7 Zifar expounds the moral to be drawn from these *exempla* in the same way as he will do later, in the *Castigos*. We are reminded of his talent as an adviser at other points in the first two books, [6] and in chapter 41 we again find him narrating a story to illustrate a didactic point. It should come as no surprise, then, when he launches into a full-scale programme of instruction in the *Castigos*.

A third way in which the *Castigos* is integrated into the work as a whole is to be seen in the constant reminders, in the midst of the abstract didacticism, of the concrete world of men and adventures we have left and to which we shall return. The author takes care to keep firmly in our minds the fact that the *Castigos* is not an irrelevant collection of moral commonplaces, but advice designed for the specific purpose of instructing Zifar's sons as they prepare to take on the responsibilities of adult life. Thus, the second person plural form of the verb is used throughout, constantly reminding us of the presence of the two silent listeners. The direct address form «míos fijos» occurs no fewer than eighty-six times in the course of the 125 pages of instruction. In almost every case this phrase is introduced by a particle such as *onde, porende, mas, pues*, etc., which links it syntactically to what has just been said, and so regularly reminds us of the direct application of the precepts to Garfín and Roboán. [7]

---

[5] The author's picture of the king settling down to instruct his sons «asý commo maestro que quiere mostrar a escolares» at the end of Book II (254.10-11) is repeated at the beginning of Book IV when Zifar tells Grima that he has been advising their sons «asý commo buen maestro con los disçípulos que ama» (382.12-13). This identity of image and near identity of wording is a further aid to the firm integration of the *Castigos* into the work as a whole.

[6] See, for example, chs 21 and 30.

[7] The distribution of «míos fijos» and the various introductory particles is as follows:

a) «(E) míos fijos» (18 occurrences): 255.3, 263.3, 263.12, 265.1, 280.7, 301.14, 301.25-26, 302.15, 305.26, 311.28, 320.19, 340.22, 344.6, 352.12, 355.26, 361.28, 362.14, 378.24.

b) «Otrosý, míos fijos» (20 occurrences): 279.4, 298.16, 306.18, 313.26, 321.17, 324.3 [*PS* only], 327.18, 329.12, 334.23, 337.3, 344.12, 352.4, 353.23 [*PS* only], 357.13, 358.22, 363.4, 367.11, 367.22 [*PS* only], 369.6, 371.18.

It is also worth noting how, as Zifar gives his advice on kingship in the later part of the *Castigos*, the idea is gently impressed upon us that the counsels are directly addressed to his sons on the assumption that they will achieve royal status. At first the father simply talks of the duties of *el rey* in much the same way as any other medieval treatise on kingship; but gradually he suggests that both his sons (not just his heir Garfín) may eventually be in a position to apply his precepts for themselves: «Onde, míos fijos, sy Dios vos diere esta onrra que vos he dicho, punad en ser justiçieros» (317.1-2). A little later there is no doubt: «Onde, míos fijos, seredes justiçieros con piedat» (320.10). After this point it is tacitly assumed that the two young knights will become kings, and the other lessons in ruling are directly aimed at them. By this simple procedure the author not only keeps the specific nature of the *Castigos* to the fore and reminds us of the real people involved, but also foreshadows the events of Book IV in which Roboán becomes an emperor, thus clothing his moral platitudes with additional relevance and helping to integrate them into the romance as a whole.

In the midst of this prolonged stay on the abstract plane of didacticism we are also reminded of the world of men and action by the frequent use of interpolated *exempla*. There are more such stories in the *Castigos* than in the rest of the work put together. [8] Whilst these *exempla* obviously fulfil their primary function of illustrating some point Zifar is making, they also serve to recall to us the world we have left and to which we must return in much the same way as the interpolated tales in the middle of the supernatural episodes of Books II and IV get us ready for the return to normality after our excursion into the marvellous (see p. 90 above).

We also noticed in the last chapter the method by which the reader is carefully prepared for the lengthy visits to the supernatural world by the

---

c) «Onde, míos fijos» (16 occurrences): 265.19, 266.20, 269.15, 292.24, 296.24, 299.16, 300.8, 301.9, 302.7, 317.1, 320.10, 350.5, 351.13, 355.18, 363.13, 376.12.

d) «(E) porende, míos fijos» (14 occurrences): 269.23, 281.6, 294.4, 296.9, 306.25, 318.16, 334.16, 339.5, 345.8, 350.12, 356.4, 358.9-10, 360.21, 364.22.

e) «Mas/pero, míos fijos» (8 occurrences): 281.12, 295.14, 338.23, 342.15, 352.22, 354.3, 358.14, 366.12.

f) «Pues, míos fijos» (3 occurrences): 297.12, 359.14, 361.9.

g) «E sabet, míos fijos» (2 occurrences): 293.20, 313.19.

h) «E asý, míos fijos» (2 occurrences): 264.6, 289.21.

i) Miscellaneous (1 occurrence each): «Por que, míos fijos», 371.3; «Çiertamente, míos fijos», 341.13; «Ca, míos fijos», 294.25.

«Míos fijos» tends to be used when a reminder of the specific nature of the advice is most necessary: *a*) immediately after an interpolated *exemplum* (e.g. 263.3, 269.23, 279.4, 289.21, 334.16); *b*) immediately after or before a borrowing from the very generalized *Flores de filosofía* (e.g. after: 265.19, 280.7, 281.6, 296.9; before: 279.4, 295.14, 318.16, 360.21); *c*) in the midst of a long *Flores* borrowing (e.g. 265.1, 293.20, 294.4, 294.25, 297.12, 340.22, 359.14).

[8]   Book I contains four stories (chs 5, 6, 41, 53); Book II contains two (chs 99, 115); Book III contains seventeen (chs 124, 125, 126, 130, 132, 135 [2], 155, 159 [2], 161, 169, 170, 171, 172, 173, 174; Book IV contains five (chs 199, 203, 209, 222 [2]).

introduction of controlled brief glimpses of the fantastic in the earlier parts of the book, and also by the way in which the author gradually moves away from the readily acceptable Christian supernatural in Book I to the less credible other-worldly adventures in Books II and IV. A similar concern for preparing the reader's mind for a complete change of tone and atmosphere can be seen both in the way short didactic digressions are introduced at several points in the books of adventures, and also, more interestingly, in the way in which the interpolated *exempla* are distributed in the *Castigos*.

Of the seventeen stories in Book III, seven occur in the first thirteen chapters (chs 123-135) and nine in the last seventeen chapters (chs 159-175). In the twenty-three chapters that make up the middle of the book there is only one *exemplum*—the gospel story of Jesus' altercation with the Pharisees concerning man's respective duties to Caesar and God (ch. 155). The conclusion that one can draw from this distribution is that the author is determined at the beginning of the *Castigos* to lead us gently and not too abruptly away from the real, earthly plane on to the abstract plane by including many concrete examples referring to the world of men we have just left. The *exemplum*, after all, stands half-way between the purely real and the purely abstract. Similarly, when the author wants to return us to the earthly plane, he once again multiplies his references to concrete things and real human situations.

This supposition about the structural function of the *exempla* in the *Castigos* is strengthened by the fact that of the seven tales in chapters 123-135 three occur in unbroken sequence right at the beginning of the book, and of the nine tales in the closing part no fewer than six occur in successive chapters at the very end. [9] If we analyse further these nine *exempla* in chapters 124-126 and 169-174, we find that the three at the beginning concern a King and a Preacher, a King and an Apothecary, and a Hunter and a Lark. In other words, the first two deal with a king and men in professions we are likely to meet in the everyday world we have just left. The last of the three, however, is a fable, which is necessarily somewhat less real and thus more abstract than a story involving human beings, more obviously intended to serve a didactic purpose. The fable of the Hunter and the Lark therefore takes us a step nearer to the purely abstract realm we are about to enter. The six stories at the end of the *Castigos* concern a Roman King and his Athenian Captors, an Emperor of Armenia, a Moorish King and his Steward, a Wolf and Leeches, a Cardinal and a Pope, and the King of Orbín. In this sequence the fable comes fourth

---

[9] The impression of piling-up is intensified by the use at both ends of the *Castigos* of the oriental device of narrating tales within tales (see ch. 2, section F (i) above). In ch. 125 the apothecary, the central figure of the previous tale told by Zifar, tells the story of the Hunter and the Lark; the tales of the Wolf and the Leeches and the Cardinal and Pope in chs 172-173 are narrated by the steward who figures in Zifar's story in ch. 171.

and so gives us a last reminder of the world of abstractions we are leaving, whereas the other five tales concern kings and other familiar figures in the world we are about to re-enter. In fact, the last *exemplum* of all features a character who has already played a part in the *Zifar* itself. The meeting between the King of Orbín and Grima is recalled for us by Zifar after he has told the story to his sons: «E míos fijos, sabet que este enxienplo oý contar a vuestra madre la reýna, que lo aprendiera quando ý fuera» (378.24-25). By this simple statement the author both reminds us of the family situation and prepares us for the reappearance of Grima at the beginning of Book IV. [10]

Despite the not inconsiderable differences of tone and subject between the *Castigos* and the rest of the *Zifar*, it is already possible to concede —as no other critic has done—that an honest attempt has been made to integrate the homily into the romance as a whole. As we have seen, it is carefully prepared for in the course of the first two books with the result that it arises naturally out of the situation existing at the end of Book II. Furthermore, various devices are used to temper the abstract nature of the *Castigos* and remind us of the world of men and adventures which forms the setting for the rest of the romance.

B. THE STRUCTURAL RELATIONSHIP OF THE «CASTIGOS» TO BOOKS I, II AND IV

In the last chapter we saw how Books I, II and IV are constructed according to a common five-part pattern (except for a slight aberration in Book II, which lacks a second series of adventures on the natural plane). If one is to argue that Book III is an intrinsic part of the romance, and not just a disposable parenthesis, it is reasonable to expect it to show at least some reflection of this pattern. Obviously, because of the abstract, static nature of the *Castigos*, the correspondence between it and the other books cannot be so close as that which exists between Books I, II and IV. Nevertheless, as we shall see, a search for structural parallels is not fruitless.

Even a cursory examination of the *Castigos* reveals that it contains three main divisions:

(i) A series of opening precepts and illustrative tales setting out the fundamental bases of morality (chs 123-130).

(ii) An exposition of the duties of a subject and the qualities of knighthood (chs 131-140).

(iii) An exposition of the duties and qualities of a king. This section

[10] This point is also noted by Scholberg, «Structure», 118.

falls into two parts: (*a*) moral qualities (chs 141-156); (*b*) practical qualities (chs 157-174). [11]

Already a basic similarity can be seen between the structure of the *Castigos* and the structure of the three books of adventures. Books I, II and IV open with a situation from which the rest of the book develops; the germ of the entire *Castigos,* as I hope to show, is contained in its initial chapters. The three other books move on next to a series of episodes in which the central character of the book appears in the role of a subject dependent on an overlord—Zifar in Galapia, Grima in Mentón, Roboán in Pandulfa; the second part of the *Castigos* sets out the special duties of a knight towards his superiors and the rest of society. In Books I, II and IV a supernatural interlude occurs at this point; there is no clear parallel to this in the *Castigos.* [12] In the books of adventures, after the protagonists have proved themselves as vassals, they all become rulers in their own right—Zifar in Mentón, Grima (after being reinstated as Zifar's wife) in Mentón, Roboán in Tigrida; the last section of the *Castigos* concerns the art and practice of kingship. Moreover, the twofold division of the necessary qualities of a king in the *Castigos* reflects the structural pattern of the other three books. It is the moral qualities of Zifar, Grima and Roboán that endear them in the first place to the people they are to rule. Since none of them inherits a throne by right of birth, they are enabled to rule primarily because they impress those who give them the power with their moral fitness to wield it. Once they have ascended the throne, however, they are faced with a series of severely practical problems of government for which they need qualifications of a different order. Finally, it is worth noting that the last part of the advice on kingship in the *Castigos* is concerned with the handling of wealth and the way in which rewards should be distributed. Here again we seem to have a clear parallel with the fifth and final section of each of the three books of adventures, which is always devoted to the settling of accounts, the repayment of debts and the grateful recompense of faithful service.

[11] This last section of the *Castigos* is by far the longest and reflects the taste of the time for treatises on the education of princes. For further details, see Lester K. Born, «The Perfect Prince: a Study in Thirteenth- and Fourteenth-Century Ideals», *Sp* III (1928), 470-504; Helen L. Sears, «The *Rimado de Palacio* and the *De Regimine Principum* Tradition of the Middle Ages», *HR* XX (1952). 1-27. It is interesting that the three categories of instruction correspond exactly to Zifar's avowed aim just before the beginning of the *Castigos:* «vos quiero consejar tan bien en fecho de cavallería [i.e. the duties of a knight] commo en guarda de vuestro estado [i.e. the practical qualities needed in a king] e de la vuestra onrra [i.e. the moral qualities needed in a king]» (254.1-3).

[12] Without attaching too much importance to the point, it is perhaps worth noting that the isolated story in the middle of the *Castigos* (ch. 155) is the one concerning a supernatural figure, Jesus. The fact that Jesus appears in it, as he does in the supernatural episode in Book I, together with the fact that it stands in isolation (it is 20 chapters since the last *exemplum*), possibly gives this tale a similar structural role to that of the supernatural episodes in the other three books.

The structural correspondences between the *Castigos* and Books I, II and IV are not confined to this similarity of their broad divisions, striking as this undoubtedly is. Justina Ruiz de Conde, as we saw, describes Book III as a *puente* between the adventures of Zifar and those of Roboán. To what extent, then, does the *Castigos* represent the fruit of Zifar's experience? There are in fact very few pieces of advice that cannot be said to reflect in some way the wisdom gained by the knight through his long years of struggle. At first sight, the *Castigos* seems to be a rather uneasy amalgam of practical, pragmatic advice and disinterested moral teaching. But it is interesting to note that even the apparently idealistic lessons given by Zifar are in fact recommended by him because they have proved *profitable* in the past. He realizes that because he made moral decisions throughout his life, his reward, far from being saved up for him in heaven, was dropped squarely into his earthly lap in the shape of wealth, power, a crown and the reunion of his family. There is no wonder that he urges his sons to follow the path of virtue! The curiously mingled idealism and materialism of the *Castigos*, then, makes sense only in the context of the whole romance. A few examples of how the precepts of Book III arise out of the experiences of Books I and II will be sufficient to illustrate this point.

Zifar preaches humility and obedience to the will of God, because he knows it has worked in his own case; never, in Books I and II, did he push himself forward, and he always accepted the will of God with fortitude. He can speak with feeling about the value of chastity as a man who renounced his conjugal rights with his second wife when it occurred to him that his first wife might still be alive. As a «reward» for this his second wife obligingly died when the term set for the vow of chastity was about to expire, leaving him as undisputed King of Mentón. He can preach obedience to one's earthly superiors without hypocrisy as one who has faithfully served a variety of rulers and, as a result of his service, inherited a kingdom. He recommends loyalty and humility and condemns greed and ambition, because he has sure knowledge of the rewards that await the humble and hardworking and of the disasters that overtake the avaricious and dissatisfied, such as Count Nasón and the other perpetrators of aggressive wars whom he has personally defeated or helped to defeat. The man who loved his wife and family urges the care of relatives on his sons; and the man who did not shrink from condemning his wife to death for suspected adultery can speak with authority on the need to chastise dependents when they appear to need it, since God will prevent any injustice. Zifar advises his sons to strive for the goodwill of kings and we know that he is speaking from the bitter experience that drove him from his homeland. He knows the value of following good advice and rejecting bad: when he adopted the Ribaldo's plan for getting into Mentón through the lines of the besiegers, he was successful; and when he refused to submit to the *huésped*'s exhortations to join the council-of-war in Galapia before he was asked, again he achieved the maximum effect when he was invited. Because he has always honoured his promises and agreements, God has been on his side when someone has broken faith with him; thus he insists on his sons being fair dealers. He urges Garfín and Roboán to confide only in tried and trusted friends, because he himself has entrusted his secrets only to his wife, the hermit and the Ribaldo, and their advice and help have always stood him in good stead. He has always been generous to those who have helped him, never forgetting his old friends; in this too he advises his sons to emulate him. Revolts against him have always been unsuccessful because he was in a state of constant preparedness and because his justice and generosity have assured him of the loyalty of his men. At this point especially the practical value of apparently idealistic behaviour is made quite clear. Finally, the very presence of the *Castigos* shows that Zifar has always tried to give good advice when asked for it, something else in which he urges his sons to follow him.

The *Castigos*, then, is by and large a faithful reflection of what Zifar has learned through long experience as a knight, as a king and as a man. Because he has followed his own precepts he has been successful, and he advises his sons to do the same so that they too may achieve greatness. The *Castigos* is thus intimately bound up with Books I and II, and we shall see that it is similarly important for an understanding of Book IV. Here again we can see how this remarkable author has kept in mind all the strands of his multi-textured work, since Roboán's success is due in no small measure to his adherence to his father's rules of conduct; and his setbacks come precisely when he ignores Zifar's advice.

Roboán scrupulously follows his father's teaching on the duties of subjects towards those set above them in earthly authority. The first test comes in Pandulfa, where the young man is required to serve not a strong king but a weak woman, whom he serves sincerely and honourably, never taking the law into his own hands or trying to assert his own will over hers. The stay in Pandulfa also puts on trial the strength of Roboán's humility and chastity, two qualities his father repeatedly urged him to cultivate. Despite his being subjected to an impertinent cross-examination by the lady-in-waiting Gallarda, the young knight does not lose his temper, and eventually wins over his opponent by his courtesy and patience. His devotion to chastity is evident in his refusal to take advantage of Seringa's obvious love for him. He makes no advances to her, and in fact renounces the possibility of an easy life with a beautiful woman in order to follow the hard road which will lead him to a greater destiny, once again showing the great influence his father's teaching has had on him.

When Roboán finally succeeds to the imperial throne of Tigrida, he is faced with many situations in which he is able to apply his father's lessons in kingship. He sets a good example; he tempers justice with mercy, but is implacable towards the really wicked; he honours his vows and obligations, and rewards those who have served him faithfully; he maintains a state of military preparedness to beat off aggressors and never plays the aggressor himself.

As we have seen, much of Zifar's advice is itself concerned with advice and advisers: how to tell good advice from bad, the people one should and should not confide in, the need to give counsel when asked for it, and so on. Roboán's handling of his father's admonitions in this area provides an interesting study. Usually the young man seeks advice only from tried and trusted friends, notably the Ribaldo; and in these cases the advice is always good and the outcome successful. On two occasions, however, he fails to distinguish between good counsel and bad, and follows the latter. At the court of the Emperor of Tigrida Roboán allows himself to be persuaded by the Conde de Lan, who is jealous of his favour with the emperor, to ask their ruler why he never laughs. As a result of this indiscretion he is banished to the *Islas Dotadas*. In this magic kingdom, despite his lapse, he is given a further chance of great happiness when he marries Nobleza, the ruler of the islands. But once again he allows himself to be swayed by evil advice and, at the instigation of the beautiful temptress, asks Nobleza for the enchanted horse. The horse carries him away from his paradise for ever. As it happens, all turns out well in the end, as Roboán succeeds the Emperor of Tigrida when the latter dies; but there seems no doubt that the setbacks are to be attributed to the young man's neglect of his father's advice. Roboán's visit to Turbia, during which he solves the count's problems by his sound advice, appears to be included in the work simply in order to show how the son has both heeded his father's admoniton to give counsel when asked and apparently inherited his talent as a counsellor. There seems to be no other purpose for the visit than to provide a thematic link between the *Castigos* and the last book. [13]

Enough evidence has been presented, I hope, to show that the *Castigos*, far from being irrelevant to the main theme of the *Zifar*, is in fact in some ways the most essential part of it, forming a meaningful link between the adventures of Zifar and those of Roboán. It represents a code of conduct that the father has lived by and formulated through his many trials and tribulations; faithful adherence to its precepts has led him from initial degradation and poverty to a position of power and honour as King of Mentón. Roboán is given the benefit of all this painfully accumulated wisdom at the start of his career as a knight, and by the conscientious application of his father's advice reaches an even higher position in society

---

[13] There is also an interesting verbal similarity between the section in the *Castigos* on the general qualities required of a knight (289.21-290.15) and the author's description of Roboán's excellence in this respect as he sets out from home (386.7-19).

than Zifar. When he observes his father's teachings he prospers, when he ignores or forgets them he is given a sharp reminder of the vulnerability of the careless. One could perhaps even go so far as to say that the three books of adventures in the *Zifar* are really representations of the *Castigos* in action.

C. THE INTERNAL COHESION OF THE «CASTIGOS»

One of the most important structural features of Books I, II and IV is the recurrence of the same series of motifs in the different sections. In the previous chapter we saw how the various sets of earthly adventures and the supernatural interludes have several elements in common—arrivals, tests, marriages, rewards, etc.—which serve to give an inner cohesion to each book. In the *Castigos* too it is possible to discern a reflection of this technique: each section puts forward basically the same pieces of advice with a different slant or emphasis.

(i) *The Opening Section*

The short opening section of the *Castigos* (chs 123-130) in fact contains in distilled form all the advice that is going to be imparted in the rest of the book. The first chapter stresses the fear of God (255.11-17), to medieval eyes at least, the basis of all morality. This admonition to fear God, adds Zifar, is good advice and should be heeded, although many people choose to follow bad advice because it suits their purposes better. These two precepts—fear God and heed good counsel—are the twin pillars upon which the *Castigos* is built. The concentration of three *exempla* in the next few chapters illustrates these two fundamental pieces of advice and, by this extensive exposure, prepares us for their development in more detail in the rest of the book. The short anecdote of the king's meeting with the preacher (ch. 124) serves as a suitable introduction to the book, since the preacher tells the king, who is in a hurry to get on with his hunting, that the truths of God are many and varied and need a considerable time to expound; it is clear from the length of the *Castigos* that Zifar subscribes to this view![14] The next two *exempla* are, to my mind, the kernel of the whole book, since they expand the implications of the fear of God and the necessity of taking notice of good advice. In the first of these stories (ch. 125) the king, who has walked away from the preacher, meets an apothecary and asks him for a prescription «para sanar e guaresçer de los pecados» (257.6-7). The *reçepta* given by the apothecary is worth quoting

---

[14] This tale forms a particularly good starting point for the *Castigos* since the king and the preacher can be regarded as a representation of the dual personality of Zifar at this juncture.

in full because it sums up virtually everything else that is said later in the book:

> Toma las raýzes del temor de Dios e meollo de los sus mandamientos, e la corteza de la buena voluntad de los querer guardar, e los mirabolanos de la homildat, e los mirabolanos de la paçiençia, e los mirabolanos de la castidad, e los mirabolanos de la caridat, e semiente de atenpramiento de mesura, e la semiente de la costança, que quiere dezir firmeza, e la semiente de la vergüença, e ponlo a cozer todo en caldera de fe e de verdat, e ponle fuego de justiçia, e sóllalo con viento de sapiençia, e cuega fasta que alçe el fervor de contriçión, e espúmalo con cuchar de penitençia, e sacarás en la espuma las orruras de vanagloria, e las orruras de la sobervia, e las orruras de la enbidia, e las orruras de la cubdiçia, e las orruras de luxuria, e las orruras de yra, e las orruras de avariçia, e las orruras de glotonía, e ponlo a enfriar al ayre de vençer tu voluntad en los viçios del mundo, e bévelo nueve días con vaso de bien fazer, e madurarán los umores endureçidos de los tus pecados de que te non repentiste nin feziste emienda a Dios, e son mucho ya endureçidos, e quieren te toller de pies e de manos con gota falaguera, comiendo e beviendo e enbolbiéndote en los viçios deste mundo, para perder el alma, de la qual as razón e entendimiento e todos los çinco sentidos del cuerpo. E después de que tomares este xarope preparativo, tomarás el riobarba fino del amor de Dios una drama, pesado con balanças de aver esperança en el que te perdonará con piedat los tus pecados. E bévelo con el suero de buena voluntad para non tornar más a ellos. E asý serás guarido e sano en el cuerpo e en el alma (257.13-258.14).

The last story of the group, the fable of the Hunter and the Lark, underlines the need to take note of good advice and act on it (ch. 126). This tale is put into the mouth of the apothecary who has just given the prescription to the king; the two stories together thus form a coherent whole illustrating the two basic tenets set out in the first chapter of the *Castigos*. The opening group of *exempla* is rounded off with the following statement:

> E el rey, quando oyó esto, tovo que el físico le dava buen consejo, e tomó su castigo e usó del xarope e de la melezina, maguer le semejava que era amarga e non la podría sofrir, e partióse de las otras lievedades del mundo, e fue muy buen rey e bien acostunbrado, e amado de Dios e de los omes (262.18-22).

In chapter 127 Zifar proceeds to urge his sons to follow the example of the king in the story, so that they too might become «amados e onrrados e preçiados de Dios e de los omes» (263.8-9). [15] He goes on to repeat the ingredients of the apothecary's prescription stressing the need to «aprender buenas costunbres» and to «usar dellas» (263.9-10). The «buenas costunbres» consist of seven virtues, «umildat, castidat, paçiençia, abstinençia, franqueza, piedat, caridat» (263.13-14), which in five cases out of seven agree with the *mirabolanos* and *simientes* of the *reçepta*. [16] In the next chapter (ch. 128) Zifar emphasizes the need to cultivate these virtues (of which humility, patience and generosity are particularly stressed) together with justice and truth, which are also included in the prescription. To qualify as a man «de buenas costunbres» one must also be *mesurado* and *franco*. [17] In short, «en amor de Dios se ayuntan todas las buenas costunbres» (265.14-15).

It is not enough, however, for a man simply to know about these qualities: he must also follow them («usar dellas»). The last two chapters of this opening section (chs 129-130) are concerned with the need to control the carnal appetites, to subject the body and the senses to the *razón* and *entendimiento* (two further ingredients of the *reçepta)* given to man by God for this purpose. Although man's nature is basically evil he can overcome it, as Zifar shows in his *exemplum* of Filemón, the physiognomist (ch. 130).

(ii) *The Duties of a Knight*

The second section of the *Castigos* (chs 131-140) is concerned with the duties of the subject knight. Throughout this section the emphasis is once again on the moral qualities set out in the apothecary's prescription. Chapters 131-133 deal with the vassal's responsibility towards his superiors, the «reys que mantienen la ley» (270.4), who have first claim—after God— on a man's loyalty and allegiance. The *exemplum* of the traitor Rages is told (ch. 132) to illustrate the wickedness of disloyalty and the severe penalties awaiting treachery; in the story God personally sends his angels to punish Rages. The next two chapters (chs 134-135) concern a man's duties and responsibilities towards his dependents. After the love of God, the love of one's family is the most important manifestation of *caridat*. But love must not exclude correction when this is necessary, since parents are responsible for the way their children turn out. Once again the truth of this concept is illustrated by an *exemplum*, the story of the Greek Lady and her Son (ch. 135). This is followed by a chapter devoted to the knight's responsibilities towards his peers and the general qualities expected of a man who practises knighthood. He must honour

---

[15] Cf. also 264.7-8. This phrase, although a cliché, sums up the mingled idealism and materialism of the *Castigos:* the virtuous are not only valued by God but emerge successful in this world also.

[16] I discuss below (pp. 132-133) why I think the lists of virtues differ at two points.

[17] *Mesura*, of course, occurs in the prescription.

women; he must be proficient in the chivalric pursuits of hunting, jousting, wrestling, fencing, chess-playing, etc.; he must be temperate in his eating and drinking, and also in his speech; he must be truthful; he must be patient with those who offend him.

These three short sections dealing with a knight's specific duties towards his superiors, his inferiors and his equals are followed by three chapters (chs 137-139) devoted to the more general moral qualities necessary for a knight, or indeed for any man. One might say that at this point the author is concerned with a man's duties towards himself. Here especially the points made in the introductory section of the *Castigos* are recalled and stressed once again. There are four things that can raise a man to great heights: being wise, being «bien acostunbrado», being «de buena creençia», and being loyal. Wisdom is the basis of courtesy, and the elements that go to make up courtesy are fear of God, self-discipline, seeking the good of others, liberality, chastity and patience. The most fundamental motivation of courtesy, however, is humility, which is also the root of both «buenas costunbres» and «buena creençia». The humble will be «amados e preçiados de Dios e de los omes» (296.10-11; cf. 296.24-25). The parallelism between these precepts and the ingredients of the apothecary's prescription does not require comment.

The section on the duties of the knight ends with a chapter (ch. 140) on the need to fight the will with «buen seso natural» in order to ensure humility. It will be remembered that the opening section of the *Castigos* also closes with an exhortation to control the body and the senses with the reason and understanding (chs 129-130).

(iii) *The Duties of a King*

The remainder of the *Castigos* is concerned with the duties and qualities of a king. Chapters 141-156 deal with moral qualities necessary in a ruler, amongst which we find repeated most of the virtues that were adjudged earlier to be essential in a knight. Some of these virtues, however, are stressed rather more at this point, presumably because the king, being a more important person, needs to give an even better example than a knight, and also because he is prey to greater temptations to abuse his power. Chapters 141-148 set out the constitution of the king's *nobleza*, which is divided into three parts—his duty to God, to himself and to his subjects. He must fear God so that his subjects, seeing him honour his superior, will be inclined to honour him. In this way he will show his «buen seso» and his «buenas costunbres». He must also recognize the truth of God and be truthful himself if he wishes to avoid being deceived by his vassals. The liar always forfeits the love of God, as various Bible stories show only too clearly. The king must also love God's goodness and model himself on God; if he does this, God will reward his efforts.

129

After his duties to God, he has duties to himself. He must keep a guard on his heart and refrain from lusting after too much wealth, power and pleasure; he must root out covetousness. His tongue must also be guarded and prevented from saying more or less than it should and from lying, blaspheming and slandering. Lies breed discord; truth breeds justice and fear of God. The king owes it to himself, then, to discipline himself so that he may prosper. Finally, the king's *nobleza* towards his subjects is shown in his ability to punish justly and without anger, tempering justice with mercy. Justice and truth are the basis of all good government, and God will support the *justiçiero*.

It will be noticed that the division of the king's duties into his responsibilities towards his superior (God), his inferiors (his subjects) and himself, parallels closely the earlier division of the knight's duties. The qualities of a good king that are most stressed—fear and love of God, truthfulness and justice—are the same as those required of the knight; and they are all ingredients of the apothecary's *reçepta*. Inevitably those who act with «justiçia e verdat» (311.12) are «onrrados e poderosos e ricos e amados de Dios e de los omes» (311.13-14). [18]

The themes of truth and justice are developed further in chapters 150-151, with particular reference to their importance in a king. A ruler must always honour his pledges and treaties; consequently he should be wary about making such agreements lightly, since the breaking of them is such a serious matter. The king must work through the law to uphold justice, because the king and the law depend on each other for their existence. The king must deal with himself in accordance with strict justice so that he is in a fair position to judge others.

At the end of chapter 151 Zifar sums up his thoughts on this whole subject of the king's *nobleza*, with its stress on the love of God, justice, truth and responsibility towards others, in the following words:

> Onde, míos fijos, seredes justiçieros con piedat allý do pecaron los omes por ocasión, e asý vos daredes por benignos; e benigno es el ome que es religioso a Dios e piadoso a sus parientes que lo meresçen, e que non faga mal a los menores, e que sea amigo a sus yguales, e aya reverençia a sus mayores, e que aya concordia con sus vezinos, e que aya misericordia a los menguados, e de buen consejo e sano adó gelo demandaren (320.10-16).

The exposition of the moral qualities required of a king continues with a discussion (chs 152-156) of another of the basic themes advanced in the opening chapters of the *Castigos*, the giving and receiving of advice.

---

[18] A further link with the previous section is found in ch. 148 in which the king is compared to the father of the people. He must behave towards them exactly as the knight must behave towards his dependents: he must love them, but he must also punish them when necessary.

It will be noticed how smoothly this topic arises out of the last sentence of chapter 151 just quoted. In chapter 152 the king is required to supply advice when asked for it, taking his time over his answer and making sure that the petitioner's motives in the matter upon which he is seeking guidance do not spring from *codiçia* (another of the recurrent themes of the *Castigos*). Although he should always be ready to advise others, a king should ask for advice as little as possible, so that his own affairs can be kept secret. However, if he has to seek advice, it should be only from old, wise and trusted friends. [19] In this matter he should always be wary of those who are self-seeking and who will give him bad counsel whilst trying to alienate him from his wise advisers. Never trust a former enemy; above all, avoid Jews.

This admonition (in ch. 156) to trust only one's real friends, who should be valued and treasured, leads smoothly into the last section of the *Castigos* (chs 157-175), which is concerned with the practical aspects of kingship such as the distribution of gifts, the advisability of military preparedness, the division of the spoils of battle, the employment of a minimum of officials, and the dangers of selling offices. Nine chapters (chs 157-165) are devoted to the virtue of generosity, which is here presented as a practical rather than a moral attribute: the author, through Zifar, stresses the solid advantages that accrue to the ruler from its practice. In chapter 157 we are told that the rich king gains the affection and respect of his subjects, whereas the poor man is despised and unheeded. Consequently a rich man has a great power to do good, both for himself and for others. However, riches must be worked for: laziness brings only poverty; and wealth, once acquired, must be looked after: moderation in expenditure is vital (ch. 158). The most important use of wealth is to reward one's vassals, and this should be done cheerfully and quickly (ch. 159). Chapters 160 and 161 remind the king of the need to treat his vassals honestly and fairly, and suggest the various types of vassal that he should be on his guard against. The next two chapters (chs 162-163) put forward further points connected with the distribution of gifts: one should not be angry with those who do not seem to appreciate one's generosity, since God will reward one; nor should the recipient be constantly reminded by the king of his gift. Promises of rewards should always be kept; the deserving should always be recompensed (ch. 163). Chapter 164 draws a distinction between liberality and extravagance, and reminds us that generosity is one of the greatest of the «buenas costunbres». The long section on generosity ends with a reminder to the king to be grateful in his turn for the gifts and services of others (ch. 165).

The next five chapters (chs 166-170) deal with the king's military responsibilities: he must always be in a state of readiness for war, but

---

[19] Similar advice is given to the knight in ch. 136.

he must never be an aggressor. In time of war he should avoid rash acts and be prepared to take advice. There are five necessary things in war: «buen seso natural», «buen esfuerço», wealth, generosity and good vassals. In this list one notes the recurrence of a number of themes that have been dealt with elsewhere in the *Castigos*. Once war has been declared the king must persevere and never despair, for God will uphold the cause of those in the right. Cowardice is unforgivable (ch. 167). After the battle the king must show his generosity in sharing the booty (ch. 168) and he must hold fast to any promises he might make to his former enemies (ch. 169). The last chapter of this homily on military virtues is a résumé of what has gone before with added emphasis on the need to protect one's own vassals with justice: if the king is a *justiçiero* he will be «amado de Dios e de los omes» (369.10). This care for justice towards one's subjects is also present in the final condemnation of aggression: it is not only morally wrong, but also unfair to one's vassals to conscript them for a war out of which they will gain nothing.

The last chapters of the *Castigos* contain warnings, illustrated by *exempla*, against the employment of too many officials to manage one's money and against the selling of offices, since both practices inevitably lead to corruption.

* * *

The main purpose of this fairly lengthy outline of the principal contents of Book III is to show that the same preoccupations are to be found in the different sections of the *Castigos*, just as the same motifs recur in the different sections of the books of adventures. The apothecary's prescription in chapter 125 contains nine main ingredients: the fear of God, the will to observe God's commandments (i.e. love of God), and a list of seven virtues which, in all but one case, agrees with the church's list of contrary virtues to the seven deadly sins—humility *(homildat)*, meekness *(paçiençia)*, chastity *(castidat)*, charity *(caridat)*, temperance *(mesura)*, diligence *(costança-firmeza)*. The last virtue given in the *Castigos* is *vergüença*, whereas the church list has liberality. In view of the prominence given to liberality in the rest of the *Castigos* and the fact that shame is never mentioned again, [20] we may be entitled to postulate some textual corruption at this point. The likelihood of this is, I think, strengthened if we compare the list given in the prescription with that offered by Zifar as a recapitulation of what constitutes «buenas costunbres» in chapter 127. This list agrees exactly at four points with the earlier one—humility, patience, chastity, charity—and *abstinençia* has obvious links with temperance. Instead of the *reçepta*'s «costança que quiere dezir firmeza», Zifar's list has *franqueza* in *M* and *P* (i.e. liberality),

[20] *Vergüença* may mean honour or loyalty, from Arabic *'ār;* see Américo Castro, *España en su historia. Cristianos, moros y judíos* (Buenos Aires, 1948), 69-70.

whereas *S* has *fortaleza*, which it also uses in the prescription, omitting «costança que quiere dezir firmeza». There appears to be, then, some confusion over *fortaleza/firmeza/franqueza* which, in the present state of the texts, it is impossible to sort out. However, it is at least a possibility that the original version of the *Zifar* had *franqueza* and *firmeza* in both lists, thus bringing it more into line with the church list and also with the contents of the *Castigos* itself. The seventh virtue in the *reçepta*, *vergüença*, is completely missing from Zifar's list in *M* and appears in *P* and *S* as *piedat*. The inclusion of *piedat* in the two later versions is presumably the work of some later copyist who wanted to make up the number of virtues to the customary seven, not realizing that the list had been reduced to six at some earlier stage by the confusion of *firmeza* and *franqueza*.

The six main virtues are treated in more detail in the next few chapters: humility, temperance, generosity (ch. 128), chastity (ch. 130), charity (ch. 134), patience (ch. 136). The fact that *piedat* and *vergüença* are not mentioned again in these chapters, together with the fact that *franqueza* occupies an important place, supports the supposition that there is some textual confusion in these lists.

According to the apothecary's prescription, after the ingredients have been assembled, they are to be mixed in the «caldera de fe e de verdat», boiled over the fire of justice, fanned by the wind of wisdom. In chapter 128 Zifar tells his sons that «el noble deve aver en sý estas syete virtudes que desuso diximos, e demás que sea amador de justiçia e de verdat» (264.8-10). In chapter 136 the two young men are urged to associate with the wise so as to learn wisdom, a counsel that is repeated in chapter 137.

The basic elements of Zifar's advice to his sons, therefore, are all firmly established at the beginning of the *Castigos*, in the introductory section in general and in the apothecary's *reçepta* in particular—fear and love of God, humility, patience, temperance, generosity, chastity, charity, justice, truth, wisdom. As we have seen, all of these, in varying degrees, become the keynotes of the whole book, recurring over and over again in the different sections. This is particularly true of the love of God (almost every piece of advice is linked in some way to the service of God), humility, patience, generosity, justice and truth. Thus, despite their apparently haphazard structure, there is at least a *prima facie* case for seeing in the *Castigos* the same care for organization that we have noticed in the other books of the *Zifar*. Once again the cohesion of the book depends on a system of parallelisms and repetitions; it is not as clear-cut in the *Castigos* as in Books I, II and IV, but I do not think there is any doubt that it is there. The author's concern for structural organization is well illustrated in his treatment of the *Flores de filosofía*, his basic source for the *Castigos*.

D. The «Castigos» and the «Flores de filosofía»

It was Hermann Knust who first pointed out that the *Zifar* author had incorporated almost *verbatim* into the *Castigos* practically the whole of the *Flores de filosofía*. [21] Despite the virtual or complete identity of many passages in the *Castigos* and the *Flores*, the author nevertheless seems to have expended considerable thought on the arrangement and disposition of his borrowings. C. P. Wagner gives a list of the parallel passages in the two works, showing how the *leyes* of the *Flores* have been broken up and dispersed in the *Castigos*. [22] In his edition of the romance Wagner prints the *Flores* borrowing in italics. Closer investigation shows, however, that the table of identities is not entirely accurate and that the italicizing is occasionally a little erratic. These two factors, combined with the fact that the references in the list of parallel passages are to the Michelant edition of the *Zifar*, [23] which is now both rare and superseded, convince me that a new comparison of the two texts is necessary. The following table gives, I trust, an accurate picture of the *Zifar*'s borrowings and their distribution in the *Castigos*.

Zifar (ed. Wagner)		*Flores* (ed. Knust) [24]	
chapter	pages	*ley*	pages
124-125	256.7-257.10	II	18-19
125	257.13-258.3	III	19-20
127	263.12-14	XVIII	46
128	264.11-14	XVIII	46
128	264.15-21	XVII	43
128	265.1-2, 6-15	XVII	44-45
131	270.13-271.11	V	22-23
133	279.5-280.6	VII	25-27
133	280.17-281.5 [25]	XI	34-35
134	281.21-282.14	XXVII	58-59
136	290.16-291.9	XIII	38-39
136	291.12-23	XIV	39-40
136	291.24-292.11	XV	40-42
137	292.24-293.1 [26]	XII	35-36
137	293.17-294.6	XXXVI	73-74

---

[21] *Dos obras didácticas y dos leyendas* (SBE XVII, Madrid, 1878), 5.
[22] «The Sources of *El Cavallero Cifar*», *RHi* X (1903), 5-104, at pp. 31-33.
[23] *Historia del Cavallero Cifar* (Bibliothek des Litterarischen Vereins in Stuttgart CXII, Tübingen, 1872).
[24] *Dos obras*, 11-83.
[25] 280.28-281.5 derive from a version of the *Flores* somewhat longer than that contained in MS. Escorial &-II-8, on which Knust bases his edition. This amplified version is preserved in MSS Escorial h-III-1 and BN 9428; see Wagner, «Sources», 34.
[26] 293.4-16 are from the longer version.

Zifar (ed. Wagner)		Flores (ed. Knust)	
chapter	pages	ley	pages
137-138	294.7-23	XII	37
138	294.25-295.8	XIX	47
139	295.16-296.8	XX	48-49
139	296.14-23	XXI	49-50
139-140	297.1-22	XXXVII	74-75
151	315.24-316.28	IV	20-21
151	317.18-318.15	VI	23-25
151	318.19-319.22	VIII	27-28
151	319.23-320.9	IX	29-32
152	323.3-20	XXV	54-55
156	335.14-336.5	XVI	42-43
156	336.8-11	XVII	43
156	336.12-25	XXIII	51-52
157	337.13-338.9 [27]	XXVI	56-57
157	338.10-12	XXXIV	70-71
158	340.14-341.11 [28]	XXIX	61-62
158	341.13-342.12 [29]	XXXI	64-65
162	352.23-353.19	XXI (appx)	82-83
164	356.17-357.10	XXVIII	60-61
166	358.25-359.21	XXIV	53-54
166	359.22-360.20	XXXII	66-67
166	360.23-361.13	XXXIII	68-69
166	362.22-28	IX	32
167	365.1-20	X	33-34
167	365.24-366.11	XXX	63-64

Certain basic points emerge clearly from the above table. First, with the exception of leyes I, XXII, XXXV, XXXVIII, and the appended ley VIII, the whole of the Flores has been incorporated into the Castigos. [30] Secondly, the borrowings from the Flores are distributed over all the four major divisions that we have noted in the Castigos: the introductory section (chs 123-130), the exposition of the duties and neccessary qualities of a knight and subject (chs 131-140), and the two-part description of the moral qualities (chs 141-156) and practical qualities (chs 157-174) required of a king. Thirdly, despite their distribution throughout the four sections, the borrowings are heavily concentrated in five main groups, covering chapters 124-128, 131-140, 151-152, 156-158 and 166-167. The only two passages from the Flores that fall outside these groupings are in

[27] 338.1-9 are from the longer version.
[28] 340.23-341.11 are from the longer version.
[29] 341.24-342.12 are from the longer version.
[30] There are, of course, a few minor omissions involving an odd phrase or sentence; but these are of no great significance.

chapters 162 and 164. Well over half the chapters in the *Castigos*, then, include no material from the earlier work, [31] and yet it is impossible to regard the third book of the *Zifar* as anything other than an elaborate gloss on the *Flores*. It is to this point that we must now turn our attention.

It is clear from the start that the *Zifar* author is basing his *Castigos* on the *Flores*, since both begin with the story of the king's encounters with the preacher and the apothecary, which serve as a pretext for the introduction of the latter's moral prescription. [32] The *reçepta* in the *Zifar*, however, is a much expanded version of *ley* III of the *Flores*, which is given in full below so that it may be compared with the corresponding passage in the *Castigos* which has already been quoted: [33]

> Toma de la rraýs del estudiar e las rraýses de aturar en ello e la cortesa de seguillo e los mirabolanos de la umildad e los mirabolanos de la caridad e los mirabolanos del miedo de Dios e la simiente de la vergüença e la symiente de la obediencia e la simiente de la esperança de Dios, e métalo a coser en una caldera de mesura, e ponle fuego de amor verdadero, e sóplalo con viento de perdón, e cuega fasta que se alce el espuma del saber, e esfríalo al ayre de vencer tu voluntad, e bévelo con devoción de buenas obras, e sigue esto, e sanarás de los pecados (19-20).

The reason for this large-scale amplification and alteration of the source material has already been suggested: the *Zifar* author expands the prescription because he wants to incorporate in it all the points that will be particularly developed in the rest of the *Castigos*; at the same time he replaces irrelevant elements with more appropriate ones.

The same creative use of his source is shown in the considerable rearrangement of the *Flores* material in the *Castigos*. Despite the almost *verbatim* transcription of the *leyes* the *Zifar* author's dependence on his model is not in the least slavish. The romance-writer's reasons for fundamentally reorganizing his borrowings from the *Flores* have so far never attracted the attention of critics, but they are surely worth investigating. It seems to me that the author's main motive for breaking up and redistributing the *leyes* of his source is once again a structural one. It has already been pointed out that the borrowings are distributed throughout the four sections of the *Castigos*; it is natural, therefore, that the author should have rearranged the *leyes* in the first instance to fit his overall pattern for Book III. A glance at the titles of some of the *leyes*

---

[31] The following chapters contain no material from the *Flores*: 123, 126, 129, 130, 132, 135, 141-150, 153-155, 159-161, 163, 165, 168-175.

[32] Before this episode there is a general introductory chapter in both the *Castigos* (ch. 123) and the *Flores* (*ley* I). The *Flores* chapter is headed «Cómmo omne deve amar a Dios» and consists of a string of moral maxims. The *Castigos* begins with Zifar's stressing the need to know and fear God.

[33] See above p. 127.

will show how appropriately they have been grouped within this pattern. *Ley* XVIII is entitled «En cómmo omne deve pugnar en ser noble»; it consists of a discussion of the seven essential virtues. This, naturally enough, is incorporated into the introductory section of the *Castigos*, in which the fundamental bases of morality are established. On the other hand, *ley* V «Cómmo los omnes deven ser leales e obedientes al rrey» and *ley* VII «De los que an de aver vida con los rreyes» clearly refer to the duties of the knight and subject; whilst *ley* IV «De la ley e del rrey que la guarda» and *ley* VIII «Del rrey que sabe bien guardar su pueblo» are appropriately placed in the section of the *Castigos* concerned with the moral qualities of kingship.

The titles of other *leyes* do not give such an unequivocal indication of the place they should occupy in the scheme of the *Castigos;* but an examination of their contents usually provides a clue. *Ley* XI, for instance, is entitled «De cómmo se canbian los tienpos», but it deals with the way in which a man's happiness depends on the goodness or otherwise of his overlord: «E los mejores tienpos del mundo son los días en que biven los omnes a sonbra del buen sennor que ama verdad e justicia e mesura» (34). If his lord is evil, however, the vassal must bear it patiently. Consequently, *ley* XI appears in chapter 133 of the *Castigos*, in the section devoted to the duties of subjects. Similarly, *ley* XXIV «Del esfuerço e de la covardía» is incorporated into chapter 166 amongst the practical qualities required in a king, because it deals mainly with the need for military preparedness.

Of particular interest are *leyes* IX and XVII, since they have been split into two parts in the *Zifar*, and the two parts appear in completely different sections of the *Castigos*. [34] *Ley* IX «Del rrey que pospone las cosas» is divided between the moral requirements of kingship (ch. 151) and the practical requirements (ch. 166). A comparison of the two passages shows how carefully the *Zifar* author has allocated his material to the appropriate place. The *Castigos* version of the part of *ley* IX in chapter 151 reads:

> E las peores maneras que el rey puede aver son, ser fuerte al flaco e flaco a los fuertes, otrosý ser escaso a quien non deve. E por esto dixieron que quatro cosas están mal a quatro personas: la una es ser el rey escaso a los que le sirven; la segunda, ser el alcalle tortizero; la terçera, ser el físico doliente e non se saber dar consejo; la quarta, ser el rey atal que non osen venir ant'él los omes que son syn culpa. Çertas más de ligero se endresçan las grandes cosas en el pueblo, que la pequeña en el rey; ca el pueblo, quando es de mejorar, mejóralo el rey, e sy el rey es de mejorar, non ay quien lo mejorar sy non Dios. E porende non deve fallar sobervia en aquél de quien atiende

---

[34] *Ley* XII is also split into two parts in the *Castigos*, but this is a rather different case, since both parts occur in ch. 137, framing *ley* XXXVI.

justiçia e derecho. Ca aquél contra quien el rey se ensaña, es en muy grant cuyta, ca le semeja que·l viene la muerte onde espera la vida. E este tal es commo el que ha grant sed e quiere bever del agua e afógase con ella (319.23-320.9).

The passage in chapter 166, however, deals with the practical problem for the king of keeping an eye on things in his kingdom:

E non deven desdeñar los reys unas cosas que conteçen de nuevo, nin las tener en poco maguer sean pequeñas; ca las mayores cosas que acaesçieron en los reynos començaron en poco e cresçieron. E esto fue porque las tovieron en poco e las desdeñaron; ca la pequeña pelea o el pequeño mal puede cresçer atanto que faría muy grant daño, asý commo el fuego que comiença de una çentella, que sy non es luego amatado, faze muy grant daño (362.22-28).

The division of *ley* XVII «De cómmo omne deve ser de buenas maneras» is even more fundamental, since part of it occurs amongst the general principles of morality in chapter 128, and the rest in chapter 156 along with the moral qualities specially relevant to kingship. Again the *Zifar* author's redistribution is completely valid, because most of *ley* XVII, as the title implies, deals with general moral precepts; but a few lines in the middle are devoted to how one should treat one's friends:

E con tres cosas gana omne claro amor de sus amigos, la primera es: que los salve do quier que los falle, la segunda es: que los rreciba bien do quier que los encontrare, la tercera es: que los rrasone bien do ellos non estudieren. [35]

It is therefore logical that this passage should be included in chapter 156 since it links up neatly with the precepts of *ley* XVI «De cómmo omne deve ser de buen talante» (which deals with winning friends) and *ley* XXIII «De cómmo omne se deve avenir con sus amigos», both of which are included in this same chapter of the *Castigos*.

The distribution of the *leyes*, then, seems to correspond broadly to the four main divisions of the *Castigos* which themselves, as we have seen, correspond to the stages in the lives of the protagonists of the three books of adventures. However, a further question arises with regard to the reorganization of the *Flores*: once the *leyes* have been allocated to their appropriate section within the *Castigos*, why does the *Zifar* author then feel it necessary to rearrange them further? To suggest an answer to this question we must examine in more detail the treatment of the *Flores* borrowings in one of the four sections of the *Castigos*. The section devoted

[35] Knust, *Dos obras*, 43; *Cauallero Zifar*, with minor variants of wording, 336.8-11.

to the qualities of knighthood (chs 131-140) includes thirteen of the earlier work's *leyes*, and the order in which they are used seems, at first sight, rather haphazard: V, VII, XI, XXVII, XIII, XIV, XV, XII, XXXVI, XIX, XX, XXI, XXXVII. Apart from the two points at which three consecutive *leyes* are grouped together in the same order in which they appear in the *Flores* (ch. 136: *leyes* XIII, XIV, XV; chs 138-139: *leyes* XIX, XX, XXI), the rest of the *Flores* borrowings appear to follow no logical sequence. A closer examination, however, reveals that the *leyes* are grouped according to their similarity of subject matter and that in fact they form a much more coherent progression in the *Castigos* than they do in the *Flores*.

The first borrowing *(ley* V, ch. 131) has the self-explanatory title «Cómmo los omnes deven ser leales e obedientes al rrey». This is followed by the long tale of Tabor and his treacherous cousin Rages (ch. 132), which illustrates perfectly the precepts of *ley* V and leads into *ley* VII «De los que an de aver vida con los rreyes» (ch. 133), which concerns the need to avoid incurring the anger of kings. A short paragraph (280.7-16) links *ley* VII to the next *Flores* borrowing, *ley* XI «De cómmo se canbian los tienpos» (ch. 133), in which the subject is urged to bear misfortunes patiently until things change for the better: he must never rebel against or anger the king, however unjust he may be. Despite the fact that *ley* VII and *ley* XI are widely separated in the *Flores*, there is a clear thematic connection between them which the *Zifar* author has noticed and exploited by juxtaposing them in the *Castigos*.

Chapter 134 begins with a short introductory paragraph (281.12-20) in which the author speaks of the duties a man has to *los suyos*. This follows on logically from the exposition of the duties he has to his overlord, and provides a link to the introduction of *ley* XXVII «Cómmo omne deve onrrar a sus parientes». At this point the *Zifar* author interpolates a section on the need to «castigar los suyos» in the «spare-the-rod-and-spoil-the-child» vein, which is illustrated by the story of the Greek Lady and her undisciplined son (ch. 135).

We return to the *Flores* in chapter 136 where, after a paragraph devoted to the general physical and social qualities necessary for the practice of knighthood (289.21-290.15), [36] the author incorporates *leyes* XIII, XIV and XV, on the various aspects of *mesura*: «De cómmo omne deve guardar su lengua», «De cómmo omne deve ser paciente», «De cómmo omne deve ser sofrido». The end of this chapter provides a link between the theme of *mesura* and the introduction of *ley* XII in the next chapter:

> E seyendo ome sofrido e paçiente non puede caer en vergüença
> .... E asý el que se quiere guardar de yerro e de vergüença,
> es dado por sabio e entendido (292.12-13 and 19-20).

[36] Such as skill in jousting, fencing, hunting, wrestling, chess-playing, etc.

Chapter 137 opens directly with *ley* XII «Del saber e de su noblesa e de la pro que viene dél». Into the middle of this borrowing the author inserts *ley* XXXVI «Qué cosa es el saber» which, as its title indicates, deals with the same subject.

At the beginning of chapter 138 the author once again carefully links his borrowings with the phrase «e asý con el saber puede ome ser cortés en sus dichos e en sus fechos» (294.23-24), which brings us naturally to *ley* XIX «De la cortesía e de su noblesa». A similar linking takes place at the opening of chapter 139 immediately before the inclusion of *ley* XX «De la humilldad e del bien que nasce della»:

> Pero, míos fijos, creed que cortés nin bien acostunbrado nin de buena creençia non puede ome ser, sy non fuese omildoso (295.14-15);

and again later in the same chapter as a preamble to *ley* XXI «De cómmo omne non deve ser orgulloso»:

> E porende, míos fijos, queret ser omildosos e non urgullosos, ca por la umildat seredes amados e preçiados de Dios e de los omes, e por orgullo seredes desamados e fuyrán los omes de vós commo de aquéllos que se quieren poner en más de lo que deven (296.9-13).

The final *Flores* borrowing in this section on the duties and qualities of knights is *ley* XXXVII «Cómmo la voluntad es enemiga del seso», which occurs in chapters 139-140. Once again a clear link is forged between what has gone immediately before and what is to come immediately after:

> Onde, míos fijos, sy queredes ser preçiados e amados de Dios e de los omes, sed omildosos al bien e non al mal, que quiere dezir, sed omildosos a vuestro seso e non a la voluntad (296.24-26).

Enough evidence has been presented to show that the *Zifar* author's use of the *Flores* is a highly intelligent and creative one. There is no doubt that the *Flores* provided the initial inspiration for the *Castigos*, since the starting point for both is the apothecary's *reçepta* and since, with five exceptions, all the *leyes* of the former are incorporated into the latter with relatively slight verbal alterations. [37] But, as we have seen, the order of the *Flores* is changed considerably to enable the structure of the *Zifar*'s Book III to parallel as nearly as possible the structure of the books of

---

[37] Most of these alterations are designed to integrate the *Flores* borrowings more completely into the romance, such as the interpolation of «míos fijos» or the recasting of verbs in the second-person plural form.

adventures. On to this basic material the author has added linking passages (some of which we have noted) to introduce a smoother flow into his work to counter the rather jerky movement of the *Flores*. He has added many illustrative *exempla* to give more reality and vitality to the abstract moral precepts and also to increase the structural and tonal cohesion between the *Castigos* and the rest of the romance. Finally, some entirely new sections of didacticism, largely derived from other contemporary works of wisdom, [38] have been included in order to make the *Castigos* a fuller treatise and to increase its relevance to the *Zifar* proper. It will be found that these additions to the basic *Flores* material are there for one of two reasons: they may be used to emphasize some precept which is treated only sketchily in the earlier work, but which is very important in the *Zifar*; or they may introduce some aspect of morality or behaviour that is not dealt with at all in the *Flores*, but which is necessary if the *Castigos* is to reflect at all accurately the experiences of Zifar in the past and of Roboán in the future.

Chapter 129 of the *Castigos* is a good example of the former type of addition. It concerns chastity and, whilst *castydad* is mentioned very briefly in *ley* XVIII as one of the seven great virtues, it is not dealt with at all as an independent topic in the *Flores*. But chastity has played an important role in Zifar's life: if he had not forsworn sexual relations with his second wife he would have been placed in an impossible moral predicament when Grima reappeared on the scene. Similarly, if Roboán had taken Seringa as soon as she showed herself willing, he would have stayed in Pandulfa and never have become Emperor of Tigrida. Both men are rewarded by God for their self-control. It is important, therefore, that the theme of chastity should have some prominence in the *Castigos*.

Chapter 165 provides a good illustration of a didactic section that is quite outside the scope of the *Flores*:

> Otrosý, míos fijos, sy algunt grant señor vos feziere bien, o sy el vuestro vasallo vos oviere fecho buen serviçio, punad en gelo reconosçer, a los señores con serviçio e a los servidores en bienfecho (357.13-16).

Once again the soundness of this advice reflects Zifar's past experience. His first overlord did not value him as he should and consequently lost the services of his finest knight. Other sovereigns, however, notably the lady of Galapia and the King of Mentón, derived great profit from his military skill and in turn rewarded him suitably. When the knight himself achieved a position of power he made a point of remembering those who had helped him along the way: the Ribaldo was given the title of Cavallero

---

[38] In particular, the *Castigos e documentos* and the *Siete partidas;* see Wagner, «Sources», 36-44.

Amigo, Garfín and Roboán were rewarded with honours, and even the hermit who prophesied his future greatness was sent money so that he could found a monastery. This theme of mutual service and appreciation is an important one in the *Zifar* and consequently had to be reflected in the teaching of the *Castigos*.

* * *

The *Castigos*, then, is not the irrelevant parenthesis or tasteless blunder that it has been called by past critics. It may be overlong, repetitive and rather boring to the modern reader who is out of sympathy with moral platitudes and has little interest in the education of princes. Nevertheless, this chapter has, I hope, demonstrated that the *Castigos* is an essential element of the *Zifar* and perhaps, from the point of view of the author and his public, the most essential element. Book III codifies in abstract form the moral and practical lessons it is possible to derive from the heroes' adventures in the rest of the romance. In other words, the *Castigos* sums up Books I and II and lays down the lines which Book IV will follow. The author has taken great care to try and integrate his long didactic treatise into the unfamiliar setting of a romance. He may not have been entirely successful in this extremely difficult task (one that was undertaken by no other European romance-writer, to my knowledge), but there can be no denying the value of the attempt.

CHAPTER FIVE: FORMULAIC STYLE IN THE *ZIFAR*

The *Zifar*'s prose style has never been fully examined, although it has evoked a few murmurs of approval, ranging from Menéndez y Pelayo's rather back-handed compliment—«hasta la ranciedad y llaneza de su estilo le pone a salvo de la retórica amanerada y enfática que corrompió estos libros desde la cuna»— [1] to Erich von Richthofen's unsubstantiated assertion that «hacen aquí su aparición los primeros intentos de una prosa artística en español». [2] Three other critics have praised the author's artistry in very general terms after examining one particular section of the work. Amado Alonso, in the course of a commentary on the story of the Wind, Water and Truth, remarks that the *Zifar* is «una de las más poéticas y menos disparatadas» romances of chivalry. [3] C. P. Wagner, discussing the author's treatment of a passage borrowed from the *Moralium Dogma Philosophorum*, calls it «a splendid example of the creative use of a source by a remarkable artist». [4] J. B. Avalle-Arce, studying the various Spanish versions of the story of the Two Friends, notes that «el autor del *Cifar* vislumbró las posibilidades novelísticas del cuento y trató de darle mayor amplitud.... Así y todo, se hacen tanteos en el aprovechamiento artístico de la fábula». [5] Finally, the *Zifar* author's inventiveness in the field of moral phraseology of the *abstractum agens* and *homo reagens* type is commented on favourably by John H. R. Polt. [6]

The most extensive study of the *Zifar*'s style is in the unpublished dissertation of James F. Burke, who discusses (in a rather generalized way) medieval stylistic theories in relation to this romance, concerning himself principally with narrative procedures, the intermingling of *sermo gravis* and

[1] *Orígenes de la novela*, ed. E. Sánchez Reyes (Edición Nacional, 2nd ed., Madrid, 1962), I, 314.

[2] *Estudios épicos medievales con algunos trabajos inéditos* (Madrid, 1954), 50.

[3] «Maestría antigua en la prosa», *Sur* XIV, no. 133 (1945), 40-43, at p. 40.

[4] «The *Caballero Zifar* and the *Moralium Dogma Philosophorum*», *RPh* VI (1952-53), 309-312, at p. 312.

[5] *Deslindes cervantinos* (Madrid, 1961), 174-175.

[6] «Moral Phraseology in Early Spanish Literature», *RPh* XV (1962), 254-268, especially pp. 258-259 and 268.

sermo humilis, parataxis and imagery.[7] Much, then, remains to be done.

The *Zifar* is, as far as we know, the first full-scale work of consciously literary prose fiction in Spanish. Before it the only story-telling in prose, apart from the sections of novelized history in some of the chronicles (such as the *Estoria de Tebas* in the *General estoria)* and some possible translations (now lost) of French romances, is to be found in the books of *exempla* such as the *Calila e Digna* and the *Libro de los engaños*. The only other vernacular prose models available to the *Zifar* author were the historical, legal and scientific writings of the great thirteenth-century translators. He had, therefore, virtually to create a new narrative style for the genre he was introducing into Spanish literature; and for his inspiration he seems to have turned, perhaps not surprisingly, more towards the earlier story-tellers in verse, the epic poets, than towards the historians and the lawyers. Recent critics have shown how both the chroniclers and the learned poets of the *mester de clerecía* borrowed extensively from the «already standard diction of the epic minstrels».[8] Since the *Zifar*, in the first two books at least, deals with a near epic subject and consequently abounds in epic motifs, it was natural that this author too should model his style to a large extent on the still popular heroic tales in verse.[9]

Some years ago Ruth Crosby drew up a set of criteria for identifying medieval works that were intended for oral presentation. She classifies the features of such literature under four main heads: phrases of direct address to the audience; «excessive repetitions» dictated by the public's fondness for the familiar; other «excessive repetitions» which show the relationship of the poet to his audience; religious openings and endings.[10] Crosby's analysis will be used as a basis for an examination of the *Zifar*'s debt to «oral» style.

[7] *A Critical and Artistic Study of the «Libro del Cavallero Cifar»* (unpubl. diss. of the University of North Carolina at Chapel Hill, 1966), ch. 5.

[8] C. C. Smith and J. Morris, «On 'Physical' Phrases in Old Spanish Epic and Other Texts», *PLPLS: Lit. and Hist. Section* XII, part v (1967), 129-190, at p. 182. For the debt of the *clerecía* poets to the minstrels, see also Ian Michael, «A Comparison of the Use of Epic Epithets in the *Poema de Mío Cid* and the *Libro de Alexandre»*, *BHS* XXXVIII (1961), 32-41; Brian Dutton, «Gonzalo de Berceo and the *Cantares de gesta»*, *BHS* XXXVIII (1961), 197-205; Dutton, *La «Vida de San Millán de la Cogolla» de Gonzalo de Berceo. Estudio y edición crítica* (London, 1967), 175-181; T. Anthony Perry, *Art and Meaning in Berceo's «Vida de Santa Oria»* (Yale Romanic Studies, Second Series 19, New Haven-London, 1968), especially chs 5 and 6. A. D. Deyermond, «Mester es sen peccado» *RF* LXXVII (1965), 111-116, produces evidence to challenge the traditional view that the *clerecía* poets in general despised the productions of the *juglares*.

[9] Peter Schon, *Studien zum Stil der frühen französischen Prosa* (Analecta Romanica 8, Frankfurt am Main, 1960), shows that there is much reminiscence of epic style in the French prose writers of the thirteenth century, such as Robert de Clari, Geoffroy de Villehardouin and Henri de Valenciennes. Cf. Jeanette M. A. Beer, «Villehardouin and the Oral Narrative», *Sp* LXVII (1970), 267-277, and *Villehardouin Epic Historian* (Etudes de Philologie et d'Histoire 7, Genève, 1968).

[10] «Oral Delivery in the Middle Ages», *Sp* XI (1936), 88-110.

A. DIRECT ADDRESS TO THE AUDIENCE

Crosby's main point is that phrases of direct address to the audience
are «the surest evidence of the intention of oral delivery». [11]   The formulas
of audience address in the *Zifar* are of two types only: those using a second-
person plural form of *oír*, and «ahévos (aquí)». [12]

There are thirty examples of phrases of direct address involving a
second-person plural form of *oír* in the *Zifar*.   Four occur in the author's
Prologue, ten in Book I, five in Book II, four in Book III, and seven in
Book IV.   Two of those in Book I, however, must be left out of the present
discussion since they do not appear in the narrative proper, but are spoken
by one of the characters when about to relate a tale (17.12, 88.10).   The
four occurrences in Book III (263.15-16, 271.12, 332.11, 350.28) must
also be disregarded, since the whole of the *Castigos del rey de Mentón*
is put into the mouth of Zifar and consequently abounds in direct address
forms such as «sabet» and «míos fijos»; but these are aimed not at us
but at the audience within the audience.   There remain, then, twenty-four
genuine examples of the author speaking directly to his public:

(*a*)   (asý) commo (ya) (lo) oyestes: 5.22, 178.21-22, 248.13-14, 503.21,
     505.24, 516.2.
(*b*)   segunt oyestes: 36.12.
(*c*)   asý commo oystes de suso: 106.21. [13]
(*d*)   (asý) commo adelante oyredes/oyredes adelante: 8.10-11, 9.9-10,
     40.3, 97.12-13, 228.16, 251.14, 430.5-6, 444.14-15.
(*e*)   que adelante oyredes: 6.14.
(*f*)   (asý) commo agora oyredes: 24.16, 36.14-15, 443.5, 471.4.
(*g*)   segunt agora oyredes: 8.17, 226.16.
(*h*)   que agora oyredes: 110.16.

---

[11]   «Oral Delivery», 100.   For support for the same point, see Crosby, «Chaucer
and the Custom of Oral Delivery», *Sp* XIII (1938), 413-432; H. J. Chaytor, *From
Script to Print. An Introduction to Medieval Vernacular Literature* (Cambridge, 1945),
ch. 2, especially pp. 11-12; Joaquín Artiles, *Los recursos literarios de Berceo* (Madrid,
1964), 32-36; Pierre Gallais, «Recherches sur la mentalité des romanciers français du
Moyen Age.   Les formules et le vocabulaire des prologues. I», *CCMe* VII (1964),
479-493; Albert C. Baugh, «The Middle English Romance: Some Questions of Creation,
Presentation and Preservation», *Sp* XLII (1967), 1-31.

[12]   All statistical evidence in this chapter and the next, unless otherwise stated, is
based on MS. *M*.   The linguistic modernizations of *P* and *S* have much affected the
archaisms of *M*.

[13]   This example is from *P*; there is a short lacuna in *M* at this point.   The paradoxical
nature of formulas such as this, which seem to combine address to a listening audience
with an adverb that indicates that the author thought of his work as a MS. in the hands
of a reader, has been pointed out by G. B. Gybbon-Monypenny, «The Spanish *Mester
de Clerecía* and its Intended Public: Concerning the Validity as Evidence of Passages
of Direct Address to the Audience», *Medieval Miscellany Presented to Eugène Vinaver*
(Manchester, 1965), 230-244, at p. 236.   Cf. also A. D. Deyermond, *Epic Poetry and
the Clergy: Studies on the «Mocedades de Rodrigo»* (London, 1969), 171.

To these may be added two further phrases which, although they do not contain a form of *oír*, use a second-person plural pronoun: «de que agora vos contará la estoria» (94.5); «e este cuento vos conté» (242.13-14).

There are six occurrences of «ahévos (aquí)» in the *Zifar*, all but the first one preceded by the stock phrase «e ellos estando en esto». All six introduce an epic-type motif: the author is calling our attention to the arrival on the scene of some new character, usually a knight or royal official bearing news or a message. This use of «ahévos (aquí)» seems to be a clear reminiscence of epic style: [14]

(a) E el cavallero e la dueña estando a la puerta esperando la repuesta de la señora de la villa, ahévos aquí un cavallero armado do venía contra la villa en su cavallo armado (41.15-18).

(b) E ellos estando en esto, ahévos el portero e un cavallero do venían (43.17-18).

(c) E ellos estando en esto, ahévos do venían seysçientos cavalleros e grant gente de pie (57.4-5).

(d) E ellos estando en esto, ahévos do venía el mayordomo con todas las nuevas çiertas (152.3-4).

(e) E ellos estando en esto, hévos un cavallero de Roboán do entró por las tiendas del rey (204.24-25).

(f) E ellos estando en esto, ahévos Roboán do asomó con toda su gente (216.16-17). [15]

The *Zifar*, of course, is not the only non-juglaresque work, or the latest, to use phrases of direct address involving *oír*. On this evidence alone it would be dangerous to postulate imitation of the minstrels, since it has been shown that such phrases were often employed as pure conventions as late as the sixteenth century. [16] The *Zifar*'s «ahévos» phrases, however, are a much rarer relic of oral style and seem more significant as evidence of the author's debt to the art of the minstrels. It is worth noting also that the modernizing scribe of *P*, writing in the fifteenth century, preserves all the *oír* constructions, sometimes with a very slight change of wording (such as the omission of «asý»), but always retaining the second-person plural form of the verb. [17] All the examples from the romance proper, with one exception (444.14-15), also appear in *S*, the sixteenth-century

---

[14] Cf. *PMC* 476, 1317, 1431, 2368, 3591. Albert B. Lord, *The Singer of Tales* (HSCL 24, Cambridge, Mass., 1960), 80-81, shows that the arrival of a messenger is still a common motif (or theme, in Lord's terminology) in the modern Yugoslav oral epic.

[15] A further example occurs in 65.28: «fe aquí los cavalleros do vienen»; but as this is used in dialogue not narrative, it cannot be counted as an instance of direct address to the audience. «Afévos», however, is frequently used in speech in the epic (e.g. *PMC* 269, 1335).

[16] See above ch. 1, n. 36.

[17] The two phrases with *vos* (94.5, 242.13-14) are also preserved in *P*.

print. [18]   On the other hand, all the «ahévos» phrases have been recast in straightforward narrative form in both *P* and *S* so as to remove the element of direct address. [19]   Thus, while the *oír* constructions became fossilized as an acceptable convention, «ahévos» came to be regarded as an intolerable archaism as the minstrels' art became a more and more distant memory.

B.   «EXCESSIVE REPETITION» - I

Crosby's second criterion for identifying oral literature is «the constant repetition of words, phrases, situations and ideas». [20]   She further defines these repetitions as:

> types of phrases occurring frequently in the works intended to be heard but showing no specific intention of uniting the poet or minstrel with his hearers. These phrases appeal rather to the fondness of the popular audience—well known, no doubt, to those who wrote for it—for hearing things said in a familiar way. [21]

Crosby lists four main types of «excessive repetition»: introductory phrases, descriptive phrases, expletives (inclusive and redundant phrases) and formulas.

(i)   *Introductory Phrases*

The commonest introductory phrase in Middle English is, according to Crosby, «on the day» or the more elaborate «on the morrow when it was day».   There are exactly similar expressions in Old French narratives: «un jor», «au matinet quant le jor vit», etc.   In the *Poema de Mío Cid* «otro día mañana» occurs twelve times, «a la mañana» three times and

---

[18]   *S* does not include the author's Prologue, but substitutes its own prefatory matter, most of which is devoted to justifying the publication of such an archaic work.   This new material contains no instance of direct address.   The editor of *S*, however, ends his introduction with a paraphrase of the last few lines of the manuscript Prologue which summarize the origins and achievements of Zifar.   In *S* these final sentences close thus: «E por ser tal, alcançó a ser rey... como aquí oyréys».   The *S* prologue is reproduced in Wagner, *Cauallero Zifar*, 517-518.   The two *vos* phrases are also preserved in *S*.

[19]   There is one curiosity in *P*: the «ahévos aquí» of 41.15-18 is changed to the different direct address phrase «catad aquí».   This, however, is the only example of such a substitution in *P*, and even this has no echo in *S* which, as in all other cases, eliminates the last trace of audience address.

[20]   «Oral Delivery», 102.

[21]   «Oral Delivery», 102.   A. C. Spearing, *Criticism and Medieval Poetry* (London, 1964), 20, also points out that oral poetry contains «a high proportion of the familiar»; but he seems to regard this as a rather negative limitation laid on the poet by the lack of sophistication in his audience, rather than as a positive attitude of mind, as Crosby appears to do.   The difference is, of course, slight; but the shift of emphasis is interesting.

«cras (a la) mañana» four times. [22] The main use of such phrases in medieval literature is to signpost a new stage in the development of the story.

The *Zifar* contains a considerable number of such introductory formulas. The simple «e otro día» occurs seven times in both manuscripts and in the 1512 print. [23] The more emphatic «e otro día en la mañana» [24] turns up twenty-five times in all three versions; [25] and there are a further seven examples in *P* and *S* which, for various reasons, do not appear in *M*. [26] Other variations on these phrases are: «E en la (grant) mañana» (28.13, 273.22); «Al terçer día después desto, en la grant mañana ante del alva» (50.8); «E quando fue el domingo en la grant mañana» (78.15); «E un día venieron a él en la mañana» (88.16); [27] «Quando fue en la mañana» (137.14); «E quando fue otro día en la mañana ante del alva» (143.10); [28] «Asý que un día en la mañana» (211.26). The *Zifar*, then, has no fewer than forty-eight examples of the commonest of these introductory clichés so beloved of the oral poets, a total which certainly qualifies for Crosby's first category of «excessive repetition».

Apart from the «otro día» phrases there are at least two other expressions that are used extensively in the *Zifar* as introductory formulas. One of these «(él/ella/ellos/ellas) estando en esto» occurs sixteen times, [29] and there are a further five examples in which *esto* is replaced by the masculine or feminine form of the demonstrative adjective with a noun. [30] In all these cases the formula is used, as in the epic, to introduce a new character to the scene or to recall the audience's attention to someone

[22] See Edmund de Chasca, *Registro de fórmulas verbales en el «Cantar de Mio Cid»* (Iowa City, 1968), 27.

[23] 18.22, 111.12, 126.15, 240.18, 438.2, 442.7, 506.10 [*M* desý o. d.]. A further example occurs only in *P* and *S* (175.4).

[24] There are a number of minor variations on this phrase, such as «otro día en la mañana», «(e) otro día en la grant mañana», «(e) otro día de (grant) mañana». These variants are of little significance since none of the three versions seems to show a marked preference for any one over the others. *P* and *S* usually, but far from invariably, agree in their readings.

[25] 21.7, 26.26, 46.7, 72.10, 83.14-15, 87.18, 89.10, 105.18, 126.6-7, 141.7, 156.9, 157.20, 175.14, 205.22, 231.23, 254.4, 384.21, 427.7, 441.3, 450.6, 451.18, 468.18, 497.4, 506.22, 510.10.

[26] In 41.1 and 157.6 *M* has simply «e otro día»; in 170.17 and 208.9 *M* reads «otro día mañana»; in 403.22 and 456.29 the examples are taken from *P* because of *lacunae* in *M* at these points; *M*'s reading in 153.6 is «e quando fue otro día en la mañana».

[27] *P* and *S* read «e un día de mañana vinieron».

[28] *P* and *S* read «otro día quando fue de mañana ante del alva».

[29] 29.5, 43.17, 44.11 (e sobre esto estando), 48.7, 57.4, 75.2, 132.19, 152.3, 165.15, 183.12, 204.24, 216.16, 374.7, 405.21, 408.30, 425.14. There are occasional insignificant variations between one version and another, such as «en esto estando», «estando ellos en esto», etc. The examples quoted occur in all three versions except 405.21 and 408.30 which occur only in *P* and *S* because of a *lacuna* in *M* at this point; there is, however, no reason to doubt that *M*, if complete, would have contained these two cases.

[30] «Estando el rey en esta guerra» (14.18); «E ellos estando en esta porfía» (44.8); «E estando en esta oración» (105.25); «Estando en este pensamiento» (165.12); «E ellas estando en esta fabla» (177.13).

who has been away from the centre of the stage for some time and is about to resume a leading role. [31] We have already noted how «ahévos (aquí)», which has an identical narrative function, is itself invariably preceded by a phrase of this kind. Although «ahévos» is eliminated from the later versions, *P* and *S*, «estando en esto» and its variants survive right through to the sixteenth-century printed edition.

The other introductory phrase worthy of note because of its frequent use in the *Zifar* is «dize el cuento». Like «otro día» and «estando en esto», «dize el cuento» is used to usher in a fresh development in the narrative. Of the thirty-three occurrences in the work only three can be said not to fulfil this function. [32] The remaining thirty can be divided into two distinct categories: those that introduce an interpolated *exemplum* and those that initiate a new phase in the main story. Thirteen of the twenty-seven *exempla* in the *Zifar* open with «dize el cuento». [33] Another one, introduced by «oý dezir que» uses «dize el cuento» later on to begin a new stage in the plot of the tale. [34] This use of the phrase is clearly a specialized one, and one of which the author is obviously very fond. [35] The other sixteen cases of «dize el cuento» occur in almost exactly similar circumstances to the «otro día» and «estando en esto» phrases. [36] «Dize el cuento», however, tends to mark a more significant break in the story, a more emphatic shift of direction. It is used particularly when the career of a character who has been out of the picture for some time is taken up again. Thus a number of examples of the phrase occur in the later chapters of Book I and in Book II, where the family has been split up and three separate sets of adventures are running side by side; another group appears in the latter half of Book IV when ends are being tied up and the principal characters brought together for the last time. The emphatic function of «dize el cuento» is underlined by the fact that in fifteen out of the sixteen cases it opens a chapter. [37] Moreover, in a number of instances, the sense of a major change of direction is strengthened by the concluding words of the immediately preceding chapter. Chapter 1, for example, ends «asý commo se puede entender e ver por esta estoria»;

[31] Cf. *PMC* 2311.

[32] 98.2, 418.36, 515.17.

[33] 17.16, 88.11, 256.7, 259.11, 266.25, 271.16, 283.15, 332.12, 346.7, 368.10, 370.14, 375.17 (dize desta guisa el cuento), 376.25.

[34] The tale is that of the Whole Friend, which covers pp. 23-32 of Wagner's edition. It is the longest and most developed *exemplum* in the work. «Dize el cuento» occurs in 24.17.

[35] A further *exemplum* is introduced by «dize la escriptura» (372.15) and yet another by «e dize asý» (235.10).

[36] 11.5, 40.6, 94.10, 106.19 (onde dize el cuento), 164.11, 178.20, 190.20, 226.20, 243.3, 429.19, 438.6, 444.20 (onde d. el c.), 506.4, 514.6, 515.17.

[37] Wagner's chapter headings in *Cauallero Zifar* are taken from *P*, which has far more rubrics than *M* or *S*. The only case in which «dize el cuento» does not open a chapter in *P* is 429.19; but both *M* and *S* have a rubric at this point. It is perhaps, therefore, reasonable to suppose that here *P*'s rubric has been misplaced by a few lines.

chapter 10 ends «así commo adelante oyredes en la su estoria»; chapter 43 ends «de que agora vos contará la estoria en cómmo pasó su fazienda»; chapter 109 ends «que fue engañado desta guisa, segunt que agora oyredes». In all these cases the following chapters begin with «dize el cuento».

To sum up. The *Zifar* author, although writing for a more learned audience, relies just as heavily on introductory phrases to indicate successive stages in his story as the poets composing for oral delivery. «Otro día» and «estando en esto» serve to link smoothly the various elements of the narrative and give warning of the appearance or reappearance of a character who is in some way to play an important part in the subsequent episode. [38] This usage reflects precisely the function of similar expressions in the epic. «Dize el cuento», however, serves to indicate a more fundamental break in the narrative, a clear change of direction or subject, or the taking up again of the main story thread after a digression. This is seen most clearly in its use as a formula to introduce interpolated *exempla*: eleven of the seventeen tales in Book III, for example, where the change from pure abstraction to concrete exemplification is very marked, begin in this way. «Dize el cuento» is also used, as we have seen, to bridge the awkward gap when the centre of interest in the main narrative in the books of adventures shifts from one character to another. The phrase does not occur very much in oral poetry, largely because this type of literature is normally distinguished by its unilinearity of plot, with few digressions or interpolations. However, the use of «dize el cuento» as an introductory formula in the *Zifar* seems to be modelled on the stereotyped techniques of episodic composition used in juglaresque works.

(ii) *Descriptive Phrases*

Crosby's second type of «excessive repetition» is the stereotyped descriptive phrase:

> These phrases are not in the nature of fixed epithets, describing a particular trait of an individual character, like Virgil's «pius Aeneus» [*sic*]. They are applied indiscriminately in one romance after another. Any knight or squire may be «doughty in dede», or «corteise, hende and fre», or «worthy under wede» (103-104).

This kind of phrase is monotonously common in the *Zifar*. In what follows only the epithets and adjectival phrases that seem to obsess the

---

[38] A further illustration of the author's care for cohesion is the way in which he quite often «motivates» the formulas «otro día» and «en la mañaña» a few lines before they occur: e.g. «mandaldes que fagan alarde cras en la mañaña» (54.2) —«E otro día en la mañaña salieron a su alarde» (54.13); «E mandóles ... que otro día en la grant mañaña que saliesen a la plaça a fazer alarde» (156.27-157.1) —«E otro día salieron ý todos aquellos cavalleros armados» (157.6); cf. 72.4, 72.10; 78.7, 78.15; 205.13, 205.22; 254.1, 254.4; etc.

author most have been included: there are many others that occur only
a few times, although they are equally stereotyped. The formulas of
character description in the *Zifar* may be divided into three main categories:
those referring to physical appearance or prowess; those denoting social
origin and accomplishments; and those indicating moral qualities, which
form the largest group.

There are three very common phrases which describe physical attributes,
of which the most frequently encountered is «(muy) buen cavallero de
armas», which occurs seventeen times. [39] A similar group of related
expressions indicating fighting prowess is «de buen/grant esfuerço», «de
esforçar» and «esforçado», of which there are twelve examples. [40] Finally,
in this category, there is «apuesto», which occurs thirteen times. [41]

Adjectival phrases are used with great frequency to denote the social
qualities of the characters. Aristocratic provenance is expressed by «de
alto/buen/grant lugar» twenty times, [42] and by «de alta sangre» a further
four times. [43] The courtly quality of fair speech is indicated by «de buena
palabra» ten times, [44] and by «bien razonado» three times. [45]

As is to be expected in such a serious didactic work as the *Zifar*, by
far the greatest number of stereotyped descriptive phrases apply to moral
qualities. The following are the most commonly encountered: «de buen
entendimiento» (34 times), [46] «de justiçia/amador de justiçia/justiçiero»
(30 times), [47] «bien acostunbrado/de buenas costunbres» (23 times), [48]
«de buen seso (natural)» (14 times), [49] «de buena/santa vida» (9 times), [50]

[39] 11.5-6, 60.16, 140.3 (buenos cav. de sus armas), 151.21, 157.11, 169.14, 208.21,
216.12, 242.9, 385.1, 386.18 (buen cav. de sus armas), 415.14-15, 415.16 (el mejor cav. de
armas), 420.29 (mejor cav. de armas), 421.8, 446.8-9, 507.23.

[40] «De esforçar»: 8.13; «de grant esfuerço»: 11.8, 385.3; «de buen esfuerço»:
126.14, 212.17, 362.3; «(muy) esforçado»: 179.23, 192.3-4, 194.22, 213.2, 227.7-8,
409.2.

[41] 71.4, 85.4, 127.26, 140.18, 162.9, 181.15-16, 185.9, 233.22, 263.25, 386.10, 389.5,
394.15, 506.8.

[42] 18.16, 24.19, 26.23, 33.26-27, 48.31, 49.10, 68.8, 68.16, 71.5, 139.21, 145.23, 146.3,
151.23, 151.26, 244.6, 296.14-15, 296.21, 403.18, 438.12, 462.4.

[43] 145.21, 145.22, 161.20, 489.25.

[44] 127.26, 140.18-19, 235.11, 386.10-11, 389.5, 394.15, 396.4, 396.6, 469.22, 489.21.

[45] 71.4, 99.16, 179.2.

[46] 6.5-6, 31.18, 34.10, 48.31, 71.26-27, 100.1, 101.25, 108.16-17, 110.7, 111.3, 126.13-14,
151.20, 155.23, 168.6-7, 169.14-15, 250.3, 251.1, 255.21, 297.16, 321.14, 328.12-13, 370.12,
373.13-14, 379.4, 389.8, 391.26-392.1, 398.14, 398.18, 427.21, 428.15-16, 456.13, 469.23,
506.14, 507.22.

[47] «de (grant) justiçia»: 8.13, 11.6-7, 12.11, 135.15, 167.19, 167.21, 187.9, 188.25-26;
«amador de justiçia»: 4.2-3, 33.19, 264.10; «justiçiero»: 87.20, 100.22, 165.2, 287.8, 308.26-
27, 309.24, 316.14, 317.2, 317.21-27 (5 occurrences), 318.6, 320.10, 332.17, 369.6, 435.24,
450.25.

[48] «bien acostunbrado»: 36.6, 40.1, 68.16, 83.5, 94.3, 178.22, 204.23, 262.22, 290.5,
294.13, 295.14, 386.8-9, 459.14, 506.8, 513.4; «de buenas costunbres»: 4.2, 33.20, 34.8,
39.20, 68.1, 264.16, 264.19-20, 264.23-24.

[49] «de buen seso»: 13.3, 139.21, 250.12, 289.22, 298.4, 384.26; «de buen seso natural»: 4.1, 8.4, 8.13, 12.10, 33.19, 143.2, 362.2, 489.20.

[50] 4.1, 9.5-6, 87.21, 179.24 (santa), 287.12, 375.13, 397.13, 427.21, 499.14.

«de buen/sano consejo» (7 times), [51] «de buen coraçón» (7 times), [52] «de buen conosçer» (6 times), [53] «de verdat» (5 times). [54]

These adjectives and adjectival phrases introduced by *de* by no means exhaust the references to these stereotyped qualities in the *Zifar*. Frequently characters are said to possess, for instance, «buen seso natural» or «buenas costunbres», to act with «esfuerço», to be capable of giving «buen consejo» when required. The following few examples are typical of many such in the work:

> E non deven creer a aquéllos en quien non paresçe buen seso natural nin verdat nin buen consejo (12.20-22)

> e con grant fuerza de bondat e de buenas costunbres se faze (33.23-24)

> E la señora de la villa pagóse del buen razonar e del buen seso e del buen sosiego del buen cavallero e de la dueña (46.21-22)

> Señor, el vuestro buen donayre, e la vuestra buena apostura, e las vuestras buenas costunbres, e el vuestro buen esfuerço, e la vuestra buena ventura, e el vuestro buen entendimiento, e la vuestra bondad... (427.23-26).

A number of interesting points arise from this analysis of the frequency and distribution of the descriptive phrases in the *Zifar*. First, Crosby's assertion that these qualifiers are not distinguishing is amply borne out: they can be applied apparently indiscriminately to many different characters. The phrase «de buena vida», for example, is applied to Doña María de Molina (Prologue, 4.1), Grima (9.5-6), the King of Orbín (87.21), a cardinal (375.13), Gallarda, Seringa's lady-in-waiting (397.13), Seringa (427.21), and the maidens who make Roboán's magic banner on the *Islas Dotadas* (499.14). To these may be added Zifar who, as King of Mentón, «fizo muy buena vida e muy santa» (172.23-24), and his second wife, whom he praises after her death because she «mantenía muy buena vida» (246.8). Similarly wide-ranging are those who are regarded as being «de buena palabra»; they include the Ribaldo (127.26), Zifar (140.18-19), a girl who tells an *exemplum* (235.11), Roboán (386.10-11, 389.4-5), Gallarda (394.15), and Nobleza, Empress of the *Islas Dotadas* (469.22).

Yet, although these qualities appear to be applied quite indiscriminately, this is not really the case in the *Zifar*. The author certainly relies heavily on descriptive formulas, but he almost always seems to take care only

---

[51] 4.1, 8.13-14, 11.6 (sano), 12.11, 63.13-14, 320.16, 384.26-385.1.
[52] 129.5, 143.2, 351.7, 364.13, 364.17, 365.15, 484.8.
[53] 6.6, 236.19, 354.13, 355.24, 358.2, 471.17.
[54] 8.14, 12.10, 188.25, 264.10, 335.22.

to use for each character ones that are fully appropriate and therefore meaningful. Thus, nearly all those represented as «de buena vida» are women, and there is no doubt that a good life in the *Zifar* means a life of sexual abstinence, a quality that distinguishes most of the women in the work, especially Grima, Seringa and Zifar's second wife.[55] Nor is it surprising to find Zifar himself (or, of course, the cardinal) in this category. Similarly, all those who are «de buen consejo» earn the right to this epithet by giving sound advice. Zifar, for instance, is three times described in this way at the beginning of the romance, which serves to prepare us for his important role as counsellor to various people later on (8.13-14, 11.6, 12.11). He himself insists that one of a knight's first duties is to «dar buen consejo» (83.5-6), a theme to which he returns in the *Castigos* (320.16). Roboán, too, is ready to «dar buen consejo quando gelo demandavan» (386.16), and he proves his ability to do so, notably to the Count of Turbia, the Emperor of Tigrida and the Ribaldo, among others. And the anonymous knight, who wisely urges his lord to raise his siege of Galapia and surrender to Zifar, is similarly designated «ome de Dios e de muy buen consejo» (63.13-14).[56]

If we accept that the *Zifar* author usually tries to find appropriate clichés for his characters, it is interesting to see how he is willing to grant certain stereotyped qualities to those who are hostile to his heroes. Significantly, however, these only involve physical or social virtues, never the more important moral ones. Thus, the sons of the king laying siege to Galapia are «muy buenos cavalleros de sus armas» (140.3); and the one who later marries the lady who rules the city is «mançebo e mucho apuesto e muy bien razonado e de muy grant logar» (71.4-5). The traitor Nasón is «muy buen cavallero e mucho esforçado» (194.21-22), and his nephew is also «muy buen cavallero de armas» (208.21). The woman on the *Islas Dotadas* who persuades Roboán to neglect his duty addresses him as «ome de grant logar e muy apuesto en todas cosas» (462.3-4), significantly refraining from attributing moral qualities to him at this point.[57]

---

[55] The *Zifar* author's equation of chastity and «buena vida» is made explicit in his description of the banner-making maidens: «las donzellas fueron sienpre de tan buena vida que non quisieron casar» (499.14-15). It is perhaps surprising to find the Queen María de Molina included in this company, since her liaison with King Sancho IV was far from an exemplary illustration of «buena vida» and even required a forged papal bull to counteract the scandal; see Peter Linehan, *The Spanish Church and the Papacy in the Thirteenth Century* (Cambridge Studies in Medieval Life and Thought, Third Series 4, Cambridge, 1971), 104 and 223. C. P. Wagner, however, suggests that the sentence containing the eulogy of Queen María is a later interpolation written after her death in 1321 and so not attributable to the writer of the romance. The *Zifar* author's generally censorious attitude towards sex is discussed briefly in my article, «Juan Ruiz's Defence of Love», *MLN* LXXXIV (1969), 292-297.

[56] See Jules Piccus, «Consejos y consejeros en el *Libro del Cauallero Zifar*», *NRFH* XVI (1962), 16-30.

[57] Eugene Vance, «Notes on the Development of Formulaic Language in Romanesque Poetry», *Mélanges offerts à René Crozet* (Poitiers, 1966), I, 427-434, points to

In connection with this distinction between moral and non-moral qualities, it in worth adding that the *Castigos* which, as we have seen, is the real *meollo* of the work, makes very little reference indeed to the physical and social attributes of knighthood. «Buen cavallero» and «buen cavallero de armas», so frequently encountered in the three books of adventures, make no appearance in Zifar's advice to his sons. The only formula of military virtue to be found in Book III is a fleeting reference to the need to be «esforçado» (362.3). The smooth-tongued and the courteous are clearly of less worth than the honest, the just and the «bien acostunbrados», since there is no mention in the *Castigos* of the advantages of being «de buena palabra» or «bien razonado». A proverb contains the only *Castigos* reference to «apuesto»: «E porende dizen que la muger apuesta non es de lo ageno conpuesta» (263.25-264.1). Nobility of birth is mentioned twice in Book III but, interestingly enough, not as a *sine qua non* of knighthood, but as something to be wary of, as it can easily lead to pride: «Ca non dizen orgulloso sy non por el que se pone en más alto logar que·l conviene» (294.14-15); «e el que se preçia mucho cae en vergüença... aunque sea de alto lugar» (296.19-21).

The *Zifar* author's use of formulas of character description reveals two of his most typical stylistic traits. First, he loves to elaborate, never to use one word or phrase where two will do, to accumulate syntactical and lexical elements. Thus, in his delineation of character, he rarely uses just one formula, and sometimes uses as many as six or eight. The following are rather extreme examples, but they are by no means untypical:

> la qual fue muy buena dueña e de muy buena vida, e de buen consejo, e de buen seso natural, e muy conplida en todas buenas costunbres e amadora de justiçia e con piedat (3.34-4.3)

> el qual cavallero era conplido de buen seso natural e de esforçar, de justiçia e de buen consejo, e de buena verdat (8.12-14)

a similar rather surprising use of formulas of praise in the *Chanson de Roland*, where the treacherous Saracen who tries to steal the sword Durendal from the dying Roland is described thus: «Bels fut e forz e de grant vasselage» (2278). Vance argues that this illustrates that «qualitative judgments apply to a person or thing only as he or it relates to a specific context. There is little intellectual carryover if these same terms are applied to another being seen in a radically opposed context.... Formulas in this poem do not attempt to convey values of an ultimate moral nature, for these distinctions have already been made and firmly agreed upon, even by the characters in the poem: 'Paien unt tort e chrestiens unt dreit'» (429). In the *Zifar*, however, a much simpler explanation than Vance's «morality of spaces» (430) is possible: physical, warlike and social qualities can be applied to anyone (it is, after all, more honourable for the hero to defeat a «buen cavallero de armas» than a cringing coward); but only the clearly «good» characters are accorded the formulas of moral and intellectual superiority. It is possible that this simple distinction might also apply to the *Roland;* it certainly holds good for 1. 2278, quoted by Vance: handsomeness and strength have no moral value, and the primary meaning of *vasselage* is not loyalty, but bravery, a military virtue; see *La Chanson de Roland*, ed. F. Whitehead, 2nd ed. (Oxford, 1946), 164.

e aver sobre todo esto la más fermosa, e de mejor donayre, e la más enseñada e de mejor palabra, e la más sosegada e de mejor entendimiento, e la más mesurada e de mejor resçebir, e la más alegre e mejor muger que en el mundo fue nasçida (469.21-25).

The same tendency towards rhetorical elaboration is to be seen in the somewhat excessive use of modifiers such as *bueno, grant, muy, mucho,* etc.

The second stylistic feature typical of the *Zifar* as a whole which is illustrated by the use of formulas of character description is the search for variety within the confines of the stereotype. Although the author uses only a limited number of these phrases, he varies the combinations so that it is rare to find the same pair used more than once or twice. Even in the longer catalogues, such as those just quoted, the order in which the various points are presented is considerably different in each case. The same desire for flexibility can also be seen in the use of these formulas by the characters themselves as well as by the author. Usually, of course, the description comes from the author in his role as omniscient creator; but there are many other cases where this is not so. Sometimes a character is described by another person in the story, either in a speech addressed directly to him or in a speech addressed to a third party. [58] At other times the descriptive formulas are put into the mind of another character in the form of his unspoken opinion. [59]

Apart from the generalizations in the *Castigos* there are also a number of cases in the narrative proper where the particular is raised to the general by the simple device of introducing the character cliché by *commo* or *a guisa de*, thus implicitly comparing the individuals in the story with the abstract ideal of, for example, the «buen cavallero» or «ome de buen seso». [60] Finally, we have already noted one of the author's main techniques of stylistic variation, the frequent avoidance of the stock adjectival phrase introduced by *de* by making the characteristic in question either the subject or object of his sentence. [61] This search for variety reveals a highly self-conscious artist.

[58] For example, the Lady of Galapia addresses Grima as «dueña de buen lugar e bien acostunbrada e sierva de Dios» (68.16-17); a father addresses his daughter as «mía fija de buen conosçer» (236.19); the *mayordomo* describes Zifar to the King of Mentón as «ome ... de buen coraçon e de buen seso natural» (143.2); a girl tells Roboán that Nobleza is «la mejor acostunbrada dueña de todo el mundo» (459.14).

[59] For example, when the foster-parents of Zifar's sons are debating the boys' future, they decide to send them to the King of Mentón (i.e. Zifar) to be knighted, because «oyeron dezir del rey de Mentón que era muy buen cavallero e muy buen rey e muy esforçado en armas e de santa vida» (179.22-24); when the sons are knighted «todos se maravillavan e judgávanlos por muy buenos cavalleros» (189.20-21); after hearing from his messenger about Grima and her mysterious boat guided by Christ «entendió el rey [de Orbín] por las repuestas que esta dueña era de Dios e de buen entendimiento» (99.26-100.1).

[60] See, for example, 101.24, 110.6-7, 155.23, 213.1-2, 251.1.

[61] See, for example, 12.20-22, 33.23-24, 46.21-22, 427.23-26, quoted on p. 152 above.

A final point of interest about the use of these stereotyped descriptive phrases is that their ubiquity helps to underline the unity of the whole work. Just as Roboán's adventures are almost a carbon copy of those of Zifar, so the son's moral and physical qualities reflect those of his father. Seringa attracts Roboán by displaying the same virtues as Zifar found in Grima. The unity of moral tone imposed by the principles set out in the *Castigos* is maintained on either side of them by the qualities of father and son, with the addition of the military virtues made necessary by the translation of abstract didacticism into terms of chivalric adventure. The seeming lack of imagination implied by the monotonous repetition of the same formulas can be seen as yet a further instance of the author's very real concern to impose a pattern and a unity on his highly heterogeneous material.

(iii) *Physical Phrases*

The third category of repetition in Crosby's analysis she calls «expletives», by which she means padding phrases, line-fillers. The first of her two main types of expletive is the «inclusive phrase», such as «day and night», «old and young», «blod and bon», «tour and toun», «high and low» (104-105). There are many of these inclusive pairs in the *Zifar*, but as they will be discussed in detail along with synonymous pairs in the next chapter, their existence is merely noted here.

The second major type of expletive is defined by Crosby as:

> certain words and phrases, entirely redundant, which serve no purpose but that of rhyme tags. Among those often repeated are «to speke with tonge», «to see with eye», «to tell in my talking» (105).

Phrases of this type are encountered with great frequency in the *Zifar* where, of course, they do not serve as rhyme tags. The classification and analysis of these and other «physical» expressions in early literature has been the subject of an important article by C. C. Smith and J. Morris, which sheds a great deal of light on one of the most constant features of medieval style. [62] Smith and Morris show that many of these phrases were of legal origin and that the *juglares* used them to make their performance more vivid for their audience, since they enabled them to avoid abstractions. They also make the fascinating suggestion that the minstrels may well have enlivened their narrative at these points with appropriate gestures with, or directed at, the parts of the body that occur in these formulas. Some parts of the body, such as the heart and the hands, have a whole series of symbolic associations that appear to be

---

[62] «On 'Physical' Phrases». The *Zifar* is not one of the texts used in this study.

more or less universal. These the *juglar* could exploit by indicating his own heart or gesticulating with his own hands in the course of his recital. In the light of Smith and Morris' thesis, then, these «physical» phrases have a much more important artistic function in orally diffused poetry than Crosby suggests: they are certainly more than mere padding.

Many of the physical phrases in the *Zifar*'s battle scenes have parallels in similar scenes in the epic. These can be divided into various categories. First, there are those which describe the taking up or positioning of weapons, of which the most frequently used is «meter mano a su espada», which occurs nine times in the *Zifar* and six times in the *Poema de Mío Cid*. [63] Obviously related to this basic formula are the phrases «metió mano al estoque» (131.16) and «metió mano a una misericordia» (148.4-5). Other physical expressions in this category include «puso la lança so el sobaco/ braço» (60.28, 194.4, 407.29), «tomó su escudo ante pechos» (197.13-14) and «teniendo alçado el braço con el espada» (200.13-14). The simple mention of a man bearing a weapon is often accompanied by the strictly superfluous «en la mano», as in «él tomó dos piedras en las manos e su espada» (138.21), «su espada en la mano» (19.3-4, 278.15). This again appears to be a reminiscence of epic style. [64]

Secondly, there are in the *Zifar* a number of references to physical action and gesture in battle that do not involve weapons, such as «non creo que con esa mano derecha me amenazedes» (207.11), «fízole fincar las manos sobre la çerviz del cavallo» (406.20), «bolvieron las espaldas» (500.5).

Thirdly, many physical phrases are used to denote the direction of a blow, the position of a wound or the nature of a punishment. The head seems to have been the favourite target for violence; apart from six cases of «cortar la cabeça», [65] and variations on the phrase «diole un golpe en la cabeça» (28.10-11, 148.10-11, 216.4-5), there also occur «le atronó la cabeça» (406.19), «fendió la cabeça fasta en los ojos» (497.15), «mandóle tajar la cabeça» (502.12-13), «arrancóle la cabeça» (503.1). Other parts of the body suffer too, however, as is illustrated by numerous gory examples of mutilation and wounding: «le metió la lança por el costado» (147.7-8), «dióvosla en la barba» (217.5), «mando que vos saquen la lengua por el pescueço» (225.2-3), «quebrantóse las çervizes» (288.25), «diole tan grand golpe sobre el braço derecho» (406.22), «cortó el braço diestro» (497.14), «quebrantóle amos adós los ojos» (216.3), «los ojos quebrados» (214.20-21, 215.2-3), «semejava que los sacava los coraçones

[63] *Zifar*: 28.10, 95.23, 129.11, 147.9, 186.15, 198.18, 198.25, 212.25, 493.12; *PMC*: 500, 746, 1722, 2387, 3642, 3648. Smith and Morris, «Phrases», 140, note that this phrase does not occur in any battle description in *clerecía* and that it appears as «poner/ echar mano a» in chronicle prosifications of epic poems. This is the form in 493.12, which comes from MS. *P*.

[64] Cf. *PMC* 757, 790, 1745, 2413.

[65] 225.4, 400.9, 401.13, 406.9, 407.12, 453.13.

e los comía» (240.4). The most extensive and graphic illustration of detailed emphasis on physical violence is the passage describing the mutilation inflicted on his permissive mother by the spoilt son as he is about to be executed:

> tomóla con amas adós las manos por las orejas a buelta de los cabellos, e fue poner la su boca con la suya, e començóla a roer e la comer todos los labros, de guisa que le non dexó ninguna cosa fasta en las narizes, nin del labro de yuso fasta en la barbiella, e fincaron todos los dientes descobiertos e ella fincó muy fea e muy desfaçada (285.27-286.6).

In the scenes of violence in his romance the *Zifar* author is drawing on the most popular crowd-pulling motifs of the epic. [66] It is natural, therefore, that his descriptions of fighting and bloodshed should also reflect the techniques and formulas of the epic poets. [67] Learned and cultured men have often been very interested in warfare; usually at a comfortable distance. The poet of the *Libro de Alexandre* and Juan de Mena are but two of the many erudite authors who have revealed a developed taste for violent action and gory detail. The writer of the *Zifar*, too, in the words of María Rosa Lida de Malkiel, is «muy amigo de golpes y de batallas». [68] If such authors loved to depict bloodshed, there is no reason to suppose that their audience of private or semi-private readers was not equally fond of hearing about it. The replacement or reinforcement of a colourless abstract verb in the *Zifar* with a physical phrase is part of the author's attempt to make the scenes of violence as vivid as possible for the armchair-soldiers in his audience.

The same desire for concreteness of texture and vividness of detail probably explains the use of many similar physical expressions in the rest of the work, outside the battle scenes. Sometimes, of course, reference to a part of the body is inevitable; it is difficult to see how else the author could have conveyed his meaning in such cases as «alçó el pie del agua e mostrógelo» (227.12-13), «alçando las coçes, e púsole las manos sobre la cabeça» (109.22), «tenía el un braço sobre el conde Nasón ... e el otro braço sobre el visavuelo» (239.18-20), «a él aviénle soltado las manos»

---

[66] The fact that the best and most nearly complete surviving Spanish epic, the *PMC*, is very restrained in this respect does not alter the truth of this general statement. All the evidence points to a Spanish epic that was every bit as gory as its French and German counterparts; one thinks immediately, for example, of the vengeance scenes in the *Siete Infantes de Lara*. The *PMC*, then, is as atypical in its sobriety as it is in its «realism». Keith Whinnom, *Spanish Literary Historiography: Three Forms of Distortion* (Exeter, 1967), 16-17, suggests that the *PMC* was probably an artistic failure in its own day for precisely those reasons that make us value it today as a masterpiece.

[67] Battle formulas other than physical phrases are discussed in the next section of this chapter.

[68] *La idea de la fama en la Edad Media castellana* (México-Buenos Aires, 1952), 259.

(285.22), «el conde que la tovo por el braço» (424.22), «díxole a la oreja» (411.16), etc.

In other cases the *Zifar* author seems to have used a physical phrase in preference to a simple abstract verb that would have expressed his meaning equally well and more succinctly but, of course, less vividly. Thus, instead of *coger* we find «meter manos a/en/sobre», [69] and instead of *ver* «aver a ojo» or «aver/tener ante los ojos». [70]   There are numerous other similar periphrastic phrases, such as «les tolliera la lunbre de los ojos» (67.5), «ella fincó los ojos en él» (71.2-3), [71] «nunca partié los ojos dél» (421.13).

A particularly interesting periphrasis involving *ojo* is «tener ojo por/para/a», which occurs ten times in the *Zifar*. Its basic literal meaning is «to keep an eye on», «to watch out for», as in the following: «e todos tengamos ojo por el señor de la hueste» (58.30-59.1); «mas [Dios] non tiene agora ojo para ti para lo fazer» (123.7); «ca yo seré el primero que terné ojo al rey señaladamente» (405.1-2). This expression appears to be rare in Old Spanish texts: the only examples earlier than the *Zifar* quoted by Smith and Morris are from the *Estoria de España*, where it has the meaning of «to observe», «to gaze upon». [72]   The only time they document its use in the sense of «to keep an eye on» is in the mid-fourteenth-century *Proverbios morales* (666ab) of Sem Tob. The other seven occurrences of the phrase in the *Zifar* are all figurative, conveying the idea of «to concern oneself with», «to take notice of»: «ca çiertamente ojo tengo para trabajar e para ganar onrra» (253.21-22); «sienpre tienen ojo los omes más por el rey que por otro ninguno» (310.21-22); «el rey non tovo más ojo por aquella batalla ... fincó las espuelas al cavallo e fuyó» (408.5-8); «ay otra cosa más grave a que ternían los omes ojo» (439.22-23). [73]

Elsewhere the *Zifar* author is content to use a prepositional phrase involving a part of the body to strengthen an abstract verb. Most of these «specifiers» are entirely or largely redundant; their only purpose can be to give added visual quality to the narrative. Those expressions in which mention of the part of the body is totally superfluous (since no other part could conceivably be involved) include «llorar de los ojos» (twelve occurrences), [74] «ver a/al/por ojo» (four occurrences), [75] and «ver

---

[69]   129.20, 138.6, 222.18-19, 277.12-13, 391.21, 447.15, 448.11, 455.22, 474.24, 501.20.

[70]   «Aver a ojo»: 205.25; «aver/tener ante los ojos»: 224.22, 292.17-18.   See Smith and Morris, «Phrases», 156.

[71]   This is a particularly interesting case as it is immediately followed by an abstract verb expressing the same thing: «e començó lo a catar» (*catar*, of course, from *captare*, itself started out as a physical expression). Cf. *PMC* 2392, 2859; *Alex* 504a, 1008a; *Apol* 164a, 631b.

[72]   *PCG* 504.a.21, 597.a.6, 601.a.8 («Phrases», 157).

[73]   Cf. also 256.13-14, 355.9-10, 355.12.

[74]   40.16, 67.19, 69.14-15, 84.22-23, 379.15, 383.15, 434.19, 435.15, 437.11, 455.28, 477.21, 499.9.

[75]   «Ver a ojo»: 242.19, 349.20; «ver al ojo»: 17.26; «ver por ojo»: 420.33-34.

ante los ojos» (two occurrences). [76] These are precisely the kind of phrase that Crosby labels expletives; and, in view of their frequency in earlier Spanish epics and other works intended for oral presentation, it would seem reasonable to assume that here again the *Zifar* author is borrowing from the style of the minstrels. [77] Some other specifying phrases at first sight appear less tautologous, but closer examination reveals that they too are largely redundant, since the context makes it abundantly clear that no other part of the body could be involved:

> e salió una leona del montezillo e tomó en la boca el mayor [fijuelo] (85.18-19)

> le dixieron que su madre lo quería saludar e besar en la boca ante que muriese (285.13-14)

> dexatvos caer del cavallo, ca yo vos resçibiré en los mis braços (477.22-23)

> E el forno estando ardiente, lançáronlo dentro, e resçibiólo Nuestro Señor Jesu Cristo en sus manos, e quantos allí estavan lo vieron estar en medio del forno, e de cómmo lo tenía una criatura en las manos (496.1-4). [78]

In none of the above would the sense be seriously impaired if the prepositional phrase were omitted; but the visual quality would certainly be much reduced.

The same might be said of a further series of physical phrases in the *Zifar* which serve as a kind of stylized stage direction, preparing the hearer or reader for what is to follow. These phrases, which are also extremely common in the epic, achieve the status of formulas because the same gesture always introduces the same action. Thus, when someone is about to pray, the action is preceded by the suppliant's raising his hands to heaven: «alçó las manos ayuntadas contra el çielo e dixo asý: 'Señora Virgen Santa María...'» (67.7-8); «La señora de la villa alçó las manos a Dios e gradesçióle quanta merçed le feziera» (68.8-10); «E por esta buena

---

[76]   13.18, 268.9.

[77]   See Smith and Morris, «Phrases», 152-154. It is worth noting that of the twelve occurrences of «llorar de los ojos» in *M*, only eight appear in *P* and only six in *S*. The later texts either omit the phrase altogether (e.g. 84.22-23, 379.15) or content themselves with «llorando» (e.g. 383.15). This latter curtailment is commoner in *S* than in *P* (e.g. 437.11, 499.9). The *Zifar* also contains one occurrence of the apparently tautologous «confesar por la boca» (224.19), which seems to be connected with the «dezir por la boca» phrases noted by Smith and Morris («Phrases», 159-160). The physical element here, however, is necessary to distinguish oral from written confession.

[78]   Other examples of similar phrases are «resçebir en los braços» (65.12, 68.22), «aver/tener en los braços» (65.8, 92.22, 92.25, 188.16), «levar en la boca» (animal: 92.16-17, 181.9, 181.19, 182.8), «tomar en la boca» (animal: 187.23), «tirar con los dientes» (animal: 373.24-25), «besar en la boca» (285.10, 287.20, 441.18).

andança alçó las manos a Nuestro Señor Dios e gradesçióle quanta merçed le feziera» (97.23-25); «e ella alçó las manos a Dios e dixo asý: 'Señor, bendito sea el tu nonbre'» (105.20-22). [79]

The common verb *ver* which, as we have seen, is frequently strengthened by the addition of a prepositional phrase («a/por ojo», etc.) or replaced by a periphrasis («aver a ojo», etc.), may also be preceded by the concrete expression «alçó los ojos», particularly if the idea of «looking up» is implied: «el otro alçó los ojos e viole» (93.1); «alçó los ojos e vio la vela tendida» (97.3-4); «el rey alçó los ojos e vido una criatura muy fermosa ençima de la vela» (101.6-7); «la buena dueña alçó los ojos ... e vio estar ençima del mástel aquella criatura» (105.18-20). [80]

The change of speaker in a debate or council is indicated some thirteen times in the *Zifar* by the formula «levantóse (en pie) ... e dixo», as, for example: «Un cavallero de los de la villa, e de los muy poderosos, levantóse entre los otros e díxole: 'Cavallero estraño ...'» (48.28-29); «Levantóse un cavallero su vasallo, ome de Dios e de muy buen consejo, e fuele besar las manos, e díxole asý: 'Señor ...'» (63.13-14). [81] This formula may be an echo of the biblical (or generally Semitic) «X arose and ...»; but the *Zifar* author could equally well have imitated its frequent use by the epic poets. Similar phrases occur sixteen times in the *PMC*, the majority indicating a change of speaker. [82]

All these formalized gestures help to set the scene in clearly defined physical terms; the abstract notions of praying, looking and advising are given a framework of concrete reference. The same can be said of the physical phrases that are used in the *Zifar* to describe the external manifestations of an inner emotion. Besides simply telling us that someone is ashamed or afraid, the author often employs in addition a physical expression which helps us to visualize the character's emotional state more vividly:

> entró en acuerdo la buena dueña, e abrió los ojos e levantóse commo muger muy lasa e muy quebrantada (183.12-14) [83]

> E desque llegó la dueña a su fijo, abrió los braços commo muger muy cuytada e fuése para él (285.20-21)

> Desý abaxó los ojos la infante e púsolos en tierra, e non lo pudo catar con grant vergüença que ovo de lo que avía dicho (428.16-18)

[79] Cf. *PMC* 216, 1340, 1617, 2476, 2829, 3185, 3508. Most of these are accompanied by a further physical phrase such as «la cara se santigó» or «a la barba se tomó», but all of them introduce either a prayer or a solemn oath.

[80] Cf. «bolvió la cabeça e vio» (60.22, 85.20).

[81] Cf. 75.2, 160.18, 161.18, 247.4, 349.17, 349.22, 394.10, 437.7, 453.7, 487.1, 491.28.

[82] See de Chasca, *Registro*, 25.

[83] Recovery from a faint brought on by fear or grief is denoted by «abrir los ojos» on three other occasions: 26.12, 26.14, 67.6-7.

161

12

commoquier que grant pesar e grant tristeza ý ovo, non pudo
ser ygual désta; ca pero non se mesavan nin se rascavan, nin
davan bozes, a todos semejava que·l quebraran por los coraçones,
dando sospiros e llorando muy fuerte e poniendo las manos sobre
los ojos (429.22-26)

Abaxó los ojos en tierra el enperador commo cuydadoso, e la
enperatris le tomó las manos e besógelas muchas vegadas (470.7-9)

Çertas bien dio a entender el enperador que avía muy grant plazer
con él, ca le traýa el braço desuso (482.20-21).

The commonest of these «externalization» phrases in the *Zifar*, however,
is «dar bozes», which occurs no fewer than thirty-three times. [84] It is
used to convey the idea of grief, and is often combined with another
expression denoting the outward signs of grief, such as «fazer llanto».

In almost all the above cases it will be noticed that the physical phrase
is accompanied by an abstract adjective or verb that specifies precisely
what emotion is being revealed through movement or gesture. In other
cases, however, such definition is unnecessary, since certain physical
actions were already invested with a rich symbolic value that dated back
many centuries. This is especially true of the stylized gestures of feudal
homage—kneeling, hand- and foot-kissing, etc. In connection with this
ceremonial Smith and Morris write:

> The essence of the homage ceremony in feudal Europe was that
> the vassal (kneeling) placed his hands between those of his
> lord, an act by which the vassal symbolized his dependence
> and submissiveness and by which the lord symbolized protection
> and his wider power. Since the fief was involved, the act
> had suggestions of a property deal about it, and there resulted
> a wealth of phrases involving symbolism of the hand.... Similar
> phraseology was evolved in those parts of Spain where feudalism
> was established. Even in Castile and the western parts of Spain,
> where a strict feudalism was never implanted, some of the outward
> show and language of feudalism was adopted.... In the usage
> of Castile the chief symbolic act of submission was the kissing
> by the vassal of the lord's hand, not only on making or breaking
> the bond between the two, but also on many lesser occasions,
> such as when the vassal asked for, and again after he received,
> any kind of gift or favour («Phrases», 145-146).

Like the *PMC*,[85] the *Zifar* is rich in homage phrases such as «dexarse caer

[84]   26.7, 28.23, 65.9, 66.8, 85.19, 85.21, 87.2, 93.1, 94.35-95.1, 109.23, 124.16, 128.19,
137.18, 138.23, 139.4, 141.14, 143.18, 143.19, 148.18, 152.17, 186.8, 186.12-13, 197.2,
197,5 197.7, 225.21, 241.4-5, 285.2, 377.13, 405.6, 429.24, 478.23, 497.8.
[85]   See de Chasca, *Registro*, 24-26.

a sus pies» (four occurrences), [86] «fincar los ynojos» (fifteen occurrences), [87] «besar las manos» (twenty-seven occurrences) [88] «besar el pie/los pies» (four occurrences), [89] and «prometer en las manos» (three occurrences), [90] Usually two or three of these are combined in a description of the act of homage:

> E fue fincar los ynojos ant'el rey e besóle la mano e díxole asý: «Señor...» (204.26-205.1)

> Allý se dexaron caer a los sus pies Garfín e Roboán, e besáronle las manos muchas vezes (210.17-18)

> E quiso le besar las manos e los pies, e ella non los quiso dar, ante le dixo: «Aun tienpo verná» que ella gelos besaría a él (429.11-13)

> E quando el infante entró por el palaçio do estava la enperadriz, fueron a él los reyes e fincaron los ynojos ant'él e besáronle los pies. E quando llegó el ynfante a la enperadriz, quiso le bessar las manos, e ella non gelas quiso dar, ante lo fue tomar por la mano e fuelo a posar cabe ella (460.1-5).

The last quotation introduces another *mano* phrase which occurs with some regularity in the *Zifar*, «tomar por la mano». This is always a symbolic ceremonial gesture implying intimacy, affection and respect, usually on the part of a superior towards a person of lower status. When the unfortunate Grima, for example, arrives in Orbín in her boat, the king and queen recognize that she is under God's protection and worthy of their respect. The author describes the scene of Grima's presentation to the Queen of Orbín thus:

> E desý salió el rey de la galea e tomó la dueña por la mano e dixo asý: «Reýna, resçebit estas donas que vos Dios enbió, ca bien fío por la su merçed que por esta dueña verná mucho bien a nós e a nuestra tierra e a nuestro regno.» «E yo en tal punto la resçibo», dixo la reýna, e tomóla por la mano, e fuéronse para el palaçio e toda la gente con ellos (101.17-23).

Intimacy between an overlord and a vassal who has rendered him, or is about to render him, special service is also denoted by «tomólo por la mano» (79.24, 239.10). When the Cavallero Atrevido arrives at the

[86] 210.17, 250.22, 379.14-15, 435.18-19.
[87] 70.8, 101.8, 175.16, 205.1, 206.1, 400.19-20, 413.34, 437.11, 439.7, 460.2-3, 477.15, 477.21, 495.14, 495.35, 499.8.
[88] 63.14, 100.15, 183.22, 199.14, 205.1, 205.2, 206.1-2, 210.8, 210.18, 229.16, 248.2, 252.4-5, 429.11-12, 457.18, 457.22, 460.4, 463.16, 463.16-17, 465.12, 465.13, 465.13-14, 465.19 (twice), 470.2, 470.6-7, 470.9, 482.8.
[89] 429.11-12, 459.29, 460.3, 488.4.
[90] 2.28-29, 3.13-14, 272.1.

163

Enchanted Lake, he is led by the hand by the queen of the underwater kingdom into her realm (227.16-17). After their wedding the fearless knight and his fairy bride are solemnly led to their marriage-bed by two *donzellas* «que tomaron por las manos la una al cavallero e la otra a la señora» (231.16-17). Finally, the symbolic linking of hands in the wedding ceremony is described with the same phrase when the female ruler of Galapia marries the son of her former enemy: «Allý se tomaron por las manos e fueron oýr misa a la capiella» (81.4-5).

Another physical phrase which, like «tomar por la mano», usually symbolizes an overlord's respect for a vassal is «levantóse a él/ella/ellos». Distinguished guests, ambassadors and visitors are greeted in this formal fashion twelve times in the *Zifar*.[91] This formula, too, has precedents in the epic.[92]

Insult, the opposite of respect, also has its appropriate physical gesture in the pulling of one's adversary's beard, the symbol of his honour and his manhood.[93] References to beard-pulling occur only twice in the *Zifar*, and in both cases it is a threat rather than an action:

> «Çertas», dixieron los otros, «bien cuyda este cavallero que desçercaremos nós este rey por sus palabras apuestas. Bien creedes que lo non faremos fasta que·l tomemos por la barva» (144.19-21)

> e avía jurado de nunca se partir de aquella çerca fasta que tomase al rey por la barba (168.17-19).

The *Zifar* author, then, seems to draw heavily on the stylistic techniques of the oral poets and minstrels in his extensive use of physical phrases not only to express action and gesture, but also to give external and visual form to abstract concepts such as grief, affection and loyalty. The appreciation of the symbolic potential of parts of the body that is involved in this latter procedure can also be seen in the many physical formulas in the *Zifar* that are purely metaphorical, an appreciation that may also derive from the study of the work of the *juglares*. Not surprisingly, most of these metaphorical phrases concern the hand and the heart, which are still the source of many figurative expressions in modern speech, such as «to lend a hand» or «to put one's heart into it».

Smith and Morris remind us that «the basic symbolic value of the hand is at all times that of 'power', since in a hand dealing a blow or wielding a sword a man's physical strength is made most visible» («Phrases», 139). The hand as the symbol of effort is seen in the *Zifar* in the phrase

---

[91]   48.14, 53.8, 73.14, 79.3, 99.1, 100.14-15, 162.11-12, 206.2, 277.12, 387.15, 391.6, 429.16.

[92]   E.g. *PMC* 3108.

[93]   See Smith and Morris, «Phrases», 161-162.

164

«poner las manos contra»: «avía a poner las manos contra aquéllos que·l querían deseheredar» (273.16-17). Elsewhere, however, *mano* represents a more abstract form of power, as in «ca en la tu mano es de me conprar o non» (492.19-20). The power, of course, may be that of an enemy, in which case the *manos* are usually qualified as *malas:* «tovo que era cayda en manos malas e que la querían escarnesçer» (94.11-12); «Dios nos guarde de malas manos de aquí adelante» (170.15-16); «rogando a Nuestro Señor Dios que ayudase a los suyos e los guardase de manos de sus enemigos» (408.28-29); «la condesa cuydó que avía caýdo en malas manos» (494.4-5).

Another aspect of hand symbolism is described by Smith and Morris thus:

> If the hand is ritually laid on a thing or a person to indicate the assertion of power over it or him, the raising of the hand indicates the ending of that power.... The idea of «release» appears frequently as *dar de mano*, a phrase deriving from a ritual movement of the hand and strongly recalling the process which produced *emancipare* and *manumittere*. [94]

«Dar de mano» occurs five times in the *Zifar*, all in the space of two pages. [95] Oddly enough, however, all these instances appear in the *exemplum* of the Hunter and the Lark; nowhere in the romance is «dar de mano» used in a military or political context.

The notion of escaping from someone's power is also expressed in phrases involving the symbolism of the hand. Unlike «dar de mano», «salir de (las) mano(s)» [96] and «escapar de sus/tus manos» [97] do occur in true epic-style episodes. One interesting point about these phrases, however, is that in the similar examples quoted by Smith and Morris («Phrases», 141) from other texts (the *Apolonio, Mocedades de Rodrigo* and various ballads), *mano* is invariably used in the singular, whereas in every case but two the *Zifar* author uses *manos*. [98] This perhaps suggests that the accepted symbolism of *mano* was on the wane by the early fourteenth century and had to be reinforced with the more «realistic» plural.

The notions of possession and protection, closely related to that of power, are also expressed in *manos* phrases: «vedes quán fermosa criatura me traxo Dios a las manos» (93.11); «E pues en vuestro poder so e me

[94] «Phrases», 141. Examples are given from *PMC* 1035b, 1040; *Alex* 577d; *PCG* 534.a.12.

[95] 259.17, 259.20-21, 260.3, 260.11, 260.18.

[96] 80.18, 361.7, 361.9, 467.1, 467.26, 476.25.

[97] 261.16, 497.11-12. There is also one example of «desapoderóse de las manos» (465.17).

[98] The exceptions are «salir de mano» in 361.9 and 476.25. The first of these occurs in a borrowing from the *Flores* (ley XXXIII), which is found in *M* only. Knust's edition of the *Flores* (in *Dos obras didácticas y dos leyendas* [SBE XVII, Madrid, 1878], 68-69) has *manos*. In 476.25 both *P* and *S* read *manos*.

tenedes [*PS* en las manos], guardatme bien e non tiredes la mano de mí e non me querades perder» (466.25-27); «mientre me tenedes entre manos, guardatme bien que vos non salga della [*sic*]» (467.24-25). The idea of possession is also present in two other interesting metaphorical phrases involving *mano:* «andar de mano en mano» (234.22) meaning «to have many lovers», and «encoger las manos» (367.16-17) which is exactly equivalent to the English idiom «tight-fisted».

It is apparent, then, that the *Zifar* author is fully conscious of the rich symbolic associations of *mano*, established by the lawyers and consecrated as a poetic device by the epic poets and minstrels. The fact that the majority of these metaphorical expressions occur in dialogue indicates further the author's concern for vividness and concreteness of texture where it is felt to matter most.

By far the most numerous metaphorical physical phrases involve the heart, which has always enjoyed and still enjoys great symbolic importance in man's language. The wide range of associations conveyed by *coraçón* in early Spanish writers [99] is strongly represented in the *Zifar*. One of the most basic concepts expressed in *coraçón* is courage or determination, as in the following examples:

> E este atal es esforçado e de buen coraçón, teniendo sienpre razón e derecho, que es cosa que esfuerça más el coraçón para yr por su fecho adelante (351.7-9)

> Ca el que una vegada bien andante es, créçele el coraçón e esfuérçase para yr enpós de las otras buenas andanças (416.14-16)

> E allí cobraron grand coraçón para servir a su señora la ynfanta (422.9-10). [100]

We have already noted that expressions such as «de buen coraçón», meaning courageous, are frequently used as formulas of character description in the *Zifar*.

The heart also symbolizes the innermost part of the being; it is used in the *Zifar*, as in other texts, to represent both the intellectual and emotional centre of the personality. First, as a symbol of mind and reason—«los sesos pobladores son del coraçón» (341.24)—*coraçón* expresses the notion of one's most secret thoughts:

> E bien es verdat que non ay cosa en el mundo tan deletosa para el ome commo aver ome buen amigo con quien pueda fablar las sus poridades e descubrir su coraçón seguramente (325.24-27)

[99]   See Smith and Morris, «Phrases», 169-174. In the analysis of the use of *coraçón* in the *Zifar* I follow the categories established by Smith and Morris.

[100]   Other examples of *coraçón* used to denote courage include «creçióle el c.» (441.2), «con fuerça de c.» (192.3), «con grant mengua de c.» (25.20). Cf. *PMC* 1655; *Alex* 12c, 2411b.

E çiertamente en el bejayre del ome se entiende muchas vegadas lo que tiene en el coraçón (399.10.12)

E el enperador quando esto oyó refrenóse e non le quiso demandar lo que tenía en coraçón (473.16-18). [101]

Secondly, *coraçón* may stand for memory:

ca el enemigo, maguer que perdona a su enemigo, non pierde del su coraçón el antigo dolor que ovo por el mal que resçibió (326.25-327.1)

E porende vos digo, míos fijos, que non olvidedes el bienfecho resçebido, ca, ¡mal pecado! pocos coraçones se mienbran de lo pasado (358.9-11).

Thirdly, *coraçón* is used as the agent of presentiments and premonitions, the voice of inner certainty:

E çertas quiero que sepades que tan aýna commo contastes estas palabras que vos dixiera vuestro avuelo, sy es cordura o locura, tan aýna me sobieron en coraçón, e creo que han de ser verdaderas (35.10-13)

mas el coraçón me da que a grant estado avedes a llegar e grant señor avedes a ser (133.16-17). [102]

Fourthly, *coraçón* is used as the equivalent of conscience:

E maravíllome seyendo tan buen cavallero commo dizen que sodes, commo vos sufre el coraçón de vos estar aquí en la cama a tal priesa commo ésta (51.6-8)

E después que a Dios ovierdes demandado consejo e ayuda sobre los vuestros fechos, luego en pos él demandaredes a vós mesmos, e escodriñaredes bien vuestros coraçones, e escogeredes lo que vierdes que sea mejor (322.15-18)

ca el que bien creyente es, en el coraçón tiene las espinas para se acordar della [de la fe] e de los mandamientos de Dios (331.1-3).

[101] For a similar usage of *coraçón*, see 17.2-3, 35.19-20, 170.5-6, 322.12, 333.25-26. Cf. also *SMill* 429a; *Milag* 190a, 345b; *Alex* 897b; *PFG* 639d.
[102] Cf. «el coraçón me da» (381.11), «el coraçón le dava» (441.1-2, 382.24), «vos subió al coraçón» (383.5), «segunt el coraçón me dize» (425.4). Cf. also *PMC* 2767; *Sacr* 177d; *Apol* 647c.

Finally, an important group of phrases, such as «aver a coraçón», «meter en coraçón» and «poner en (el) coraçón», express the idea of will, desire or intention:

> Mas el diablo que se trabaja sienpre de mal fazer, metióme en coraçón en esta noche que le fuese matar (30.5-7)

> e creo que el que estas merçedes me fizo me puso en el coraçón de andar en esta demanda que vos diré en confesión (33.6-8)

> gradesco mucho a Dios quanta merçed ha fecho a vós e a nós oy en este día, en vos querer poner en coraçón de conosçervos que tenedes tuerto a esta dueña (63.15-17)

> mas los señores lo consentieron que fuese asý, porque los omes oviesen más a coraçón de yr en pos los enemigos por la ganançia que cuydavan ý fazer (203.24-27). [103]

There are a number of other expressions in the *Zifar* in which *coraçón* has this meaning of intention or will:

> ¿Qué coraçón te movió a conosçer la muerte de aquel ome bueno, pues en culpa non eras? (30.19-20)

> e non prometades lo que non podierdes conplir nin tovierdes en coraçón de dar (265.7-9). [104]

As well as being the seat of the intellect and reason, the heart is also, perhaps somewhat paradoxically, the seat of the emotions. [105] But, of course, not all emotions are evil, as the *Zifar* author himself tells us: «del coraçón salen todas las malas cosas e las buenas» (303.20-21). Nevertheless, the *Castigos del rey de Mentón* in particular is full of warnings about the wicked tendencies of the heart and the need to control them:

> E punad en ser con omes de buena fe, ca ellos raen de los coraçones la orín de los pecados (265.10-11)

> La guarda del coraçón es guardarse de grant codiçia de onrras e de riquezas e deleytes (303.1-2) [106]

---

[103] There are many other examples of these phrases: «aver a coraçón»: 3.29, 51.4, 277.4-5; «meter/poner en (el) coraçón»: 89.14, 95.14, 101.1-2, 272.4, 272.5, 273.2, 275.15, 275.19, 287.21, 381.18, 466.22.

[104] Other phrases in which *coraçón* is used in the same way are to be found in 34.17, 354.25, 486.11-12.

[105] Medieval and Renaissance medical writers devote much space to describing the physical effects on the heart of various emotions; see J. B. Bamborough, *The Little World of Man* (London-New York-Toronto, 1952), especially pp. 88-90, 120-129.

[106] Variations of the phrase «guardar el coraçón» are also found in 302.27-28, 303.7, 303.12, 303.25-26.

Refrene en sý el rey primeramente la luxuria, e apremie la avariçia, e abaxe la sobervia, e eche de su coraçón todas las otras manziellas (303.16-18).

The wicked impulses must be replaced by good ones:

sola nobleza es aquélla que guarneçe e orna el coraçón de buenas costunbres (263.18-19)

non partades los vuestros coraçones de la bondat de Dios (301.10).

The references to the heart as the seat of the emotions, however, are not confined to generalities. In the Middle Ages, as now, the heart was regarded as the home of love. The *Zifar* contains a number of illustrations of this idea:

a las vegadas estando con el un amador, tiene el coraçón en el otro que vee pasar (237.1-3)

mas nunca a tal ora yredes que las telas del mi coraçón non levedes conbusco, e fincaré triste e cuytada pensando sienpre en vós (384.5-7) [107]

E veo que vós queredes yr, non aviendo piedat de mí mesquina cuytada, desanparada de las cosas que más amo, cuyo amor del mi coraçón non se puede partir en ningunt tienpo fasta la muerte (475.26-476.2). [108]

The heart is also the symbolic centre of many other emotions and instincts:

Fear

con reçelo que tenía en mi coraçón (69.1)

por justiçia se aseguran los coraçones de los medrosos (308.19).

Anger

ca con la saña está torvado el coraçón del ome (322.21).

Greed/Envy

quedará la codiçia del coraçón; ca lo que vee el ojo desea el coraçón (115.9-10) [109]

---

[107] The phrase «telas del coraçón» also occurs in *PMC* 2578, 2785.

[108] Other references to *coraçón* as the seat of love include 237.4-6, 313.12, 370.4-5, 385.14-15, 472.25-26, 472.28.

[109] Other instances of «codiçia del coraçón» include 303.4, 303.10, 303.13-14.

el dar quebranta e vençe los coraçones muy rezios de los omes, mayormente de los codiçiosos; ca los dones grandes enlazan los coraçones de los cubdiçiosos e de los cabdiellos muy fuertes e crueles (366.18-22).

Cruelty

Atán grant es la crueldat en vuestro coraçón contra mí (477.8-9).

Pain/Grief

tomavan grant pesar en sus coraçones (87.10)

E sy en la uña del pie vos dolierdes, dolermê yo en el coraçón (166.7-8)

commoquier que en algunas palabras que vos yo dixe me fería cruelmente en el coraçón (238.19-20)

E la enperatris ovo muy grant pesar en su coraçón (474.20-21). [110]

Joy

tomando grant plazer en su coraçón (34.13-14)

ca bien así commo el coraçón se deleta con las buenas obras, así el alma se deleta con los consejos del buen amigo (325.22-24)

aquél que non puede aver folgura en su coraçón (513.14).

Finally, there is considerable use of the adverbial phrase «de coraçón» in the *Zifar*. Smith and Morris discuss its function in Old Spanish:

> This phrase is used with a great variety of verbs, and serves to intensify any emotion or act expressed.... The use of the adverbial *de corazón* must have begun when it was attached to certain verbs of emotion, a gesture to the heart accompanying the spoken word («Phrases», 172).

In the *Zifar*, as in the earlier texts, «de coraçón» occurs most frequently with *plazer* and *pesar:* «plazer de coraçón» appears twelve times, [111] «pesar de coraçón» seventeen times. [112] A little surprisingly, perhaps, *amar* is only once reinforced by «de coraçón» (206.3). When used with

---

[110] There are many other references to pain and grief being felt in the heart: e.g. 94.13, 104.13, 335.10, 363.11, 411.9-10, 429.25, 433.12, 468.11-12, 469.2, 476.16.

[111] 31.24, 42.11, 46.3, 93.16-17, 190.1, 193.4, 248.18, 251.16, 252.8, 390.22, 430.21, 511.20. Cf. *PMC* 1184, 1355, 1455, 1947, 2648, 2881, 3019, 3120, 3434.

[112] 15.28, 18.18, 24.8, 42.5, 66.5, 84.1 [*PS*], 87.5, 93.26-27, 150.9, 183.4, 394.25, 424.14, 434.20, 454.16, 475.19, 482.14-15, 497.17. Cf. *PMC* 2317, 2815, 2821, 2954, 2959.

non-emotional verbs such as *dezir* (210.19-20), *morder* (351.10) or *reýr* (483.20), the phrase has clearly lost much of its original force and means little more than modern English «heartily», although some emotional content probably survives in «perdonar de coraçón» (79.7) and «obedesçer de coraçón» (318.7). The adverbial phrase «de un coraçón», signifying agreement, occurs twice in the *Zifar* (203.1, 403.15). [113]

Apart from *mano* and *coraçón*, there are a few other parts of the body that are used in metaphorical expressions in the *Zifar*. Just as the heart must be *guardado* against evil thoughts and desires, so the tongue must be kept from speaking evil words: «la lengua del rey mucho deve ser çerrada e guardada en lo que oviere a dezir» (304.25-26). [114] On one occasion *braços* is used in the sense of supporters, «right-hand men»: when his two sons are killed in battle the King of Ester is said to have lost «los mejores dos braços que él avía» (154.10). The metaphorical use of *braço* occurs three times in the *PMC* (753, 810, 3063) but, except for the prosification of line 753 in the *PCG*, nowhere else in the chronicles, the ballads or the works of the *mester de clerecía*. [115]

The evidence suggests that in his widespread use of physical phrases, literal, symbolic and figurative, the *Zifar* author is imitating an important aspect of the style of his epic predecessors. A very large proportion of these formulas, as we have seen, occur in epic-type situations—battles, councils, homage ceremonies, etc. Their effectiveness, of course, is bound to be less in a work intended for private or semi-private consumption than in a poem designed for mass oral dissemination by a professional *juglar* who would have both the training and the opportunity to underline his physical references by the use of his own body, thus making his narrative more immediate and visual to his rapt audience. A gentleman's library does not lend itself to extravagant pantomimic gesture to anything like the same extent as the market place or even the large baronial hall. Nevertheless, the *Zifar* author, by a controlled imitation of the minstrels' technique in the matter of physical phrases, has achieved a vividness and concreteness that would have been difficult to achieve by other means. By using the familiar formulas that his readers would presumably be well acquainted with, he exploits already formed habits of mind and so perhaps manages to convey in his own very different work something of the excitement and stark grandeur of the epic.

Of the physical phrases in the *Zifar* outside epic-type situations most occur in the *Castigos*, where they have an equally important but somewhat different role to play. The predominant tone of this third book is necessarily abstract and static, in striking contrast to the chivalric narratives

---

[113] Cf. also «los entendimientos e las voluntades e los coraçones serán unos» (472.24-25). The phrase «de un coraçón» occurs in *PFG* 252d, 308c 368c; *PCG* 353.b.11.

[114] Cf. also 290.15, 302.28, 304.4.

[115] Smith and Morris, «Phrases», 150.

surrounding it. We have already noted (in chapter 4) how the author prepares the reader as carefully as possible for the journey to the abstract plane, so that the change of ambience is not too abrupt. Moreover, it is no accident that seventeen of the work's twenty-eight *exempla* are to be found in the *Castigos*, where their function is not only to express abstract concepts in more concrete form, but also to keep in the reader's mind the everyday world of flesh and blood creatures that he has temporarily left, but to which he will return. The constantly recurring address to «míos fijos» fulfils much the same purpose. The greater incidence of concrete similes and metaphors in the *Castigos* again seems the result of deliberate policy, [116] and the same policy probably lies behind the inclusion in Book III of so many physical phrases, especially the figurative use of *coraçón:* their function is to reduce an abstract concept to more concrete and visual terms, and at the same time to remind us of the real world. The *Zifar* author seems to have learned much from the *Flores de filosofía* in this respect. The *Flores* abounds in metaphors and similes and physical phrases, many of which are simply incorporated into the *Castigos*. [117] But the romance-writer has also made some interesting contributions of his own along the same lines, as, for example:

> E sabet que la lengua es sergenta del coraçón, e es atal commo el pozal que saca el agua del pozo (305.28-30)

> ca bien commo la grant llaga del cuerpo non puede sanar, sy non con grandes e fuertes melezinas, asý commo por fierro o por quemas, asý la maldat de aquéllos que son endureçidos en pecado, non se pueden toller sy non en grandes sentençias syn piedat (312.5-9)

> bien asý commo el rayo del çielo quebranta por fuerça las peñas, asý el dar quebranta e vençe los coraçones muy rezios de los omes (366.17-20).

(iv) *Other Formulas*

Crosby's fourth type of excessive repetition is what she calls formulas, by which she means the stock expressions that are not phrases of direct address, introduction or description, or expletives, but which, like all these, are common to a number of poets and betray heavy reliance on a

---

[116] A very rough count shows that Book I contains some thirteen similes and metaphors, Book II four, Book III twenty-five and Book IV four.

[117] E.g. metaphors and similes: 293.17-19 (*ley* XXXVI), 294.3-4 (XXXVI), 294.10-11 (XII), 295.20-296.1 (XX), 296.6-8 (XX), 297.5-7 (XXXVII), 297.14-15 (XXXVII); physical phrases: 338.12 (XXXIV), 290.16 (XIII), 360.23 (XXXIII), 291.4 (XIII), 318.7-8 (VI), 341.24 (XXXI), 265.10-11 (XVII).

traditional store of ready-made clichés. [118] The *Zifar* contains many formulas and formulaic phrases other than the ones already discussed, but a full analysis of these would enlarge the present chapter beyond reasonable limits. It will be sufficient to examine some of the more significant stereotyped expressions in the romance, which again suggest a stylistic debt to the earlier oral poets.

As with the physical phrases, a good place to start the examination is the battle scenes where, in view of the epic motifs present, one would expect most reflections of epic style. The spurring on of horses, for example, is a common element in both the *PMC* and the *Zifar*, either as a prelude to battle or to convey the notion of great haste. In the *PMC* we find «aguijan a espolón» (232-233, 2009, 2693, 2775), «batién los cavallos con los espolones» (3618), «espolonó el cavallo» (711). The *Zifar* also has a basic formula for this activity and a number of variants: «fincó/fincaron las espuelas al cavallo» occurs six times, [119] and «ferió de las espuelas al cavallo» (198.3), «espoloneando el cavallo» (213.13) and «tocó un poco del espuela al cavallo» (478.6-7) occur once each.

A group of formulaic expressions that is not found in the *PMC* concerns falling to the ground during battle. The phrase «(dexarse) caer en tierra» appears nineteen times altogether in the *Zifar*, [120] «(dexarse) caer del cavallo» appears five times, [121] and «caer de la siella» once (288.24-25). The *PMC*'s «en tierra lo echó» (3686) is reflected in the *Zifar*'s four occurrences of «dio con él en la tierra» [122] and one occurrence of «sacudiólo en tierra» (495.20).

The delivery of blows is expressed through a variety of formulas. In the *PMC* the most frequent are «dar (grandes) golpes» (nine occurrences) and «irlos ferir» (three occurrences). [123] In the *Zifar* there are fifteen examples, including variations, of the basic formula «dar golpes». [124] Sometimes the weapon used to strike the blow is mentioned: for instance, «dieron seños golpes con las lanças» (147.4), «diéronse muy grandes golpes de las espadas» (213.20). [125] In other cases the target of the blows is explicitly stated: «diole un golpe en la cabeça» (28.10-11), «tan grand

---

[118] «Oral Delivery», 105-106. The term «formula» is used now according to the classic definition of Milman Parry, «Studies in the Epic Technique of Oral Verse Making. I: Homer and Homeric Style», *HSCP* XLI (1930), 73-147, at p. 80: «a group of words which is regularly employed under the same metrical conditions to express a given essential idea.» But see also Edmund de Chasca, «Toward a Redefinition of Epic Formula in the Light of the *Cantar de Mio Cid*», *HR* XXXVIII (1970), 251-263.

[119] 43.7-8, 61.3, 61.11-12, 147.2, 408.7-8.

[120] 40.16, 43.10-11, 65.10-11, 66.7-8, 82.21, 88.24-89.1, 107.7, 108.5, 149.11, 182.22-23, 200.16, 200.18-19, 214.4, 218.12-13, 262.14-15, 405.28, 406.26, 407.36-408.1, 497.16 [PS].

[121] 198.24-25, 201.15, 405.28, 477.22-23, 497.12.

[122] 61.5-6, 142.5, 147.8-9, 407.31.

[123] See de Chasca, *Registro*, 19-20.

[124] 28.10-11, 147.4, 147.10, 148.10-11, 198.25-26, 199.24, 200.14-15, 213.7, 213.20, 213.22-23, 216.4-5, 406.17-22 (3 times), 497.15.

[125] Cf. «dar una espadada» (216.2), «dar una lançada» (61.4, 147.7, 198.19).

golpe le dio ... ençima del yelmo» (406.18-19), «diole tan grand golpe sobre el braço derecho» (406.22). [126]   In a few instances both the weapon used and the target are specified: «que·l dio un golpe del espada ençima de la cabeça» (216.4-5).   Clearly related to the «dar golpes» group of formulas is the phrase «fazer un golpe/golpes», which occurs six times, twice accompanied by «con la espada». [127]

Ferir is used in a number of apparently formulaic expressions in the *Zifar*, of which the commonest is «fuelo ferir» (ten occurrences). [128] Variants involving *golpe(s)* also appear, as in the following: «començólo a ferir en la cabeça de muy grandes golpes con la misericordia sobr'el almofa» (148.8-9); «el conde ferió del espada un grant golpe al cavallo de Garfín en el espalda» (198.22-23); «ferió el puerco al cavallo en la mano diestra» (465.4-5).   Reciprocal wounding is twice expressed by *ferirse* (142.1, 408.2).

It will already be apparent that one of the notable features of the *Zifar* author's use of formulas is the variety that he introduces into the basic stereotype, an element of his technique we have already noted in connection with other aspects of his style.   This diversity can be seen very clearly in a group of phrases concerned with the piercing of an opponent's defences in battle.   The following obviously related expressions appear only once in the work: «falsar el escudo» (198.20), «fender el escudo» (199.1), «pasar el escudo» (142.1-2), «falsar las guarniçiones» (147.8), «pasar las guarniçiones» (142.4), «cortar las guarniçiones» (406.23), «enpesçer por las guarniçiones» (148.3-4), «enpesçer por las armaduras» (213.21).   Because of their infrequency none of these can be called formulaic in themselves, but they fairly clearly derive from a single basic formulaic concept. [129]

The same is true of the adverbial phrase «de rezio» which, in the *Zifar*, seems to fulfil the same function as the epic formula «d'alma e de coraçón». [130]   «Ferir (muy) de rezio», which occurs eleven times, [131] is clearly formulaic, but there is a whole series of derivatives used only once or twice that the author appears to have devised along the lines of the basic model: «(a)cometer de rezio» (68.3, 362.4), «conbatir de rezio» (158.24), «defender de rezio» (59.21, 405.15), «aguijar de rezio» (197.2). There are a few other expressions, such as «comer de rezio» (21.20, 21.26), «rascar de rezio» (215.9) and «sobir de rezio» (240.10-11), which fall

---

[126]   Cf. «dar una pescoçada» (217.3, 217.26, 420.14, 440.8).

[127]   216.4, 350.20-21, 350.26, 497.10; with «con la espada» (405.22, 406.2-3).

[128]   61.3, 61.12, 63.2-3, 95.22-23, 194.4-5, 212.20, 407.29, 465.4, 497.13, 500.4.

[129]   Albert B. Lord, *The Singer of Tales*, considers a phrase formulaic if it occurs twice; Ruth House Webber, *Formulistic Diction in the Spanish Ballad* (UCPMPh XXXIV, 2, Berkeley-Los Angeles, 1951) only classes an expression as a formula if it occurs five times; Edmund de Chasca's criterion for his *Registro* is three occurrences (owing to the much smaller number of lines in the *PMC* than in the *romancero*).

[130]   See de Chasca, *Registro*, 39-40.

[131]   59.10, 132.18, 147.22-23, 158.18, 212.20, 212.22, 405.1, 405.8, 406.2, 407.35, 497.19.

outside the military sphere, but which nevertheless seem to have been formed by analogy with the formula «ferir de rezio».

This brief analysis of some of the formulas in the romance's battle scenes illustrates once more the stylistic similarities between the *Zifar* and earlier epic poetry. But this is not a case of blind imitation: although the author apparently borrows much of the basic formulaic language of his predecessors, one suspects that this is not primarily because he lacks imagination but because he wants his audience to orient itself easily within the familiar battle situation. His creative talents show in the way he uses a much wider variety of expression than the oral poets, ringing the changes on the familiar and creating new quasi-formulas on the basis of existing models.

In conclusion it will be enough to note a few other epic-type formulas that are extensively used in the *Zifar*. First, the phrase «pedir merçed», which occurs five times in the *PMC*, [132] turns up six times in the *Zifar*. [133] Much more frequent, however, is the variant form «pedir por merçed», which appears on no fewer than forty occasions. [134]

Another extremely common formula is «parar mientes en/a», of which the *PMC* provides us with only one example, [135] but which occurs on at least sixty-nine occasions in the *Zifar*. [136] This appears to be a more modern form of the phrase «meter mientes en», which is found in many thirteenth-century texts, [137] but which survives in only three places in the *Zifar*, all within the space of three pages. [138] It is noteworthy, however, that in all these cases the author is quoting from the *Flores de filosofía* (a thirteenth-century text) which frequently uses «meter mientes en». In other places where parts of the *Flores* are incorporated into the romance *meter* has been changed to *parar*, [139] which suggests that by the early fourteenth century «meter mientes en» was regarded as something of an archaism. This seems to be borne out by the fact that the three relics of the old idiom that survive in *M* have all been altered to «parar mientes en» in the later versions *P* and *S*.

---

[132] 1885, 2031, 2594, 3430, 3504.

[133] 3.21, 121.9, 285.5, 382.22, 488.21, 498.10.

[134] 93.14-15, 102.12, 102.16, 104.6-7, 147.20-21, 153.21, 176.22, 188.23-24, 188.24, 199.17, 205.3, 210.20, 240.22-23, 248.16, 249.21, 252.18, 253.6, 253.20, 275.1, 285.9-10, 288.5-6, 289.4, 401.7, 415.26, 417.6, 420.5, 422.10, 428.25, 429.4, 432.18, 433.12-13, 435.19, 437.26-27, 446.13, 474.23-24, 477.22, 496.11, 498.16, 506.11-12, 509.24.

[135] 2218. But cf. also *PFG* 525a.

[136] 1.10, 9.23, 12.8, 13.5-6, 22.19, 29.14-15, 57.19, 59.14-15, 62.23, 64.24, 90.3-4, 113.19, 119.2, 144.23, 145.1, 148.16, 151.17, 161.21, 175.18, 181.4, 215.3-4, 234.12, 258.26, 260.6, 263.3-4, 264.18, 273.3, 273.9-10, 273.13, 274.8-9, 275.13, 275.16, 290.1, 298.16, 300.6, 307.3-4, 322.3, 323.13-14, 326.15-16, 328.10, 339.9, 339.18, 344.6, 347.17, 350.14-15, 351.13, 356.3, 358.22, 368.19, 371.3, 373.3-4, 382.20, 391.10, 399.8, 411.7, 411.13, 420.31, 427.10-11, 465.16, 468.3, 471.1, 472.13, 476.17, 487.23, 489.3, 490.9-10, 491.29, 496.12, 500.17.

[137] E.g. *PMC* 3137; *Milag* 424b; *SMill* 1c; *Apol* 68c; *Alex* 13d.

[138] 359.14, 360.16, 361.10.

[139] E.g. 264.18, 323.13-14.

A common formula of honorific greeting in the *PMC* is «salir (a) reçebir». [140] The same stock phrase is used on twelve occasions in the *Zifar*. [141] It occurs no fewer than five times in the author's Prologue where he is describing the honour paid to the body of Cardinal García Gudiel on its journey through Spain.

The formula of assent «plazme», which is found throughout the *PMC*, [142] is also used extensively by the *Zifar* author. «Plázeme» or «plázenos» or «bien/mucho me plaze» occurs forty times in the romance, in exactly the same circumstances as in the *PMC*. [143] There is, however, one interesting difference: the epic poet tends to reinforce his «plazme» with the addition of «de coraçón» or «de veluntad», combinations which never occur in the *Zifar*, despite its wealth of *coraçón* phrases. The most usual form of the cliché is «mucho me plaze», which accounts for some seventeen of the forty examples in the work. [144]

Finally, both in the epic and in the *Zifar* there are a number of common phrases in which the name of God is invoked. «Por amor del Criador», for example, occurs seven times in the *PMC*; [145] «por amor de Dios» occurs ten times in the *Zifar*. [146] «Grado a Dios/al Criador/a Christus» appears twenty-nine times in the *PMC*; [147] the *Zifar* contains three examples of the exactly parallel «gradesco a Dios». [148] «(Asý) lo mande Dios/el Criador» turns up five times in the *PMC*, [149] and three times in the *Zifar*. [150] In both works every one of these phrases involving *Dios* is used in dialogue.

C. «EXCESSIVE REPETITION» - II

Crosby writes:

> The second group of repetitions is more significant in our study of oral delivery since it consists of those types of phrases which

[140] 1478, 1583, 1917, 2015, 2649, 2882, 2886.
[141] 4.25-26, 5.2, 5.3-4, 5.18, 5.21, 78.25, 216.18, 228.19-20, 385.18, 430.11, 457.21, 482.8.
[142] E.g. 180, 1355, 1947, 3052, 3434.
[143] 19.12, 23.2, 56.14, 63.25, 70.9, 74.19, 78.3, 80.1, 82.13, 85.12, 89.21, 111.24, 125.7, 125.12, 131.19, 135.6, 140.9, 142.24, 143.15, 155.20, 156.20-21, 157.12, 160.9, 176.24, 177.10, 177.23, 203.12, 232.23, 247.23, 259.19-20, 394.8, 395.6, 397.6, 420.7, 425.21-22, 447.23, 454.6, 462.29, 492.15, 499.29.
[144] There is also one example of «plázeme mucho» and one of «mucho nos plaze».
[145] 720, 1321, 2787, 2792, 3490, 3504, 3580.
[146] 15.23, 119.5, 138.5, 153.9, 252.24-25, 381.9, 409.9, 411.4, 423.15, 424.12.
[147] See de Chasca, *Registro*, 29-30.
[148] 22.22, 63.15, 130.21-22. Cf. also «gradéscavos(lo) Dios»: 35.8-9, 79.16, 455.17, 463.26.
[149] 1404, 1437, 2055, 2630, 3491.
[150] 89.9, 108.24, 110.13.

actually further the purpose of oral delivery by showing the relation of the poet or minstrel to his audience. This group consists of transitions, asseverations, and oaths («Oral Delivery», 106).

It is thus extremely interesting to find that in the case of these three types of repetition the *Zifar* is significantly less rich than in the other features of oral style so far examined in this chapter. If, as Crosby suggests, these three techniques underline the fact that the text is being presented orally to a mass audience, then their very inconspicuous presence or almost total absence in the *Zifar* perhaps strengthens her point that these are the really significant criteria by which to judge whether a work was orally diffused or not.

By «transitions» Crosby means such phrases as «Now we leave X and return to Y» which, as we have already seen (ch. 3, section D), abound in those romances with complex interwoven structures, where they serve as signposts when the narrative is about to take a significant new direction. We also noted, however, that the *Zifar* also employs a more subtle type of transitional technique and that the only examples of the simple bald formula, like those quoted by Crosby, are to be ascribed to a later copyist who incorporated them at various points in his chapter headings.

«Asseverations» are the frequently repeated assurances by a poet or minstrel that the story he is telling is a true one. Sometimes these assurances take the form of simple adverbs or adverbial phrases such as «certes», «douteless», «for sothe», etc. On other occasions they are a little more elaborate and refer to the source of the story, the authoritative Book, as in «als saith the book», «in romance as we rede», «l'escrit recorde», etc. The very frequent use of *çertas* has already been noted (ch. 2, section D (i)), but in almost every case, as we saw, this adverb occurs in dialogue and does not therefore form part of a direct statement of the author himself to his audience. Even when it is not used in conversation, *çertas* almost invariably introduces some moral platitude, the truth of which is self-evident, and which is not at all concerned with the reliability or otherwise of the story the author is telling us. The following examples illustrate this point:

> Çertas, vergüença e mayor mengua es en querer guardar el prometimiento dañoso e con desonrra, que en lo revocar (14.5-7)

> Çertas mucho se deven esforçar señores en dar buen galardón a aquéllos que lo meresçen (202.11-12)

> Çertas mester sería un infante commo éste en todo tienpo en las casas de las reýnas e de las dueñas de grant lugar que casas tienen (397.14-16).

177

Only very occasionally is *çertas* used to reinforce some comment made by the author on his story, and it is in this handful of cases that there is perhaps some echo of the minstrels' asseveration. The Ribaldo, for example, lights a fire to frighten off the wolves, an action which provokes the following comment from the author:

> E çertas bien sabidor era el ribaldo, ca de ninguna cosa non han los lobos tan grant miedo commo del fuego (133.4-6).

Again, after describing Seringa's virtues and qualities, the author remarks:

> E çertas mucho era de loar quando bien se mantovo después de la muerte de su padre, e quando bien mantovo su regno (390.7-9).

References to the work's source—which are very frequent in, for example, Berceo— [151] are confined in the *Zifar* to the stock phrase «dize el cuento», with the occasional variant «cuenta la estoria». But these, as we have seen, are not used to assert the truth and authority of the source, as they are in Berceo and other texts intended for oral diffusion; in the *Zifar* they serve largely as *incipit* formulas, signposting a new direction in the narrative or introducing a digression in the form of an *exemplum* or a supernatural episode (see ch. 3, section D). The only expressions in the work that invoke the authority of the Book are those such as «dize (en) la Santa Escriptura», «dize el sabio», «palabra es del sabio», etc. (see ch. 2, section D (ii)). But these phrases do not, of course, stress the truth of the narrative as a whole, but serve only to give the stamp of authority to the moral maxim they introduce. In any case, phrases of this type seem to derive from the tradition of wisdom literature, not from the oral poets.

Finally, Crosby notes the frequency in medieval literature of oaths such as «par ma foie», «pardee», «by Cristes ore», etc., and adds that «it is not only in conversation that the romances abound in oaths. They are used commonly in the narrative itself, another mark of its colloquial character» (108). In the *Zifar* we find two such expressions used with a certain regularity, «par/por Dios» and «mal pecado». But the forty-eight examples of the first of these occur without exception in dialogue, [152] and only seven of the twenty-two instances of the second are to be found in the mouth of the author himself. [153] Other expressions such as «por

---

[151] See Joaquín Artiles, *Los recursos literarios de Berceo*, 28-31.

[152] 15.29, 24.10, 40.20, 49.17, 51.18, 52.10, 56.17-18, 68.2, 104.14, 133.8, 150.25. 151.11, 151.24, 157.13, 159.23, 166.22, 170.9, 173.21, 176.16, 198.12, 203.11, 207.2-3, 207.22, 216.1, 234.8, 397.2, 400.6, 403.4, 409.14-15, 420.21, 420.30, 421.15-16, 422.33, 425.18, 425.21, 432.9, 436.2, 448.22, 462.29, 463.21, 464.11, 466.6, 472.16, 473.15-16, 490.9, 491.32, 502.24, 512.1.

[153] 13.10, 25.21, 35.2, 156.12-13, 168.4, 234.10, 234.20, 255.19, 275.3, 287.18, 321.9, 330.11, 337.9, 358.10, 384.8, 391.9, 397.19, 398.8, 432.3, 433.17, 455.3, 486.9.

amor de Dios», «bendito/loado sea Dios» and «en el nonbre de Dios», which are frequently encountered in the *Zifar*, [154] are used without exception in direct speech and with full realization of their seriousness.

D. CONCLUSIONS

From the material presented in this chapter it seems that the author of the *Zifar*, faced with the problem of creating a style for writing the first long prose romance in the vernacular, relied heavily for a considerable part of his literary technique on the conventions of the epic poets. All the features regarded by Crosby as typical of literature intended for oral diffusion are, as we have seen, to be found in this romance. Like his thirteenth-century predecessors, the learned poets of the *mester de clerecía* and the equally learned chroniclers directed by Alfonso X, the *Zifar* author chose to draw on the only existing vernacular style that had been developed into a successful vehicle for the narration of tales of heroic action; and certain advantages accrued.

First, the extensive use of formulas enabled the author to give his audience, already no doubt familiar with oral literature, a clear orientation. The *Zifar*, after all, is concerned with the great epic themes of prowess and honour and the glorification of a military hero of mythical proportions. It also, naturally enough, draws heavily on the epic motifs of battles, stratagems, distribution of rewards, councils, homage ceremonies, and so on. It is therefore not surprising that the author should use a style that also owes much to the epic, so that his audience should both feel at home in a familiar setting and also lend their assent to his story more readily. The minstrels and their poets had evolved a set of techniques and formulas that had proved adequate over and over again for the narration of epic deeds; for the *Zifar* author to try to ignore them or invent a totally new set would have been unnecessary at best and imprudent at worst.

Secondly, the large-scale use of those epic formulas which emphasize the concrete and the physical helps to give the narrative a vividness and «realism» that it might not otherwise have had. Smith and Morris have suggested that many of these stock phrases were deliberately used by the minstrels to give them an opportunity for gesture and mime during their performance. These «visual aids», as it were, would presumably be absent from a private or semi-private reading of the *Zifar*, but such things

---

[154] «Por amor de Dios» occurs ten times: 15.23, 119.5, 138.5, 153.9, 252.24-25, 381.9, 409.9, 411.4, 423.15, 424.12. «Bendito sea Dios», etc., occurs sixteen times: 63.4, 67.11, 77.26-27, 86.22, 90.18, 103.27, 103.28, 105.21-22, 147.18-19, 151.2-3, 193.5, 207.13-14, 288.13, 380.2, 409.33, 510.16. «Loado sea Dios» occurs nine times: 24.11, 66.1, 83.2, 105.6, 152.6, 253.6, 383.20, 387.19, 493.10. «En el nonbre de Dios» occurs sixteen times: 56.24, 64.8-9, 76.9-10, 100.11, 106.2, 142.20, 144.5, 158.4, 170.8, 196.20-21, 211.17, 322.14, 384.16, 404.32-33, 440.12, 447.16.

as the physical phrases and the battle formulas would still lend a more immediate quality and concrete texture to the work, which would increase its appeal to an audience living at a time when genuine oral delivery was still very much alive. Clearly the effect of these clichés would be less striking in a written text, but they would still amount to more than «dead remains of what had previously been a flourishing epic convention». [155] All the evidence suggests that the *Zifar* author is too conscious and thoughtful an artist to use anything that is merely a meaningless relic of an outmoded tradition.

Thirdly, since the basic structural pattern of the *Zifar* is one of parallelism and balance of episodes and motifs, the repetition of the same formulas in virtually identical situations in different parts of the work serves to underline the parallelism and to recall earlier events to the reader's mind.

There would seem to be, then, no need to make apologies for the *Zifar* author's use of formulas: they fulfil useful functions within the work and can be justified at least on the grounds outlined above. In view of this extensive indebtedness to the techniques of the minstrels, however, it may seem at first sight a little curious that the author largely ignores the last group of oral devices in Crosby's classification—transitions, asseverations and oaths. But it is precisely these, as Crosby points out, that emphasize the «conversational» nature of oral delivery, the intimate *rapport* between the minstrel and his listening public; and, since the *Zifar* was intended to be presented under quite different circumstances and to a different type of audience, its author presumably felt no need of such devices. In this respect, as in many others, the *Zifar* is a transitional work, a product of the age of script and reading aloud, the age which links the long tradition of oral composition and delivery with the modern tradition of print and private reading.

It was Northrop Frye who coined the term «radical of presentation» to define the role of the composer of literature in relation to his public, pointing out that it is in this particular that oral literature differs most completely and fundamentally from written and printed literature. In Frye's category of «epos» the radical of presentation is the minstrel's personal recitation to an audience that he has before him; in «fiction», on the other hand, the radical of presentation is the printed page destined for an absent and unknown readership. [156] The author of the *Zifar*, along with many other medieval writers, stands between these two radicals of presentation, and he consequently uses elements of both at the same time. The problems faced by these transitional artists have recently been well defined in an important book on the theory of literature:

[155] Ian Michael, «A Comparison of the Use of Epic Epithets», 41.
[156] *Anatomy of Criticism. Four Essays* (Princeton, 1957), 246-251.

> The greatest of the medieval romances were not orally composed, although they depended heavily on traditional elements, some of which may even have been taken directly from oral tradition or from transcribed versions of oral narratives.... The sudden acquisition by medieval narrative artists of the new role of authorship found them unprepared and somewhat ill at ease. Like all authors they attempted to «refine themselves out of existence». The most natural course was found to be a fairly straightforward imitation of a teller reciting his story to an audience. [157]

This would seem to be a fair summary of the situation in the *Zifar:* the author addresses his audience directly in the manner of the minstrels; he employs many of the oral narrator's techniques to make his story vivid and real; but he uses sparingly or not at all those devices that emphasize the minstrel's radical of presentation: in a book destined for private or semi-private reading, these would be out of place.

In addition to ignoring some of the more «conversational» features of the «epos», the *Zifar* author also introduces many positive elements into his style that come from the academic, written tradition, which came into contact with the popular tradition of oral delivery and eventually produced the modern radical of presentation characterized by the printed page and the private reader. The learned tradition influencing the *Zifar* is a twofold one, deriving from both Latin and Arabic culture.

We have already noted some of the features of the *Zifar*'s style that seem fairly certainly indicative of Arabic influence (ch 2, section D). Many of these Semitic elements are, in fact, formulas, occurring, as they do, frequently and in identical circumstances. Arabic revels in artificial balanced repetitions, as its most typical verse form, the monorhymed *qaṣida*, bears eloquent witness. In the *Zifar*, the almost monotonous introduction of interpolated *exempla* by «dize el cuento», the signposting of *sententiæ* by «dize el sabio» or «palabra es del sabio» and of proverbs by «dizen que», the opening of speeches by «'Çertas,' dixo», all seem reflections of the mannered formulaic nature of Arabic prose, modelled of course primarily on the Koran, and influencing the *Zifar*'s style either directly, or indirectly through the thirteenth-century translations of wisdom literature and books of *exempla*.

The *Zifar*, then, derives its formulaic phrases from two quite distinct sources—vernacular oral poetry and learned Arabic wisdom literature. But controlling the borrowing from these two traditions is a mind trained in the principles of medieval Latin rhetoric as exemplified in the *Artes Poeticæ*. It is the application of these precepts above all that gives the romance its learned air and, despite its epic-type subject, clearly distinguishes it from the productions of the *juglares* and those who composed for them.

---

[157] Robert Scholes and Robert Kellogg, *The Nature of Narrative* (New York, 1966), 55.

The way in which the material is elaborated, the careful balance of phrases and clauses within the sentence, the learned digressions, the repetitions of the same thing in a slightly different form, the developed taste for antithesis, all these betray the influence of a rhetorical education. They also make the *Zifar*, in this respect at least, typical of medieval romance in general which, in Eugène Vinaver's words, «was primarily a *literary* genre in the strict and perhaps somewhat narrow sense of the term: it was the product of trained minds, not of an uncritical and ingenuous imagination». [158]

---

[158] «From Epic to Romance», *BJRL* XLVI, 1 (March 1964), 476-503, at p. 488.

CHAPTER SIX: BINARY EXPRESSIONS IN THE *ZIFAR*

One of the most striking stylistic features of the *Zifar* author's style is his habit of using binary expressions or «pairs». This tendency to write in pairs of words joined by a simple conjunction is by no means peculiar to the *Zifar*, however, or even to Old Spanish literature; similar binary expressions turn up so frequently in, for example, medieval Latin and Old French that they seem to be more than a mere stylistic device and to reflect a habit of mind that was prevalent throughout medieval Europe. The phenomenon has been studied by a number of critics, although none of them has considered its occurrence in the *Zifar*, one of the medieval Spanish works richest in pairs. [1]

The pairs are of two basic types, inclusive and synonymous. The latter, which are much more frequent in medieval literature, consist of the coupling together by means of a conjunction, such as (in Spanish) *e, o* or *nin*, of two nouns, adjectives, adverbs or verbs that are either exactly or almost synonymous in meaning. Such pairs as «alegre e pagado», «rico

[1] See, for example, E. R. Curtius, «Zur Literarästhetik des Mittelalters, II», *ZRP* LVIII (1938), 129-232; Erich von Richthofen, *Estudios épicos medievales y algunos trabajos inéditos* (Madrid, 1954), ch. 2; Peter M. Schon, *Studien zum Stil der frühen französischen Prosa* (Analecta Romanica 8, Frankfurt am Main, 1960), especially 205-238; S. G. Nichols, Jr, *Formulaic Diction and Thematic Composition in the «Chanson de Roland»* (UNCSRLL 36, Chapel Hill, 1961), especially appendix I; Erwin Bernhard, «Abstractions médiévales ou critique abstraite?», *Studi Mediolatini e Volgari* IX (1961), 19-70; Richthofen, «Style and Chronology of the Early Romance Epic», *Saggi e Ricerche in Memoria di Ettore li Gotti* (Palermo, 1962), III, 83-96. Specifically concerned with pairs in Spanish writers are: E. Kullmann, «Die dichterische und sprachliche Gestalt des *Cantar de Mio Cid*», *RF* XLV (1931), 1-65; Ruth H. Webber, *Formulistic Diction in the Spanish Ballad* (UCPMPh XXIV, 2, Berkeley-Los Angeles, 1951), especially 218-223; Joaquín Artiles, *Los recursos literarios de Berceo* (Madrid, 1964), 109-118; Carmelo Gariano, *Análisis estilístico de los «Milagros de Nuestra Señora» de Berceo* (Madrid, 1965), 95-99; Edmund de Chasca, *El arte juglaresco en el «Cantar de Mio Cid»* (Madrid, 1967), ch. 10; *id.*, *Registro de fórmulas verbales en el «Cantar de Mio Cid»* (Iowa City, 1968), 38-40, 45-46; T. Anthony Perry, *Art and Meaning in Berceo's «Vida de Santa Oria»* (New Haven-London, 1968), 154-164; C. C. Smith, «Latin Histories and Vernacular Epic in Twelfth-Century Spain: Similarities of Spirit and Style», *BHS* XLVIII (1971), 1-19, at pp. 10-13.

e abonado», «falso e traidor» are to found in numerous Old Spanish texts. These synonymous pairs will be discussed in the second part of this chapter. We turn our attention first to the inclusives.

A. INCLUSIVE PAIRS

The inclusive pairs, although less common than the synonymous pairs, are in some ways more interesting, because of what they can tell us about medieval modes of thought, the influences at work on a medieval writer's style, and the effects he wanted to achieve through that style. The idea behind the inclusive pair is that, by reference to two notions that are either antithetical or at opposite extremes, all the intermediate stages are automatically included in the concept. Medieval writers use this device to express the idea of «all» (or, if negative, «none»). Thus «grandes e pequeños» = «everyone», «yermo e poblado» = «everywhere», «día e noche» = «all the time», «continuously». The reasons why authors should choose to employ these periphrastic pairs in preference to simpler equivalents, such as *todos* or *por todas partes*, are worth examining.

In the first place, the medieval Romance vernaculars are somewhat weak in abstractions, and Latin, their parent language, itself shows a constant preference for periphrases which avoid an abstract. [2] Many abstract nouns that exist in the modern languages are in fact the coinage of medieval scholastic Latin which do not enter day-to-day vernacular speech until much later. Moreover, a number of the abstractions that did exist in Classical Latin became extinct during the evolution to Romance. Consequently, without a derivative of *quisque* or *omnes*, for example, the vernaculars had to make do with such phrases as «grandes e pequeños» (since *todos* would not always be unambiguous) until such a time as they borrowed the metaphorical *todo el mundo* from the French. In other words, in some cases the use of inclusive pairs represents the only way of expressing a particular concept.

Secondly, since the majority of medieval authors wrote with a largely illiterate audience in mind, they naturally tried as far as possible to avoid abstractions and express themselves in concrete terms in order to make their work both more vivid and more comprehensible to people whose uneducated minds were unfitted to cope with abstractions. A learned author might well have been in a position to coin *culto* abstract words from contemporary Latin, but his audience would have been in no position to understand them. The great use of concrete inclusive pairs is almost certainly to some extent a result of the basic need for comprehensibility.

[2] E.g. «ab urbe condita», «from the *foundation* of the city»; «regnante X», «in the *reign* of X».

184

· · A third factor which probably contributes to the medieval writer's fondness for pairs is the influence of legal language. Lawyers have always used expressions of this kind in order to achieve greater precision and minimize the chance of loopholes being found in their decrees or contracts. At no time in the history of the law was this tendency more prevalent than in the Middle Ages, where the need for concrete precision in a largely illiterate society was allied to a taste for rolling rhetoric. The influence of legal language on medieval literary style is only just beginning to be seriously studied, [3] but there can be little doubt that, since many of the greatest authors are known to have been connected with the law (one thinks immediately of Chaucer, Berceo and Rojas), some reflection of their professional style is likely to be present in their creative writing. This is especially likely if we bear in mind that writers in the Middle Ages were not concerned with inventing new material but with organizing and clarifying an existing *matière* and persuading their audience of the *sens* that they had given it. [4] Clarification and persuasion are still the major pursuits of the legal profession. [5]

Fourthly, one cannot discount the probable influence of the *Artes Poeticæ* on the medieval writer's taste for pairs. Although these manuals of rhetoric, whose precepts for literary composition were the standard fare of medieval education, cover many points, the majority of them devote most space to *amplificatio*, the technique of expanding and elaborating one's material. For the Middle Ages, in the words of Edmond Faral, «l'amplification est la grande chose; elle est la principale fonction de l'écrivain». [6] One of the leading preceptists, Geoffrey of Vinsauf, in both his *Poetria Nova* and his *Documentum de Arte Versificandi*, lists eight main types of *amplificatio*, including *circumlocutio* or periphrasis. To say «the old men and the young men» or «the great and the small» instead of «everybody» is obviously an elementary form of circumlocution. Another topic in the textbooks that may also have influenced medieval writers in their use of inclusive pairs is the «colour of rhetoric» known

[3] An important work in this respect is C. C. Smith and J. Morris, «On 'Physical' Phrases in Old Spanish Epic and Other Texts», *PLPLS: Lit. and Hist. Section* XII, part v (1967), 129-190.

[4] The terms are those used by Chrétien de Troyes in the opening lines of his *Chevalier de la Charrete*.

[5] Clarity and persuasion were in fact the basis of all medieval education, not just that of the lawyers. Robert O. Payne, «Chaucer and the Art of Rhetoric», *Companion to Chaucer Studies*, ed. Beryl Rowland (Toronto-New York-London, 1968), 38-57, points out that all the rhetorics —the *ars poetica, ars prædicandi* and *ars dictaminis*—, despite their different aims, all had the same basis, «an elegant and orderly style and the use of language to persuade» (38).

[6] *Les Arts poétiques du XIIᵉ et du XIIIᵉ siècle. Recherches et documents sur la technique littéraire du Moyen Age* (BÉHÉ 238, Paris, 1924), 61. Towards the end the Middle Ages, however, brevity *(abbreviatio)*, the direct opposite of amplification, became much more seriously considered as a stylistic ideal; see, for instance, Keith Whinnom, «Diego de San Pedro's Stylistic Reform», *BHS* XXXVII (1960), 1-15, and A. C. Spearing, *Criticism and Medieval Poetry* (London, 1964), 123-131.

as *contentio*. Geoffrey, in his short treatise *De Coloribus Rhetoricis*, defines *contentio* thus: «est quando ex contrariis rebus conficitur oratio, hoc modo: 'Res homo vana: placet, sordebit; abundat, egebit; / Floret, marcebit; stat, cadet; est, nec erit'».[7] E. R. Curtius also points to the occurrence of the inclusive pair «omnis sexus et aetas» in many examples of the rhetorical *topos* of inexpressibility.[8]

When all this has been said, however, it is probable that the tendency to express the notions of «all» and «none» through the medium of inclusive pairs rather than by some other means is ascribable to something more fundamental than the gaps in the language, the pedantry of the lawyers, the precepts of the rhetoricians or the simple desire to avoid the abstract: quite simply it reflects medieval man's way of looking at the world in terms of mutually exclusive opposites, the famous polarized dualisms of God and man, heaven and hell, good and evil, angel and devil, body and soul, cortex and nucleus. It is, therefore, not impossible that the lawyers, the literary theorists and the poets could have derived their taste for inclusive pairs from this common habit of mind of their age.

Whatever their origin, inclusive pairs are certainly much in evidence in early Spanish literature. The epics abound in them, and the poets of the *mester de clerecía*, who drew on the heroic poems for much of their method of composition and presentation,[9] were quick to avail themselves of this device, which had for them the double advantage of expressing the abstract in concrete terms and also of providing them very often with a ready-made hemistich. The chroniclers too, whether writing in the vernacular or in Latin, were familiar with the compositions of the epic poets and tended to imitate in places their stylistic vitality. Consequently the pages of the *Historia Roderici*, the *Chronica Adefonsi Imperatoris* and Alfonso X's *Estoria de España* abound in inclusive pairs.[10] The most thorough study of the use of pairs (both inclusive and synonymous) in early Spanish literature has been made by C. C. Smith and J. Morris in a monograph to be published shortly, entitled *Reality and Rhetoric: An Aspect of Medieval Linguistics*.[11] Their work goes beyond that of earlier critics (Webber, Artiles, Gariano, de Chasca—see n. 1 above) because it studies the use of pairs in a large number of texts and delves into the origin as well as the function of the pair. Much of the evidence from epic, *clerecía* and chronicle texts given below is taken from this monograph, which has been used as a starting point for the investigation of the binary expressions in the *Zifar*.

[7] Faral, *Les Arts poétiques*, 322.

[8] *European Literature and the Latin Middle Ages*, trans. W. R. Trask (New York, 1953), 160.

[9] See ch. 5, n. 8.

[10] See Smith, «Latin Histories», 10-13.

[11] I am greatly indebted to Dr Smith and Dr Morris for allowing me to read the typescript of their monograph.

(i) *Persons*

A very large number of inclusive pairs refer to persons and express the idea of «everyone» (or, of course, «no one»). The principal ways of denoting «everyone» have been classified by Smith and Morris as follows: [12]

(*a*) By rank and age: «grandes e chicos», «grandes e pequeños», «altos e baxos», «mozos e viejos», «ricos e pobres», etc.

(*b*) By military rank: «cavalleros e peones», «escuderos e peones», etc.

(*c*) By sex: «omnes e mugeres», «mugeres e varones», «vecinos e vecinas», «cristianos e cristianas», etc.

(*d*) By race and religion: «moros e cristianos».

(*e*) Miscellaneous: «justos e pecadores» (by virtue); «enfermos e sanos» (by health); «virgen e viuda» (by marital status), etc.

The *Zifar* has a large number of such pairs, but only a few of them fully deserve the title of inclusive. There are, for example, only four cases of «grandes e pequeños», [13] and it is interesting that none of these is allowed to speak for itself, as it were: all four are preceded by *todos*. Two slight variants of this pair are «non solamente los grandes mas los pequeños» (146.6-7, also preceded by *todos*) and «en el grande nin en el pequeño» (299.14). A second inclusive denoting «everyone», common elsewhere, is «buenos e malos»; this occurs only twice in the *Zifar* (56.8, 328.23).

A rather special inclusive pair is «de Dios e de los omes». This expression is not mentioned at all by Smith and Morris, but it is the commonest of the true inclusives in the *Zifar*, where it appears at least twelve times. [14] A further point of interest about this pair is that it illustrates the author's apparent preoccupation with the rhythm and balance of his prose. In every case the strictly superfluous second *de* is retained, presumably so as to achieve the satisfying slow rhythm with the longer element towards the end of the clause. Furthermore, in seven of the twelve cases a further pair (in one case a triplet) precedes «de Dios e de los omes»:

> ca sabed que dos cosas son por qué los omes pueden ser amados e onrrados e preçiados de Dios e de los omes (263.7-9)

[12] I have somewhat altered the order in which these categories are presented in Smith and Morris' work so as to make them fit my own classification of the *Zifar*'s pairs more easily.

[13] 137.18, 164.22, 289.24, 506.9. Unless there is some special reason for doing so, I have not distinguished in the following pages between «*x* e *y*» and «*y* e *x*». For convenience, such variants as «*x* o *y*», «nin *x* nin *y*», «el *x* e el *y*», are included under «*x* e *y*».

[14] 219.26-27, 221.25, 262.22, 263.8-9, 264.7-8, 296.10-11,296. 24-25, 311.13-14, 369.1-2, 369.10, 509.12, 509.17. Not surprisingly, eight of these appear in the *Castigos*, which also contains one example of «a Dios e a los omes» (294.26).

E así, míos fijos, aprendiendo buenas costunbres e usando bien dellas seredes nobles e amados e preçiados de Dios e de los omes (264.6-8)

ca por la umildat seredes amados e preçiados de Dios e de los omes (296.10-11)

Onde, míos fijos, sy queredes ser preçiados e amados de Dios e de los omes, sed omildosos al bien e non al mal (296.24-25)

e los que así fazen son onrrados e poderosos e ricos e amados de Dios e de los omes (311.13-14)

así serán más amados e más preçiados de Dios e de los omes (369.1-2)

ca es onrrado e loado de Dios e de los omes por el bien que faze (509.12-13).

It will be noticed that the pairs preceding «de Dios e de los omes» are not inclusive but synonymous; they add little or nothing to the meaning, but they strengthen the rhythmic balance of the sentence. The fifth example (311.13-14) is a particularly interesting one, since the inclusive is preceded by *two* synonymous pairs—«onrrados e amados» and «poderosos e ricos»— both of which are common enough to be called clichés (the first occurs three times in the *Zifar*, the second twelve times). However, by avoiding simple juxtaposition and inserting the second pair between the constituent elements of the first, the author has succeeded, maybe unconsciously, in introducing an element of variety into the stereotyped material at his disposal. This point will be discussed in more detail later in the present chapter.

The many other pairs used to denote «everyone» in the *Zifar* are not true inclusives in the sense that «grandes e pequeños», «buenos e malos» and «de Dios e de los omes» are true inclusives: they do not cover the whole of mankind or society from the highest to the lowest, but consist of two elements drawn from within the same broad upper or lower social bracket. Thus «condes e omes buenos» (or «omes ricos» or «omes grandes»), [15] «cavalleros e omes buenos», [16] «cavalleros e escuderos», [17] «condes e duques», [18] «condes e cavalleros», [19] denote ranks within the aristocracy or the officer class. «Vallesteros e peones» is the unique pair representative of the lower orders. [20] The occurrence of a pair, such as

[15] 150.5-6, 150.12, 153.6-7, 156.5-6, 161.19-20, 208.10, 419.31, 419.35, 460.20.
[16] 71.24, 156.1-2.
[17] 284.6, 463.12, 464.2-3.
[18] 229.15.
[19] 422.4-5.
[20] 50.10, 54.3-4, 58.13-14.

«los cavalleros e la gente» (51.26-27), which embraces both the upper and lower classes is very rare indeed in the *Zifar*. Even the tripartite phrase «condes e duques e omes buenos/ricos/grandes», which the author uses three times, [21] covers only one social grade. Other very occasional triplets, however, are more like true inclusives: «cavalleros e vallesteros e peones» (58.4-5), «los condes e los omes buenos e toda la gente de la çibdat» (156.9-10). «Everybody» is also sometimes expressed by a pair of pairs, the first covering the upper strata, the second the lower, as in «tan bien cavalleros commo escuderos e vallesteros e peones» (54.3-4); but again these double pairs are very rare. Even the one five-part phrase in the *Zifar* used to denote «everybody» is not fully inclusive: «los reys e los condes e los vizcondes e todos los grandes omes e los procuradores» (460.8-9). [22]

Outside the military sphere, once again we find the same tendency to draw the constituents of the pair not from the basic divisions of humanity into male and female, rich and poor, etc., but from one half of this duality. Governors, for example, are not coupled with the governed to embrace two fundamentally opposed political realities; instead two different types of governor make up the pair, as in «governadores e consejeros» (308.10), «reys e prínçipes» (311.11) or «privados e consejeros» (327.11). Similarly, women are not linked with men to show one of the clearest divisions of human kind, but are themselves separated into «dueñas e donzellas», a pair that occurs twenty-two times in the *Zifar*, [23] whereas pairs of the «omes e mugeres» type do not appear at all. [24] As in the case of social and military divisions, the nearest the author gets to a real inclusive covering both sexes is in tripartite expressions such as «todos los cavalleros e los omes buenos e las dueñas» (48.12-13) or «se espedió della e de todas las otras dueñas e donzellas e de todos los otros omes buenos» (429.16-18). [25]

Although this use of pairs to denote a duality within a basic duality is not unknown in earlier Spanish texts, [26] the *Zifar* author's taste for it to the virtual exclusion of the truer inclusives seems to be unusual. As we

[21] 121.2-3, 245.6, 369.26.

[22] The author's Prologue provides some interesting examples of inclusives that have no echo elsewhere in the romance. There is, for instance, a division of men into clergy and laity (very common in Berceo) in «fue resçebido ... de toda la clerezía e de las órdenes e de los omes buenos de la villa» (4.29-31). The triplet «cristiano nin moro nin judío» is the unique trace in the *Zifar* of the expression «moros e cristianos» frequently encountered in the texts studied by Smith and Morris.

[23] 65.16, 65.17, 78.26, 101.10-11, 102.21, 102.24, 103.2, 103.11, 163.4, 289.24, 386.19, 388.8-9, 389.3-4, 391.2, 397.16-17, 398.26-27, 402.4, 409.23, 442.9-10, 478.18, 513.3, 513.12.

[24] The nearest approach to such a pair occurs in the following sentence: «ca Dios non fizo los omes yguales nin de un seso nin de un entendimiento, mas departidos, tan bien varones commo mugeres» (32.23-24).

[25] Cf. 393.22-23, 482.17.

[26] E.g. «reyes e potestades» (*PFG* 134a), «cuemdes e infançones» (*PMC* 2964), etc. Smith and Morris suggest that the origins of such inclusive pairs of ranks within the nobility and royalty lie in elaborate formulas of address.

have seen, the romance contains few of the pairings by age, sex, wealth, race or religion that abound in the works studied by Smith and Morris. In the *Zifar* there appears to be a love of pairs for their own sake, a luxuriant taste for rhetorical *amplificatio*, which has turned a once vital oral procedure into little more then an elegant cliché.

There remains one rather special case of «everyone» expressed as an inclusive pair to be examined—the three obviously related phrases «parientes e amigos», «parientes e vasallos», «amigos e vasallos». [27] Smith and Morris, noting the frequent use of these and similar pairs as forms of direct address to the audience in the *clerecía* poets, suggest that since they form convenient hemistichs and were also probably in common everyday use, any distinction that had once existed between the two elements had become blurred. They therefore consider «parientes e amigos», etc. as synonymous, not inclusive, pairs. In the *Zifar*, however, when these formulas are used for direct address (never, incidentally, to the reader) they are always put into the mouth of someone in authority who can legitimately claim to be able to distinguish between his relatives, his friends and his vassals, in a way that Berceo, for instance (or his *juglar*), obviously cannot do. [28] Moreover, the occurrences of these pairs in narrative again show a consciousness, in most cases, of the distinction between these various grades of intimates. [29] Here, then, it would seem that the *Zifar* author has restored life to a set of phrases that elsewhere had degenerated into rather meaningless clichés.

(ii) *Time*

The abstract notion of «always», «all the time», «continuously», is also frequently expressed in Old Spanish by means of the inclusive pair «(de) día e (de) noche», and the negative idea «never», «at no time» by «de día nin de noche». Smith and Morris show that in the texts they studied the phrase has a general sense and two more restricted applications, all of which are of common occurrence. The *Zifar* contains six examples

[27] «Parientes e amigos»: 63.5, 104.8, 113.1, 114.5, 114.19-20, 348.7, 348.11-12 (twice), 485.6, 500.2-3; «parientes e vasallos»: 190.22, 219.2-3; «amigos e vasallos»: 245.18, 300.21. There is one occurrence of a triplet combining all three elements, «amigos e parientes e vasallos» (69.15-16).

[28] For example, the formula of address «amigos e parientes» is put into the mouth of the count who is attacking Galapia (63.5). It is also used by another count to his intimates when about to teach the King of Efeso a lesson in how to treat his subordinates (348.7). Zifar, as King of Mentón, addresses his subjects as «amigos e vasallos leales» (245.18). The female ruler of Galapia appeals to her «amigos e parientes e vasallos buenos e leales» (69.15-16).

[29] Count Nasón rebels with the aid of «mill cavalleros de sus parientes e vasallos» (190.21-22), a fact of which his nephew reminds him (219.2-3). The counts who rebel against Roboán do so «con parientes e con amigos» (485.6). Grima asks leave of the King of Orbín to return «para su tierra a ver sus parientes e sus amigos e murir entr'ellos» (104.7-8); here any mention of vassals, however stereotyped, would clearly be out of place.

of the pair, three of them used in the general sense: «e aý estava de día e de noche veyendo aquellas maravillas» (226.25-227.1); «E porende sienpre avía de andar armado de día e de noche» (433.6-7); «ove sienpre de andar armado de día e de noche» (435.7-8). [30] The first of the more restricted uses noted by Smith and Morris is the association of the pair with prayers or appeals for divine assistance. There is one example of this usage in the *Zifar:* «e allý rogava a Dios de día e de noche que·l oviese merçed» (97.27-98.1). The second specialized use of the phrase is to convey the idea of great haste and urgency in the description of a journey. Again the *Zifar* provides one instance of this usage, in the Prologue: «e veyendo que el Arçidiano avía mucho a coraçón este fecho, non quedando de día nin de noche, e que andava mucho afincadamente en esta demanda...» (3.28-31).

The other time pairs discussed by Smith and Morris, such as «invierno e verano», «en caliente e en frío», «en paz e en guerra», are not found at all in the *Zifar*. There are, however, two examples of «en vida e en muerte», an expression not documented by Smith and Morris: «ca lealtad les faze acordarse del bienfecho que resçebieron en vida e en muerte» (6.9-10); «ca reconosçen bienfecho en vida e en muerte de aquél que gelo faze» (277.21-23). A variant of this pair also occurs once: «ca conbusco seremos a vida o a muerte» (277.5-6).

Finally, the *Zifar* contains two examples of the accumulated inclusive pairs often found in medieval legal documents to convey the idea of «at any time» or «in any circumstances»:

> sy vós ý llegásedes yrado o pagado, o sano o enfermo, muerto o bivo, con pocos o con muchos, que vos acogiesen (219.13-15)

> ca tal fuero era en aquella tierra que sy el enperador ... viniese a la tierra, que lo avían de resçibir, yrado o pagado, con pocos o con muchos (503.6-9). [31]

(iii) *Place*

There are a number of inclusive pairs in Old Spanish which express the abstract notion of «everywhere» (or «nowhere»). Although the one to which Smith and Morris devote most space, «yermo e poblado», is not found in the *Zifar*, the romance is rich in pairs of the type «çibdades e villas», «villas e castiellos», «castiellos e torres». We have already noted the *Zifar* author's apparent preference for pairs that are not strictly

[30] It will be noticed that the latter two are preceded by the abstract word *sienpre*, just as many of the pairs denoting «everyone» are preceded by *todos*.

[31] Cf. example quoted by Smith and Morris: «que el acogiera en el dicho alcaçar a nuestro sennor el Rey de noche o de día, ayrado o pagado, con pocos o con muchos» (*Colección de fórmulas jurídicas castellanas de la Edad Media (c. 1400)* in *Anuario de Historia del Derecho Español* III [1926], 501).

speaking fully inclusive since they draw both elements from one half of
the basic division: thus «condes e omes buenos» is much commoner than
«los cavalleros e la gente», and «dueñas e donzellas» than«omes e mugeres».
The same tendency is to be found in the inclusives of place: all of them
refer only to different kinds of settlements or buildings (the *poblado)* and
completely ignore uninhabited areas (the *yermo)*. There are two examples
of «çibdades e villas» and one of «çibdades e castiellos» used in the general
sense of «everywhere»:

> Ca de tal donario era él e aquella gente que levava, que los de
> las otras çibdades e villas que lo oýan avían muy grant sabor de
> lo ver (385.28-386.2)

> E luego los reys e los condes e los vizcondes e todos los grandes
> omes e los procuradores de las çibdades e de las villas, le fizieron
> omenaje (460.8-10) [32]

> cayeron muchas torres e muchas casas en las çibdades e en los
> castiellos (240.13-14). [33]

The notion of «everywhere» is also occasionally conveyed by a tripartite
expression of the same type:

> e mandóles que feziesen cartas para todos los condes e duques e
> ricos omes, e para todas las çibdades e villas e castiellos de todo
> su señorío (245.5-7). [34]

The following sentence, involving both a triplet and a pair, hovers between
the general sense of «everywhere» and the literal meaning of «cities, towns
and castles»:

> e veen çibdades e villas e castiellos muy fuertes conbatiendo los
> unos a los otros e dando fuego a los castiellos e a las çibdades
> (226.7-9).

It is noteworthy, however, that the pair «villas e castiellos», which
occurs in one form or another no fewer than twenty-seven times in the
Zifar, is used only once to denote the general idea of «everywhere»:
«E el rey le dixo ... que'l reçebrían en las villas e castiellos del regno syn
duda ninguna» (503.4-6). [35] Elsewhere it is used quite literally to mean

---

[32] The elaborate five-part expression to denote «everyone» has already been noted.
[33] There is only one example of «torres e casas» in the *Zifar* (240.13), but it recalls
similar pairs in earlier texts, such as «nin cámara abierta nin torre» *(PMC* 2287) or
«nin torre nin cabaña» *(PFG* 137b).
[34] Note the careful balance of the two triplets used to express «everyone» and
«everywhere».
[35] 418.8 seems at first sight a similar case; but in fact at this point specific «villas
e castiellos» are being discussed.

specific towns and castles, as in «esta villa e los otros castiellos» (71.22) or «me dará las villas e los castillos que me tiene tomados» (417.15-16). [36] At times this specificity is underlined by the addition of numerals: «vos ha tomado seys castiellos e dos villas» (391.13-14). [37]

In seven further cases «villas e castiellos» at first sight appears to carry its literal meaning. Closer examination reveals, however, that we are dealing here with a separate category in which «villas e castiellos» is, in fact, a different type of inclusive pair, not signifying «everywhere», but symbolizing power and wealth, a man's sovereignty over a whole country, as in the following examples:

> «Conde», dixo el rey, «mandatme dar las villas e los castiellos del condado» (219.9-10)

> «Señor», dixo el conde, «a este mi sobrino fezieron todos omenaje, tan bien de las villas commo de los castiellos» (219.10-12)

> mas, señor, ¿cómmo me darían a mí las villas e los castiellos pues vieren que non so en mi poder e estó en presión? (219.20-21)

> Desý el enperador mandó al rey de Safira que·l feziese entregado luego de todas las villas e los castiellos del reyno (503.3-4).

Alternatively, «villas e castiellos» may represent a generous gift from a ruler as a reward to one of his vassals:

> por que vos ruego que escojades en este mi reyno villas e castillos e aldeas quales vós quisierdes (410.28-29)

> ca non me cunplen agora villas nin castillos, sy non tan solamente la vuestra graçia que me dedes liçençia para que me vaya (410.31-33)

> e era muy católico ... en fazer muchas graçias a las eglesias, dotándolas de villas e de castiellos (508.20-23).

(iv) Wealth and Property

The commonest inclusive pair denoting wealth and property in the earlier texts is not «villas e castiellos» but «oro e plata». This pair, which abounds in the *PMC*, *clerecía*, chronicles and legal documents, occurs seven times in the *Zifar*, each time with the generic meaning of «money», «property». [38] In a further case gold and silver form part of

[36] Cf. 83.16-17, 103.6-7, 164.18-19, 416.33, 417.32, 419.28, 420.1, 420.3, 421.20, 512.16.
[37] Cf. 417.20, 418.27-28.
[38] 25.19, 25.21-22, 325.28-29, 366.15, 384.22, 385.8, 414.28.

14

a series of nouns used to describe the treasure on the ship of which Grima finds herself the unexpected mistress in Book I:

> e falló ý cosas muy nobles e de grant preçio, e mucho oro, e mucha plata, e mucho aljófar e muchas piedras preçiosas, e paños preçiados e muchas otras mercadurías de muchas maneras (97.15-18). [39]

There are a few other pairs denoting richness in the *Zifar*, but these have no inclusive value at all and are to be taken literally. The princess of Mentón wears «una guirnalda en la cabeça lleña de robís e de esmeraldas» (163.6-7); for his knighting ceremony Roboán is brought «una camisa grande de sirgo e de aljófar» (441.11-12); Seringa is accompanied by a hundred ladies «vestidas de paño de oro e de seda» (513.5). Not surprisingly, a number of these literal pairs are to be found in the descriptions of the marvellous other-world kingdoms visited by the Cavallero Atrevido and Roboán. The roofs of the houses in the Enchanted Lake are covered with «robís e esmeraldas e çafires» (229.8); the table from which the Cavallero Atrevido eats has legs «todos de esmeraldas e çafires» (229.20); the whole of the city on the *Islas Dotadas* is «encortinada de paños de oro e de seda muy nobles» (461.11); the hawk which Nobleza presents to Roboán wears jesses that are «bien obradas de oro e de aljófar» (468.21-22). None of these pairs has the same general *meaning* of wealth conveyed by «oro e plata», although of course they do give an *impression* of richness, an impression that is intensified by the use of two elements rather than just one. The binary habit has apparently influenced the author at these points, but the phrases are probably his own invention and owe only their syntactical form to the inclusive-pairs tradition.

The notion of «all one's property» (as distinct from simply «one's money») is expressed in Old Spanish works by pairs such as «cuerpo e aver» or «tierra e onor», in which material possessions are linked with more vitally personal possessions such as life and reputation. The *Zifar* provides occasional echoes of this usage:

> E porende vos devedes guardar de tales omes commo éstos, e non fiar vuestros cuerpos nin vuestras faziendas mucho en ellos (328.19-21)
>
> porque avía mucho de librar en su casa de la su fazienda e pro del regno (254.6-7)
>
> yo en vós pongo todo el mi fecho e la mi fazienda (423.22-23). [40]

---

[39] Smith and Morris quote examples from medieval Latin works that show similar elaboration of the basic *aurum-argentum* division: e.g. «unde nostri multa attulerunt spolia, aurum et argentum videlicet, et vestes pretiosas» (*España sagrada*, ed. R. Flórez [Madrid, 1747-(1879)], XIV, 453).

[40] «Guardó su fama e su alma» (368.24-25) should perhaps also be included in this category.

«One's whole being», without any reference to one's possessions, is expressed by the inclusive pair «alma e cuerpo», a phrase with an obviously legal, and ultimately religious, origin, implying as a penalty both the death of the body through execution and the damnation of the soul through excommunication. [41] This pair appears no fewer than eleven times in the third book of the *Zifar*, the ponderously didactic *Castigos del rey de Mentón*. [42] The other three books contain five further examples, [43] not counting the following fine illustration of the author's penchant for elaboration and almost pedantic precision:

> Puedes entender que ay tres maneras de amigos: ca la una es el que quiere ser amigo del cuerpo e non del alma, e la otra es el que quiere ser amigo del alma e non del cuerpo, e la otra el que quiere ser amigo del cuerpo e del alma, así commo este preso postrimero, que fue amigo de su alma e de su cuerpo, dando buen enxienplo de sý, e non queriendo que su alma fuese perdida por escusar el martirio del cuerpo (32.9-15).

The only other point of interest about the use of «alma e cuerpo» in the *Zifar* is that the author seems to feel the need for another pair in the same sentence to complement it. As in the case of the pairs used with «de Dios e de los omes», this is usually a couple of synonyms which add little to the meaning but perfect the balance of the sentence. The following are good examples of this tendency:

> ca me consejades muy bien, a onrra e a pro del cuerpo e del alma (63.25-26)

> E del mal puede aver desonrra e daño para el cuerpo e para el alma (221.5-6)

> E asý serás guarido e sano en el cuerpo e en el alma (258.14).

(v) *Military Activities*

An important series of inclusive phrases in the *Zifar* concerns the military profession, the equipment and occupation of knights, and their fate in battle. [44] Knights are fitted out with «cavallos e armas», an inclusive pair denoting the main instruments of chivalry: «aguisóse el

---

[41] For a discussion of the origins of this phrase, see my article, «'Con miedo de la muerte la miel non es sabrosa': Love, Sin and Death in the *Libro de buen amor*», «*Libro de Buen Amor*» *Studies*, ed. G. B. Gybbon-Monypenny (London, 1970), 231-252, at pp. 238-243; Smith and Morris, «Phrases», 164-168.

[42] 258.14, 266.2, 290.24, 292.5, 296.19, 313.3, 313.8-9, 313.22, 318.20, 339.3-4, 351.25. Three of these (on pp. 292, 296, 318) are taken from the *Flores de filosofía*.

[43] 63.26, 77.26, 166.24, 221.6, 516.22-23.

[44] Although these pairs abound in epic and *clerecía* verse, Smith and Morris do not discuss them in their study.

cavallero muy bien de su cavallo e de sus armas» (141.7-8); «tomó su cavallo e sus armas» (157.23-24). [45] These two fundamental pieces of equipment are always specified, whilst the rest of the knight's accoutrements tend to be dismissed in the vaguest of terms: «guisávalo muy bien de cavallos e de armas e de todas las cosas que avía mester» (11.20-21); «E mandóle dar muy bien de vestir, e buen cavallo e buenas armas e todo conplimiento de cavallero» (139.17-18). [46]

The *Zifar* author's fondness for sub-dividing inclusive pairs into other pairs embracing only one of the two basic categories is also to be seen in connection with horses and arms. The knight's weapons are classed as «lorigas e armas» (78.10), «espada e cuchiello» (312.23-24, twice), «escudo e lança» (386.6), «espada e lança» (442.5); and his mounts as «cavallos e bestias» (11.16, 11.27-28, 82.25). Before battle he will «ensellar e armar» his horses (192.21, 192.24); in times of peace he rides a palfrey that is gorgeously «ensellado e enfrenado» (229.1, 233.4, 457.17-18, 475.2-3). His rest and recreations are also frequently described by means of inclusive pairs. After a battle he will «desarmar e folgar», [47] «dormir e folgar», [48] «comer e folgar», [49] or, most frequently of all, «comer e bever». [50] For amusement he will take part in tournaments and «bafordar e lançar», [51] or «correr e luchar», [52] or play «tablas e axadres». [53]

The most numerous inclusive pairs connected with military affairs in the *Zifar* are those used to describe the various misfortunes that can overtake soldiers in battle. They may be defeated *(ganado, vençido)*, captured *(preso)*, wounded *(ferido)*, killed *(muerto)*, despoiled *(astragado)*. For the defeated in the *Zifar* disasters never seem to come singly: almost invariably the author uses a pair of participial adjectives to describe the fate of his armies. The most frequently encountered of such pairs involve permutations of *preso*, *ferido* and *muerto*. At one point all three are used in a tripartite expression four times within the space of a few pages, [54] but normally they are used in pairs. Thus «muerto e/o ferido» occurs thirteen times, [55] «muerto e/o preso» eight times, [56] and «ferido e preso»

---

[45] Cf. 53.24, 59.13, 179.26, 202.3-4, 409.16.
[46] Cf. 82.28-29, 140.13-14.
[47] 410.6, 501.4.
[48] 132.17, 155.12, 193.1, 472.15, 472.21, 473.9-10.
[49] 68.11, 109.20, 120.23.
[50] 69.7, 95.7, 95.12-13, 124.2, 138.7, 258.7, 290.10, 290.11, 328.4, 356.10, 451.1, 473.22, 473.24, 507.10, 507.12, 514.11. Not all of these refer to knights after battle. There are also three examples of the related pair «pan e vino» (21.19-20, 132.6, 138.1).
[51] 81.6, 81.14, 178.24, 290.5, 386.5, 442.7-8, 442.14.
[52] 290.6.
[53] 179.1, 290.6, 386.11.
[54] 408.11-12, 409.4, 409.7-8, 415.1-2. In only two cases, however, is the order of the elements the same.
[55] 57.14, 197.19, 197.22, 197.25, 213.5, 214.10, 215.12, 407.36-408.1, 408.7, 415.6, 497.7, 497.12, 497.23.
[56] 61.20, 61.27, 62.9, 198.4, 214.9, 215.16, 406.1, 500.8.

196

once (408.23-24). Other inclusives in the same category are «muerto e astragado», [57] «vençido e preso», [58] «ganado e preso». [59]

The corresponding verbs are also used frequently in pairs in the *Zifar*'s battle scenes. *Prender*, *ferir* and *matar*, like *preso*, *ferido* and *muerto*, are the most often encountered. Only once, however, do they occur all together in a triplet. [60] Of the pairs «matar e ferir», like «muerto e ferido», is by far the commonest, with seven occurrences, [61] whereas «ferir e prender» and «matar e prender» turn up only once each. [62] Other unique verbal pairs in the same category are «tomar e guardar» (410.22-23), «matar e astragar» (431.11), «matar e deseheredar» (433.4), «prender e guardar» (451.8), and «desanparar e matar» (478.25); «desaforar e matar» occurs twice (432.1, 433.3-4).

(vi) *Miscéllaneous*

The *Zifar* also contains a number of other inclusive pairs that cannot be included in any of the categories already discussed. Most of these are found only once in the work, such as «natura e razón» (40.22), «vieja e podrida» (105.1), «parir e criar» (286.22-23), «ley e natura» (299.1), «razón e esfuerço» (351.6-7). A few others occur twice, but so close together that they may to all intents and purposes be counted as unique examples: «nasçer e floresçer» (232.3, 232.9), «poblado e mantenido» (307.26, 308.17), «provechosa e onesta» (320.26, 321.8). There are, however, two other related inclusives that have a sufficiently high incidence to be worth noting. «Dezir e fazer» (fourteen occurrences) [63] and «dicho e fecho» (five occurrences) [64] are used to convey the notion of «all one's activity». They appear to be of legal origin.

The *Zifar*, then, is very rich in inclusive pairs. Some are clearly derived from the stylistic repertoire of earlier writers, who were themselves undoubtedly influenced by the techniques of the *juglares*, by the precepts of the rhetoricians, by the language of the law, and by a desire or need to present their material in concrete terms. Other inclusive pairs in the *Zifar* seem to be the author's own creations and reflect both his love of rhetoric and the general medieval tendency to think in terms of dualities. His taste for rhetorical amplification is to be seen even more clearly in the

[57] 274.9-10, 300.26, 432.8.
[58] 301.2, 421.6-7, 421.7-8.
[59] 418.23. This pair is, of course, almost synonymous. The fully synonymous pair «presa e cativa» (only used of women) occurs twice (65.21, 69.3).
[60] 408.10-11; but cf. «derribando e firiendo e matando» (421.2) and «los ovieron a ferir e a matar e vençer» (197.16-17).
[61] 158.18, 158.21, 158.27-28, 179.9, 197.11, 408.2-3, 500.6-7.
[62] 420.32 and 407.35 respectively.
[63] 29.15, 223.9, 224.1-2, 238.6, 300.9, 307.2, 309.8, 310.21, 333.4, 346.16-17, 351.6, 397.25, 427.6, 450.27. Half of these occur in the *Castigos*.
[64] 291.13, 294.24, 346.20, 414.14-15, 509.16.

vast number of synonymous and near-synonymous pairs in the work, to which we now turn our attention.

B. SYNONYMOUS PAIRS

The *Zifar* contains one of the richest collections of synonymous pairs in medieval Spanish literature, and the difficulties of classifying them according to some logical system are consequently very great. Most of the critics who have concerned themselves with synonymous pairs in medieval writers have been content to categorize their pairs according to their grammatical function (nouns, adjectives, adverbs, verbs) or according to their particular role in the work in which they occur. The only scholars to have established a classification for synonymous pairs according to their origins are Smith and Morris: they discuss their material under four main headings—social, legal, religious and literary. These categories are an eminently suitable basis for a study of the synonymous pairs in the *Zifar*.

(i) Social

Some of the synonymous pairs in the *Zifar* have a clear social origin. Smith and Morris define such pairs as those «which it is easy to imagine arising 'naturally' from a social situation». «Rey e señor», for example, originally reflected a social reality, the dual role of the king as the ruler of his country and as the feudal lord of his vassals. Such a distinction has a clear point in a work like the *PMC* which is concerned with the conflict between Alfonso and the Cid. [65] In time, however, this subtle distinction became blurred as the phrase acquired everyday currency and became used as a courtesy title without its users being fully aware of its original force. The *Zifar* contains twelve examples of «rey e señor», [66] seven of them in the *Castigos* at the point where the hero is outlining the duties of kingship to his sons. Of the others, three appear in the *exemplum* of the struggle for power between Tabor and Rages (ch. 132; also in the *Castigos*), and two in the section dealing with Zifar's accession to the throne of Mentón. In all cases in the *Zifar*, then, «rey e señor» turns up in a clearly defined «social» situation, and could well be used with full knowledge of its pristine significance. This assumption is strengthened by the fact that the *Zifar* author also employs the much less common pairs «señor e enperador» and «señora e reýna», and apparently invents a

[65] The phrase in the *PMC* is «commo a rey e a señor»; it occurs eight times: 1885, 1952, 2109, 3118, 3146, 3430, 3488, 3574.
[66] To avoid a multiplicity of notes and parenthetical references in the text, all synonymous pairs and their occurrences are listed in appendix 2.

verbal pair «regnar e señorear» to cover the separate functions of the king's twin offices.

Another type of «social» pair is that which reflects courtesy and respect on the part of one person towards another. «To take the trouble to be long-winded is of itself courteous, even if it be in a rather set manner» (Smith and Morris). Thus, although the constituent elements of such phrases as «serviçio e amor», «merçed e graçia» or «serviçio e onor» may originally have been subtly differentiated and not fully synonymous in the language of feudal law and custom, it is reasonable to suppose, as Smith and Morris suggest, that the frequent use of these pairs in direct address reduced them to the level of mere clichés. [67] The *Zifar* abounds in pairs of this type: «onrra e pro(vecho)» (21), [68] «bien e merçed» (16), «onrra e bien» (7), «pres e onrra» (7), «graçia e merçed» (3), «onrra e estado» (2), «pres e fama» (2), «bien e don» (2), «ayudas e onrras» (2), «bien e amor», «fama e onrra», «serviçio e onrra», «onrra e merçed», «onrra e guarda», «onrra e nobleza», «onrra e poder», «merçed e ayuda» (1 each). Some of these pairs are undoubtedly used as courtesy formulas in the *Zifar*, as the following examples show:

> e enbiat dezir a la señora de la villa que el domingo de grant mañaña, a ora de prima, seré con ella, sy Dios quisiere, e non commo guerrero, mas commo buen amigo de su onrra e de su pro (78.4-7)

> E bien es verdat que quando una vegada nos consejastes, e vos toviemos en merçed el bien e la merçed que nos faziedes (379.19-21)

> Señor... queriendo vuestro bien e vuestra onrra pensé en una cosa qual vos agora diré (424.2-5)

> Çiertamente la quiero muy grant bien e préçiola e ámola muy verdaderamente, queriendo la guardar su pro e su onrra (424.14-16). [69]

The majority of such pairs in the romance, however, are not used as formulas of respect, but as simple clichés of narrative or in the construction of didactic commonplaces; for instance:

> e ganó muy grant pres e grant onrra por costunbres e por cavallería (40.1-2)

[67] E.g. «Recebí de ti siempre serviçio e amor» (*Milag* 126c).

[68] The figures in parentheses refer to the number of occurrences of the pair in the *Zifar*.

[69] The first and last quotations are particularly good examples of elaborate medieval courtesy.

sienpre parat mientes a los consejos que vos dieren los que
viéredes que son en razón e pueden ser a vuestra pro e a vuestra
onrra (263.3-5)

e fízole mucho bien e mucha merçed sobre todos los del su reyno
(271.21-22)

metiéndovos a saña contra aquéllos que quesieren vuestro serviçio
e vuestra onrra (328.5-6).

The literary evolution of these pairs from clarity to courtesy to cliché
can be traced fairly accurately. The original precise distinctions become
blurred, but the resulting near-synonymous pairs are retained in forms
of address to show respect. The next stage seems to be the use of these
pairs to show indirect respect, as when A tells B that C is working for the
«onrra e pro» of B. [70] They can then also be used by an author, as third-
person narrator and commentator, to imply his own and his readers'
respect for his characters. By this stage these binary expressions have
come a long way from their original feudal usage, and they are free to
begin a new life—or half-life—as simple rhetorical clichés which an author
can draw on whenever he needs to fill out a half-line of verse or, if writing
in prose, to achieve a more elegant balance in his sentence.

(ii) *Legal*

A similar fate seems to have befallen many of the other synonymous
pairs that have their source in the language of the law. Subtle legal
distinctions were probably once conveyed in such noun pairs as «desonrra
e daño» (10), «daño e mal» (7), «desonrra e mal» (4), «mal e desafuero» (4),
«daño e enojo» (3), «pérdida e desonrra» (2), «pérdida e daño» (2), «enojos
e peligros» (2), «peligro e daño» (2), «peligros e desonrra», «desonrra
e enbargo», «daño e menoscabo», «perdiçión e destruymiento», «discordias
e enamistad», «enamistad e desamor», «daño e robo» (1 each). The
Zifar also contains a number of related adjectival and verbal pairs which,
unless otherwise indicated, occur only once in the course of the work:
«desonrrado e perdido», «perdido e astragado», «despechado e astragado»,
«desaforado e astragado», «menospreçiado e desechado»; «despechar
e astragar», «desonrrar e abiltar», «confonder e astragar», «quemar e
astragar» (2), «enojar e arrebatar», «deseheredar e desterrar», «desfazer
e desapoderar», «desfazer e toller», «despechar e desterrar», «arrancar

[70] This is especially true in references to God. Synonymous pairs are not only
used in addressing God, as in «Dios Señor, yo non te lo podría gradesçer quanto bien e
quanta merçed me has fecho» (469.25-26; cf. 147.18-20), but also when a character refers
to God, as in «a nós fizo Dios mucho bien e mucha merçed» (251.23-24; cf. 252.2-4,
394.11-12).

e desbaratar» (2), «derribar e sacar», «quebrantar e vençer», «quebrantar e abaxar».

With these pairs it is again very difficult to decide where the desire for precise coverage of the different classes of damage and dishonour ends and the sheer love of rhetoric takes over. There certainly seem to be some traces of legalistic hairsplitting in a few places where these pairs are used in the *Zifar*. When ambassadors from the count who is besieging Galapia are invited inside the city, for instance, they ask the welcoming committee: «¿E vós segurádesnos ... que non resçibamos daño nin desonrra por esta entrada?» (73.8-10). A little later, when the same ambassadors deliver their lord's message to the ruler of Galapia, a similar careful choice of words is evident:

> [Nuestro señor] dize que fue mucho su amigo [of the lady's late husband] en toda su vida, e qu'él vos ha fecho guerra e mucho daño e mucho mal en aquesta vuestra tierra. E porende tiene que sy mayores enbargos le diese e mayores desonrras de quantas le ha fecho fasta el día de oy, con grant derecho gelo faría (74.2-7).

Apart from such moments, however, when threats are being issued or treaties negotiated—moments at which both solemnity and precision are essential—the pairs such as «daño e mal» seem to function purely as narrative rhetorical clichés.

Rather less of a cliché are the synonymous pairs that deal with the bonds of feudal loyalty. Clearly taking an oath of allegiance was a very serious business; for this reason medieval legal language abounds in pairs to suit such a solemn occasion. In the *Zifar*, apart from the triplet «verdat e fialdat e lealtad» (222.26-27), we find «verdat e lealtad» (6), «fe e verdat» (5), «bondat e lealtad» (3), «fialdat e lealtad» (2), «jura e omenage» (3), «pleito e omenage» (3), «tregua e omenage» (3). There are also a number of corresponding adjectival pairs: «bueno e leal» (8), «verdadero e bueno» (2), «leal e verdadero» (2), «verdadero e fiel» (2). On one occasion the act of swearing itself merits a pair: «prometer e jurar» (301.1).

The author may have been conscious of the minute differences between the constituent elements of the various pairs denoting allegiance, but it seems more likely that his main reason for using them was not one of precision but one of solemnity. The relative infrequency of these pairs points to a rather more conscious and deliberate usage than is perhaps the case with some of the more common pairs we have examined, and lifts them above the simple level of the cliché. The fact that the phrase «fazer omenage» is employed twenty-three times without the addition of a second noun, [71] whereas «fazer pleito e omenage» and «fazer jura

[71]   43.27, 44.7-8, 44.12, 44.14, 44.17, 73.5, 219.11, 219.16, 219.23 220.4, 220.8, 243.6, 248.2, 314.8, 315.2, 400.7, 400.9, 401.2-3, 418.30, 437.24, 457.23, 460.10, 484.21.

e omenage» occur only six times altogether, indicates that the pairs seem to have been reserved for special occasions. And so it proves: in five out of the six cases the solemn pairs are used by a character when he wishes to impress his hearers forcibly with his seriousness. Two examples will be sufficient to illustrate this point. After the capture of the rebel Nasón, he is arraigned before Zifar, now King of Mentón, and formally charged with treason by the king in these words:

> Onde, commo vós, conde, fuestes mío vasallo e heredado en el mío regno, e teniendo de mí tierra grande de que me avíedes a fazer debdo, e muy grande aver cada año por que érades tenudo de me servir, e aviéndome fecho jura e omenage de me guardar fialdat e lealtad, asý commo buen vasallo deve fazer a buen señor... (223.21-224.1).

In Book IV the Cavallero Amigo (the former Ribaldo), having been sold into captivity by Count Farán, persuades his purchaser, a merchant, to go to the palace of the emperor Roboán, assuring him of the safety of his investment in these terms: «Yo vos fago pleito e omenaje ... que de vós non me parta ffasta que cobredes todo lo vuestro e más» (493.25-27).

The various duties of vassals towards their lords and lords towards their vassals, of children towards their parents and parents towards their children, of men towards their fellows and towards God, all these are frequently expressed by means of legalistic pairs. Once again the purpose of the pair is at best to underline the seriousness of the obligation rather than to draw any meaningful distinctions; and in most cases it serves merely as a rhetorical cliché. The *Zifar* is particularly rich in verbal pairs of this type: «guiar e endresçar» (6), «conortar e esforçar» (5), [72] «anparar e defender» (5), «amar e preçiar» (4), «guardar e defender» (4), «guardar e servir» (3), «amar e onrrar» (3), «seguir e guardar» (3), «castigar e consejar» (3), «amar e guardar» (2), «conortar e ayudar» (2), «esforçar e ayudar» (2), «guiar e mantener» (2), «servir e gradesçer» (2), «castigar e dotrinar» (2), «onrrar e defender», «preçiar e onrrar», «heredar e onrrar», «onrrar e loar», «amar e servir», «servir e defender», «aconpañar e onrrar», «aconpañar e guiar», «ayudar e acorrer», «ayudar e defender», «endresçar e ayudar», «ayudar e guiar», «guardar e endresçar», «guardar e onrrar», «guardar e castigar», «guardar e catar», «salvar e guardar», «governar e criar», «castigar e emendar», «castigar e refrenar», «enseñar e consejar», «mandar e aconsejar», «enseñar e castigar», «demostrar e enseñar» (1 each).

This already large group of synonymous pairs is augmented still further by other pairs from the same lexical roots but with different grammatical

---

[72] Included in this total are pairs which have *dar conorte* or *dar esfuerço* as one of their components. Cf. also «tomad buen esfuerço e buen conorte» (69.25).

functions. We find the following adjectival pairs: «amado e preçiado» (7), «anparado e defendido» (4), «onrrado e poderoso» (3), «guardado e servido» (3), «onrrado e amado» (3), «guardado e mantenido» (2), «amado e ensalçado», «defendido e onrrado», «onrrado e loado», «onrrado e preçiado», «guardado e asegurado», «servido e ayudado», «sostenido e mantenido», «aconpañado e servido» (1 each). Related noun pairs include: «guardador e defendedor» (2), «anparador e defendedor», «guiador e endreçador», «guiador e ordenador», «lidiador e defendedor» (1 each); «ayuda e consejo» (3), «guarda e anparamiento», «guarda e endresçamiento» (1 each).

Also probably of ultimately legal provenance are the numerous pairs denoting the moral qualities that a good lord (or sometimes just a good man) must possess, qualities such as honesty, justice, clemency and restraint: «justiçia e verdat» (9), «justiçia e derecho» (4), «misericordia e piedat» (2), «merçed e mesura» (2), «verdat e derecho», «verdat e razón», «verdat e bien», «sapiença e verdat», «duelo e piedat», «merçed e piedat», «misericordia e merçed», «mesura e seso», «mesura e bondat», «mesura e cordura», «mesura e piedat», «mesura e vergüença» (1 each).

If loyalty and feudal obligations were taken seriously, so too were disloyalty and treachery. We have already seen, in the case of Nasón, the elaborate solemnity of phrasing in the accusation and condemnation of a traitor. The *Zifar* uses several pairs to denote the contravention of oaths and deception and treachery in general, some of them of clear legal ancestry and all of them, it seems, of legal inspiration. There are a few adjectival pairs: «falso e traydor» (2), «mintroso e falso», «mentiroso e desvariado», «falaguero e engañoso» (1 each); and a couple of verb pairs: «mentir e engañar» and «fallesçer e mentir» (1 each). The majority of pairs in this category, however, are noun pairs: «maestría e engaño» (6), [73] «falsedat e enemiga» (2), «mal e engaño» (2), «sobervia e engaño» (2), «falsedat e mentira», «fealdat e trayçión», «mal e trayçión», «trayçión e enemiga», «mal e enemiga», «maldat e deslealtad», «engaño e sotileza», «maestría e sotileza», «mentira e enemiga», «mentira e lisonja», «mentira e ynfinta», «mentira e sobervia», «lisonja e maestría» (1 each).

Other verb pairs in the *Zifar* that seem to have a legal origin are «valer e meresçer» (2); «guardar e tener» (1), which recalls the «habere, tenere et possidere» formula dating back to Justinian; the pairs signifying agreement «fazer e otorgar», «dar e galardonar», «querer e consentir» (1 each). A very interesting group of pairs involves *dezir* as one of the elements: «fablar e dezir» (2), «dezir e consejar», «dezir e mandar», «dezir e pregonar», «confesar e dezir» (1 each). Here one senses the lawyer's desire to be specific in the context of an illiterate society where the spoken word was much more important in agreeing contracts, truces, decrees, etc.

---

[73] *Maestría* tends to be used throughout the *Zifar* with this rather unusual meaning of «deception».

than a signature on a piece of paper. [74] The large number of near-synonymous verbal pairs of thinking, understanding, learning and knowing are also probably derived from the emphatic overprecision of legal style: «entender e ver» (13), «saber e poder» (4), «saber e conosçer» (3), «saber e entender» (2), «entender e creer» (2), «ver e conosçer» (2), «catar e conosçer» (2), «conosçer e judgar» (2), «catar e pensar», «pensar e cuydar», «catar e ver», «ver e sentir», «pensar e entender», «saber e aprender», «oýr e aprender», «fallar e conosçer», «escudriñar e adevinar» (1 each).

Finally, the language of the lawyers has also contributed some noun pairs used with an adverbial function to denote the speaker's willingness. Smith and Morris quote «de bon corazón y voluntad» from a legal document, and there are several similar phrases in the epic and ballads. [75] The *Zifar* has only two such pairs, each used only once: «por voluntad e por sabor» and «de coraçón e de voluntad». [76]

(iii) *Religious*

Despite the *Zifar* author's obvious religious background and preoccupations, only very few of the synonymous pairs in the work seem to have a specifically religious origin. Faith is subdivided into «la gran fe e la gran devoçión», «buena fe e buena creençia» and «fuzía e esperança». «Onrra e gloria», applied to God, occurs once, in a quotation from the Bible: «E por eso dizen las palabras santas que por él, e con él, e en él, es toda onrra e gloria para sienpre» (301.21-22). Many of the pairs which have been classified here as being of legal origin could, of course, have an ultimately religious inspiration, bearing in mind the close connections between religion and the law in the Middle Ages and the frequent use of similar pairs by the Jewish lawgivers of the Old Testament. One has only to consider such phrases as «Custodite legitima mea atque judicia» *(Leviticus* XVIII.26) or «Non facietis vobis idolum et sculptile» (*ibid.* XXVI.1) to appreciate this possibility.

(iv) *Literary*

The remainder of the *Zifar*'s synonymous pairs fit into the category defined by Smith and Morris as those «pairs which seem not to have been incorporated into literature from some other and pre-existing 'real' sphere, but to have originated in a literary tradition». The nature of this

[74] See Smith and Morris, «Phrases», especially 135-136.
[75] E.g. «de voluntad e de grado» (*PMC* 149, 1005, 1056), «de amor e de voluntad» (*PMC* 1139, 1692), «de amor e de grado» (*PMC* 2234).
[76] Smith and Morris point out that such pairs are rare in *clerecía* verse; the only examples found by them are «de amor e de grado» (*SOria* 34b, 66b) and «de sabor e de grado» (*Apol* 618c). There are, however, in the *Zifar* quite a number of examples of *de coraçón* used on its own after a verb: e.g. «perdonar de coraçón» (79.7), «amar de coraçón» (206.3), «obedesçer de coraçón» (318.7).

tradition and the *Zifar* author's dependence on it and contribution to it will be dealt with later in this chapter.

The first type of literary pair noted by Smith and Morris is that in which the second element adds little or nothing to the meaning expressed by the first. They cite as examples «lumbres e candelas», «cena e yantar», «rico e abondado», «soportar e sofrir», «robar e correr». The existence of such pairs can be ascribed either to a simple love of rhetoric or, in the poets, to the more practical consideration of filling up half a line of verse. The *Zifar* abounds in such pairs. Amongst the nouns we find (arranged in rough semantic groups): «aver e riqueza» (1); «fuerça e poder», «poder e esfuerço», «señorío e poder» (1 each); «razón e entendimiento» (6), «seso e entendimiento»(3); «locura e sobervia»(2), «atrevimiento e locura», «locura e braveza» (1 each); «paçiençia e sufrençia» (1); «razón e derecho» (11); «enxienplo e castigo» (2), «enxienplo e consejo» (1); «copas e vasos» (2); «cuenta e razón», «razón e ocasión» (1 each); «ora e sazón» (1); «ymagen e semejança» (1); «muerte e pasyón» (1); «gestos e adamanes» (1); «conpaña e gente», «ayuntamientos e conpañías» (1 each); «escatima e reprehensión» (1); «mandamientos e mandaderías» (1); «ofiçios e ordenamientos» (1); «yerro e pecado» (4), «yerro e vergüença» (2), «yerro e estropieço» (1). Adjectival pairs in the same category include: «cocho e asado» (3); «feo e malo» (2), «feo e cruo» (1); «abonado e abastado», «largo e abonado» (1 each); «fecho e adobado» (1); «esquivo e estraño» (1); «fresco e abibado» (1); «público e manifiesto» (1). Similar verbal pairs are: «sofrir e pasar» (5), «sofrir e conplir», «sofrir e mantener» (1 each); «guarneçer e ornar» (1); «abraçar e besar» (4), «saludar e besar» (3); «aperçibir e aguisar», «poner e ordenar» (1 each); «abibar e despertar» (1); «comer e roer» (1); «mudar e canbiar» (1); «dexar e olvidar» (1); «tardar e recabdar» (2), «dudar e tardar», «alongar e detardar» (1 each); «amar e cobdiçiar», «querer e codiçiar», «demandar e cobdiçiar», «demandar e querer», «rogar e demandar» (1 each); «amansar e atenprar» (1).

Smith and Morris' second category of literary synonymous pairs consists of those pairs in which the second element adds something to the meaning and/or intensifies the emotional impact. Not surprisingly most of the pairs they assign to this category concern feelings and emotions, such as grief (e.g. «pesar e duelo», «triste e penado»), anger (e.g. «sannoso e irado», «sañudo e irado»), joy (e.g. «alegre e pagado», «savor e alegría»). They also include under this heading pairs such as «bivo e sano» and «salvo e seguro», which express security and general well-being.

In the *Zifar* both adjectival and noun pairs of this type are extremely common. A large number denote sadness or grief: «triste e cuytado» (8), «triste e lloroso», «cuytado e lazrado», «desconortado e triste», «demudado e triste», «deseheredado e lazrado» (1 each); «tristeza e pesar» (4), «pesar e trabajo» (2), «ruydo e llanto» (2), «cuydado e pesar», «cuydado e tristeza», «cuyta e pesar», «llanto e pesar», «lloro e llanto», «lloro e pesar», «lazerío e cuydado», «lazerío e servidunbre», «trabajo e cuydado», «mal e pesar» (1 each). Other similar pairs denote weariness: «cansado e quebrantado» (2), «laso e quebrantado» (1); or a combination of grief and weariness: «cansado e lazrado» (2), «cuytado e cansado», «quebrantado e triste» (1 each); «cuyta e quebranto», «quebranto e lazerío», «quebranto e pesar» (1 each). A few pairs denoting poverty, all occurring only once, are also worth noting: «pobre e desfecho», «pobre e fanbriento», «pobre e menguado»; «pobredat e lazería», «pobredat e mengua».

The related notion of danger and hardship is also often expressed through pairs: «peligroso e dañoso» (2), «malo e peligroso», «áspero e grave», «grave e duro», «grave e peligroso», «vil e dañoso» (1 each); «trabajo e peligro» (2), «premia e priesa» (2), «priesa e peligro», «afán e trabajo», «bolliçio e escándalo», «escándalo e duda» (1 each).

Pairs conveying the emotion of fear also clearly come into this category: «temido e dubdado», «medroso e vergoñoso» (1 each); «miedo e vergüeña» (4), «miedo e reçelo» (3), «miedo e lisonja» (2), «miedo e sospecha», «mal e reçelo», «cuyta e reçelo» (1 each).

On the more positive side there are many pairs used to denote joy and pleasure in the *Zifar*: «ledo e pagado» (5), «alegre e pagado» (4), «loçano e alegre», «alegre e bien andante», «entregado e pagado» (1 each); «alegría e plazer» (7), «plazer e solás» (6), «alegría e amor», «alegría e trebejo», «alegría e conorte», «sabor e plazer», «trebejo e solás», «viçios e deleytes», «consolaçión e plazer», «viçio e folgura», «bien e plazer» (1 each). [77] The kindred ideas of peace and security also have their pairs: «folgado e seguro», «folgado e asosegado», «viçioso e folgado», «çierto e seguro», [78] «adormido e descuydado», «descuydado e perezoso» (1 each); «pas e justiçia» (5), «pas e concordia» (2), «pas e sosiego» (1), «tregua e segurança» (2). Occasionally the notions of joy and security are combined in a pair: «viçioso e abondado» (2); «pas e alegría» (2). Pairs denoting physical well-being, some of which are possibly legal in inspiration, also occur: «bivo e sano» (5), «bivo e razonable», «guarido e sano» (1 each); «vida e salud» (2); but almost as common are pairs that link this concept with the general idea of joy: «sano e alegre» (5), «leydo e sano» (1).

In these intensifying emotional expressions verbal pairs are very much rarer than noun or adjectival pairs. I have found only eight verbal pairs in the entire romance that can be fitted into this category; all of them occur only once: «cuytar e presurar», «llorar e dar bozes», «dar bozes e fazer llanto», «llorar e fazer llanto»; «folgar e asosegar», «folgar e trebejar», «trebejar e jugar»; [79] «sanar e guaresçer». The reason for

---

[77] Smith and Morris only encountered one noun pair denoting joy, «savor e alegría» (*Milag* 313c, 332d).

[78] Another instance of «çierto e seguro» (410.20) denotes «certainty», not «security».

[79] Note also the inclusives «dormir e folgar», etc. listed above in section A (v).

this scarcity of verbal pairs is probably that states of emotion are much more readily expressed substantively and adjectivally than through verbs, which of course denote action far more frequently than they describe state.

Smith and Morris' third category of literary pairs comprises the adjectival pairs used to describe landscapes, swords, horses, persons, etc., in which the two terms «are not fully synonymous but have a kind of natural association». They quote such phrases as «linpio e claro», «gruesos e corredores», «maravilloso e grand», «dulz e sabrido». In the *Zifar* we find two fountains and a day described as «fermoso e claro» and water as «clara e linpia». The city of the King of Brez is «apuesto e viçioso»; the lake kingdom is «fermoso e viçioso» and its palaces «grandes e fermosos». Jewels are «finos e virtuosos» and gold «fino e puro». The beauty of persons is conveyed through a number of pairs involving *fermoso* or *apuesto:* «blanco e fermoso» (3), [80] «apuesto e bien vestido» (2), «mançebo e apuesto», «fermoso e leydo», «fermoso e bien vestido», «fermoso e bien andante» (1 each). There are also occasional pairs denoting contrary qualities: «feo e desfaçado» (2), «negro e feo» (1).

The commonest pairs in this category in the *Zifar* are those made up of a very common adjective denoting quality (such as *bueno, rico, grande, fuerte*) and another adjective which is semantically associated with the first. In some cases the second element further defines the particular nuance of goodness, greatness or strength that is involved; but usually these pairs seem to have little more than a purely rhetorical function. Pairs involving *bueno* include «bueno e leal» (8), «bueno e onesto» (7), «bueno e santo» (5), «bueno e verdadero» (2), «bueno e acabado», «bueno e apuesto», «bueno e conplido», «bueno e entendido», «bueno e escogido», «bueno e provado», «bueno e sano» (1 each). *Rico* occurs in the following combinations: «rico e poderoso» (12), «rico e bien andante» (4), «rico e viçioso» (2), «rico e abonado» (2), «rico e apuesto» (2), «rico e de grant lugar» (2), «rico e fermoso», «rico e reçelado», «rico e anparado» (1 each). With *grande* we find «grande e grave» (2), «grande e poderoso» (2), «grande e fermoso», «grande e noble», «grande e sazonado», «grande e desesperado», «alto e grande» (1 each). *Fuerte* is involved in the following pairs: «fuerte e rezio» (2), «fuerte e firme» (2), «bravo e fuerte», «fuerte e cruel», «fuerte e desesperado», «duro e fuerte», «fuerte e lazrado», «fuerte e alto» (1 each). There are also a number of pairs that combine two of the «basic» adjectives *bueno, rico, grande* and *fuerte:* «grande e bueno» (5), «grande e rico» (4), «grande e fuerte» (3), «bueno e rico» (3), «bueno e fuerte» (2).

An important point made by Smith and Morris is that the adjectival pairs used in «static» descriptions of persons are of special interest since

---

[80] One of these (475.2) describes a horse.

they may reflect the teachings of the *Artes Poeticæ* preceptists, who recommend the use of pairs in the description of character. Although such pairs are common in Old French, [81] they tend to be much rarer in Old Spanish because of Spain's «cultural belatedness», to use Curtius' phrase, which meant that the influence of the *Artes* was not felt so much in the earliest vernacular literature of the Peninsula. Such rhetorical pairs, however, are relatively common in the *Zifar*, which of course is late enough to have submitted to the authority of the preceptists. The only Spanish pairs quoted by Smith and Morris in this part of their study come from the *Vida de San Ildefonso* and the *Libro de buen amor*, both of which are later than the *Zifar*. The romance contains a wide variety of adjectival pairs denoting moral qualities and defects, not counting those involving *bueno*, *rico*, *grande* and *fuerte* or those concerning specifically feudal virtues such as loyalty, which have already been listed: «firme e estable» (4); [82] «escaso e covarde» (1); «obediente e mandado» (1); «sabio e entendido» (2), «sabio e sotil», «sotil e agudo» (1 each); «torpe e nesçio» (1); «loco e atrevido» (4), «desmesurado e sobervio» (2), «bravo e loco», «malo e desmesurado», «orgulloso e sobervio», «sobervio e cruo», «sobervioso e loco» (1 each); «franco e mesurado» (2), «cortés e mesurado» (1); «omildoso e paçiente» (3), «sofrido e paçiente» (1); «noble e poderoso», «poderoso e bien andante» (1 each); «codiçioso e malo» (1). It will be noticed that in many of these pairs the second element adds little or nothing to the meaning expressed by the first.

C. CONCLUSIONS

What general conclusions are we to draw from this long catalogue of the *Zifar*'s multitudinous pairs? First, an examination of this material can tell us much about the author's literary inspiration. Although a large number of the synonymous and inclusive pairs in the work derive *ultimately* from the stylised language of social relationships, the law and religion, it would appear, for various reasons, that the author did not take his pairs directly from the linguistic conventions and habits of feudalism and medieval Christianity, but got them at second-hand from a thriving literary tradition. Although occasionally he may have been aware of the subtle distinctions that were once involved in such pairs as «rey e señor» or «desonrra e daño», for the most part he seems to appreciate them not for their precision, but for their impressiveness and, above all, for their

---

[81]   E.g. in the *Chanson de Roland*, «E Oliver li proz e li curteis» (596), «E en bataille est fiers e orgoillus» (3175).

[82]   This phrase is probably of legal origin. Smith and Morris note its use in the *Fuero juzgo* (38) and in a document of 1187 in T. Muñoz y Romero, *Colección de fueros municipales y cartas pueblas* (Madrid, 1847), 244.

rhetorical and rhythmic possibilities. These considerations, of course, as was pointed out long ago, were not ignored by the orators and the lawyers; [83] but it was the poets who turned the pair into a major stylistic device and exploited its literary potential to the full. Furthermore, since a very large proportion of the *Zifar*'s synonymous pairs owe nothing (except their form) to social, legal or religious modes of expression, as we have seen, it seems reasonable to postulate a predominantly literary inspiration, rather than a «real» one, for the others as well.

This literary inspiration comes, I think, from three different sources. In the first place, there can be no doubt that the great use of synonymous and inclusive pairs by earlier vernacular writers influenced the author of the *Zifar*. The binary expression is such a common feature of, for example, all the *clerecía* poets that no reader could fail to be struck by it. [84] We have no direct evidence that the *Zifar* author was familiar with early narrative poetry, but it would be surprising if he had not read—or had read to him—such works as the *Libro de Alexandre*, which was widely known in the late thirteenth and early fourteenth centuries.

A second incentive to use pairs was undoubtedly provided by the preceptists of the *Artes Poeticæ*. We have already seen how they might have encouraged the use of inclusives through the devices of *circumlocutio* and *contentio*. They also advocate the practice of *interpretatio*, which consists of saying the same thing in different words; this might well have been taken as an invitation to use synonymous pairs. Furthermore, apart from the general exhortation «varius sis et tamen idem», [85] Geoffrey of Vinsauf specifically urges the use of synonymous pairs:

> Vel mobile sic geminemus:
> Mensa fuit pauper et parvula, mappa vetusta
> Et contrita, cibus incoctus et horridus, ipse
> Potus acetosus et turbidus, assecla mensae
> Vilis et illepidus. [86]

And Matthew of Vendôme speaks of the importance of synonyms for varying the expression:

> Sequitur de permutatione verborum et non sententiarum, in qua plurimum sunt necessaria synonyma. Synonymorum enim eadem est significatio ex diversis rationibus, unde alterum alterius

---

[83] See, for example, M. Chassan, *Essai sur la symbolique du droit* (Paris, 1847), especially xxix ff. The examples quoted by Smith and Morris from medieval documents and legal texts support his point.

[84] Artiles, *Los recursos literarios*, 111, claims to have noted over 1000 «expresiones bimembres» in Berceo, over 400 of them in the *Milagros*.

[85] *Poetria Nova*, 1. 225 (Faral, *Les Arts poétiques*, 204).

[86] *Poetria Nova*, 11. 1770-74 (Faral, 251).

15

plerumque poterit esse vicarium. Nec vacat quod dictum est «plerumque». Multa enim synonyma sunt, quae, quia diversa significant, mutuam non sortiuntur positionem, immo significatum unius significatio alterius potest attribui. [87]

A third possible inspiration for the use of pairs could well have been provided by Arabic literary conventions. The Koran, the stylistic model for all Arabic writers, has frequent recourse to both inclusive and synonymous pairs. Each *sūra*, for example, opens with a phrase which includes two synonymous adjectives: «In the name of God, the Compassionate, the Merciful». [88] The following two extracts, chosen at random, contain examples of both types of pair:

> There is no God but He; the Living, the Eternal; nor slumber seizeth Him, nor sleep; His, whatsoever is in the Heavens and whatsoever is in the Earth (366)

> They who give away their substance in alms, by night and day, in private and in public, shall have their reward with their Lord: no fear shall come on them, neither shall they be put to grief (369). [89]

An examination of any of the wisdom books translated from Arabic into Spanish in the thirteenth century shows that both inclusive and synonymous pairs remained as striking a feature of the translation as they were of the original. The *Poridat de las poridades*, for instance contains the following pairs: [90]

> *Inclusives*: «Dios et los omes» (36.14), «en comer ny en bever» (38.14-15), «omes et bestias» (40.3), «dezir et fazer» (41.9), «en vuestro dicho ny en vuestro fecho» (41.11-12), «vuestro cuerpo et vuestro aver» (41.12), «non comer nyn bever» (41.23), «con cuerpo et con aver» (47.15), «cuerpo et alma» (55.12), «fazer et dezir» (57.23).

> *Synonymous*: «de bon seso et de buen entendimiento» (29.8), «justiçia et verdad» (29.10), «leal et verdadero» (30.11), «roguel et pedil merçed» (31.10), «el pesar et el cuydado» (31.18), «viejo et flaco» (31.23), «guardar et aguysar» (33.16), «el gastador et el

---

[87] *Ars Versificatoria*, IV, § 24 (Faral, 186).

[88] All quotations from the Koran are from the translation of J. M. Rodwell (Everyman's Library 380, London, 1909; frequently reprinted).

[89] Pairs seem to be a feature of all Semitic religious writing. The Old Testament, particularly the books of prophecy, contains many fine examples.

[90] Ed. Lloyd A. Kasten (Madrid, 1957). Only the clearest pairs have been included in the list. The forms of *u*, *v*, *i* and *j* have been regularized. Page and line numbers are given.

dannador» (34.3), «fiel et franco» (34.5-6), «partir et dar» (34.6), «ordenamiento et endreçamiento» (34.22-35.1), «grand gozo et grand sabor (et grand alegria)» (37.22), «amarle et obedeçerle» (37.25), «el bien et la merçed» (40.4), «por leal et por verdadero» (41.12), «en pensar et en cuydar» (49.2-3), «vuestro seso et vuestro entendimiento» (50.6), «ninguno mal nin sobervia» (51.4-5), «de seso et de entendimiento» (51.20), «fiel et verdadero» (52.1-2), «fieldad et lealtad» (52.17-18), «sin lazerio et sin trabajo» (53.22-23), «grand ondra et grand prez» (54.22), «sin verguença de vos et sin miedo» (63.17-18), «clara et fermosa» (65.4), «mayor sabor et mayor voluntad» (68.18), «onrrado et noble» (71.8), «viçioso et folgado» (71.17).

At least some of these pairs, of course, may be the result of the translator's rhetorical elaboration of his material; it is not unlikely that his style, like that of the *Zifar* author, would be influenced by the flourishing vernacular pairs tradition of the epic and *clericía* poets. But there is no doubt that pairs were a feature of the style of Arabic works other than the Koran. Álvaro Galmés de Fuentes prints a chapter from the *Calila e Digna* alongside the Arabic text, which enables us to see quite clearly that many of the pairs in the two Escorial manuscripts of the *Calila* derive directly from the original. [91] The following *Calila* pairs are faithful translations of the Arabic: «verdadera nin derecha» (247 [48]), [92] «prendiólos e firiólos» (254 [93]), «alegría e folgura» (263 [148]), «tinebla e angostura» (264 [163]), «ocasiones e miedos» (274 [211]). Thus, in view of the other Arabic influences on the *Zifar*'s style (set out in chapter 2), it would be rash to discount the possibility of such influence on the author's taste for pairs.

One of the most striking features, however, of the *Zifar*'s synonymous pairs is their apparent originality: very few of them turn up in earlier Spanish works. The findings of Artiles, Gariano, Perry, de Chasca, Smith and Morris, and my own researches, show that only a small minority of the pairs in the romance seem to have been taken over from previous authors in the Latin or vernacular tradition. The only «established» pairs in the *Zifar* would appear to be the following:

alegre e loçano	*Milag* 824a.
alegre e pagado	*Milag* 213d, 359a, 612a, 731a; *Signos* 50c; *SOria* 46b; *SMill* 249a, 457d; *SDom* 303d, 396d, 556d, 605d; *Apol* 163d, 177b, 194b.
bivo e sano	*PMC* 2866.
defender e guardar	*SMill* 199b.

[91] «Influencias sintácticas y estilísticas del árabe en la prosa medieval castellana», *BRAE* XXXV (1955), 213-275.

[92] The first number refers to the page in «Influencias», the second to the sections within the text established by Galmés de Fuentes.

falso e traidor [93]	*Milag* 419a; *Apol* 388b.
firme e estable	*Loores* 192b.
fuerte e grand	*PMC* 554.
fuerte e lazrado	*SMill* 70b.
lazerío e quebranto	*SOria* 173c.
ledo e pagado	*PFG* 686c.
lloro e llanto	*PFG* 243d, 244a, 250a.
malo e perigloso	*SMill* 103d.
pobre e menguado	*SLor* 13c.
rey e señor	*PMC* 1885, 1952, 2109, 3118, 3146, 3430, 3488, 3574; *SMill* 131c.
rico e abon(d)ado	*Milag* 656b; *SDom* 283c; *Apol* 124b, 240a; *PCG* 524.b.22.
rico e bien andante	*PCG* 592.b.28.
sano e alegre	*SDom* 291a, 314c, 548d; *SLor* 83d; *PCG* 594.b.23.
sano e guarido	*SDom* 476d.
serviçio e onor [94]	*Milag* 487d.

The above list, of course, makes no claim to be exhaustive, but it is probably sufficiently complete to support the contention that the *Zifar* author's direct borrowings from the purely vernacular tradition are much fewer than one might expect in a work so rich in pairs. A study of the binary expressions in translations of Arabic wisdom literature (not dealt with at all by Smith and Morris) would show that some of the *Zifar*'s pairs, particularly those expressing abstract moral and intellectual concepts, derive from this tradition. If one takes only the examples extracted from *Poridat de las poridades*, listed above, one can see a good deal of common ground. But even works of this type do not account for more than a small proportion of the vast number of pairs in the *Zifar*.

Moreover, many of the commonest pairs in the earlier texts, which were certainly established as stylistic clichés by 1300, make no appearance at all in the *Zifar*. In view of the abundance of pairs in the romance, it is perhaps a little surprising that it contains no echo of, for example, «triste e desarrado», which occurs seven times in Berceo and at least twice in the *PFG*. [95] The same might be said of the absence of other similar pairs such as «triste e pesado» (e.g. *Apol* 333c) and «triste e dolorido» (e.g. *PFG* 161c, 243c). Nor does the *Zifar* have any examples of the «anger» pairs «sannoso e irado» and «sañudo e irado», so common in *clerecía*. [96] Of the common descriptive adjectival pairs in the *PMC* with

[93] Much more usual is the epithetical expression «falso traidor» (e.g. *Milag* 479a, 723b, 757a, 841a).

[94] The form in the *Zifar* is «serviçio e onrra».

[95] See Artiles, *Los recursos literarios*, 116, n. 4, for the Berceo references; *PFG* 386a, 540c.

[96] E.g. «sannoso e irado»: *Milag* 466c, 560b; *SLor* 98c; *Signos* 31a; «sañudo e irado»: *PFG* 198b; *AlexO* 1928a; cf. *PCG* 541.a.49.

grand as one of the components, [97] only «fuerte e grand» is found in the *Zifar;* and there is not a single example in the whole work of the very common pairs in Berceo formed with *dulz* and another adjective. [98]

All this is particularly interesting when we remember that in the various categories from which these examples have been chosen the *Zifar* is very rich in pairs. There are, for instance, as we have seen, six adjectival pairs (three of them involving *triste)* that express grief; altogether they provide thirteen occurrences. *Grande* combined with another adjective gives ten different pairs which occur a total of twenty-one times. Other pairs made up of common adjectives such as *rico, bueno* and *fuerte* are also extremely frequent, which makes it perhaps all the more puzzling that *dulce* is never present as an element in any of them. [99] This would suggest that in his use of pairs the *Zifar* author is more than a mere borrower and imitator of the creations of his predecessors. His concern for originality is seen in his avoidance of many of the established cliché pairs, his invention of numerous new pairs and his apparent distaste for repeating the same pair too often. Most of the synonymous pairs in the romance, it will have been noticed, occur only once or twice in the entire work.

The *Zifar* author, then, although he uses pairs in much the same way and to express much the same things as earlier writers, seems to try to avoid the established cliché and invent new binary expressions. It is worth examining in some detail the ways in which he does this. One of the simplest methods of ringing the changes on the old pairs is to find a third synonym which can be separately combined with the individual elements of the original pair and so create immediately two new ones. In the following list the pairs in the first column occur in earlier texts as well as in the *Zifar;* those in the second and third columns are, so far as I have been able to ascertain, new creations built up by the method just outlined:

lloro e llanto	lloro e pesar	llanto e pesar
amar e onrrar	amar e preçiar	onrrar e preçiar
onrra e pres	onrra e fama	pres e fama.

In some cases the author discovers so many synonyms or near synonyms that he is able to produce a very large number of permutations of the same basic idea. For example, the following matrix, showing the distribution of the adjectival pairs denoting grief and weariness, reveals that by using a wide range of synonyms the author had at his disposal

[97] De Chasca, *Registro*, 45, notes five instances of «maravilloso e grand», two of «fiera e grand», and one each of «espessa e grand» and «fuerte e grand».

[98] Artiles, *Los recursos literarios*, 117, n. 11, lists nine cases of pairs involving *dulz;* but there are certainly others (e.g. *Himnos* 9b).

[99] Although Berceo seems to be the poet most fond of *dulce* pairs, their use was not confined to him; cf. *Apol* 105d.

ninety possible combinations of adjectives and 180 possible pairs, if we take into account variations in the position of the constituent elements. In fact, he avails himself of only twelve of these permutations, but nine of them occur only once. The one pair that might be called a cliché because of its frequent appearance is «triste e cuytado».

	cansado	cuytado	demudado	desconortado	fuerte	laso	lazrado	lloroso	quebrantado	triste
cansado								2	2	
cuytado	1								1	1
demudado										1
desconortado										1
fuerte						1				
laso							1			
lazrado										
lloroso										
quebrantado										1
triste	7					1				

In the corresponding matrix for noun pairs we can see that here, out of a possible total of 132 combinations, the author uses seventeen, none of them more than twice in the whole work.

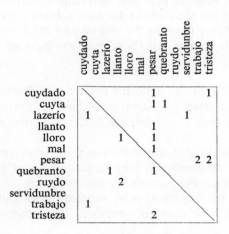

	cuydado	cuyta	lazerío	llanto	lloro	mal	pesar	quebranto	ruydo	servidunbre	trabajo	tristeza
cuydado							1					1
cuyta							1	1				
lazerío	1								1			
llanto							1					
lloro						1	1					
mal							1					
pesar											2	2
quebranto		1					1					
ruydo		2										
servidunbre												
trabajo	1											
tristeza								2				

Twenty-one verbs denoting the various obligations of lord to vassal, vassal to lord and man to man (not including *castigar*, *consejar*, etc.) are used in the *Zifar* as components of synonymous pairs. Out of a possible 420 permutations the author uses thirty-five. The most that any one pair is used is four times, as the following matrix shows.

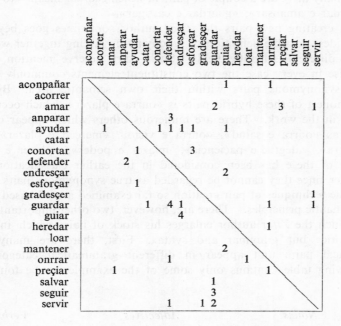

These matrices show how much variety can be introduced into the basic cliché by the simple expedient of extending the number of components from which pairs can be constructed.

The *Zifar* author also increases his stock of pairs by coupling a rather vague generalized word with a wide range of meaning together with a word that denotes one specific aspect of the general meaning. We have already noted this technique of constructing pairs by natural association in the case of the adjectives *bueno, grande, fuerte* and *rico;* but the practice is also common with nouns and verbs. A good illustration is provided by the pairs involving *bien* and *mal,* two words with an extremely wide range of possible meanings: «bien e amor», «bien e don», «bien e merçed», «bien e plazer», «bien e onrra», «bien e verdat»; «mal e crueldat», «mal e desafuero», «mal e enemiga», «mal e engaño», «mal e pesar», «mal e reçelo», «mal e trayçión». Of particular interest in this connection are the pairs containing *guardar,* a verb which has evolved several quite distinct meanings and entered a number of different semantic fields. In the *Zifar* we find pairs in which *guardar* means «to guard», «to protect», such as «guardar e defender», «guardar e endresçar», «salvar e guardar», «seguir e guardar»; in other pairs *guardar* means «to respect»: «guardar e catar», «guardar e onrrar», «guardar e servir»; a third group has *guardar* meaning «to have», «to keep»: «guardar e tener», «guardar e retener»; and finally there are a couple of pairs in which *guardar* means «to restrain»: «guardar e amansar», «guardar e castigar».

In creating new pairs the *Zifar* author sometimes goes beyond even the widest possible definition of synonymy by linking together words from quite different semantic fields. Such pairs deserve mention, however, because in every case the two constituent elements commonly appear in true synonymous pairs within their own semantic area. By far the commonest of these hybrid pairs is «onrra e plazer», which occurs eleven times in the work. There are numerous others which appear only once, such as «onrra e salud», «onrra e viçio», «merçed e plazer», «alegría e onrra», «alegría e paçiençia», «plazer e poder», «plazer e serviçio». None of these has been considered in the earlier classifications in this chapter since they cannot be regarded as true synonymous pairs. [100]

The techniques of pair creation so far examined are all based on lexical or semantic principles. There are, however, two other important processes by which the *Zifar* author enlarges his stock of pairs which involve not semantics but grammar and syntax. First, there are many lexically identical pairs that appear in different grammatical categories. The following table contains only some of the examples to be found in the work:

Nouns	*Adjectives*	*Verbs*
anparador e defendedor	anparado e defendido	anparar e defender
onrra e pres	onrrado e preçiado	onrrar e preçiar
rey e señor		regnar e señorear
pobredat e mengua	pobre e menguado	
peligro e daño	peligroso e dañoso	
guiador e endresçador		guiar e endresçar
bondat e lealtad	bueno e leal	
falsedat e mentira	mintroso e falso	
sobervia e locura	sobervioso e loco	

A second useful technique for creating pairs is to use two words of directly opposite meaning, one in the affirmative and the other in the negative. Such «syntactical» pairs are common in the *Zifar;* for example: «sienpre dezía verdat e non mentira» (11.11), «calló e non le dixo más» (18.14), «conosçido sería del diablo e non de Dios» (31.21-22), «ella calló e non le respondió ninguna cosa» (76.24-25), «muere viejo e non mançebo»

[100] All, however, are listed in appendix 2.

(114.29), «a tuerto e syn derecho» (128.23), «en el mal fablar ay daño e non pro» (290.23-24), «queret ser omildosos e non urgullosos» (296.9), «nos ha fecho mucho mal e non bien» (348.16-17), «fue enemigo e non amigo» (478.2). [101] This is the rhetorical device of *aferre contrarium*, one of the sub-varieties of *expolitio*. It is similar to the more common device of *oppositum* (or *oppositio*), the only difference being that in the latter the opposite is denied first:

> Rem certam pono, cujus contraria primo
> Tollitur: haec dempta cedit, et illa manet:
> Non placeat, sed displiceat tibi gloria mundi:
> Decipit, et vitam non parit, immo necem. [102]

Indeed, Geoffrey of Vinsauf seems to have confused the two devices since his alleged illustrations of *oppositum* are in fact examples of *aferre contrarium:*

> Sapiens est illa juventa:
> Ista juventutis est et non forma senilis:
> Pone juventutem vultus vel tolle senectam.
> Pone senectutem mentis vel tolle juventam:
> Ista senectutis est mens et non juvenilis. [103]

There are occurrences of this device in Spanish texts earlier than the *Zifar*, [104] and there are some in Old French. [105] Once again, however, the *Zifar* author seems to develop the germs of a tradition much more than any of his predecessors.

The author's apparent concern for variety in the use of pairs is also to be seen in the way in which he changes the order of the components of a pair if it occurs more than once within a few lines:

> Amigos, a los que tienen en priesa e en premia, non se deven dar vagar, mas deven fazer quanto pudieren por salir de aquella premia e priesa (55.11-13)

> e ninguno non puede judgar nin conosçer a otro si ante non sabe conosçer e judgar a sý mesmo (145.26-146.1)

> ca Dios non fizo el ome commo las otras animalias mudas, a quien non dio razón nin entendimiento.... E por eso dio Dios al ome entendimiento e razón (266.10-14)

[101] Cf. 16.6, 79.18-19, 221.8, 289.7-8, 300.16-17, 310.9-10, 375.18, 420.24, 433.6-7.
[102] Everhard the German, *Laborintus*, 11. 333-336 (Faral, 348).
[103] *Poetria Nova*, 11. 674-678 (Faral, 218). Geoffrey's full discussion of *oppositum* covers 11. 668-686.
[104] E.g. «Por muertas las dexaron, sabed, que non por bivas» (*PMC* 2752), «faze mal ca non bien» (*Sacr* 60d), «en paz e sin contienda» (*Himnos* 5b).
[105] Faral, 85, quotes an example from *Songe d'enfer* and one from *Voie de paradis*.

> sienpre tiene ojo por aquél que gelo da, para lo guardar e
> para lo servir... e non cata por servir e aguardar âquél que
> gelo dio (355.9-14)

> e tomava en ello muy grand plazer e grand solaz.... E todo
> ome que quesiere aver solaz e plazer... (459.19-23).[106]

Another way of avoiding the exact repetition of the same pair within
the space of a few lines is to change the grammatical category for the
second occurrence:

> E asý que todos los reys e príncipes del mundo deven mucho
> amar justiçia e verdat... ca todos los de su regno se asegurarán
> en el rey justiçiero e verdadero (311.11-15)

> despechando e astragando la vuestra tierra... do el vuestro
> pueblo fuese despechado e astragado (371.8-11).

Apart from the desire for variety, there seems to be another important
literary consideration governing the use of pairs in the *Zifar*—the search
for balance and rhythm in the prose. The occurrence of pairs of
synonymous pairs to balance the structure of the sentence is fairly common
as, for example, «aviéndome fecho jura e omenage de me guardar fialdat
e lealtad» (223.24-25); but the majority of double pairs involve one
inclusive and one synonymous pair. [107] The reason for this is that the
very nature of inclusives makes it impossible to omit one of the components,
whereas the true synonymous pair expresses little more in actual meaning
than either one of its constituent elements used singly. The occurrence
of many synonymous pairs, then, would seem to be dictated purely by
the desire to provide balance for an inclusive, as the following examples
show: «dioles mesura e bondat en manera e en seso» (39.14), «el duelo
e las bozes de las dueñas e de las donzellas» (65.15-16), «a pro e a onrra
de mí e de mi fijo» (72.3).

The use of pairs of pairs is particularly common in antithetical sentences,
where a perfect balance of the two parts contributes greatly to the
effectiveness of the whole. Clearly, a matching or contrasting pair in
each half is an even more striking device for underlining this balance
than matching or contrasting single words. A simple illustration of
this is «e agora vos abría yo por pecador e enemigo de Dios, e estonçe
vos abré syn pecado e amigo de Dios» (166.24-25). But the *Zifar* abounds
in much more complex examples of pairs in antithetical expressions.

---

[106] Cf. the similar technique with some inclusives: e.g. «feriendo e matando» (158.18),
«matando e feriendo» (158.27-28); «muertos e feridos» (197.19), «feridos e muertos»
(197.25).
[107] We have already noticed the tendency to introduce a balancing synonymous
pair before the inclusives «de Dios e de los omes» and «alma e cuerpo».

In the following, for instance, the duality of *mal* and *bien* introduced in the first clause splits into its constituent elements, each of which introduces a clause containing a synonymous pair followed by an inclusive pair. Moreover, the synonymous pairs are directly opposite in meaning («onrra e pro» and «desonrra e daño»), whilst the second inclusive («cuerpo e alma») recalls the double life of man expressed in the first («este mundo e el otro»):

> E asý bien aventurado es el que fuye del mal e se llega al bien, ca del bien puede ome aver onrra e pro en este mundo e en el otro. E del mal puede aver desonrra e daño para el cuerpo e para el alma (221.3-6). [108]

In some of the most impressive antithetical statements synonymous or near-synonymous triplets are used as well as pairs. [109] An excellent example of such elaboration is the following:

> (*a*) mas pero la bondat e lealtad e buen consejo es más de preçiar e de onrrar que la maldat e la deslealtad e el mal consejo, (*b*) ca los buenos e leales e de buen consejo guardarvos-hán de yerro e de vergüença, (*c*) e sienpre punarán de acresçentar vuestra onrra e vuestra [*sic*] bien. (*d*) E los malos[*PS add* e los] desleales e de mal consejo, plazerles-há quando en yerro e en vergüença cayerdes, (*e*) e serán en consejo de amenguar vuestra onrra e el vuestro poder (328.25-329.6).

In (*a*) two absolutely parallel contrasting triplets surround a pair. The triplets have their own internal balance, with the number of syllables increasing with each element $(2 + 3 + 4)$. The bipartite third element of the triplets *(buen/mal consejo)* serves to break the possible monotony of a series of three single-word synonyms. One notes too how the rhythm at the end of this section (*a*) is slowed down by the introduction of the definite article before *each* of the nouns in the second triplet. Section (*b*) opens with another triplet, each component of which is the exact adjectival equivalent of the nouns in the first triplet of (*a*). Once again there is

---

[108] Another good example of multiple pairing is 312.23-25.

[109] Although there are a number of synonymous triplets in the work (e.g. 222.26-27, 247.10), the author makes less use of them than he does of inclusive triplets. The reason is that the third element of an inclusive can add something significant to the meaning —e.g. «matando e firiendo e prendiendo» (408.10-11), «los cavalleros e los omes buenos e las dueñas» (48.12-13)— whereas a third synonym usually seems just wearisome pedantry. That the *Zifar* author seems to have been aware of this is shown by the frequency with which he disguises a synonymous triplet either by elaborating the final element, as in «para los defender e para los anparar e para los sacar de la premia en que están» (136.13-14), or by changing his syntactical structure, as in «ca muy fea e muy crua cosa sería e contra natura» (22.20-21).

a rhythmic development within the triplet, owing to the progressive increase in the number of syllables in each element $(2 + 3 + 5)$. The use of an adjectival phrase introduced by *de* as the third component serves to break the monotony of the triplet and also to connect it firmly with the first triplet of (*a*) by the repetition of *buen consejo*. This second section closes with a pair («yerro e vergüença»). In section (*c*), joined to (*b*) by the simple copulative *e*, the future *punarán* echoes the *guardarvos-hán* of the preceding section, with a mild variation of grammatical structure. The pair which closes (*c*) («onrra e bien») balances the contrasting pair which closes (*b*) («yerro e vergüença»), and one of its elements recalls the *onrrar* of the pair in section (*a*). Section (*d*) is closely linked with both (*a*) and (*b*): it opens with an adjectival triplet which parallels exactly both the second triplet in (*a*) (notionally) and the triplet in (*b*) (syntactically). The same pair («yerro e vergüença») closes both (*b*) and (*d*), with a subtle alteration of the supporting preposition from *de* to *en*. In section (*e*), attached to (*d*) by the conjunction *e* (cf. (*b*) and (*c*)), *amenguar* contrastingly parallels *acresçentar* in (*c*), and the closing pair «vuestra onrra e el vuestro poder» parallels «vuestra onrra e vuestra bien» in (*c*). Exact repetition is avoided here not by changing the supporting elements of the pair (like *de ... de* to *en ... en)*, but by substituting one of the basic components, a change which is emphasized by the introduction of the article *el*. The element which remains common to the pairs of (*c*) and (*e*) is *onrra*, which also links up, as we saw, with the *onrrar* of the pair in (*a*), and thus serves to bind the whole elaborate passage together. Finally, one notes the use of *consejo* in (*e*), which echoes its use, although in different grammatical circumstances, in (*a*), (*b*) and (*d*). This too helps to cement the structural and thematic fabric of the whole passage. This analysis, which could be repeated for dozens of other passages in the *Zifar*, illustrates very clearly what appear to be the author's twin preoccupations, balance and variety.

As a last point it is worth mentioning that pairs such as «firme e fuerte», «grande e grave», «premia e priesa», «mandamientos e mandaderías», have a special effect because of their alliteration. The *Zifar* author employs alliteration sparingly, but there are a few good examples of its effective use. In the clause «pero muchas vegadas los malos son firmes e fuertes en sus fechos malos» (363.18-19), for instance, the alliterative effect of the pair «firmes e fuertes» is strengthened by the *f* of *fechos* and the less insistent, because more spaced-out, fourfold recurrence of *m*. A more elaborate example is:

> e falló ý cosas muy nobles e de grant preçio, e mucho oro, e mucha plata, e mucho aljófar e muchas piedras preçiosas, e paños preçiados e muchas otras mercadurías de muchas maneras (97.15-18).

It is in passages like this that the influence of the rhetoricians is at its most obvious: in the space of three lines we have fully developed examples of *frequentatio, repetitio* and *paranomasia*, as well as a complicated alliterative pair «piedras preçiosas e paños preçiados», whose effect the author carefully preserves by omitting the expected *muchos* before *paños*. The repetition of *mucho* throughout the passage also leads into the burst of alliteration with which the sentence closes, «muchas otras mercadurías de muchas maneras». [110]

In conclusion, then, one must admit that, although the *Zifar* author is not the first or the only Spanish writer of the Middle Ages to use pairs, he is certainly not content merely to tread blindly the path beaten by his predecessors. In his work we seem to have a fusion of, on the one hand, the Latin and vernacular pairs tradition and, on the other, the literary conventions of Arabic, reaching him both through the translations of wisdom literature and probably through direct contact with Semitic sources. This dual influence, exaggerated by the precepts of the *Artes Poeticæ* and the creative imagination of the author, makes the *Zifar* one of the richest mines of pairs in medieval literature. To our modern taste the use of pairs may appear excessive and rather monotonous; but one must nevertheless grant that the author, whilst accepting with open arms and ready pen the pair as a stylistic device, seems to have done his utmost to introduce variety into the stereotype and exploit the rhythmic possibilities of the pair and the triplet to the full.

---

[110] There are, besides alliterative pairs, a few rhyming pairs in the *Zifar:* e.g. «carrera e manera» (334.3), «locura o cordura» (383.4), and the near-rhyme «la carrera e la tierra» (393.1).

CHAPTER SEVEN: CONCLUSION

The major conclusion to emerge from our study of the *Zifar* must be that it is very much a product of its time and place. Like Toledo in the later Middle Ages, the romance stands at the crossroads of two civilizations, one basically Moslem and Arabic, the other essentially Christian and Latin. Islamic culture had long ago absorbed the riches of the civilizations of India, Asia Minor, the Middle East and Greece, and by the beginning of the fourteenth century, Christian culture included, besides its classical heritage and a rich Latin literature of its own, several literary monuments in the vigorous aspirant vernaculars. On all these riches the *Zifar* author has drawn.

In the course of this book, we have seen how the evidence points to the author's having taken as his starting point some Arabic version of a story that derives ultimately from an Indian archetype; to this he has added details from a Graeco-Latin christianized version of the same archetype, elaborating the whole from his own imagination and the vernacular epic and romance traditions. We have seen how a thirteenth-century Castilian translation of an oriental wisdom book, augmented with borrowings from other works of didacticism, and biblical and Christian moralists, has been recast and reorganized, and incorporated into the unlikely framework of a romance. In the last book particularly the author seems to have drawn on elements from the courtly and chivalric tradition of the French romances.

Our analysis has also revealed that the *Zifar*'s style, like its content, is an amalgam of many influences. There is no doubt that the author has drawn extensively on the techniques of the epic poets, his main predecessors in the field of the heroic tale. But, by the early fourteenth century, epic diction had also been taken over, and in some ways fossilized, by the poets of the *mester de clerecía* and the chroniclers of Alfonso X. It is impossible to say how much the *Zifar* author took directly from the epics and how much he borrowed at second hand from the learned writers of *cuaderna vía* poems and the historians. However, as we have seen,

222

the epics and the *Zifar* have elements in common that are found only sporadically or not at all in *clerecía*. Moreover, a number of the stylistic devices retain in the romance some of the vitality they had in heroic poetry, but which they had largely lost in *clerecía*. It seems, then, that the *Zifar* author knew the epic tradition at first hand.

But the heroic poems are responsible for only a part of the elements that go to make up the *Zifar*'s style. Almost as important appears to be the influence of the thirteenth-century translations of oriental wisdom literature, which forced the developing vernacular into new patterns and created a whole new series of formulas. The traces of Arabic stylistic features in the *Zifar*, however, are not confined to the *Castigos del rey de Mentón*, which is completely within this didactic tradition, but are to be found throughout the romance. It seems reasonably certain that the author was familiar with Semitic literature and Semitic literary conventions at first hand.

The *Zifar*, then, draws on a great variety of sources both for its content and for its style, and the author's achievement in fusing all these heterogeneous elements into a coherent and aesthetically satisfying whole is a considerable one. The qualities in the work that have been most emphasized in the course of this book are balance and variety. An attempt has been made to show how the author sought to weld together his huge compilation by a complex system of structural and thematic parallels that unifies such disparate elements as chivalric adventures and didactic *exempla*, the ponderous *Castigos* and the fantastic Other Worlds of the Enchanted Lake and the *Islas Dotadas*. The use of constant themes and motifs on all planes of the narrative, and the careful preparations for the shift from one plane to another, impose pattern and order on the miscellaneous content.

The same is true of the style: once again we discern a search for harmony and elegant balance. Fusing all the diverse stylistic registers is a mind trained in the principles of medieval rhetoric. The leisurely unfolding of *interpretatio*, the emphatic punch of *repetitio*, the carefully contrived balance of antithesis, give a sophistication and polish to the raw materials which make up the style of the romance.

Unity, balance, order, harmony; but also variety. The elaborate structural pattern serves to bind the various elements together, but it does not destroy their diversity. Part of the charm of this romance is the absence, for the most part, of monotony: adventures, wars, dialogues, humorous interludes, supernatural extravaganzas, moral sermons, well-told *exempla*, all have their allotted place within the carefully designed structure. There are also, besides the constant motifs occurring in the same place in each section of the romance, free-ranging motifs that serve to bend the rigidity of the basic patterning without breaking it.

In the style, too, the patterns of the pair and the stock formula are imbued with enormous variety. No stereotyped phrase is abused; many new ones are created to be used only once or twice. The order of the elements in the clichés is frequently altered in the constant search for variety. The harmony that patterning gives is not disturbed, but monotony is avoided.

The aim of this book has been to single out some of the more important literary qualities of a much maligned and neglected romance. It can scarcely claim, of course, to stand beside the greatest productions of medieval Spanish literature, such as the *Poema de Mío Cid*, the *Libro de buen amor* or the *Celestina;* but it certainly deserves more than a passing glance and sneer. The modern distaste for works like the *Zifar* was certainly not shared by the Middle Ages, and our evidence suggests that this romance was popular for a very long time. Apart from its historical importance, however, the *Zifar* is worthy of study in its own right. Its fusion of so many cultural streams and stylistic conventions makes it unlike any other medieval romance that I know. It stands as a bridge between the dying epic and *clerecía* traditions and the nascent *novela de caballerías*, handing on to its successors in its prose style a newly-forged literary instrument of elegance and flexibility.

This examination of the *Zifar* certainly makes no claim to be an exhaustive one; much work remains to be done before the romance can be fully rehabilitated. A thorough investigation of its moral tone, for example, would be worthwhile, with its interplay of Christian and Islamic attitudes and its strange, yet eminently modern, mingling of materialism and idealism, all conveyed by a wide variety of means—direct preaching, *exempla, sententiæ*, proverbs, the actions and reactions of the characters. More needs to be done, too, in the almost totally neglected area of the *Zifar*'s literary influence, particularly its relationship with the later romance of chivalry. In a wider field there is valuable work to be carried out on the development of the vernacular literary prose style in the fourteenth century.

In this study the main concern has been to show how a remarkable literary artist handled the riches that he inherited from the complex of traditions that he found around him in Toledo. In his own modest way the *Zifar* author has done what Thomas Aquinas and Dante did; one hopes they would be willing to admit him to their company.

APPENDIX ONE: THE OCCURRENCES OF ÇERTAS, ÇIERTAS, ÇIERTO, ÇIERTAMENTE

All references are to *çertas* unless otherwise indicated

2.3 *(çiertas)*, 6.2 *(çiertas)*, 6.22, 14.5, 15.25, 16.20, 17.8, 18.8, 19.12, 20.18, 21.2, 22.1 *(çierto, from PS)*, 23.2, 25.21, 25.24, 29.20, 33.22, 34.2, 35.10, 35.21 *(çiertas)*, 39.10 *(çiertamente)*, 42.1, 42.6, 42.23, 43.3, 43.24, 44.6, 44.26, 45.5, 45.9, 47.25, 48.5, 48.16 *(çierto, from PS)*, 49.18, 51.1, 51.14, 51.20, 52.3, 52.11, 52.23, 53.5, 53.11, 54.5, 54.18, 55.26, 56.2, 56.9, 56.12, 60.15, 61.2, 62.9 *(çierto, from PS)*, 62.11, 63.1, 63.24, 68.7 *(çiertamente)*, 68.19, 68.24, 70.2, 70.10, 70.12, 70.15, 70.20 *(çierto, from S)*, 70.25, 73.7, 74.19, 75.25, 77.16, 77.22, 77.25, 78.3, 79.7, 80.15, 80.18, 81.16, 81.19 *(çierto, from P)*, 81.26, 84.4, 86.21, 87.1, 88.2, 89.22, 90.7, 91.20, 91.23, 92.11, 93.14, 93.19, 95.19, 98.25, 99.5, 100.26, 104.24, 106.1, 107.2, 107.12, 108.5, 108.11, 111.7, 111.13, 111.18, 111.27, 112.16, 112.28, 113.10, 114.6, 115.6, 115.20, 117.4, 117.16, 118.9, 120.9, 121.16, 123.1, 124.23, 125.6, 128.9, 128.16, 129.4, 129.7, 130.17, 131.9, 131.12, 133.5, 133.15, 134.10, 134.24, 135.3, 135.14, 135.19, 136.9, 138.4, 138.9, 139.3, 139.16, 139.25, 140.6, 144.1, 144.12, 144.19, 145.22, 146.5, 146.17, 146.20, 148.22, 149.5, 151.18, 153.11, 153.18, 154.19 *(çierto, from PS)*, 155.5, 156.1, 160.7, 161.23, 165.18, 166.6, 169.5, 172.15 *(çiertamente)*, 174.19, 176.1, 183.24, 185.2, 193.1, 195.7, 195.20 *(çierto, from PS)*, 196.4, 196.15 *(çierto, from PS)*, 196.19, 198.8 *(çiertas)*, 198.13, 199.4, 199.7, 199.14, 200.2, 200.7, 200.22, 200.24, 201.10, 202.11, 202.24, 203.15, 203.24, 204.20, 205.8, 206.7, 206.12, 206.18, 207.12, 207.25, 208.3, 210.4 *(çiertamente)*, 211.24, 215.6, 215.13, 215.16, 215.21, 215.22, 216.11, 216.23, 217.7, 217.11, 217.22, 218.1, 218.4, 218.15, 218.18, 219.8, 219.12, 219.17, 222.24, 225.18, 228.12, 231.7, 232.8, 232.12, 233.12, 233.16, 234.7, 234.23, 236.1, 236.9, 237.23, 238.9, 238.13, 238.17, 239.9, 240.24, 241.5, 241.9, 241.13, 242.5, 242.23 *(çiertamente)*, 248.17, 249.1, 249.25, 250.3, 252.22, 253.11, 253.18 *(çiertamente, from PS)*, 258.15, 258.21, 259.19, 260.2, 260.26, 261.15, 261.25, 264.13, 266.5, 266.17 *(çiertamente)*, 275.23, 278.12 *(çiertamente)*, 283.4, 284.20, 286.13, 287.11, 288.7, 289.13, 295.9 *(çiertamente)*, 299.4, 302.6, 302.17, 303.20 *(çiertamente)* 305.17, 306.2, 308.15, *(çiertamente)*, 308.26, 309.13, 312.1, 314.23 *(çiertamente)*, 317.11, 320.2, 322.27 *(çiertamente)*, 324.20, 326.2 *(çierto, from PS)*,

225

16

326.9, 328.1, 330.1, 331.15, 339.21, 340.2, 340.16, 341.13 *(çiertamente)*, 341.16 *(çiertamente)*, 343.27, 344.1, 344.8, 344.19, 345.2, 345.19, 348.24, 349.19, 350.1, 354.7, 356.2, 358.1, 360.1, 363.21, 364.8, 365.7, 365.27, 368.5, 371.13, 372.4 *(çertamente* [*sic*]), 377.19 *(çiertamente)*, 378.25, 381.1, 381.12, 381.16, 382.26, 383.9, 385.2 *(çiertamente)*, 387.20, 387.23, 389.6, 389.10, 389.20, 390.7, 391.7-8, 392.6, 392.11, 392.13, 394.1, 394.8, 394.22, 395.1, 395.28, 397.5, 397.10, 397.14, 397.24, 398.10, 399.8, 399.10 *(çiertamente)*, 400.9, 401.14, 402.18, 403.2, 404.23 *(çierto,* from *PS)*, 411.4 *(çiertamente,* from *PS)*, 411.20 *(çiertamente,* from *PS)*, 421.11 *(çierto,* from *PS)*, 421.18 *(çiertamente,* from *PS)*, 423.11, 424.8, 424.14-15 *(çiertamente)*, 425.1, 428.10 *(çiertamente)*, 430.26, 431.28 *(çiertamente)*, 432.15, 433.15-16, 434.15, 434.22, 436.23, 439.12, 439.24, 439.27, 447.12, 448.11, 449.4, 449.13, 450.17, 451.13 *(çiertamente)*, 451.21, 452.3 *(çiertamente)*, 452.21, 453.3, 458.29 *(çierto,* from *PS)*, 459.20 *(çiertamente,* from *PS)*, 464.14, 468.5, 470.4, 470.19 *(çiertamente)*, 471.15, 472.5 *(çiertamente)*, 473.12, 477.11, 479.14, 481.28, 482.20, 484.7, 499.29, 501.22, 502.15, 502.20, 507.14 *(çiertamente)*, 508.12, 509.7 *(çiertas)*, 510.19, 511.12, 511.23, 513.17 *(çiertamente)*, 514.24 *(çiertamente)*, 515.15, 515.21-22 *(çiertamente)*.

abibar e despertar 273.11.
abonado e abastado 390.3.
abraçar e besar 93.5, 188.19, 285.27, 440.25.
aconpañado e servido 362.7.
aconpañar e guiar 120.2.
aconpañar e onrrar 512.27-513.1.
adormido e descuydado 273.10-11.
afán e trabajo 118.4.
alegre e bien andante 423.2.
alegre e pagado 77.13, 240.22, 243.11, 397.10.
alegría e amor 336.24.
alegría e conorte 47.9.
alegría e onrra 91.14.
alegría e paçiença 111.28.
alegría e plazer 91.14, 248.4, 463.14, 477.6, 479.8, 479.14, 515.16.
alegría e trebejo 101.15-16.
alongar e detardar 343.28.
alto e grande 16.19.
amado e ensalçado 302.20.
amado e preçiado 263.8, 264.7, 296.10, 296.24, 369.1, 379.9-10, 490.13.
amansar e atenprar 265.22.
amar e codiçiar 510.17-18.
amar e guardar 282.26, 476.19.
amar e onrrar 102.7, 488.10, 491.14.
amar e preçiar 32.4, 356.17, 424.15, 429.1.
amar e servir 255.11.
anparado e defendido 234.15-16, 247.10, 378.22, 428.4.
anparador e defendedor 409.36-410.1.
anparar e defender 136.13-14, 204.4, 271.25-26, 326.2, 484.27.
aperçibir e aguisar 487.8.
apuesto e bien vestido 249.25, 457.16.
apuesto e viçioso 413.29-30.

arrancar e desbaratar 169.1, 169.17.
áspero e grave 108.7.
atrevimiento e locura 509.7.
aver e riqueza 159.6.
ayuda e consejo 274.3-4, 321.23, 322.15.
ayudar e acorrer 326.4.
ayudar e defender 369.19.
ayudar e guiar 105.23.
ayudas e onrras 3.28, 190.6.
ayuntamientos e conpañías 305.8.
bien e amor 478.3.
bien e don 66.20, 255.4.
bien e merçed 2.33, 6.6, 147.19, 251.23-24, 271.21, 272.8-9, 278.1, 278.21, 293.23, 328.22-23, 379.20-21, 394.12, 428.20, 446.17, 469.26, 485.11.
bien e plazer 470.17.
bivo e razonable 269.3.
bivo e sano 63.4-5, 205.7-8, 242.4, 409.34, 482.9.
blanco e fermoso 97.7, 227.14, 475.2.
bolliçio e escándalo 332.19.
bondat e lealtad 328.25.
bravo e fuerte 420.19.
bravo e loco 407.16-17.
bueno e acabado 321.27.
bueno e apuesto 438.20.
bueno e conplido 270.1.
bueno e entendido 413.11-12.
bueno e escogido 320.21.
bueno e fuerte 148.4, 168.1.
bueno e leal 6.8, 22.18, 63.24, 69.15-16, 270.15, 329.2, 350.5-6, 402.7.
bueno e onesto 7.16, 7.33, 23.25, 251.18, 321.4-5, 321.11, 322.3.
bueno e provado 408.15.
bueno e rico 170.20-21, 283.16, 446.6-7.
bueno e sano 434.4.

bueno e santo 96.18, 172.24, 244.12, 288.20, 499.16.

cansado e lazrado 28.2, 316.16.

cansado e quebrantado 422.30-31, 423.1.

castigar e consejar 209.26-27, 380.5, 382.13-14.

castigar e dotrinar 396.20-21, 397.20.

castigar e emendar 312.3.

castigar e refrenar 272.22.

catar e conosçer 250.21-22, 435.4.

catar e pensar 13.5.

catar e ver 358.7.

çierto e seguro 10.6.

claro e linpio 221.10.

cocho e asado 20.25, 21.3, 21.10.

codiçioso e malo 371.24-25.

comer e roer 306.19-20.

confesar e dezir 317.7.

confonder e astragar 453.10.

conortar e ayudar 90.23, 96.25.

conortar e esforçar 68.4, 68.6-7, 96.24-25, 405.34, 497.18.

conosçer e judgar 145.26, 146.1.

conpaña e gente 249.16-17.

consolaçión e plazer 383.21.

copas e vasos 229.23, 460.29.

de coraçón e de voluntad 318.7-8.

cortés e mesurado 494.5-6.

cuenta e razón 224.24.

cuydado e pesar 15.25.

cuydado e tristeza 14.25.

cuyta e pesar 94.12-13.

cuyta e quebranto 384.10.

cuyta e reçelo 68.25-69.1.

cuytado e cansado 28.5.

cuytado e lazrado 28.17.

cuytar e presurar 516.9.

daño e enojo 76.12, 334.27, 456.22.

daño e mal 70.23, 74.4, 76.11-12, 211.21, 391.17, 456.18, 509.18.

daño e menoscabo 373.13.

daño e robo 303.11.

dar bozes e fazer llanto 66.8-9.

dar e galardonar 342.20.

defendido e onrrado 428.4-5.

demandar e cobdiçiar 461.18.

demandar e querer 417.28-29.

demostrar e enseñar 333.11-12.

demudado e triste 185.21.

derribar e sacar 479.9.

desaforado e astragado 371.12-13.

desconortado e triste 478.18-19.

descuydado e perezoso 340.3.

deseheredar e desterrar 432.2.

deseheredado e lazrado 371.2.

desfazer e desapoderar 327.21-22.

desfazer e toller 350.23.

desmesurado e sobervio 406.8, 407.16.

desonrra e daño 13.24-25, 23.18, 71.19, 73.9, 79.11, 221.5-6, 334.29, 335.3, 335.7, 397.28-398.1.

desonrra e enbargo 74.5-6.

desonrra e mal 284.12, 403.16, 453.11, 494.11.

desonrrado e perdido 14.2-3.

desonrrar e abiltar 348.18-19.

despechado e astragado 371.11.

despechar e astragar 371.8.

despechar e desterrar 435.3.

dexar e olvidar 236.17-18.

dezir e consejar 372.11.

dezir e mandar 299.7.

dezir e pregonar 117.8.

discordias e enamistades 313.28-314.1.

dudar e tardar 129.6.

duelo e piedat 348.14.

duro e fuerte 113.19-20.

enamistad e desamor 336.25.

endreçar e ayudar 175.17.

engaño e sotileza 334.2.

enojar e arrebatar 361.24.

enojos e peligros 1.13-14.

enseñar e castigar 271.26-272.1.

enseñar e consejar 382.13.

entender e creer 10.15, 302.8.

entender e ver 10.25, 96.26, 211.11, 255.22, 259.22, 261.5-6, 273.3-4, 273.8, 274.5-6, 298.8-9, 379.17, 394.21, 440.13.

entregado e pagado 422.6.

enxienplo e castigo 10.14, 10.24.

enxienplo e consejo 10.5.

escándalo e duda 246.17.

escaso e covarde 365.4.

escatima e reprehensión 290.3-4.

escudriñar e adevinar 339.11.

esforçar e ayudar 267.22-23, 278.16.

esquivo e estraño 213.11-12.

fablar e dezir 227.21, 230.10.

falaguero e engañoso 484.1-2.

falsedat e enemiga 94.25, 118.12-13.

falsedat e mentira 185.15.

falso e traydor 277.13, 431.16.

fallar e conosçer 343.17.

fallesçer e mentir 368.24.

fama e onrra 221.20.

fazer e otorgar 245.9.

fe e creençia 39.22.

fe e devoçión 1.12.

fe e verdat 237.13-14, 257.20, 489.31-32, 490.4, 490.11.

fealdat e trayçión 332.2-3.

fecho e adobado 103.20.

feo e cruo 22.20.

feo e desfaçado 286.5-6, 286.20.

feo e malo 284.13, 322.9-10.

fermoso e bien andante 461.33-462.1.

fermoso e bien vestido 461.5.

fermoso e claro 85.8-9, 88.17-18, 483.9.

fermoso e leydo 235.10-11.

fermoso e viçioso 227.19.

fialdat e lealtad 222.27, 223.25, 224.21.

fino e puro 450.11-12.

finos e virtuosos 507.15.

firme e estable 4.5, 309.23, 317.10, 363.5.

folgado e asosegado 470.22.

folgado e seguro 340.3, 350.15.

folgar e asosegar 204.20.

folgar e trebejar 106.7.

franco e mesurado 258.21, 258.25.

fresco e abibado 423.4.

fuerça e poder 276.26-27.

fuerte e alto 125.15.

fuerte e cruel 366.21-22.

fuerte e desesperado 434.5.

fuerte e lazrado 433.11.

fuerte e rezio 106.4, 134.21.

fuzía e esperança 403.3.

gestos e adamanes 427.11.

governar e criar 318.25.

graçia e merçed 319.9-10, 319.10, 371.27.

grande e bueno 124.5, 184.7, 312.1, 430.20-21, 499.21.

grande e desesperado 434.10-11.

grande e fermoso 229.3-4.

grande e fuerte 214.3, 240.5, 312.6.

grande e grave 274.6, 275.7.

grande e noble 12.9.

grande e poderoso 69.22-23, 463.23.

grande e rico 41.7, 83.18, 414.20, 469.20.

grande e sazonado 241.6.

de grant lugar e rico 24.19, 49.10-11.

grave e duro 117.22.

grave e peligroso 299.21.

guarda e anparamiento 174.7.

guarda e endresçamiento 298.9-10.

guardado e asegurado 372.10.

guardado e mantenido 176.12-13, 308.5.

guardado e servido 345.10, 454.22, 485.2.

guardador e defendedor 64.19, 384.11-12.

guardar e amansar 303.12-13.

guardar e castigar 238.15.

guardar e catar 304.21, 354.26-27.

guardar e defender 104.21-22, 203.1-2, 273.5, 308.1.

guardar e endresçar 170.18.

guardar e onrrar 372.3.

guardar e retener 334.23-24, 334.25-26.

guardar e servir 355.10, 355.13, 409.14.

guardar e tener 368.27.

guarido e sano 258.14.

guarneçer e ornar 263.19.

guiador e endreçador 402.26-27.

guiador e ordenador 276.3.

guiar e endresçar 50.2, 105.23, 245.19, 383.8, 457.32, 458.1.

guiar e mantener 99.8, 99.9.

heredar e onrrar 508.6.

jura e omenage 223.24, 368.20, 475.24.

justiçia e derecho 309.26, 310.12, 313.7, 320.6.

justiçia e verdat 188.25-26, 264.10, 298.12, 298.23, 307.27, 308.14, 311.12, 311.17, 316.21.

laso e quebrantado 183.13-14.

lazerío e cuydado 258.24.

lazerío e servidunbre 258.23.

leal e verdadero 270.14, 475.26.

ledo e pagado 167.4, 201.23-24, 238.24, 248.11, 508.18.

leydo e sano 152.6.

lidiador e defendedor 511.26.

lisonja e maestría 111.5-6.

loçano e alegre 463.28.

loco e atrevido 240.6, 283.7, 400.24, 406.10.

locura e braveza 365.27.

locura e sobervia 317.8, 392.20.

llanto e pesar 154.4-5.

llorar e dar bozes 26.7.

llorar e fazer llanto 66.23-24.

lloro e llanto 385.23.

lloro e pesar 114.18.

maestría e engaño 334.5, 345.10-11, 345.15, 348.17, 480.12, 490.28.

maestría e sotileza 330.16.

mal e crueldat 287.5.

mal e desafuero 432.4-5, 432.12-13, 433.22-23, 434.18.

mal e enemiga 287.1.

mal e engaño 345.18, 349.7 (?).

mal e pesar 154.6.

mal e reçelo 434.10.

mal e trayçión 273.4.

maldat e deslealtad 329.1.

malo e desmesurado 413.10.

malo e peligroso 75.17.

mançebo e apuesto 389.5.
mandamientos e mandaderías 489.17-18.
mandar e aconsejar 272.20.
medroso e vergoñoso 15.10.
menospreçiado e desechado 355.1-2.
mentir e engañar 350.11.
mentira e enemiga 304.14-15.
mentira e lisonja 13.17.
mentira e sobervia 436.13.
mentira e ynfinta 461.3.
mentiroso e desvariado 354.18.
merçed e ayuda 49.8.
merçed e mesura 318.13, 433.13.
merçed e piedat 488.22.
merçed e plazer 93.27.
mesura e bondat 144.18, 491.6.
mesura e cordura 51.13.
mesura e piedat 435.1-2.
mesura e seso 39.11.
mesura e vergüença 407.17.
miedo e lisonja 327.4, 327.5.
miedo e reçelo 308.25, 308.30, 432.9.
miedo e sospecha 501.14.
miedo e vergüeña 15.9, 217.8, 287.4, 490.12.
mintroso e falso 277.1.
misericordia e merçed 91.4-5.
misericordia e piedat 90.22, 105.24-25.
mudar e canbiar 300.11.
muerte e pasyón 496.10.
negro e feo 241.26.
noble e poderoso 264.12.
obediente e mandado 38.23-24.
ofiçios e ordenamientos 308.5.
omildoso e paçiente 258.20, 258.24, 298.3-4.
onrra e bien 79.16, 329.4, 424.4, 424.8, 461.20-21, 476.27, 480.7.
onrra e estado 254.3, 263.11.
onrra e gloria 301.22.
onrra e guarda 322.25.
onrra e merçed 252.3-4.
onrra e nobleza 122.11.
onrra e plazer 47.5, 64.22, 73.11, 91.14, 166.23, 183.7, 348.9, 430.12, 461.23, 483.15, 494.8.
onrra e poder 329.6.
onrra e pro(vecho) 13.12-13, 13.18, 35.3, 63.26, 72.3, 78.6-7, 116.10, 166.23, 221.4-5, 263.5, 335.8, 351.24-25, 411.25-26, 424.16, 426.16, 453.6, 455.1-2, 459.8, 512.10-11, 516.7, 516.21.
onrra e salud 73.22.
onrra e viçio 476.27.
onrrado e amado 104.5, 263.8, 379.3.

onrrado e loado 509.12.
onrrado e poderoso 172.5, 311.13, 438.9-10.
onrrado e preçiado 263.8.
onrrar e defender 365.1.
onrrar e loar 190.7.
ora e sazón 291.1.
orgulloso e sobervio 298.3.
oýr e aprender 256.17.
paçiençia e sufrençia 291.10.
pas e alegría 461.14-15, 506.8-9.
pas e concordia 172.2, 173.5.
pas e justiçia 169.13-14, 172.2, 173.5, 484.27, 506.8-9.
pas e sosiego 470.20-21.
peligro e daño 398.9, 398.11.
peligros e desonrra 366.14-15.
peligroso e dañoso 310.22, 398.16-17.
pensar e cuydar 16.9.
pensar e entender 264.21.
perdiçión e destruymiento 484.17-18.
pérdida e daño 114.21, 416.8.
pérdida e desonrra 478.2-3, 500.1-2.
perdido e astragado 247.14.
pesar e trabajo 184.4, 383.8.
plazer e poder 478.13.
plazer e serviçio 173.13.
plazer e solás 7.5, 7.8, 79.6, 459.20, 459.23, 483.21.
pleito e omenage 42.22, 76.15, 493.25.
pobre e desfecho 24.8.
pobre e fanbriento 375.3.
pobre e menguado 175.11.
pobredat e lazería 339.1.
pobredat e mengua 340.7-8.
poder e esfuerço 315.28-316.1.
poderoso e bien andante 458.23.
poner e ordenar 6.15.
preçiar e onrrar 328.25-329.1.
premia e priesa 55.11, 55.13.
pres e fama 186.10, 234.13.
pres e onrra 11.26, 12.12-13, 40.1-2, 118.2, 211.9, 413.18, 416.11-12.
priesa e peligro 215.7.
prometer e jurar 301.1.
público e manifiesto 312.22.
quebrantado e triste 27.18.
quebrantar e abaxar 392.17-18.
quebrantar e vençer 366.18-19.
quebranto e lazerío 295.9.
quebranto e pesar 114.20.
quemar e astragar 209.2, 404.7-8.
querer e codiçiar 301.12.
querer e consentir 272.33.
razón e derecho 4.6, 7.14, 14.7, 129.5,

183.20, 223.5-6, 278.6, 292.3, 307.23, 351.8, 435.4.
razón e entendimiento 10.12-13, 255.12, 258.8-9, 266.12, 266.14, 491.3.
razón e ocasión 299.5.
regnar e señorear 118.16.
rey e señor 164.15-16, 169.20, 272.2-3, 273.15, 273.21, 298.17, 298.20, 300.19, 302.26, 304.16, 315.21, 342.17-18.
rico e abonado 249.8, 390.3.
rico e anparado 171.24.
rico e apuesto 85.4, 506.8.
rico e bien andante 171.8-9, 230.11, 379.4-5, 463.24.
rico e fermoso 54.21.
rico e poderoso 24.1, 27.3, 30.22-23, 32.3, 36.9-10, 49.10-11, 92.10, 311.13, 346.3, 458.3, 469.16, 486.4-5.
rico e reçelado 427.27.
rico e viçioso 414.20, 430.3.
rogar e demandar 322.9.
ruydo e llanto 45.17-18, 142.11.
saber e aprender 231.10.
saber e conosçer 211.10, 448.27, 458.26.
saber e entender 99.17, 266.12.
saber e poder 127.11, 151.21, 151.23, 262.14.
sabio e entendido 292.20, 326.13 (M sabido e e.).
sabio e sotil 334.9-10.
sabor e plazer 469.18-19.
saludar e besar 285.10, 285.14, 287.19-20.
salvar e guardar 458.9.
sanar e guaresçer 257.7.
sano e alegre 66.1, 67.21, 222.28, 302.12-13, 409.34.
sapiença e verdat 321.26.
seguir e guardar 158.2, 158.5, 310.12.
señor e enperador 460.10-11, 484.20.
señora e reýna 247.19.
señorío e poder 316.26.
serviçio e onrra 328.6.
servido e ayudado 379.7-8.
servir e defender 422.12.
servir e gradesçer 180.11, 428.19-20.
seso e entendimiento 123.6, 182.23, 483.14.
sobervia e engaño 490.25-26, 490.28.

sobervio e cruo 168-1.2.
sobervioso e loco 224.5.
sofrido e paçiente 292.12.
sofrir e conplir 12.2.
sofrir e mantener 103.4.
sofrir e pasar 113.18, 133.14, 165.24, 398.10, 484.10.
sostenido e mantenido 299.22-23.
sotil e agudo 12.24.
tardar e racabdar 274.18, 276.9.
temido e dubdado 365.17.
torpe e nesçio 289.26.
trabajo e cuydado 7.9.
trabajo e peligro 9.19, 253.2.
trayçión e enemiga 92.5.
trebejar e jugar 109.15-16.
trebejo e solás 327.8.
tregua e omenage 314.3, 314.26, 315.4.
tregua e segurança 414.13, 426.14.
triste e cuytado 27.24, 85.26-86.1, 86.18, 243.15, 260.22, 384.7, 477.10, 481.11.
triste e lloroso 165.16.
tristeza e pesar 105.14, 244.9, 429.23, 479.16.
valer e meresçer 367.13, 422.8.
ver e conosçer 195.12, 333.20-21.
ver e sentir 468.9.
verdadero e bueno 326.1, 350.5-6.
verdadero e fiel 325.27-28, 372.6.
verdat e bien 436.22.
verdat e derecho 431.22.
verdat e lealtad 199.12, 221.22, 222.26-27, 318.25-26, 336.5, 422.17, 466.28.
verdat e razón 436.12.
viçio e folgura 253.12.
viçios e deleytes 265.22-266.1.
viçioso e abondado 434.26, 478.14.
viçioso e folgado 253.10.
vida e salud 396.29, 477.1-2.
vil e dañoso 220.24-25.
por voluntad e por sabor 421.22.
yerro e estropieço 470.14-15.
yerro e pecado 78.14, 324.8, 329.16, 435.8-9.
yerro e vergüença 329.2-3, 329.5.
ymagen e semejança 255.6.

BIBLIOGRAPHY

Aben Ragel, Aly: *El libro conplido en los iudizios de las estrellas de Aly Aben Ragel*, ed. Gerold Hilty (Madrid, 1954).

Alborg, Juan Luis: *Historia de la literatura española*, 2nd ed., I (Madrid, 1970).

Alfonso X: *Primera crónica general*, ed. Ramón Menéndez Pidal, 2nd ed. 2 vols (Madrid, 1955).

— — *El libro de las cruzes*, ed. Lloyd A. Kasten and Lawrence B. Kiddle (Madrid-Madison, 1961).

— — *Antología de Alfonso X el Sabio*, ed. A. G. Solalinde, 5th ed. (Austral 169, Madrid, 1965).

— — *Lapidario*, ed. María Brey Mariño (Odres Nuevos, Madrid, 1968).

Alfonso, Martha: «Comparación entre el *Félix* de Ramón Llull y *El caballero Cifar*, novela caballeresca a lo divino», *ELu* XII (1968), 77-81.

Alonso, Amado: «Maestría antigua en la prosa», *Sur* XIV, no. 133 (1945), 40-43.

Amadís de Gaula, ed. Edwin B. Place, 4 vols (Madrid, 1959-69).

Amador de los Ríos, José: *Historia crítica de la literatura española*, 7 vols (Madrid, 1861-75).

Arias y Arias, Ricardo: *El concepto del destino en la literatura medieval española* (Madrid, 1970).

Aristotle, Horace, Longinus. Classical Literary Criticism, trans. and ed. T. S. Dorsch (Harmondsworth, 1965).

Artiles, Joaquín: *Los recursos literarios de Berceo* (Madrid, 1964).

Avalle-Arce, Juan Bautista: *Deslindes cervantinos* (Madrid, 1961).

Baist, Gottfried: «Die Spanische Litteratur», *Grundriss der Romanischen Philologie*, ed. Gustav Gröber, II (Strassburg, 1898).

Baldwin, Charles Sears: *Medieval Rhetoric and Poetic (to 1400)* (New York, 1928).

Bamborough, J. B.: *The Little World of Man* (London-New York-Toronto, 1952).

Baugh, Albert C.: «The Middle English Romance: Some Questions of Creation, Presentation and Preservation», *Sp* XLII (1967), 1-31.

Beer, Gillian: *The Romance* (The Critical Idiom 10, London, 1970).

232

Beer, Jeanette M. A.: *Villehardouin, Epic Historian* (Études de Philologie et d'Histoire 7, Genève, 1968).
— — «Villehardouin and the Oral Narrative», *SP* LXVII (1970), 267-277.
Bell, Aubrey F. G.: *Castilian Literature* (Oxford, 1938).
Berceo, Gonzalo de: *Milagros de Nuestra Señora*, ed. A. G. Solalinde (CC 44, Madrid, 1922).
— — See also Dutton, Brian; *Poetas castellanos...*
Bernhard, Erwin: «Abstractions médiévales ou critique abstraite?» *Studi Mediolatini e Volgari* IX (1961), 19-70.
Bischoff, Bernhard: «The Study of Foreign Languages in the Middle Ages», *Sp* XXXVI (1961), 209-224.
Bohigas Balaguer, Pedro: «Orígenes de los libros de caballería», *Historia general de las literaturas hispánicas*, ed. Guillermo Díaz-Plaja, I (Barcelona, 1949), 521-541.
Bonilla, Adolfo: see *Libros de caballerías.*
Book of the Thousand Nights and a Night, The; see Burton, Richard F.
Born, Lester Kruger: «The Perfect Prince: a Study in Thirteenth- and Fourteenth-Century Ideals», *Sp* III (1928), 470-504.
Brewer, D. S.: see Coghill, Nevill; Schlauch, Margaret.
Brey Mariño, María: see Alfonso X.
Brodie, Fawn M.: *The Devil Drives. A Life of Sir Richard Burton* (London, 1967).
Buceta, Erasmo: «Algunas notas históricas al prólogo del *Cauallero Zifar*», *RFE* XVII (1930), 18-36.
— — «Nuevas notas históricas al prólogo del *Cauallero Zifar*», *ibid.*, 419-422.
Burke, James F.: *A Critical and Artistic Study of the «Libro del Cavallero Cifar»* (unpubl. Ph.D. diss. of the University of North Carolina at Chapel Hill, 1966; abstract in *Dissertation Abstracts* XXVII [1966-67]. 2525-A).
— — «Names and the Significance of Etymology in the *Libro del Cavallero Cifar*», *RR* LIX (1968), 161-173.
— — «Symbolic Allegory in the Portus Salutaris Episode in the *Libro del Cavallero Cifar*», *KRQ* XV (1968), 69-84.
— — «The Meaning of the *Islas Dotadas* Episode in the *Libro del Cavallero Cifar*», *HR* XXXVIII (1970), 56-68.
— — *History and Vision. The Figural Structure of the «Libro del Cavallero Zifar»* (Tamesis, London, 1972).
Burton, Richard F.: *The Book of the Thousand Nights and a Night*, repr. and ed. Leonard C. Smithers, 12 vols (London, 1894).
Cancionero de Palacio, El. (Manuscrito no. 594), ed. Francisca Vendrell de Millás (Barcelona, 1945).
Carmody, F.: «Les Sources orientales du *Perceval* de Chrétien de Troyes», *RLC* XXXIX (1965), 497-545.
Castigos e documentos: see Rey, Agapito.
Castro, Américo: *España en su historia. Cristianos, moros y judíos* (Buenos Aires, 1948).
Cervantes Saavedra, Miguel de: *Don Quijote*, 19th ed. (Austral 150, Madrid, 1956).

Chandler, Richard E. and Schwarz, Kessel: *A New History of Spanish Literature* (Baton Rouge, La., 1961).

Chanson de Roland, La, ed. F. Whitehead, 2nd ed. (Oxford, 1946).

Charland, Th.-M.: *Artes Prædicandi. Contribution à l'histoire de la rhétorique au Moyen Age* (Publications de l'Institut d'Études Médiévales d'Ottowa VII, Paris-Ottawa, 1936).

Chassan, M.: *Essai sur la symbolique du droit* (Paris, 1847).

Chaytor, H. J.: *From Script to Print. An Introduction to Medieval Vernacular Literature* (Cambridge, 1945).

Cipolla, Carlo M.: *Literacy and Development in the West* (Harmondsworth, 1969).

Cirot, G.: rev. of C. P. Wagner (ed.), *El Libro del Cauallero Zifar* (*q.v.*), *BH* XXXIII (1931), 58-59.

Coghill, Nevill: «Chaucer's Narrative Art in *The Canterbury Tales*», *Chaucer and Chaucerians. Critical Studies in Middle English Literature*, ed. D. S. Brewer (London, 1966), 114-139.

Corominas, J.: *Diccionario crítico etimológico de la lengua castellana*, 4 vols (Berna, 1954-57).

Cronica Najerense, ed. A. Ubieto Arteta (Textos Medievales 15, Valencia, 1966).

Crosby, Ruth: «Oral Delivery in the Middle Ages», *Sp* XI (1936), 88-110.

— — «Chaucer and the Custom of Oral Delivery», *Sp* XIII (1938), 413-432.

Curschmann, Michael: «Oral Poetry in Medieval English, French, and German Literature: Some Notes on Recent Research», *Sp* XLII (1967), 36-52.

Curtius, Ernst Robert: «Zur Literarästhetik des Mittelalters, II», *ZRP* LVIII (1938), 129-232.

— — *European Literature and the Latin Middle Ages*, trans. Willard R. Trask (New York, 1953).

De Chasca, Edmund: *El arte juglaresco en el «Cantar de Mio Cid»* (Madrid, 1967).

— — *Registro de fórmulas verbales en el «Cantar de Mio Cid»* (Iowa City, 1968).

— — «Toward a Redefinition of Epic Formula in the Light of the *Cantar de Mio Cid*», *HR* XXXVIII (1970), 251-263.

De Rougemont, Denis: *Passion and Society*, 2nd ed. (London, 1956).

Delehaye, Hippolyte: *Les Passions des martyrs et les genres littéraires* (Bruxelles, 1921).

Deyermond, A. D.: «Mester es sen peccado», *RF* LXXVII (1965), 111-116.

— — *Epic Poetry and the Clergy: Studies on the «Mocedades de Rodrigo»* (Tamesis, London, 1969).

— — *A Literary History of Spain. The Middle Ages* (London-New York, 1971).

— — «*Exemplum, Allegoria, Figura*», *Iberoromania* (in press).

— — and Walker, Roger M.: «A Further Vernacular Source for the *Libro de buen amor*», *BHS* XLVI (1969), 193-200.

Díaz del Castillo, Bernal: *Historia verdadera de la conquista de la Nueva España*, ed. Joaquín Ramírez Cabañas, 5th ed. (México, 1967).

Díaz-Plaja, Guillermo: see Bohigas Balaguer, Pedro.

Dorsch, T. S.: see *Aristotle*...

Doutrepont, Georges: *Les Mises en prose des épopées et des romans chevaleresques du XIVᵉ au XVIᵉ siècle* (Bruxelles, 1939).

Du Cange, Charles: *Glossarium Mediae et Infimae Latinitatis*, 10 vols (Niort, 1883-87).

Durán, Armando: «La 'amplificatio' en la literatura caballeresca española», *MLN* LXXXVI (1971), 123-135.

Dutton, Brian: «Gonzalo de Berceo and the *Cantares de gesta*», *BHS* XXXVIII (1961), 197-205.

—— (ed.) *La «Vida de San Millán de la Cogolla» de Gonzalo de Berceo. Estudio y edición crítica* (Tamesis, London, 1967).

—— and Walker, Roger M.: «El *Libro del Cauallero Zifar* y la lírica castellana», *Fi* IX (1963), 53-67.

Entwistle, William J.: *The Arthurian Legend in the Literatures of the Spanish Peninsula* (London-Toronto, 1925).

Escritores en prosa anteriores al siglo XV (BAE 51).

Escudero y Perosso, Francisco: *Tipografía hispalense* (Madrid, 1894).

Everett, Dorothy: «Some Reflections on Chaucer's 'Art Poetical'», *Essays on Middle English Literature*, ed. Patricia Kean (Oxford, 1955), 149-174.

Faral, Edmond: *Recherches sur les sources latines des contes et romans courtois du Moyen Age* (Paris, 1913).

—— *Les Arts poétiques du XIIᵉ et du XIIIᵉ siècle. Recherches et documents sur la technique littéraire du Moyen Age* (BÉHÉ 238, Paris, 1924).

Fernández Llera, V.: *Gramática y vocabulario del «Fuero juzgo»* (Madrid, 1929).

Fiore, Silvestro: «Nouvelles considérations sur la fusion des éléments orientaux et cambriens dans la formation du roman courtois», *AION, Sez. Rom.* XI (1969), 33-51.

Flutre, Louis-Fernand: *Table des noms propres avec toutes leurs variantes figurant dans les romans du Moyen Age, écrits en français ou en provençal et actuellement publiés ou analysés* (Publications du CÉSCM II, Poitiers, 1962).

Foulché-Delbosc, R.: «La plus ancienne mention d'*Amadis*», *RHi* XV (1906), 815.

Frye, Northrop: *Anatomy of Criticism. Four Essays* (Princeton, 1957).

Gallais, Pierre: «Recherches sur la mentalité des romanciers français du Moyen Age. Les formules et le vocabulaire des prologues. I», *CCMe* VII (1964), 479-493.

Gallardo, Bartolomé José: *Ensayo de una biblioteca española de libros raros y curiosos*, 4 vols (Madrid, 1863-89).

Galmés de Fuentes, Alvaro: «Influencias sintácticas y estilísticas del árabe en la prosa medieval castellana», *BRAE* XXXV (1955), 213-275 and 415-451, *ibid.* XXXVI (1956), 65-131 and 255-307.

Gariano, Carmelo: *Análisis estilístico de los «Milagros de Nuestra Señora»* (Madrid, 1965).

Gayangos, Pascual de: (ed.) *Libros de caballerías* (BAE 40).

Ghali, Wacyf Boutros: *La Tradition chevaleresque des Arabes* (Paris, 1919).

Gifford, D. J. and Hodcroft, F. W.: *Textos lingüísticos del medioevo español*, 2nd ed. (Oxford, 1966).

González Palencia, Angel: *Historia de la literatura arábigo-española*, 2nd ed. (Barcelona, 1945).

— — See also Hurtado, Juan; Pedro Alfonso.

Green, Otis H.: *Spain and the Western Tradition. The Castilian Mind in Literature from «El Cid» to Calderón*, I (Madison, 1963).

Gröber, Gustav: see Baist, Gottfried.

Groussac, P.: «Le Livre des *Castigos e documentos* attribué au Roi D. Sancho IV», *RHi* XV (1906), 212-239.

Gybbon-Monypenny, G. B.: «The Spanish *Mester de Clerecía* and its Intended Public: Concerning the Validity as Evidence of Passages of Direct Address to the Audience», *Medieval Miscellany Presented to Eugène Vinaver* (Manchester, 1965), 230-244.

Hava, J. G.: *Al-Faraid Arabic-English Dictionary* (Beirut, 1964).

Hernández, F.-X.: «Sobre el *Zifar* y una versión latina de la *Poridat*», *Homenaje Universitario a Dámaso Alonso* (Madrid, 1971).

Hilty, Gerold: see Aben Ragel, Aly.

Historia Apollonii Regis Tyri, ed. Alexander Riese (Lipsiae, 1871).

Hodcroft, F. W.: see Gifford, D. J.

Hurtado y J. de la Serna, Juan and González Palencia, Angel: *Historia de la literatura española*, 5th ed. (Madrid, 1943).

Jordan, Robert M.: *Chaucer and the Shape of Creation. The Aesthetic Possibilities of Inorganic Structure* (Cambridge, Mass., 1967).

— — «Chaucerian Narrative», *Companion to Chaucer Studies*, ed. Beryl Rowland (Toronto-New York-London, 1968), 84-102.

Kärde, S.: *Quelques manières d'exprimer l'idée d'un sujet indéterminé ou général en espagnol* (Uppsala, 1943).

Kasten, Lloyd A.: (ed.) *Seudo-Aristóteles: Poridat de las poridades* (Madrid, 1957).

— — See also Alfonso X.

Kean, Patricia: see Everett, Dorothy.

Keller, John E.: *Motif-Index of Mediæval Spanish Exempla* (Knoxville, Tenn., 1949).

— — (ed.) *El libro de los engaños*, 2nd ed. (UNCSRLL 20, Chapel Hill, 1959).

— — *Alfonso X, el Sabio* (TWAS 12, New York, 1967).

— — and Linker, Robert White: (eds) *El libro de Calila e Digna* (Clásicos Hispánicos XIII, Madrid, 1967).

Keller, J. P.: «The Hunt and Prophecy Episode of the *Poema de Fernán González*», *HR* XXIII (1955), 251-258.

Kellogg, Robert: see Scholes, Robert.

Kelly, Douglas: «The Scope of the Treatment of Composition in the Twelfth- and Thirteenth-Century Arts of Poetry», *Sp* XLI (1966), 261-278.

Kiddle, Lawrence B.: see Alfonso X.

Knust, Hermann: (ed.) *Dos obras didácticas y dos leyendas, sacadas de manuscritos de la Biblioteca del Escorial* (SBE XVII, Madrid, 1878).

— — (ed.) *Mittheilungen aus dem Eskurial* (Bibliothek des Litterarischen Vereins in Stuttgart CXLI, Tübingen, 1879).

— — (ed.) *Geschichte der Legenden der h. Katharina von Alexandrien und der h. Maria Aegyptiaca* (Halle, 1890).

Koran, The, trans. J. M. Rodwell (Everyman's Library 380, London, 1909).

Krappe, Alexander Haggerty: «La leggenda di S. Eustachio», *Nuovi Studi Medievali* III (1926-27), 223-258.

— — «Le Mirage celtique et les sources du *Chevalier Cifar*», *BH* XXXIII (1931), 97-103.

— — «Le Lac enchanté dans le *Chevalier Cifar*», *BH* XXV (1933), 107-125.

Kullmann, E.: «Die dichterische und sprachliche Gestalt des *Cantar de Mio Cid*», *RF* XLV (1931), 1-65.

Lanchetas, Rufino: *Gramática y vocabulario de las obras de Gonzalo de Berceo* (Madrid, 1900).

Langlois, Ernest: *Table des noms propres de toute nature compris dans les chansons de geste imprimées* (Paris, 1904).

Leavitt, S. E.: «Lions in Early Spanish Literature and on the Spanish Stage», *HBalt* XLIV (1961), 272-276.

Legge, M. Dominica: see Vinaver, Eugène.

Levi, Ezio: «Il giubileo del MCCC nel più antico romanzo spagnuolo», *Archivio della Reale Società Romana di Storia Patria* LVI-LVII (1933-34), 133-155.

Lewis, C. S.: *An Experiment in Criticism* (Cambridge, 1961).

— — *The Discarded Image. An Introduction to Medieval and Renaissance Literature* (Cambridge, 1964).

Libro de Alexandre, El, ed. Raymond S. Willis Jr (EMRLL 32, Princeton-Paris, 1934).

Libro de Apolonio, ed. C. Carroll Marden, I, 2nd ed. (EMRLL 6, Princeton, 1937).

Libro de Calila e Digna, El: see Keller, John E.

Libro de los cien capítulos, El: see Rey, Agapito.

Libro de los engaños, El: see Keller, John E.

Libro del Cavallero Zifar, El: see Michelant, Heinrich; Riquer, Martín de; Wagner, Charles P.

Libro del consejo e de los consejeros: see Rey, Agapito.

Libros de caballerías, ed. Adolfo Bonilla y San Martín, I (NBAE 6, Madrid, 1907).

Lida de Malkiel, María Rosa: «La visión de trasmundo en las literaturas hispánicas», addendum to Howard R. Patch, *El otro mundo en la literatura medieval*, trans. J. H. Campos (México-Buenos Aires, 1956), 369-449.

— — rev. of Justina Ruiz de Conde, *El amor y el matrimonio...* (*q.v.*), *RPh* III (1949-50), 224-225.

— — *La idea de la fama en la Edad Media castellana* (México-Buenos Aires, 1952).

— — «Arthurian Literature in Spain and Portugal», *Arthurian Literature*

237

in the Middle Ages. A Collaborative History, ed. Roger S. Loomis (Oxford, 1959), 406-418.

Linehan, Peter: *The Spanish Church and the Papacy in the Thirteenth Century* (Cambridge Studies in Medieval Life and Thought, Third Series 4, Cambridge, 1971).

Linker, Robert White: see Keller, John E.

Lofmark, C. J.: «Name Lists in *Parzival*», *Medieval German Studies Presented to Frederick Norman* (London, 1965), 157-173.

Loomis, Roger S.: see Lida de Malkiel, María Rosa.

López-Morillas, Consuelo: «A Broad View of *Calila e Digna* Studies on the Occasion of a New Edition», *RPh* XXV (1971-72), 85-96.

Lord, Albert B.: *The Singer of Tales* (HSCL 24, Cambridge, Mass., 1924).

Lot, Ferdinand: *Etude sur le «Lancelot» en prose* (BÉHÉ 226, Paris, 1918).

Malory, Sir Thomas: see Vinaver, Eugène.

Marden, C. Carroll: see *Libro de Apolonio*.

Menéndez y Pelayo, Marcelino: *Orígenes de la novela*, ed. E. Sánchez Reyes (Edición Nacional, 2nd ed., Madrid, 1962), I.

Menéndez-Pidal, Gonzalo: «Cómo trabajaron las escuelas alfonsíes», *NRFH* V (1951), 364-380.

Menéndez Pidal, Ramón: (ed.) *Reliquias de la poesía épica española* (Madrid, 1951).

—— (ed.) *Antología de prosistas españoles*, 8th ed. (Austral 110, Madrid, 1964).

—— See also Alfonso X; *Poema de Mío Cid*.

M[eyer] P[aul]: rev. of C. P. Wagner, «The Sources of *El Cavallero Cifar*» (*q.v.*), *R* XXXIII (1904), 314.

Michael, Ian: «A Comparison of the Use of Epic Epithets in the *Poema de Mio Cid* and the *Libro de Alexandre*», *BHS* XXXVIII (1961), 32-41.

—— «A Parallel between Chrétien's *Erec* and the *Libro de Alexandre*», *MLR* LXII (1967), 620-628.

Michelant, Heinrich: (ed.) *Historia del Cavallero Cifar* (Bibliothek des Litterarischen Vereins in Stuttgart CXII, Tübingen, 1872).

Millares Carlo, Agustín: *Literatura española hasta fines del siglo XV* (México, 1950).

Millás Vallicrosa, José M.: *Las traducciones orientales en los manuscritos de la Biblioteca Catedral de Toledo* (Madrid, 1942).

Moldenhauer, Gerhard: *Die Legende von Barlaam und Josaphat auf der iberischen Halbinsel. Untersuchungen und Texte* (Romanistische Arbeiten XIII, Halle, 1929).

—— «La fecha del origen de la *Historia del Caballero Cifar* y su importancia para la historia de la literatura española», *Investigación y Progreso* V (1931), 175-176.

Moore, Arthur K.: «Medieval English Literature and the Question of Unity», *MP* LXV (1967-68), 285-300.

Morel-Fatio, A.: *Catalogue des manuscrits espagnols de la Bibliothèque Nationale*, 2 vols (Paris, 1882-84).

Morris, J.: see Smith, C. C.

Mullen, Edward J.: «The Role of the Supernatural in *El libro del cavallero Zifar*», *REH* V (1971), 257-268.

Murdoch, Iris: «Against Dryness. A Polemical Sketch», *Encounter* XVI, 1 (Jan. 1961), 16-20.

Muscatine, Charles: «Locus of Action in Medieval Narrative», *RPh* XVII (1963-64), 115-122.

Navarro-González, Alberto: *El mar en la literatura medieval castellana* (La Laguna, 1962).

Nichols, S. G., Jr: *Formulaic Diction and Thematic Composition in the «Chanson de Roland»* (UNCSRLL 36, Chapel Hill, 1961).

Northup, George Tyler: *An Introduction to Spanish Literature* (Chicago, 1925).

— — (ed.) *El cuento de Tristan de Leonis. Edited from the Unique Manuscript Vatican 6428* (Chicago, 1928).

O'Kane, Eleanor S. (Sister M. Katharine Elaine): *Refranes y frases proverbiales españolas de la Edad Media* (*BRAE* anejo II, Madrid, 1959).

Oliver Asín, J.: *Historia de la lengua española*, 3rd ed. (Madrid, 1939).

Painter, Sidney: *French Chivalry. Chivalric Ideas and Practices in Mediaeval France* (Ithaca, N.Y., 1940).

Panofsky, Erwin: *Gothic Architecture and Scholasticism* (Latrobe, Pa., 1951).

Parry, Milman: «Studies in the Epic Technique of Oral Verse Making. I: Homer and Homeric Style», *HSCP* XLI (1930), 73-147.

Patch, Howard Rollin: *The Other World according to Descriptions in Medieval Literature* (Smith College Studies in Modern Languages, New Series 1, Cambridge, Mass., 1950).

Pauphilet, Albert: see *Queste del Saint Graal*.

Payne, John: *Tales from the Arabic of the Breslau and Calcutta Editions of the Book of the Thousand Nights and One Night not Occurring in the Other Printed Texts of the Work*, 3 vols (London, 1884).

Payne, Robert O.: «Chaucer and the Art of Rhetoric», *Companion to Chaucer Studies*, ed. Beryl Rowland (Toronto-New York-London, 1968), 38-57.

Pedro Alfonso: *Disciplina Clericalis*, ed. and trans. A. González Palencia (Madrid-Granada, 1948).

Peirce, Helen J.: «Aspectos de la personalidad del rey español en la literatura hispano-arábiga», *Smith College Studies in Modern Languages* X, 2 (Jan, 1929), 1-39.

Perry, T. Anthony: *Art and Meaning in Berceo's «Vida de Santa Oria»* (Yale Romanic Studies, Second Series 19, New Haven-London, 1968).

Petrus Alphonsi: see Pedro Alfonso.

Piccus, Jules: «Consejos y consejeros en el *Libro del Cauallero Zifar*», *NRFH* XVI (1962), 16-30.

— — «Refranes y frases proverbiales en el *Libro del Cavallero Zifar*», *NRFH* XVIII (1965-66), 1-24.

Place, Edwin B.: see *Amadís...*

Poema de Fernán González, ed. Alonso Zamora Vicente, 2nd ed. (CC 128, Madrid, 1954).

Poema de Mío Cid, ed. Ramón Menéndez Pidal (CC 24, Madrid, 1911).

Poetas castellanos anteriores al siglo XV (BAE 57).

Polt, John H. R.: «Moral Phraseology in Early Spanish Literature», *RPh* XV (1961-62), 254-268.

Prestage, Edgar: (ed.) *Chivalry. A Series of Studies to Illustrate its Historical Significance and Civilizing Influence* (London, 1928).

Queste del Saint Graal, La (Roman du XIIIᵉ siècle), ed. Albert Pauphilet (CFMA 33, Paris, 1949).

Ramírez Cabañas, Joaquín: see Díaz del Castillo, Bernal.

Ramsden, H.: «The Use of *A + Personal Pronoun* in Old Spanish», *BHS* XXXVIII (1961), 42-54.

Rey, Agapito: (ed.) *Castigos e documentos* (IUHS 24, Bloomington, Ind., 1952).

— — (ed.) *El libro de los cien capítulos* (IUHS 44, Bloomington, Ind., 1960).

— — *Libro del consejo e de los consejeros* (Zaragoza, 1962).

Richard, Jean: «La Vogue de l'orient dans la littérature occidentale du Moyen Age», *Mélanges offerts à René Crozet* (Poitiers, 1966), I, 557-561.

Richthofen, Erich von: *Estudios épicos medievales con algunos trabajos inéditos*, trans. J. Pérez Riesco (Madrid, 1954).

— — «Style and Chronology of the Early Romance Epic», *Saggi e ricerche in memoria di Ettore Li Gotti* (Palermo, 1962), III, 83-96.

Rico, Francisco: *El pequeño mundo del hombre. Varia fortuna de una idea en las letras españolas* (Madrid, 1970).

Riese, Alexander: see *Historia Apollonii...*

Riley, E. C.: *Cervantes's Theory of the Novel* (Oxford, 1962).

Riquer, Martín de: (ed.) *«El Cavallero Zifar» con un estudio*, 2 vols (Barcelona, 1951).

Rocamora, José María: *Catálogo abreviado de los manuscritos de la biblioteca del Excmo. Señor Duque de Osuna e Infantado* (Madrid, 1882).

Rodón Binué, E.: *El lenguaje técnico del feudalismo en el siglo XI en Cataluña* (Barcelona, 1947).

Rodwell, J. M.: see *Koran*.

Romera-Navarro, M.: *Historia de la literatura española* (New York, 1928).

Round, N. G.: «Renaissance Culture and its Opponents in Fifteenth-Century Castile», *MLR* LVII (1962), 204-215.

Rowland, Beryl: see Jordan, Robert M.; Payne, Robert O.

Rubió y Balaguer, J.: *La vida española en la época gótica* (Barcelona, 1943).

Ruiz de Conde, Justina: *El amor y el matrimonio secreto en los libros de caballerías* (Madrid, 1948).

Runciman, Steven: *A History of the Crusades*, 2nd ed., 3 vols (Harmondsworth, 1965).

Russell, P. E.: rev. of J. M. Millás Vallicrosa, *Las traducciones orientales...* (*q.v.*), *MLR* XLII (1947), 392-395.

Salcedo Ruiz, Angel: *La literatura española* (Madrid, 1915).

Sampson, Margaret: «Africa in Medieval Spanish Literature: its Appearance in *El Caballero Cifar*», *Negro History Bulletin* XXXII, 8 (Dec. 1969), 14-18.

Sánchez Reyes, E.: see Menéndez y Pelayo, Marcelino.

Schiff, Mario: *La Bibliothèque du Marquis de Santillane* (BÉHÉ 153, Paris, 1905).

Schlauch, Margaret: *Chaucer's Constance and Accused Queens* (New York, 1927).

—— «The Art of Chaucer's Prose», *Chaucer and Chaucerians. Critical Essays in Middle English Literature*, ed. D. S. Brewer (London, 1966), 140-163.

Scholberg, Kenneth R.: «A Half-Friend and a Friend and a Half», *BHS* XXXV (1958), 187-198.

—— «The Structure of the *Caballero Cifar*», *MLN* LXXIX (1964), 113-124.

—— «La comicidad del *Caballero Zifar*», *Homenaje a Rodríguez-Moñino* (Madrid, 1966), II, 157-163.

Scholes, Robert and Kellogg, Robert: *The Nature of Narrative* (New York, 1966).

Schon, Peter M.: *Studien sum Stil der frühen französischen Prosa (Robert de Clari, Geoffroy de Villehardouin, Henri de Valenciennes)* (Analecta Romanica 8, Frankfurt am Main, 1960).

Schwarz, Kessel: see Chandler, Richard E.

Scudieri Ruggieri, Jole: «Due note di letteratura spagnola del s. XIV. 1) La cultura francese nel *Caballero Zifar* e nell'*Amadis*; versioni spagnole del Tristano in prosa. 2) 'De ribaldo'», *CN* XXVI (1966), 233-252.

Sears, Helen L: «The *Rimado de Palacio* and the *De Regimine Principum* Tradition of the Middle Ages», *HR* XX (1952), 1-27.

Simón Díaz, José: *Bibliografía de la literatura española*, 2nd ed., III, i-ii (Madrid, 1963).

Smith, C. C.: «Latin Histories and Vernacular Epic in Twelfth-Century Spain: Similarities of Spirit and Style», *BHS* XLVIII (1971), 1-19.

—— and Morris, J.: «On 'Physical' Phrases in Old Spanish Epic and Other Texts», *PLPLS: Lit. and Hist. Section*, XII, part v (1967), 129-190.

—— *Reality and Rhetoric: an Aspect of Medieval Linguistics* (unpublished).

Smithers, Leonard C.: see Burton, Richard F.

Solalinde, A. G.: see Alfonso X; Berceo, Gonzalo de.

Spearing, A. C.: *Criticism and Medieval Poetry* (London, 1964).

Stamm, James R.: *A Short History of Spanish Literature* (New York, 1967).

Taylor, G. Rattray: *Sex in History* (London, 1953).

Thomas, Henry: *Spanish and Portuguese Romances of Chivalry. The Revival of the Romance of Chivalry in the Spanish Peninsula, and its Extension and Influence Abroad* (Cambridge, 1920).

Ticknor, George: *History of Spanish Literature*, 3rd ed., 3 vols (London, 1863).

Tyssens, Madeleine: «Le jongleur et l'écrit», *Mélanges offerts à René Crozet* (Poitiers, 1966), I, 685-695.

Ubieto Arteta, A.: see *Cronica Najerense*.

Valbuena Prat, Angel: *Historia de la literatura española*, 3rd ed., 3 vols (Barcelona, 1950).

17

Vance, Eugene: «Notes on the Development of Formulaic Language in Romanesque Poetry», *Mélanges offerts à René Crozet* (Poitiers, 1966), I, 427-434.

Vendrell de Millás, Francisca: see *Cancionero de Palacio*.

Vinaver, Eugène: Introduction to *Le Roman de Balain*, ed. M. Dominica Legge (Manchester, 1942).

—— (ed.) *The Works of Sir Thomas Malory*, 3 vols (Oxford, 1947).

—— «Flaubert and the Legend of Saint Julian», *BJRL* XXXVI, 1 (1953), 228-244.

—— (ed.) *The Tale of the Death of King Arthur by Sir Thomas Malory* (Oxford, 1955).

—— «From Epic to Romance», *BJRL* XLVI, 1 (1964), 476-503.

—— «Critical Approaches to Medieval Romance», *Literary History and Literary Criticism* (Acta of the 9th Congress: International Federation for Modern Languages and Literature, New York, 1965), 16-27.

—— *Form and Meaning in Medieval Romance* (Presidential Address of the Modern Humanities Research Association, 1966).

Wagner, Charles Philip: «The Sources of *El Cavallero Cifar*», *RHi* X (1903), 5-104.

—— (ed.) *El Libro del Cauallero Zifar (El Libro del Cauallero de Dios)*, Part I: Text (Univ. of Michigan Publications, Language and Literature V, Ann Arbor, 1929).

—— «The *Caballero Zifar* and the *Moralium Dogma Philosophorum*», *RPh* VI (1952-53), 309-312.

Walker, Roger M.: «The Unity of *El libro del Cavallero Zifar*», *BHS* XLII (1965), 149-159.

—— «The Genesis of *El libro del Cavallero Zifar*», *MLR* LXII (1967), 61-69.

—— «Juan Ruiz's Defence of Love», *MLN* LXXXIV (1969), 292-297.

—— «'Con miedo de la muerte la miel non es sabrosa': Love, Sin and Death in the *Libro de buen amor*», *«Libro de Buen Amor» Studies*, ed. G. B. Gybbon-Monypenny (Tamesis, London, 1970), 231-252.

—— «Oral Delivery or Private Reading? A Contribution to the Debate on the Dissemination of Medieval Literature», *FMLS* VII (1971), 36-42.

—— «Did Cervantes Know the *Cavallero Zifar*?», *BHS* XLIX (1972), 120-127.

—— See also Deyermond, A. D.; Dutton, Brian.

Wardropper, B. W.: «Don Quixote: Story or History?», *MP* LXIII (1965-66), 1-11.

Webber, Edwin J.: «A Lexical Note on *afortunado* 'unfortunate'», *HR* XXXIII (1965), 347-359.

Webber, Ruth House: *Formulistic Diction in the Spanish Ballad* (UCPMPh XXXIV, 2, Berkeley-Los Angeles, 1951).

Whinnom, Keith: «Diego de San Pedro's Stylistic Reform», *BHS* XXXVII (1960), 1-15.

—— *Spanish Literary Historiography: Three Forms of Distortion* (Exeter, 1967).

Whitehead, F.: see *Chanson de Roland*.

Willis, Raymond S., Jr: *The Phantom Chapters of the «Quijote»* (New York, 1953).

—— See also *Libro de Alexandre*.

Wilson, Edward M.: *Some Aspects of Spanish Literary History* (Oxford, 1967).

Wright, John Kirtland: *The Geographical Lore of the Time of the Crusades. A Study in the History of Medieval Science and Tradition in Western Europe* (New York, 1925).

Wright, Thomas: *The Life of Sir Richard Burton*, 2 vols (London, 1906).

—— *The Life of John Payne* (London, 1919).

Wright, W.: *A Grammar of the Arabic Language*, 3rd ed., 2 vols (Cambridge, 1962-64).

Yates, Frances: *The Art of Memory* (London, 1966).

Zamora Vicente, Alonso: see *Poema de Fernán González*.

Zapata y Torres, Miguel: «Breves notas sobre el *Libro de los cien capítulos* como base de las *Flores de filosofía*», *Smith College Studies in Modern Languages* X, 2 (Jan. 1929), 43-54.

INDEX

245

COLECCION TAMESIS

SERIE A - MONOGRAFIAS

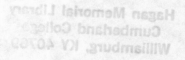

SERIE C - FUENTES PARA LA HISTORIA DEL TEATRO EN ESPAÑA

SERIE D - REPRODUCCIONES EN FACSIMIL

CRITICAL GUIDES TO SPANISH TEXTS

(Publicadas en colaboración con Grant and Cutler Limited)